The Translator's Invisibility

The Translator's Invisibility provides a thorough and critical examination of translation from the seventeenth century to the present day. It shows how fluency prevailed over other translation strategies to shape the canon of foreign literatures in English, and it interrogates the ethnocentric and imperialist cultural consequences of the domestic values that were simultaneously inscribed and masked in foreign texts during this period.

In tracing the history of translation, Lawrence Venuti locates alternative translation theories and practices which make it possible to counter the strategy of fluency, aiming to communicate linguistic and cultural differences instead of removing them. Using texts and translations from Britain, America and Europe he elaborates the theoretical and critical means by which translation can be studied and practiced as a locus of difference, recovering and revising forgotten translations to establish an alternative tradition.

Lawrence Venuti is Professor of English at Temple University, Philadelphia, and has been a professional translator for the past fifteen years. He is the editor of *Rethinking Translation: Discourse, Subjectivity, Ideology.*

Translation Studies
General editors: Susan Bassnett and André Lefevere

The Translator's Invisibility

A History of Translation

Lawrence Venuti

London and New York

First published 1995
by Routledge
11 New Fetter Lane, London EC4P 4EE

Simultaneously published in the USA and Canada
by Routledge
29 West 35th Street, New York, NY 10001

© 1995 Lawrence Venuti

Typeset in Baskerville by Solidus (Bristol) Limited
Printed and bound in Great Britain by
T. J. Press (Padstow) Ltd, Padstow, Cornwall

British Library Cataloguing in Publication Data
A catalogue record for this book is available from the British Library.

Library of Congress Cataloging in Publication Data
Venuti, Lawrence.
   The Translator's Invisibility: A History of Translation / Lawrence
Venuti.
      p.   cm. – (Translation studies)
   Includes bibliographical references and index.
   1. Translating and interpreting–History.   2. English language–
Translating–History.   I. Title.   II. Series: Translation studies
(London, England)
P306.2.V46   1995
418 ' .02 ' 09–dc20   94–6477

ISBN 0–415–11537–X (hbk)
      0–415–11538–8 (pbk)

Contents

General editors' preface

The growth of translation studies as a separate discipline is a success story of the 1980s. The subject has developed in many parts of the world and is clearly destined to continue developing well into the twenty-first century. Translation studies brings together work in a wide variety of fields, including linguistics, literary study, history, anthropology, psychology, and economics. This series of books will reflect the breadth of work in translation studies and will enable readers to share in the exciting new developments that are taking place at the present time.

Translation is, of course, a rewriting of an original text. All rewritings, whatever their intention, reflect a certain ideology and a poetics and as such manipulate literature to function in a given society in a given way. Rewriting is manipulation, undertaken in the service of power, and in its positive aspect can help in the evolution of a literature and a society. Rewritings can introduce new concepts, new genres, new devices, and the history of translation is the history also of literary innovation, of the shaping power of one culture upon another. But rewriting can also repress innovation, distort and contain, and in an age of ever increasing manipulation of all kinds, the study of the manipulative processes of literature as exemplified by translation can help us toward a greater awareness of the world in which we live.

Since this series of books on translation studies is the first of its kind, it will be concerned with its own genealogy. It will publish texts from the past that illustrate its concerns in the present, and will publish texts of a more theoretical nature immediately address-ing those concerns, along with case studies illustrating manipula-tion through rewriting in various literatures. It will be comparative in nature and will range through many literary traditions, both

Western and non-Western. Through the concepts of rewriting and manipulation, this series aims to tackle the problem of ideology, change and power in literature and society and so assert the central function of translation as a shaping force.

Susan Bassnett
André Lefevere

Preface and acknowledgements

The Translator's Invisibility originates in my own work as a professional translator since the late 1970s. But any autobiographical elements are subsumed in what is effectively a history of English-language translation from the seventeenth century to the present. My project is to trace the origins of the situation in which every English-language translator works today, although from an opposing standpoint, with the explicit aim of locating alternatives, of changing that situation. The historical narratives presented here span centuries and national literatures, but even though based on detailed research, they are necessarily selective in articulating key moments and controversies, and frankly polemical in studying the past to question the marginal position of translation in contemporary Anglo-American culture. I imagine a diverse audience for the book, including translation theorists, literary theorists and critics, period specialists in various literatures (English-language and foreign), and reviewers of translations for periodicals, publishers, private foundations, and government endowments. Most of all, I wish to speak to translators and readers of translations, both professional and nonprofessional, focusing their attention on the ways that translations are written and read and urging them to think of new ones.

A project with this sort of intention and scope will inevitably come to rely on the help of many people in different fields of literary and critical expertise. Assembling the list of those who over the past several years read, discussed, criticized, or otherwise encouraged my work is a special pleasure, making me realize, once again, how fortunate I was: Antoine Berman, Charles Bernstein, Shelly Brivic, Ann Caesar, Steve Cole, Tim Corrigan, Pellegrino D'Acierno, Guy Davenport, Deirdre David, Milo De Angelis,

Rachel Blau DuPlessis, George Economou, Jonathan Galassi, Dana Gioia, Barbara Harlow, Peter Hitchcock, Susan Howe, Suzanne Jill Levine, Philip Lewis, Harry Mathews, Jeremy Maule, Sally Mitchell, Daniel O'Hara, Toby Olson, Douglas Robinson, Stephen Sartarelli, Richard Sieburth, Alan Singer, Nigel Smith, Susan Stewart, Robert Storey, Evelyn Tribble, William Van Wert, Justin Vitiello, William Weaver, Sue Wells, and John Zilcosky. Others assisted me by providing useful and sometimes essential information: Raymond Bentman, Sara Goldin Blackburn, Robert E. Brown, Emile Capouya, Cid Corman, Rob Fitterman, Peter Glassgold, Robert Kelly, Alfred MacAdam, Julie Scott Meisami, M. L. Rosenthal, Susanne Stark, Suzanna Tamminen, Peter Tasch, Maurice Valency, and Eliot Weinberger. Of course none of these people can be held responsible for what I finally made of their contributions.

For opportunities to share this work with various audiences in the United States and abroad, I thank Carrie Asman, Joanna Bankier, Susan Bassnett, Cedric Brown, Craig Eisendrath, Ed Foster, Richard Alan Francis, Seth Frechie and Andrew Mossin, Theo Hermans, Paul Hernadi, Robert Holub, Sydney Lévy, Gregory Lucente, Carol Maier, Marie-José Minassian, Anu Needham, Yopie Prins, Marilyn Gaddis Rose, Sherry Simon, William Tropia, and Immanuel Wallerstein. I am grateful to the staffs of the libraries where much of the research was carried out: the British Library; the Archive for New Poetry, Mandeville Department of Special Collections, University of California, San Diego; Rare Books and Manuscripts, Butler Library, Columbia University; the Library Company, Philadelphia; the Nottingham City Archive; the Inter-Library Loan Department, Paley Library, Temple University; and the Collection of American Literature, Beinecke Rare Book and Manuscript Library, Yale University. I am especially thankful to Bett Miller of the Archive for New Poetry, who did a special job of helping me secure copies of many documents in the Paul Blackburn Collection, and to Adrian Henstock of the Nottingham City Archive, who enabled me to consult Lucy Hutchinson's commonplace book. Philip Cronenwett, Chief of Special Collections at Dartmouth College Library, kindly answered my questions about the Ramon Guthrie papers.

Various individuals and institutions have granted permission to quote from the following copyrighted materials:

Excerpts from Mary Barnard, *Sappho: A New Translation*, copyright © 1958 by The Regents of the University of California, ©

renewed 1984 by Mary Barnard; and from *Assault on Mount Helicon: A Literary Memoir*, copyright © 1984 by Mary Barnard.

Excerpts from Paul Blackburn's correspondence, translations, and nonfiction, copyright © 1995 by Joan Miller-Cohn. Excerpts from *The Collected Poems of Paul Blackburn*, copyright © 1985 by Joan Blackburn. Reprinted by permission of Persea Books, Inc.

Excerpts from the writings of Macmillan employees: editor Emile Capouya's letter to John Ciardi, Capouya's letter to Ramon Guthrie, Guthrie's report on Paul Blackburn's *Anthology of Troubadour Poetry*. Reprinted by permission of Macmillan College Publishing Company, New York: 1958. All rights reserved.

Excerpts from *End of the Game and Other Stories* by Julio Cortázar, translated by Paul Blackburn, copyright © 1967 by Random House, Inc. Reprinted by permission of Pantheon Books, a division of Random House, Inc.

Excerpts from "Translator's Preface" by Robert Fagles, from *Homer: The Iliad*, translated by Robert Fagles, translation copyright © 1990 by Robert Fagles. Introduction and notes copyright © 1990 by Bernard Knox. Used by permission of Viking Penguin, a division of Penguin Books USA, Inc.

Excerpts from *Poems from the Greek Anthology*, translated by Dudley Fitts, copyright © 1938, 1941, 1956, by New Directions Publishing Corporation.

Excerpts from Dudley Fitts's essay, "The Poetic Nuance," reprinted by permission from *On Translation* edited by Reuben A. Brower, Cambridge, Massachusetts: Harvard University Press, copyright © 1959 by the President and Fellows of Harvard College.

Excerpts from Ramon Guthrie's poetry and translations, used by permission of Dartmouth College.

Eugenio Montale's poem, "Mottetti VI," is reprinted by permission from *Tutte le poesie* edited by Giorgio Zampa, copyright © 1984 by Arnoldo Mondadori Editore SpA, Milano.

Excerpts from the works of Ezra Pound: *The ABC of Reading*, all rights reserved; *Literary Essays*, copyright © 1918, 1920, 1935 by Ezra Pound; *The Letters of Ezra Pound 1907–1941*, copyright © 1950 by Ezra Pound; *Selected Poems*, copyright © 1920, 1934, 1937 by Ezra Pound; *The Spirit of Romance*, copyright © 1968 by Ezra Pound; *Translations*, copyright © 1954, 1963 by Ezra Pound. Used by permission of New Directions Publishing Corporation and Faber & Faber Ltd. Previously unpublished material by Ezra Pound, copyright © 1983 and 1995 by the Trustees of the Ezra Pound Literary

Property Trust; used by permission of New Directions Publishing Corporation and Faber & Faber Ltd, agents.

The tables, "U.S. Book Exports, 1990," "U.S. Book Exports to Major Countries, 1989–1990," and "World Translation Publications: From Selected Languages, 1982–1984." Reprinted (as Tables 1 and 2) from the 5 July 1991 issue of *Publishers Weekly*, published by Cahners Publishing Company, a division of Reed Publishing USA. Copyright © 1991 by Reed Publishing USA.

The Best Seller List for Fiction from *The New York Times Book Review*, 9 July 1967, copyright © 1967 by The New York Times Company. Reprinted by permission.

Excerpts from the agreement between myself and Farrar, Straus & Giroux for the translation of *Delirium* by Barbara Alberti, used by permission of Farrar, Straus & Giroux, Inc.

Grateful acknowledgement is made to the following journals, where some of this material appeared in earlier versions: *Criticism, Journal of Medieval and Renaissance Studies, SubStance, Talisman: A Journal of Contemporary Poetry and Poetics, Textual Practice, To: A Journal of Poetry, Prose, and the Visual Arts*, and *TTR Traduction, Terminologie, Rédaction: Études sur le texte et ses transformations*. An earlier version of chapter 4 appeared in my anthology, *Rethinking Translation: Discourse, Subjectivity, Ideology* (Routledge, 1992). My work was supported in part by a Research and Study Leave, a Summer Research Fellowship, and a Grant in Aid from Temple University. My thanks to Nadia Kravchenko, for expertly preparing the typescript and computer disks, and to Don Hartman, for assisting in the production process.

The graphs displaying patterns in translation publishing (Figures 1 and 2) were prepared by Chris Behnam of Key Computer Services, New York City.

All unattributed translations in the following pages are mine.

Come la sposa di ogni uomo non si sottrae a una teoria del tradurre (Milo De Angelis), I am reduced to an inadequate expression of my gratitude to Lindsay Davies, who has taught me much about English, and much about the foreign in translation.

L.V.
New York City
January 1994

Chapter 1

Invisibility

I see translation as the attempt to produce a text so transparent that it does not seem to be translated. A good translation is like a pane of glass. You only notice that it's there when there are little imperfections – scratches, bubbles. Ideally, there shouldn't be any. It should never call attention to itself.

Norman Shapiro

I

"Invisibility" is the term I will use to describe the translator's situation and activity in contemporary Anglo-American culture. It refers to two mutually determining phenomena: one is an illusion-istic effect of discourse, of the translator's own manipulation of English; the other is the practice of reading and evaluating translations that has long prevailed in the United Kingdom and the United States, among other cultures, both English and foreign-language. A translated text, whether prose or poetry, fiction or nonfiction, is judged acceptable by most publishers, reviewers, and readers when it reads fluently, when the absence of any linguistic or stylistic peculiarities makes it seem transparent, giving the appearance that it reflects the foreign writer's personality or intention or the essential meaning of the foreign text – the appearance, in other words, that the translation is not in fact a translation, but the "original." The illusion of transparency is an effect of fluent discourse, of the translator's effort to insure easy readability by adhering to current usage, maintaining continuous syntax, fixing a precise meaning. What is so remarkable here is that this illusory effect conceals the numerous conditions under which the translation is made, starting with the translator's crucial intervention in the foreign text. The more fluent the translation, the more invisible the translator, and, presumably, the more visible the writer or meaning of the foreign text.

The dominance of fluency in English-language translation becomes apparent in a sampling of reviews from newspapers and periodicals. On those rare occasions when reviewers address the translation at all, their brief comments usually focus on its style, neglecting such other possible questions as its accuracy, its intended audience, its economic value in the current book market, its relation to literary trends in English, its place in the translator's career. And over the past fifty years the comments are amazingly consistent in praising fluent discourse while damning deviations from it, even when the most diverse range of foreign texts is considered.

Take fiction, for instance, the most translated genre worldwide. Limit the choices to European and Latin American writers, the most translated into English, and pick examples with different kinds of narratives – novels and short stories, realistic and fantastic, lyrical and philosophical, psychological and political. Here is one possible list: Albert Camus's *The Stranger* (1946), Françoise Sagan's *Bonjour Tristesse* (1955), Heinrich Böll's *Absent Without Leave* (1965), Italo Calvino's *Cosmicomics* (1968), Gabriel García Márquez's *One Hundred Years of Solitude* (1970), Milan Kundera's *The Book of Laughter and Forgetting* (1980), Mario Vargas Llosa's *In Praise of the Stepmother* (1990), Julia Kristeva's *The Samurai* (1991), Gianni Celati's *Appearances* (1992), Adolfo Bioy Casares's *A Russian Doll* (1992). Some of these translations enjoyed considerable critical and commercial success in English; others made an initial splash, then sank into oblivion; still others passed with little or no notice. Yet in the reviews they were all judged by the same criterion – fluency. The following selection of excerpts comes from various British and American periodicals, both literary and mass-audience; some were written by noted critics, novelists, and reviewers:

> Stuart Gilbert's translation seems an absolutely splendid job. It is not easy, in translating French, to render qualities of sharpness or vividness, but the prose of Mr. Gilbert is always natural, brilliant, and crisp.
>
> (Wilson 1946:100)

> The style is elegant, the prose lovely, and the translation excellent.
>
> (*New Republic* 1955:46)

In *Absent Without Leave,* a novella gracefully if not always flawlessly translated by Leila Vennewitz, Böll continues his stern and sometimes merciless probing of the conscience, values, and imperfections of his countrymen.

(Potoker 1965:42)

The translation is a pleasantly fluent one: two chapters of it have already appeared in *Playboy* magazine.

(*Times Literary Supplement* 1969:180)

Rabassa's translation is a triumph of fluent, gravid momentum, all stylishness and commonsensical virtuosity.

(West 1970:4)

His first four books published in English did not speak with the stunning lyrical precision of this one (the invisible translator is Michael Henry Heim).

(Michener 1980:108)

Helen Lane's translation of the title of this book is faithful to Mario Vargas Llosa's – "Elogio de la Madrastra" – but not quite idiomatic.

(Burgess 1990:11)

The Samurai, a transparent *roman à clef,* fluently translated by Barbara Bray, chronicles Ms. Kristeva's – and Paris's – intellectual glory days.

(Steiner 1992:9)

In Stuart Hood's translation, which flows crisply despite its occasionally disconcerting British accent, Mr. Celati's keen sense of language is rendered with precision.

(Dickstein 1992:18)

Often wooden, occasionally careless or inaccurate, it shows all the signs of hurried work and inadequate revision. [...] The Spanish original here is 10 words shorter and incomparably more elegant.

(Balderston 1992:15)

The critical lexicon of post-World War II literary journalism is filled with so many terms to indicate the presence or absence of a fluent translation discourse: "crisp," "elegant," "flows," "gracefully," "wooden." There is even a group of pejorative neologisms designed to criticize translations that lack fluency, but also used, more generally, to signify badly written prose: "translatese," "translationese," "translatorese." In English, fluent translation is recommended for an extremely wide range of foreign texts – contemporary and archaic, religious and scientific, fiction and nonfiction.

> Translationese in a version from Hebrew is not always easy to detect, since the idioms have been familiarised through the Authorized Version.
>
> *(Times Literary Supplement* 1961:iv)

> An attempt has been made to use modern English which is lively without being slangy. Above all, an effort has been made to avoid the kind of unthinking "translationese" which has so often in the past imparted to translated Russian literature a distinctive, somehow "doughy," style of its own with little relation to anything present in the original Russian.
>
> (Hingley 1964:x)

> He is solemnly reverential and, to give the thing an authentic classical smack, has couched it in the luke-warm translatese of one of his own more unurgent renderings.
>
> (Corke 1967:761)

> There is even a recognizable variant of pidgin English known as "translatorese" ("transjargonisation" being an American term for a particular form of it).
>
> *(Times Literary Supplement* 1967:399)

> Paralysing woodenness ("I am concerned to determine"), the dull thud of translatese ("Here is the place to mention Pirandello finally") are often the price we more or less willingly pay for access to great thoughts.
>
> (Brady 1977:201)

A gathering of such excerpts indicates which discursive features produce fluency in an English-language translation and which do not. A fluent translation is written in English that is current ("modern") instead of archaic, that is widely used instead of specialized ("jargonisation"), and that is standard instead of colloquial ("slangy"). Foreign words ("pidgin") are avoided, as are Britishisms in American translations and Americanisms in British translations. Fluency also depends on syntax that is not so "faithful" to the foreign text as to be "not quite idiomatic," that unfolds continuously and easily (not "doughy") to insure semantic "precision" with some rhythmic definition, a sense of closure (not a "dull thud"). A fluent translation is immediately recognizable and intelligible, "familiarised," domesticated, not "disconcerting[ly]" foreign, capable of giving the reader unobstructed "access to great thoughts," to what is "present in the original." Under the regime of fluent translating, the translator works to make his or her work "invisible," producing the illusory effect of transparency that simultaneously masks its status as an illusion: the translated text seems "natural," i.e., not translated.

The dominance of transparency in English-language translation reflects comparable trends in other cultural forms, including other forms of writing. The enormous economic and political power acquired by scientific research during the twentieth century, the postwar innovations in advanced communications technologies to expand the advertising and entertainment industries and support the economic cycle of commodity production and exchange – these developments have affected every medium, both print and electronic, by valorizing a purely instrumental use of language and other means of representation and thus emphasizing immediate intelligibility and the appearance of factuality.[1] The American poet Charles Bernstein, who for many years worked as a "commercial writer" of various kinds of nonfiction – medical, scientific, technical – observes how the dominance of transparency in contemporary writing is enforced by its economic value, which sets up acceptable "limits" for deviation:

> the fact that the overwhelming majority of steady paid employment for writing involves using the authoritative plain styles, if it is not explicitly advertising; involves writing, that is, filled with preclusions, is a measure of why this is not simply a matter of stylistic choice but of social governance: we are not free to choose the language of the workplace or of the family we are born into, though we are free, within limits, to rebel against it.
> (Bernstein 1986:225)

The authority of "plain styles" in English-language writing was of course achieved over several centuries, what Bernstein describes as "the historical movement toward uniform spelling and grammar, with an ideology that emphasizes nonidiosyncratic, smooth transition, elimination of awkwardness, &c. – anything that might concentrate attention on the language itself" (ibid.:27). In contemporary Anglo-American literature, this movement has made realism the most prevalent form of narrative and free, prose-like verse the most prevalent form of poetry:

> in contrast to, say, Sterne's work, where the look & texture – the opacity – of the text is everywhere present, a neutral transparent prose style has developed in certain novels where the words seem meant to be looked through – to the depicted world beyond the page. Likewise, in current middle of the road poetry, we see the elimination of overt rhyme & alliteration, with metric forms retained primarily for their capacity to officialize as "poetry."
>
> (ibid.)[2]

In view of these cultural trends, it seems inevitable that transparency would become the authoritative discourse for translating, whether the foreign text was literary or scientific/technical. The British translator J. M. Cohen noticed this development as early as 1962, when he remarked that "twentieth-century translators, influenced by science-teaching and the growing importance attached to accuracy [...] have generally concentrated on prose-meaning and interpretation, and neglected the imitation of form and manner" (Cohen 1962:35). Cohen also noticed the domestication involved here, "the risk of reducing individual authors' styles and national tricks of speech to a plain prose uniformity," but he felt that this "danger" was avoided by the "best" translations (ibid.:33). What he failed to see, however, was that the criterion determining the "best" was still radically English. Translating for "prose-meaning and interpretation," practicing translation as simple communication, rewrites the foreign text according to such English-language values as transparency, but entirely eclipses the translator's domesticating work – even in the eyes of the translator.

The translator's invisibility is also partly determined by the individualistic conception of authorship that continues to prevail in Anglo-American culture. According to this conception, the author freely expresses his thoughts and feelings in writing, which is thus viewed as an original and transparent self-representation, unmediated by transindividual determinants (linguistic, cultural, social) that might complicate authorial originality. This view of authorship carries two disadvantageous implications for the translator. On the one hand, translation is defined as a second-order representation: only the foreign text can be original, an authentic copy, true to the author's personality or intention, whereas the translation is derivative, fake, potentially a false copy. On the other hand, translation is required to efface its second-order status with transparent discourse, producing the illusion of authorial presence whereby the translated text can be taken as the original. However much the individualistic conception of authorship devalues translation, it is so pervasive that it shapes translators' self-presentations, leading some to psychologize their relationship to the foreign text as a process of identification with the author. The American Willard Trask (1900–1980), a major twentieth-century translator in terms of the quantity and cultural importance of his work, drew a clear distinction between authoring and translating. When asked in a late interview whether "the impulse" to translate "is the same as that of someone who wants to write a novel" (a question that is clearly individualistic in its reference to an authorial "impulse"), Trask replied:

> No, I wouldn't say so, because I once tried to write a novel. When you're writing a novel [...] you're obviously writing about people or places, something or other, but what you are essentially doing is expressing yourself. Whereas when you translate you're not expressing yourself. You're performing a technical stunt. [...] I realized that the translator and the actor had to have the same kind of talent. What they both do is to take something of somebody else's and put it over as if it were their own. I think you have to have that capacity. So in addition to the technical stunt, there is a psychological workout, which translation involves: something like being on stage. It does something entirely different from what I think of as creative poetry writing.
> (Honig 1985:13–14)

In Trask's analogy, translators playact as authors, and translations pass for original texts. Translators are very much aware that any sense of authorial presence in a translation is an illusion, an effect of transparent discourse, comparable to a "stunt," but they nonetheless assert that they participate in a "psychological" relationship with the author in which they repress their own "personality." "I guess I consider myself in a kind of collaboration with the author," says American translator Norman Shapiro; "Certainly my ego and personality are involved in translating, and yet I have to try to stay faithful to the basic text in such a way that my own personality doesn't show" (Kratz 1986:27).

The translator's invisibility is thus a weird self-annihilation, a way of conceiving and practicing translation that undoubtedly reinforces its marginal status in Anglo-American culture. For although the past twenty years have seen the institution of translation centers and programs at British and American universities, as well as the founding of translation committees, associations, and awards in literary organizations like the Society of Authors in London and the PEN American Center in New York, the fact remains that translators receive minimal recognition for their work – including translators of writing that is capable of generating publicity (because it is prize-winning, controversial, censored). The typical mention of the translator in a review takes the form of a brief aside in which, more often than not, the transparency of the translation is gauged. This, however, is an infrequent occurrence. Ronald Christ has described the prevailing practice: "many newspapers, such as *The Los Angeles Times*, do not even list the translators in headnotes to reviews, reviewers often fail to mention that a book is a translation (while quoting from the text as though it were written in English), and publishers almost uniformly exclude translators from book covers and advertisements" (Christ 1984:8). Even when the reviewer is also a writer, a novelist, say, or a poet, the fact that the text under review is a translation may be overlooked. In 1981, the American novelist John Updike reviewed two foreign novels for *The New Yorker*, Italo Calvino's *If On a Winter's Night a Traveller* and Günter Grass's *The Meeting at Telgte*, but the lengthy essay made only the barest reference to the translators. Their names appeared in parentheses after the first mention of the English-language titles. Reviewers who may be expected to have a writerly sense of language are seldom inclined to discuss translation as writing.

The translator's shadowy existence in Anglo-American culture is further registered, and maintained, in the ambiguous and unfavorable legal status of translation, both in copyright law and in actual contractual arrangements. British and American law defines translation as an "adaptation" or "derivative work" based on an "original work of authorship," whose copyright, including the exclusive right "to prepare derivative works" or "adaptations," is vested in the "author."[3] The translator is thus subordinated to the author, who decisively controls the publication of the translation during the term of the copyright for the "original" text, currently the author's lifetime plus fifty years. Yet since authorship here is defined as the creation of a form or medium of expression, not an idea, as originality of language, not thought, British and American law permits translations to be copyrighted in the translator's name, recognizing that the translator uses another language for the foreign text and therefore can be understood as creating an original work (Skone James *et al.* 1991; Stracher 1991). In copyright law, the translator is and is not an author.[4]

The translator's authorship is never given full legal recognition because of the priority given to the foreign writer in controlling the translation – even to point of compromising the translator's rights as a British or American citizen. In subscribing to international copyright treaties like the Berne Convention for the Protection of Literary and Artistic Works, the United Kingdom and the United States agree to treat nationals of other member countries like their own nationals for purposes of copyright (Scarles 1980:8–11). Hence, British and American law holds that an English-language translation of a foreign text can be published only by arrangement with the author who owns the copyright for that text – i.e., the foreign writer, or, as the case may be, a foreign agent or publisher. The translator may be allowed the authorial privilege to copyright the translation, but he or she is excluded from the legal protection that authors enjoy as citizens of the UK or US in deference to another author, a foreign national. The ambiguous legal definition of translation, both original and derivative, exposes a limitation in the translator's citizenship, as well as the inability of current copyright law to think translation across national boundaries despite the existence of international treaties. The Berne Convention (Paris 1971) at once assigns an authorial right to the translator and withdraws it: "Translations, adaptations, arrangements of music and other alterations of a literary or artistic work shall be protected as original works without prejudice to the copyright in the original work" held by the foreign "author," who "shall enjoy the exclusive right of making and of authorising the translation" (articles 2(3), 8).[5] Copyright law does not define a space for the translator's authorship that is equal to, or in any way restricts, the foreign author's rights. And yet it acknowledges that there is a material basis to warrant some such restriction.

Translation contracts in the postwar period have in fact varied widely, partly because of the ambiguities in copyright law, but also because of other factors like changing book markets, a particular translator's level of expertise, and the difficulty of a particular translation project. Nonetheless, general trends can be detected over the course of several decades, and they reveal publishers excluding the translator from any rights in the translation. Standard British contracts require the translator to make an out-and-out assignment of the copyright to the publisher. In the United States, the most common contractual definition of the translated text has not been "original work of authorship," but "work made for hire," a category in American copyright law whereby "the employer or person for whom the work was prepared is considered the author [...] and, unless the parties have expressly agreed otherwise in a written instrument signed by them, owns all the rights comprised in the copyright" (17 US Code, sections 101, 201(6)). Work-for-hire contracts alienate the translator from the product of his or her labor with remarkable finality. Here is the relevant clause in Columbia University Press's standard contract for translators:

> You and we agree that the work you will prepare has been specially ordered and commissioned by us, and is a work made for hire as such term is used and defined by the Copyright Act. Accordingly, we shall be considered the sole and exclusive owner throughout the world forever of all rights existing therein, free of claims by you or anyone claiming through you or on your behalf.

This work-for-hire contract embodies the ambiguity of the translator's legal status by including another clause that implicitly recognizes the translator as an author, the creator of an "original" work: "You warrant that your work will be original and that it will not infringe upon the copyright or violate any right of any person or party whatsoever."

Contracts that require translators to assign the copyright, or that define translations as works made for hire, are obviously exploitative in the division of earnings. Such translations are compensated by a flat fee per thousand English words, regardless of the potential income from the sale of books and subsidiary rights (e.g., a periodical publication, a license to a paperback publisher, an option by a film production company). An actual case will make clear how this arrangement exploits translators. On 12 May 1965, the American translator Paul Blackburn entered into a work-for-hire arrangement with Pantheon in which he received "$15.00 per thousand words" for his translation of *End of the Game*, a collection of short stories by the Argentine writer Julio Cortázar.[6] Blackburn received a total of $1200 for producing an English-language translation that filled 277 pages as a printed book; Cortázar received a $2000 advance against royalties, 7.5 percent of the list price for the first 5000 copies. The "poverty level" set by the Federal government in 1965 was an annual income of $1894 (for a male). Blackburn's income as an editor was usually $8000, but to complete the translation he was forced to reduce his editorial work and seek a grant from arts agencies and private foundations – which he failed to receive. Ultimately, he requested an extension of the delivery date for the translation from roughly a year to sixteen months (the contracted date of 1 June 1966 was later changed to 1 October 1966).

Blackburn's difficult situation has been faced by most freelance English-language translators throughout the postwar period: below-subsistence fees force them either to translate sporadically, while working at other jobs (typically editing, writing, teaching), or to undertake multiple translation projects simultaneously, the number of which is determined by the book market and sheer physical limitations. By 1969, the fee for work-for-hire translations increased to $20 per thousand words, making Blackburn's Cortázar project worth $1600, while the poverty level was set at $1974; by 1979, the going rate was $30 and Blackburn would have made $2400, while the poverty level was $3689.[7] According to a 1990 survey conducted by the PEN American Center and limited to the responses of nineteen publishers, 75 percent of the translations surveyed were contracted on a work-for-hire basis, with fees ranging from $40 to $90 per thousand words (Keeley 1990:10–12; *A Handbook for Literary Translators* 1991:5–6). A recent estimate puts the translation cost of a 300-page novel between $3000 and $6000 (Marcus 1990:13–14; cf. Gardam 1990). The poverty level in 1989 was set at $5936 for a person under 65 years. Because this economic situation drives freelance translators to turn out several translations each year, it inevitably limits the literary invention and critical reflection applied to a project, while pitting translators against each other – often unwittingly – in the competition for projects and the negotiation of fees.

Contracts since the 1980s show an increasing recognition of the translator's crucial role in the production of the translation by referring to him or her as the "author" or "translator" and by copyrighting the text in the translator's name. This redefinition has been accompanied by an improvement in financial terms, with experienced translators receiving an advance against royalties, usually a percentage of the list price or the net proceeds, as well as a portion of subsidiary rights sales. The 1990 PEN survey indicated that translators' royalties were "in the area of 2 to 5 percent for hardcover and 1.5 to 2.5 percent for paperback" (*Handbook* 1991:5). But these are clearly small increments. While they signal a growing awareness of the translator's authorship, they do not constitute a significant change in the economics of translation, and it remains difficult for a freelance translator to make a living solely from translating. A typical first printing for a literary translation published by a trade press is approximately 5000 copies (less for a university press), so that even with the trend toward contracts offering royalties, the translator is unlikely to see any income beyond the advance. Very few translations become bestsellers; very few are likely to be reprinted, whether in hardcover or paperback. And, perhaps most importantly, very few translations are published in English.

As Figures 1 and 2 indicate, British and American book production increased fourfold since the 1950s, but the number of translations remained roughly between 2 and 4 percent of the total – notwithstanding a marked surge during the early 1960s, when the number of translations ranged between 4 and 7 percent of the total.[8] In 1990, British publishers brought out 63,980 books, of which 1625 were translations (2.4 percent), while American publishers brought out 46,743 books, including 1380 translations (2.96 percent). Publishing practices in other countries have generally run in the opposite direction. Western European publishing also burgeoned over the past several decades, but translations have always amounted to a significant percentage of total book production, and this percentage has consistently been dominated by translations from English. The translation rate in France has varied between 8 and 12 percent of the total. In 1985, French publishers brought out 29,068 books, of which 2867 were translations (9.9 percent), 2051 from English (Frémy 1992). The translation rate in Italy has been higher. In 1989, Italian publishers brought out 33,893 books, of which 8602 were translations (25.4 percent), more than half from English (Lottman 1991:S5). The German publishing industry is somewhat larger than its British and American counterparts, and here too the translation rate is considerably higher. In 1990, German publishers brought out

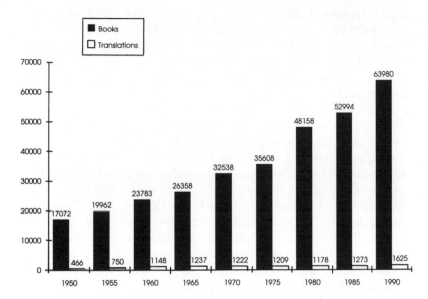

Figure 1   British publishing: Total book output vs. translations

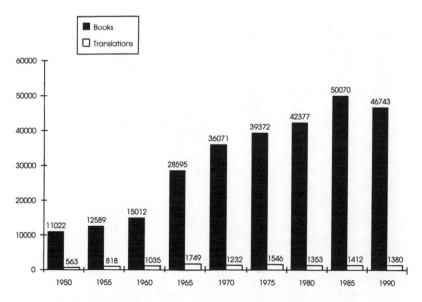

Figure 2   American publishing: Total book ouput vs. translations

61,015 books, of which 8716 were translations (14.4 percent), including about 5650 from English (Flad 1992:40). Since World War II, English has been the most translated language worldwide, but it isn't much translated into, given the number of English-language books published annually (Table 1 provides the most recent data).

These translation patterns point to a trade imbalance with serious cultural ramifications. British and American publishers travel every year to international markets like the American Booksellers Convention and the Frankfurt Book Fair, where they sell translation rights for many English-language books, including the global bestsellers, but rarely buy the rights to publish English-language translations of foreign books. British and American publishers have devoted more attention to acquiring bestsellers, and the formation of multinational publishing conglomerates has brought more capital to support this editorial policy (an advance for a predicted bestseller is now in the millions of dollars) while limiting the number of financially risky books, like translations (Whiteside 1981; Feldman 1986). The London literary agent Paul Marsh confirms this trend by urging publishers to concentrate on

Table 1 World translation publications: from selected languages, 1982–1984

	1982	*1983*	*1984*
English	22,208	24,468	22,724
French	6,205	6,084	4,422
German	4,501	4,818	5,311
Russian	6,238	6,370	6,230
Italian	1,433	1,645	1,544
Scandinavian[a]	1,957	2,176	2,192
Spanish	715	847	839
Classical, Greek, Latin	839	1,116	1,035
Hungarian	703	665	679
Arabic	298	322	536
Japanese	208	222	204
Chinese	159	148	163
World totals	52,198	55,618	52,405

[a]Swedish, Danish, Norwegian, Islandic
Source: Grannis 1991, p. 24

selling translation rights instead of buying them: "any book with four or five translation sales in the bag at an early stage stands a good chance of at least nine or 10 by the end of the process" (Marsh 1991:27). Marsh adds that "most translation rights deals are done for a modest return" (ibid.), but the fact is that British and American publishers routinely receive lucrative advances for these deals, even when a foreign publisher or agent pressures them to consider other kinds of income (viz. royalties). The Milan-based Antonella Antonelli is one such agent, although the figure she cites as an imprudent Italian investment in an English-language book – "If you pay a \$200,000 advance, you can't make it back in Italy" – actually suggests how profitable translation rights can be for the publishers involved, foreign as well as British and American (Lottman 1991:S6). The sale of English-language books abroad has also been profitable: in 1990, American book exports amounted to more than \$1.43 billion, with the export–import ratio at 61 to 39.

The consequences of this trade imbalance are diverse and far-reaching. By routinely translating large numbers of the most varied English-language books, foreign publishers have exploited the global drift toward American political and economic hegemony in the postwar period, actively supporting the international expansion of Anglo-American culture. This trend has been reinforced by English-language book imports: the range of foreign countries receiving these books and the various categories into which the books fall show not only the worldwide reach of English, but the depth of its presence in foreign cultures, circulating through the school, the library, the bookstore, determining diverse areas, disciplines, and constituencies – academic and religious, literary and technical, elite and popular, adult and child (see Table 2). British and American publishing, in turn, has reaped the financial benefits of successfully imposing Anglo-American cultural values on a vast foreign readership, while producing cultures in the United Kingdom and the United States that are aggressively monolingual, unreceptive to the foreign, accustomed to fluent translations that invisibly inscribe foreign texts with English-language values and provide readers with the narcissistic experience of recognizing their own culture in a cultural other. The prevalence of fluent domestication has supported these developments because of its economic value: enforced by editors, publishers, and reviewers, fluency results in translations that are eminently readable and therefore consumable on the book market, assisting in their commodification and

Table 2 US book exports to major countries, 1990: shipments valued at $2500 or more

Country	($)	Type of book	($)
Canada 45%	664,448	Dictionaries	4,659
United Kingdom 12%	171,391	Encyclopedias 3%	39,369
Australia 7%	106,274	Atlases	6,725
Japan 6	87,562	Textbooks 9%	128,431
Germany, West 3	42,244	Bibles & other	
Netherlands 2	33,715	religious 4%	55,341
Mexico 2	32,337	Technical, scientific,	
Singapore 2	31,321	professional 23%	322,647
France 1	20,144	Art & pictorial	12,242
India	17,576	Music	17,502
Taiwan	15,304	Children's picture,	
Hong Kong	12,853	coloring, drawing	12,875
Brazil	12,451	Other hardbound	42,194
South Africa	11,378	Rack-size	
Philippines	10,560	paperbound	49,956
Switzerland	9,854	Other	736,063
Italy	9,799		
Spain	9,687	Total	1,428,004
New Zealand	9,600		
Korea, South	8,245		
Ireland	7,946		
Sweden	6,597		
Argentina	5,746		
Finland	5,095		
Venezuela	4,772		
Israel	4,321		
Denmark	4,012		
Malaysia	3,998		
Portugal	3,881		
Total	1,428,003		

Source: Grannis 1991, pp. 21 and 22

insuring the neglect of foreign texts and English-language translation discourses that are more resistant to easy readability.

The translator's invisibility can now be seen as a mystification of
troubling proportions, an amazingly successful concealment of the
multiple determinants and effects of English-language translation,
the multiple hierarchies and exclusions in which it is implicated.
An illusionism produced by fluent translating, the translator's
invisibility at once enacts and masks an insidious domestication of

foreign texts, rewriting them in the transparent discourse that prevails in English and that selects precisely those foreign texts amenable to fluent translating. Insofar as the effect of transparency effaces the work of translation, it contributes to the cultural marginality and economic exploitation that English-language translators have long suffered, their status as seldom recognized, poorly paid writers whose work nonetheless remains indispensable because of the global domination of Anglo-American culture, of English. Behind the translator's invisibility is a trade imbalance that underwrites this domination, but also decreases the cultural capital of foreign values in English by limiting the number of foreign texts translated and submitting them to domesticating revision. The translator's invisibility is symptomatic of a complacency in Anglo-American relations with cultural others, a complacency that can be described – without too much exaggeration – as imperialistic abroad and xenophobic at home.

The concept of the translator's "invisibility" is already a cultural critique, a diagnosis that opposes the situation it represents. It is partly a representation from below, from the standpoint of the contemporary English-language translator, although one who has been driven to question the conditions of his work because of various developments, cultural and social, foreign and domestic. The motive of this book is to make the translator more visible so as to resist and change the conditions under which translation is theorized and practiced today, especially in English-speaking countries. Hence, the first step will be to present a theoretical basis from which translations can be read as translations, as texts in their own right, permitting transparency to be demystified, seen as one discursive effect among others.

II

Translation is a process by which the chain of signifiers that constitutes the source-language text is replaced by a chain of signifiers in the target language which the translator provides on the strength of an interpretation. Because meaning is an effect of relations and differences among signifiers along a potentially endless chain (polysemous, intertextual, subject to infinite linkages), it is always differential and deferred, never present as an original unity (Derrida 1982). Both foreign text and translation are derivative: both consist of diverse linguistic and cultural materials that neither the foreign writer nor the translator originates, and that destabilize the work of signification, inevitably exceeding and possibly conflicting with their intentions. As a result, a foreign text is the site of many different semantic possibilities that are fixed only provisionally in any one translation, on the basis of varying cultural assumptions and interpretive choices, in specific social situations, in different historical periods. Meaning is a plural and contingent relation, not an unchanging unified essence, and therefore a translation cannot be judged according to mathematics-based concepts of semantic equivalence or one-to-one correspondence. Appeals to the foreign text cannot finally adjudicate between competing translations in the absence of linguistic error, because canons of accuracy in translation, notions of "fidelity" and "freedom," are historically determined categories. Even the notion of "linguistic error" is subject to variation, since mistranslations, especially in literary texts, can be not merely intelligible but significant in the target-language culture. The viability of a translation is established by its relationship to the cultural and social conditions under which it is produced and read.

This relationship points to the violence that resides in the very purpose and activity of translation: the reconstitution of the foreign text in accordance with values, beliefs and representations that preexist it in the target language, always configured in hierarchies of dominance and marginality, always determining the production, circulation, and reception of texts. Translation is the forcible replacement of the linguistic and cultural difference of the foreign text with a text that will be intelligible to the target-language reader. This difference can never be entirely removed, of course, but it necessarily suffers a reduction and exclusion of possibilities – and an exorbitant gain of other possibilities specific to the translating language. Whatever difference the translation conveys is now imprinted by the target-language culture, assimilated to its positions of intelligibility, its canons and taboos, its codes and ideologies. The aim of translation is to bring back a cultural other as the same, the recognizable, even the familiar; and this aim always risks a wholesale domestication of the foreign text, often in highly self-conscious projects, where translation serves an appropriation of foreign cultures for domestic agendas, cultural, economic, political. Translation can be considered the communication of a foreign text, but it is always a communication limited by its address to a specific reading audience.

The violent effects of translation are felt at home as well as abroad. On the one hand, translation wields enormous power in the construction of national identities for foreign cultures, and hence it potentially figures in ethnic discrimination, geopolitical confrontations, colonialism, terrorism, war. On the other hand, translation enlists the foreign text in the maintenance or revision of literary canons in the target-language culture, inscribing poetry and fiction, for example, with the various poetic and narrative discourses that compete for cultural dominance in the target language. Translation also enlists the foreign text in the maintenance or revision of dominant conceptual paradigms, research methodologies, and clinical practices in target-language disciplines and professions, whether physics or architecture, philosophy or psychiatry, sociology or law. It is these social affiliations and effects – written into the materiality of the translated text, into its discursive strategy and its range of allusiveness for the target-language reader, but also into the very choice to translate it and the ways it is published, reviewed, and taught – all these conditions permit translation to be called a cultural political practice, constructing or critiquing ideology-stamped identities for foreign cultures, affirming or transgressing discursive values and institutional limits in the target-language culture. The violence wreaked by translation is partly inevitable, inherent in the translation process, partly potential, emerging at any point in the production and reception of the translated text, varying with specific cultural and social formations at different historical moments.

The most urgent question facing the translator who possesses this knowledge is, What to do? Why and how do I translate? Although I have construed translation as the site of many determinations and effects – linguistic, cultural, economic, ideological – I also want to indicate that the freelance literary translator always exercises a choice concerning the degree and direction of the violence at work in any translating. This choice has been given various formulations, past and present, but perhaps none so decisive as that offered by the German theologian and philosopher Friedrich Schleiermacher. In an 1813 lecture on the different methods of translation, Schleiermacher argued that "there are only two. Either the translator leaves the author in peace, as much as possible, and moves the reader towards him; or he leaves the reader in peace, as much as possible, and moves the author towards him" (Lefevere 1977:74). Admitting (with qualifications like "as much as possible") that translation can never be completely adequate to the foreign text, Schleiermacher allowed the translator to choose between a domesticating method, an ethnocentric reduction of the foreign text to target-language cultural values, bringing the author back home, and a foreignizing method, an ethnodeviant pressure on those values to register the linguistic and cultural difference of the foreign text, sending the reader abroad.

Schleiermacher made clear that his choice was foreignizing translation, and this led the French translator and translation theorist Antoine Berman to treat Schleiermacher's argument as an ethics of translation, concerned with making the translated text a place where a cultural other is manifested – although, of course, an otherness that can never be manifested in its own terms, only in those of the target language, and hence always already encoded (Berman 1985:87–91).[9] The "foreign" in foreignizing translation is not a transparent representation of an essence that resides in the foreign text and is valuable in itself, but a strategic construction whose value is contingent on the current target-language situation. Foreignizing translation signifies the difference of the foreign text, yet only by disrupting the cultural codes that prevail in the target language. In its effort to do right abroad, this translation method must do wrong at home, deviating enough from native norms to stage an alien reading experience – choosing to translate a foreign text excluded by domestic literary canons, for instance, or using a marginal discourse to translate it.

I want to suggest that insofar as foreignizing translation seeks to restrain the ethnocentric violence of translation, it is highly desirable today, a strategic cultural intervention in the current state of world affairs, pitched against the hegemonic English-language nations and the unequal cultural exchanges in which they engage their global others. Foreignizing translation in English can be a form of resistance against ethnocentrism and racism, cultural narcissism and imperialism, in the interests of democratic geopolitical relations. As a theory and practice of translation, however, a foreignizing method is specific to certain European countries at particular historical moments: formulated first in German culture during the classical and romantic periods, it has recently been revived in a French cultural scene characterized by postmodern developments in philosophy, literary criticism, psychoanalysis, and social theory that have come to be known as "poststructuralism."[10] Anglo-American culture, in contrast, has long been dominated by domesticating theories that recommend fluent translating. By producing the illusion of transparency, a fluent translation masquerades as true semantic equivalence when it in fact inscribes the foreign text with a partial interpretation, partial to English-language values, reducing if not simply excluding the very difference that translation is called on to convey. This ethnocentric violence is evident in the translation theories put forth by the prolific and influential Eugene Nida, translation consultant to the American Bible Society: here transparency is enlisted in the service of Christian humanism.

Consider Nida's concept of "dynamic" or "functional equivalence" in translation, formulated first in 1964, but restated and developed in numerous books and articles over the past thirty years. "A translation of dynamic equivalence aims at complete naturalness of expression," states Nida, "and tries to relate the receptor to modes of behavior relevant within the context of his own culture" (Nida 1964:159). The phrase "naturalness of expression" signals the importance of a fluent strategy to this theory of translation, and in Nida's work it is obvious that fluency involves domestication. As he has recently put it, "the translator must be a person who can draw aside the curtains of linguistic and cultural differences so that people may see clearly the relevance of the original message" (Nida and de Waard 1986:14). This is of course a relevance to the target-language culture, something with which foreign writers are usually not concerned when they write their texts, so that relevance can be established in the translation process only by replacing source-language features that are not recognizable with target-language ones that are. Thus, when Nida asserts that "an easy and natural style in translating, despite the extreme difficulty of producing it [...] is nevertheless essential to producing in the ultimate receptors a response similar to that of the original receptors" (Nida 1964:163), he is in fact imposing the English-language valorization of transparent discourse on every foreign culture, masking a basic disjunction between the source- and target-language texts which puts into question the possibility of eliciting a "similar" response.

Typical of other theorists in the Anglo-American tradition, however, Nida has argued that dynamic equivalence is consistent with a notion of accuracy. The dynamically equivalent translation does not indiscriminately use "anything which might have special impact and appeal for receptors"; it rather "means thoroughly understanding not only the meaning of the source text but also the manner in which the intended receptors of a text are likely to understand it in the receptor language" (Nida and de Waard 1986:vii–viii, 9). For Nida, accuracy in translation depends on generating an equivalent effect in the target-language culture: "the receptors of a translation should comprehend the translated text to such an extent that they can understand how the original receptors must have understood the original text" (ibid.:36). The dynamically equivalent translation is "interlingual communication" which overcomes the linguistic and cultural differences that impede it (ibid.:11). Yet the understanding of the foreign text and culture which this kind of translation makes possible answers fundamentally to target-language cultural values while veiling this domestication in the transparency evoked by a fluent strategy. Communication here is initiated and controlled by the target-language culture, it is in fact an interested interpretation, and therefore it seems less an exchange of information than an appropriation of a foreign text for domestic purposes. Nida's theory of translation as communication does not adequately take into account the ethnocentric violence that is inherent in every translation process – but especially in one governed by dynamic equivalence.

Nida's advocacy of domesticating translation is explicitly grounded on a transcendental concept of humanity as an essence that remains unchanged over time and space. "As linguists and anthropologists have discovered," Nida states, "that which unites mankind is much greater than that which divides, and hence there is, even in cases of very disparate languages and cultures, a basis for communication" (Nida 1964:2). Nida's humanism may appear to be democratic in its appeal to "that which unites mankind," but this is contradicted by the more exclusionary values that inform his theory of translation, specifically Christian evangelism and cultural elitism. From the very beginning of his career, Nida's work has been motivated by the exigencies of Bible translation: not only have problems in the history of Bible translation served as examples for his theoretical statements, but he has written studies in anthropology and linguistics designed primarily for Bible translators and missionaries. Nida's concept of dynamic equivalence in fact links the translator to the missionary. When in *Customs and Cultures: Anthropology for Christian Missions* (1954) he asserted that "a close examination of successful missionary work inevitably reveals the correspondingly effective manner in which the missionaries were able to identify themselves with the people – 'to be all things to all men' – and to communicate their message in terms which have meaning for the lives of the people" (Nida 1975:250), he was echoing what he had earlier asserted of the Bible translator in *God's Word in Man's Language* (1952): "The task of the true translator is one of identification. As a Christian servant he must identify with Christ; as a translator he must identify himself with the Word; as a missionary he must identify himself with the people" (Nida 1952:117). Both the missionary and the translator must find the dynamic equivalent in the target language so as to establish the relevance of the Bible in the target culture. But Nida permits only a particular kind of relevance to be established. While he disapproves of "the tendency to promote by means of Bible translating the cause of a particular theological viewpoint, whether deistic, rationalistic, immersionistic, millenarian, or charismatic" (Nida and de Waard 1986:33), it is obvious that he himself has promoted a reception of the text centered in Christian dogma. And although he offers a nuanced account of how "diversities in the backgrounds of receptors" can shape any Bible translation, he insists that "translations prepared primarily for minority groups must generally involve highly restrictive forms of language, but they must not involve substandard grammar or vulgar wording" (ibid.:14). Nida's concept of dynamic equivalence in Bible translation goes hand in hand with an evangelical zeal that seeks to impose on English-language readers a specific dialect of English as well as a distinctly Christian understanding of the Bible. When Nida's translator identifies with the target-language reader to communicate the foreign text, he simultaneously excludes other target-language cultural constituencies.

To advocate foreignizing translation in opposition to the Anglo-American tradition of domestication is not to do away with cultural political agendas – such an advocacy is itself an agenda. The point is rather to develop a theory and practice of translation that resists dominant target-language cultural values so as to signify the linguistic and cultural difference of the foreign text. Philip Lewis's concept of "abusive fidelity" can be useful in such a theorization: it acknowledges the abusive, equivocal relationship between the translation and the foreign text and eschews a fluent strategy in order to reproduce in the translation whatever features of the foreign text abuse or resist dominant cultural values in the source language. Abusive fidelity directs the translator's attention away from the conceptual signified to the play of signifiers on which it depends, to phonological, syntactical, and discursive structures, resulting in a "translation that values experimentation, tampers with usage, seeks to match the polyvalencies or plurivocities or expressive stresses of the original by producing its own" (Lewis 1985:41). Such a translation strategy can best be called *resistancy*, not merely because it avoids fluency, but because it challenges the target-language culture even as it enacts its own ethnocentric violence on the foreign text.

The notion of foreignization can alter the ways translations are read as well as produced because it assumes a concept of human subjectivity that is very different from the humanist assumptions underlying domestication. Neither the foreign writer nor the translator is conceived as the transcendental origin of the text, freely expressing an idea about human nature or communicating it in transparent language to a reader from a different culture. Rather, subjectivity is constituted by cultural and social determinations that are diverse and even conflicting, that mediate any language use, and that vary with every cultural formation and every historical moment. Human action is intentional, but determinate, self-reflexively measured against social rules and resources, the heterogeneity of which allows for the possibility of change with every self-reflexive action (Giddens 1979:chap. 2). Textual production may be initiated and guided by the producer, but it puts to work various linguistic and cultural materials which make the text discontinuous, despite any appearance of unity, and which create an unconscious, a set of unacknowledged conditions that are both personal and social, psychological and ideological. Thus, the translator consults many different target-language cultural materials, ranging from dictionaries and grammars to texts, discursive strategies, and translations, to values, paradigms, and ideologies, both canonical and marginal. Although intended to reproduce the source-language text, the translator's consultation of these materials inevitably reduces and supplements it, even when source-language cultural materials are also consulted. Their sheer heterogeneity leads to discontinuities – between the source-language text and the translation and within the translation itself – that are symptomatic of its ethnocentric violence. A humanist method of reading translations elides these discontinuities by locating a semantic unity adequate to the foreign text, stressing intelligibility, transparent communication, the use value of the translation in the target-language culture. A symptomatic reading, in contrast, locates discontinuities at the level of diction, syntax, or discourse that reveal the translation to be a violent rewriting of the foreign text, a strategic intervention into the target-language culture, at once dependent on and abusive of domestic values.

This method of symptomatic reading can be illustrated with the translations of Freud's texts for the *Standard Edition*, although the translations acquired such unimpeachable authority that we needed Bruno Bettelheim's critique to become aware of the discontinuities. Bettelheim's point is that the translations make Freud's texts "appear to readers of English as abstract, depersonalized, highly theoretical, erudite, and mechanized – in short, 'scientific' – statements about the strange and very complex workings of our mind" (Bettelheim 1983:5). Bettelheim seems to assume that a close examination of Freud's German is necessary to detect the translators' scientistic strategy, but the fact is that his point can be demonstrated with no more than a careful reading of the English text. Bettelheim argues, for example, that in *The Psychopathology of Everyday Life* (1960), the term "parapraxis" reveals the scientism of the translation because it is used to render a rather simple German word, *Fehlleistungen*, which Bettelheim himself prefers to translate as "faulty achievement" (Bettelheim 1983:87). Yet the translator's strategy may also be glimpsed through certain peculiarities in the diction of the translated text:

> I now return to the forgetting of names. So far we have not exhaustively considered either the case-material or the motives behind it. As this is exactly the kind of parapraxis that I can from time to time observe abundantly in myself, I am at no loss for examples. The mild attacks of migraine from which I still suffer usually announce themselves hours in advance by my forgetting names, and at the height of these attacks, during which I am not forced to abandon my work, it frequently happens that all proper names go out of my head.
>
> (Freud 1960:21)

The diction of much of this passage is so simple and common ("forgetting"), even colloquial ("go out of my head"), that "parapraxis" represents a conspicuous difference, an inconsistency in word choice which exposes the translation process. The inconsistency is underscored not only by Freud's heavy reliance on anecdotal, "everyday" examples, some – as above – taken from his own experience, but also by a footnote added to a later edition of the German text and included in the English translation: "This book is of an entirely popular character; it merely aims, by an accumulation of examples, at paving the way for the necessary assumption of *unconscious yet operative* mental processes, and it avoids all theoretical considerations on the nature of the unconscious" (Freud 1960: 272n.). James Strachey himself unwittingly called attention to the inconsistent diction in his preface to Alan Tyson's translation, where he felt it necessary to provide a rationale for the use of "parapraxis": "In German '*Fehlleistung,*' 'faulty function.' It is a curious fact that before Freud wrote this book the general concept seems not to have existed in psychology, and in English a new word had to be invented to cover it" (Freud 1960:viiin.). It can of course be objected (against Bettelheim) that the mixture of specialized scientific terms and commonly used diction is characteristic of Freud's German, and therefore (against me) that the English translation in itself cannot be the basis for an account of the translators' strategy. Yet although I am very much in agreement with the first point, the second weakens when we realize that even a comparison between the English versions of key Freudian terms easily demonstrates the inconsistency in kinds of diction I have located in the translated passage: "id" vs. "unconscious"; "cathexis" vs. "charge," or "energy"; "libidinal" vs. "sexual."

Bettelheim suggests some of the determinations that shaped the scientistic translation strategy of the *Standard Edition*. One important consideration is the intellectual current that has dominated Anglo-American psychology and philosophy since the eighteenth century: "In theory, many topics with which Freud dealt permit both a hermeneutic–spiritual and a positivistic–pragmatic approach. When this is so, the English translators nearly always opt for the latter, positivism being the most important English philosophical tradition" (Bettelheim 1983:44). But there are also the social institutions in which this tradition was entrenched and against which psychoanalysis had to struggle in order to gain acceptance in the post-World War II period. As Bettelheim concisely puts it, "psychological research and teaching in American universities are either behaviorally, cognitively, or physiologically oriented and concentrate almost exclusively on what can be measured or observed from the outside" (ibid.:19). For psychoanalysis this meant that its assimilation in Anglo-American culture entailed a redefinition, in which it "was perceived in the United States as a practice that ought to be the sole prerogative of physicians" (ibid.:33), "a medical specialty" (ibid.:35), and this redefinition was carried out in a variety of social practices, including not only legislation by state assemblies and certification by the psychoanalytic profession, but the scientistic translation of the *Standard Edition*:

> When Freud appears to be either more abstruse or more dogmatic in English translation than in the original German, to speak about abstract concepts rather than about the reader himself, and about man's mind rather than about his soul, the probable explanation isn't mischievousness or carelessness on the translators' part but a deliberate wish to perceive Freud strictly within the framework of medicine.
>
> (ibid.:32)

The domesticating method at work in the translations of the *Standard Edition* sought to assimilate Freud's texts to the dominance of positivism in Anglo-American culture so as to facilitate the institutionalization of psychoanalysis in the medical profession and in academic psychology.

Bettelheim's book is of course couched in the most judgmental of terms, and it is his negative judgment that must be avoided (or perhaps rethought) if we want to understand the manifold significance of the *Standard Edition* as a translation. Bettelheim views the work of Strachey and his collaborators as a distortion and a betrayal of Freud's "essential humanism," a view that points to a valorization of a concept of the transcendental subject in both Bettelheim and Freud. Bettelheim's assessment of the psychoanalytic project is stated in his own humanistic versions for the *Standard Edition*'s "ego," "id," and "superego": "A reasonable dominance of our I over our it and above-I – this was Freud's goal for all of us" (Bettleheim 1983:110). This notion of ego dominance conceives of the subject as the potentially self-consistent source of its knowledge and actions, not perpetually split by psychological ("id") and social ("superego") determinations over which it has no or limited control. The same assumption can often be seen in Freud's German text: not only in his emphasis on social adjustment, for instance, as with the concept of the "reality principle," but also in his repeated use of his own experience for analysis; both represent the subject as healing the determinate split in its own consciousness. Yet insofar as Freud's various psychic models theorized the ever-present, contradictory determinations of consciousness, the effect of his work was to decenter the subject, to remove it from a transcendental realm of freedom and unity and view it as the determinate product of psychic and familial forces beyond its conscious control. These conflicting concepts of the subject underlie different aspects of Freud's project: the transcendental subject, on the one hand, leads to a definition of psychoanalysis as primarily therapeutic, what Bettelheim calls a "demanding and potentially dangerous voyage of self-discovery [...] so that we may no longer be enslaved without knowing it to the dark forces that reside in us" (ibid.:4); the determinate subject, on the other hand, leads to a definition of psychoanalysis as primarily hermeneutic, a theoretical apparatus with sufficient scientific rigor to analyze the shifting but always active forces that constitute and divide human subjectivity. Freud's texts are thus marked by a fundamental discontinuity, one which is "resolved" in Bettelheim's humanistic representation of psychoanalysis as compassionate therapy, but which is exacerbated by the scientistic strategy of the English translations and their representation of Freud as the coolly analyzing physician.[11] The inconsistent diction in the *Standard Edition*, by reflecting the positivistic redefinition of psychoanalysis in Anglo-American institutions, signifies another, alternative reading of Freud that heightens the contradictions in his project.

It can be argued, therefore, that the inconsistent diction in the English translations does not really deserve to be judged erroneous; on the contrary, it discloses interpretive choices determined by a wide range of social institutions and cultural movements, some (like the specific institutionalization of psychoanalysis) calculated by the translators, others (like the dominance of positivism and the discontinuities in Freud's texts) remaining dimly perceived or entirely unconscious during the translation process. The fact that the inconsistencies have gone unnoticed for so long is perhaps largely the result of two mutually determining factors: the privileged status accorded the *Standard Edition* among English-language readers and the entrenchment of a positivistic reading of Freud in the Anglo-American psychoanalytic establishment. Hence, a different critical approach with a different set of assumptions becomes necessary to perceive the inconsistent diction of the translations: Bettelheim's particular humanism, or my own attempt to ground a symptomatic reading of translated texts on a foreignizing method of translation that assumes a determinate concept of subjectivity. This sort of reading can be said to foreignize a domesticating translation by showing where it is discontinuous; a translation's dependence on dominant values in the target-language culture becomes most visible where it departs from them. Yet this reading also uncovers the domesticating movement involved in any foreignizing translation by showing where its construction of the foreign depends on domestic cultural materials.

Symptomatic reading can thus be useful in demystifying the illusion of transparency in a contemporary English-language translation. In some translations, the discontinuities are readily apparent, unintentionally disturbing the fluency of the language, revealing the inscription of the domestic culture; other translations bear prefaces that announce the translator's strategy and alert the reader to the presence of noticeable stylistic peculiarities. A case in point is Robert Graves's version of Suetonius's *The Twelve Caesars*. Graves's preface offered a frank account of his domesticating translation method:

> For English readers Suetonius's sentences, and sometimes even groups of sentences, must often be turned inside-out. Wherever his references are incomprehensible to anyone not closely familiar with the Roman scene, I have also brought up into the text a few words of explanation that would normally have appeared in a footnote. Dates have been everywhere changed from the pagan to the Christian era; modern names of cities used whenever they are more familiar to the common reader than the classical ones; and sums in sesterces reduced to gold pieces, at 100 to a gold piece (of twenty denarii), which resembled a British sovereign.
>
> (Graves 1957:8)

Graves's vigorous revision of the foreign text aims to assimilate the source-language culture (Imperial Rome) to that of the target language (the United Kingdom in 1957). The work of assimilation depends not only on his extensive knowledge of Suetonius and Roman culture during the Empire (e.g. the monetary system), but also on his knowledge of contemporary British culture as manifested by English syntactical forms and what he takes to be the function of his translation. His "version," he wrote in the preface, was not intended to serve as a "school crib," but to be readable: "a literal rendering would be almost unreadable" (ibid.:8) because it would adhere too closely to the Latin text, even to the Latin word order.

Graves sought to make his translation extremely fluent, and it is important to note that this was both a deliberate choice and culturally specific, determined by contemporary English-language values and not by any means absolute or originating with Graves in a fundamental way. On the contrary, the entire process of producing the translation, beginning with the very choice of the text and including both Graves's textual moves and the decision to publish the translation in paperback, was conditioned by factors like the decline in the study of classical languages among educated readers, the absence of another translation on the market, and the remarkable popularity of the novels that Graves himself created from Roman historians like Suetonius – *I, Claudius* and *Claudius the God*, both continuously in print since 1934. Graves's version of *The Twelve Caesars* appeared as one of the "Penguin Classics," a mass-market imprint designed for both students and general readers.

As J. M. Cohen has observed, the translations in Penguin Classics were pioneering in their use of transparent discourse, "plain prose uniformity," largely in response to cultural and social conditions:

> The translator [...] aims to make everything plain, though without the use of footnotes since the conditions of reading have radically changed and the young person of today is generally reading in far less comfortable surroundings than his father or grandfather. He has therefore to carry forward on an irresistible stream of narrative. Little can be demanded of him except his attention. Knowledge, standards of comparison, Classical background: all must be supplied by the translator in his choice of words or in the briefest of introductions.
>
> (Cohen 1962:33)

Graves's version of Suetonius reflects the cultural marginality of classical scholarship in the post-World War II period and the growth of a mass market for paperback literature, including the bestselling historical novels by which he made a living for many years. His translation was so effective in responding to this situation that it too became a bestseller, reprinted five times within a decade of publication. As Graves indicated in an essay on "Moral Principles in Translation," the "ordinary" reader of a classical text (Diodorus is his example) "wants mere factual information, laid out in good order for his hasty eye to catch" (Graves 1965:51). Although Apuleius "wrote a very ornate North African Latin," Graves translated it "for the general public in the plainest possible prose." Making the foreign text "plain" means that Graves's translation method is radically domesticating: it requires not merely the insertion of explanatory phrases, but the inscription of the foreign text with values that are anachronistic and ethnocentric. In the preface to his Suetonius, Graves made clear that he deliberately modernized and Anglicized the Latin. At one point, he considered adding an introductory essay that would signal the cultural and historical difference of the text by describing key political conflicts in late Republican Rome. But he finally omitted it: "most readers," he felt, "will perhaps prefer to plunge straight into the story and pick up the threads as they go along" (Graves 1957:8), allowing his fluent prose to turn transparent and so conceal the domesticating work of the translation.

This work can be glimpsed in discontinuities between Graves's translation discourse and Suetonius's particular method of historical and biographical narrative. Graves's reading of Suetonius, as sketched in his preface, largely agreed with the contemporary academic reception of the Latin text. As the classicist Michael Grant has pointed out, Suetonius

> gathers together, and lavishly inserts, information both for and against [the rulers of Rome], usually without adding any personal judgment in one direction or the other, and above all without introducing the moralizations which had so frequently characterized Greek and Roman biography and history alike. Occasionally conflicting statements are weighed. In general, however, the presentation is drily indiscriminate. [...] the author's own opinions are rarely permitted to intrude, and indeed he himself, in collecting all this weird, fascinating material, appears to make little effort to reach a decision about the personalities he is describing, or to build up their characteristics into a coherent account. Perhaps, he may feel, that is how people are: they possess discordant elements which do not add up to a harmonious unity.
>
> (Grant 1980:8)

Grant's account suggests that the Latin text does not offer a coherent position of subjectivity for the reader to occupy: we are unable to identify with either the author ("the author's own opinions are rarely permitted to intrude") or the characters ("the personalities" are not given "a coherent account"). As a result, Suetonius's narrative may seem to possess a "relatively high degree of objectivity," but it also contains passages that provoke considerable doubt, especially since "his curiously disjointed and staccato diction can lead to obscurity" (ibid.:7–8). Graves's fluent translation smooths out these features of the Latin text, insuring intelligibility, constructing a more coherent position from which the Caesars can be judged, and making any judgment seem true, right, obvious.

Consider this passage from the life of Julius Caesar:

> Stipendia prima in Asia fecit Marci Thermi praetoris contubernio; a quo ad accersendam classem in Bithyniam missus desedit apud Nicomeden, non sine rumorem prostratae regi pudicitiae; quem rumorem auxit intra paucos rursus dies repetita Bithynia per causam exigendae pecuniae, quae deberetur cuidam libertino clienti suo. reliqua militia secundiore fama fuit et a Thermo in expugnatione Mytilenarum corona civica donatus est.
>
> (Butler and Cary 1927:1–2)

> Caesar first saw military service in Asia, where he went as aide-de-camp to Marcus Thermus, the provincial governor. When Thermus sent Caesar to raise a fleet in Bithynia, he wasted so much time at King Nicomedes' court that a homosexual relationship between them was suspected, and suspicion gave place to scandal when, soon after his return to headquarters, he revisited Bithynia: ostensibly collecting a debt incurred there by one of his freedmen. However, Caesar's reputation improved later in the campaign, when Thermus awarded him the civic crown of oak leaves, at the storming of Mytilene, for saving a fellow soldier's life.
>
> (Graves 1957:10)

Both passages rest on innuendo instead of explicit judgment, on doubtful hearsay instead of more reliable evidence ("rumorem," "suspicion"). Yet the English text makes several additions that offer more certainty about Caesar's motives and actions and about Suetonius's own estimation: the translation is not just slanted

against Caesar, but homophobic. This first appears in an inconsistency in the diction: Graves's use of "homosexual relationship"
to render "prostratae regi pudicitiae" ("surrendered his modesty to
the king") is an anachronism, a late nineteenth-century scientific
term that diagnoses same-sex sexual activity as pathological and is
therefore inappropriate for an ancient culture in which sexual acts
were not categorized according to the participants' sex (*OED*;
Wiseman 1985:10–14). Graves then leads the reader to believe that
this relationship did in fact occur: not only does he increase the
innuendo by using "suspicion gave place to scandal" to translate
"rumorem auxit" ("the rumor spread"), but he inserts the loaded
"ostensibly," entirely absent from the Latin text. Graves's version
implicitly equates homosexuality with perversion, but since the
relationship was with a foreign monarch, there are also political
implications, the hint of a traitorous collusion which the ambitious
Caesar is concealing and which he may later exploit in a bid for
power: the passage immediately preceding this one has the dictator
Sulla associating Caesar with his archenemy Marius. Because the
passage is so charged with lurid accusations, even the conclusive
force of that "however," promising a rehabilitation of Caesar's
image, is finally subverted by the possible suggestion of another
sexual relationship in "saving a fellow soldier's life."

Suetonius later touches on Caesar's sexual reputation, and here
too Graves's version is marked by a homophobic bias:

> Pudicitiae eius famam nihil quidem praeter Nicomedis con-
> tubernium laesit.
>
> (Butler and Cary 1927:22)

> The only specific charge of unnatural practices ever brought
> against him was that he had been King Nicomedes' catamite.
>
> (Graves 1957:30)

Where the Latin text makes rather general and noncommittal
references to Caesar's sexuality, Graves chooses English words that
stigmatize same-sex sexual acts as perverse: a question raised about
"pudicitiae eius famam" ("his sexual reputation") becomes a
"specific charge of unnatural practices," while "contubernium"
("sharing the same tent," "companionship," "intimacy") makes
Caesar a "catamite," a term of abuse in the early modern period for
boys who were the sexual objects of men (*OED*). As an archaism,
"catamite" deviates from the modern English lexicon used

throughout this and other Penguin Classics, a deviation that is symptomatic of the domesticating process in Graves's version. His prose is so lucid and supple that such symptoms can well be overlooked, enabling the translation to fix an interpretation while presenting that interpretation as authoritative, issuing from an authorial position that transcends linguistic and cultural differences to address the English-language reader. Graves's interpretation, however, assimilates an ancient Latin text to contemporary British values. He punctures the myth of Caesar by equating the Roman dictatorship with sexual perversion, and this reflects a postwar homophobia that linked homosexuality with a fear of totalitarian government, communism, and political subversion through espionage. "In the Cold War," Alan Sinfield notes, "prosecutions for homosexual 'offences' rose five times over in the 15 years from 1939," and "communist homosexual treachery was witch-hunted close to the heart of the high-cultural establishment" (Sinfield 1989:66, 299). Graves's fluently translated Suetonius participated in this domestic situation, not just by stigmatizing Caesar's sexuality, but by presenting the stigma as a historical fact. In the preface, Graves remarked that Suetonius "seems trustworthy," but he also suggested inadvertently that this Roman historian shared sexual and political values currently prevailing in Britain: "his only prejudice being in favour of firm mild rule, with a regard for the human decencies" (Graves 1957:7).

Foreignizing translations that are not transparent, that eschew fluency for a more heterogeneous mix of discourses, are equally partial in their interpretation of the foreign text, but they tend to flaunt their partiality instead of concealing it. Whereas Graves's Suetonius focuses on the signified, creating an illusion of transparency in which linguistic and cultural differences are domesticated, Ezra Pound's translations often focus on the signifier, creating an opacity that calls attention to itself and distinguishes the translation both from the foreign text and from prevailing values in the target-language culture.

In Pound's work, foreignization sometimes takes the form of archaism. His version of "The Seafarer" (1912) departs from modern English by adhering closely to the Anglo-Saxon text, imitating its compound words, alliteration, and accentual meter, even resorting to calque renderings that echo Anglo-Saxon phonology: "bitre breostceare"/"bitter breast-cares"; "merewerges"/ "mere-weary"; "corna   caldast"/"corn   of   the   coldest";

"floodwegas"/"flood-ways"; "hægl scurum fleag"/"hail-scur flew"; "mæw singende fore medodrince"/"the mews' singing all my mead-drink." But Pound's departures from modern English also include archaisms drawn from later periods of English literature.

> ne ænig hleomæga
> feasceaftig ferð frefran meahte.
> Forþon him gelyfeð lyt, se þe ah lifes wyn
> gebiden in burgum, bealosiþa hwon,
> wlonc ond wingal, hu ic werig oft
> in brimlade bidan sceolde.
> (Krapp and Dobbie 1936:144)

> Not any protector
> May make merry man faring needy.
> This he littles believes, who aye in winsome life
> Abides 'mid burghers some heavy business,
> Wealthy and wine-flushed, how I weary oft
> Must bide above brine.
> (Pound 1954:207)

The word "aye" ("always") is a Middle English usage that later appeared in Scottish and northern dialects, while "burghers" first emerges in the Elizabethan period (*OED*). The words "'mid" (for "amid") and "bide" are poeticisms used by such nineteenth-century writers as Scott, Dickens, Tennyson, Arnold, and Morris. Pound's lexicon in fact favors archaisms that have become poetical: "brine," "o'er," "pinion," "laud," "ado."

Such textual features indicate that a translation can be foreignizing only by putting to work cultural materials and agendas that are *domestic*, specific to the target language, but also, in this case, anachronistic, specific to later periods. "The Seafarer" is informed by Pound's knowledge of English literature from its beginnings, but also by his modernist poetics, by his favoring, notably in *The Cantos*, an elliptical, fragmentary verse in which subjectivity is split and determinate, presented as a site of heterogeneous cultural discourses (Easthope 1983:chap. 9). The peculiarities of Pound's translation – the gnarled syntax, the reverberating alliteration, the densely allusive archaism – slow the movement of the monologue, resisting assimilation, however momentarily, to a coherent subject (whether "author" or "seafarer") and foregrounding the various English dialects and literary discourses that get elided beneath the

illusion of a speaking voice. This translation strategy is foreignizing
in its resistance to values that prevail in contemporary Anglo-
American culture – the canon of fluency in translation, the
dominance of transparent discourse, the individualistic effect of
authorial presence.

And yet Pound's translation reinscribes its own modernist brand
of individualism by editing the Anglo-Saxon text. As the medievalist
Christine Fell has remarked, this text contains "two traditions, the
heroic, if we may so define it, preoccupation with survival of
honour after loss of life – and the Christian hope for security of
tenure in Heaven" (Fell 1991:176). However these conflicting
values entered the text, whether present in some initial oral version
or introduced during a later monastic transcription, they project
two contradictory concepts of subjectivity, one individualistic (the
seafarer as his own person alienated from mead-hall as well as
town), the other collective (the seafarer as a soul in a metaphysical
hierarchy composed of other souls and dominated by God).
Pound's translation resolves this contradiction by omitting the
Christian references entirely, highlighting the strain of heroism in
the Anglo-Saxon text, making the seafarer's "mind's lust" to "seek
out foreign fastness" an example of "daring ado,/So that all men
shall honour him after." In Susan Bassnett's words, Pound's
translation represents "the suffering of a great individual rather
than the common suffering of everyman [...] a grief-stricken exile,
broken but never bowed" (Bassnett 1980:97). The archaizing
translation strategy interferes with the individualistic illusion of
transparency, but the revisions intensify the theme of heroic
individualism, and hence the recurrent gibes at the "burgher" who
complacently pursues his financial interests and "knows not [...]
what some perform/Where wandering them widest draweth"
(Pound 1954: 208). The revisions are symptomatic of the domestic
agenda that animates Pound's foreignizing translation, a peculiar
ideological contradiction that distinguishes modernist literary
experiments: the development of textual strategies that decenter
the transcendental subject coincides with a recuperation of it
through certain individualistic motifs like the "strong personality."
Ultimately, this contradiction constitutes a response to the crisis of
human subjectivity that modernists perceived in social developments like monopoly capitalism, particularly the creation of a mass
work force and the standardization of the work process (Jameson
1979:110–114).

The examples from Graves and Pound show that the aim of a symptomatic reading is not to assess the "freedom" or "fidelity" of a translation, but rather to uncover the canons of accuracy by which it is produced and judged. Fidelity cannot be construed as mere semantic equivalence: on the one hand, the foreign text is susceptible to many different interpretations, even at the level of the individual word; on the other hand, the translator's interpretive choices answer to a domestic cultural situation and so always exceed the foreign text. This does not mean that translation is forever banished to the realm of freedom or error, but that canons of accuracy are culturally specific and historically variable. Although Graves produced a free translation by his own admission, it has nonetheless been judged faithful and accepted as the standard English-language rendering by academic specialists like Grant. In 1979, Grant published an edited version of Graves's translation that pronounced it accurate, if not "precise":

> [It] conveys the peculiarities of Suetonius's methods and character better than any other translation. Why, then, have I been asked to "edit" it? Because Robert Graves (who explicitly refrained from catering for students) did not aim at producing a precise translation – introducing, as he himself points out, sentences of explanation, omitting passages which do not seem to help the sense, and "turning sentences, and sometimes even groups of sentences, inside-out." [...] What I have tried to do, therefore, is to make such adjustments as will bring his version inside the range of what is now generally regarded by readers of the Penguin Classics as a "translation" – without, I hope, detracting from his excellent and inimitable manner.
>
> (Grant 1980:8–9)

In the twenty-two years separating Graves's initial version from the revised edition, the canons of accuracy underwent a change, requiring a translation to be both fluent and exact, to make for "vivid and compulsive reading" (ibid.:8), but also to follow the foreign text more closely. The passages quoted earlier from the life of Caesar were evidently judged accurate in 1979, since Grant made only one revision: "catamite" was replaced by "bedfellow" (ibid.:32). This change brings the English closer to the Latin ("contubernium"), but it also improves the fluency of Graves's prose by replacing an archaism with a more familiar contemporary usage. The revision is obviously too small to minimize the homo-phobia in the passages.

Pound's version of "The Seafarer" also cannot be simply ques-tioned as too free because it is informed by the scholarly reception of the Anglo-Saxon text. As Bassnett has suggested, his omission of the Christian references, including the homiletic epilogue (ll. 103–124), is not so much a deviation from the text preserved in the Exeter Book, as an emendation that responds to a key question in historical scholarship: "Should the poem be perceived as having a Christian message as an integral feature, or are the Christian elements additions that sit uneasily over the pagan foundations?" (Bassnett 1980:96). In *English Literature from the Beginning to the Norman Conquest,* for example, Stopford Brooke asserted that "it is true, the *Seafarer* ends with a Christian tag, but the quality of its verse, which is merely homiletic, has made capable persons give it up as a part of the original poem" (Brooke 1898:153). Pound's translation can be considered accurate according to early twentieth-century academic standards, a translation that is simulta-neously a plausible edition of the Anglo-Saxon text. His departures from the Exeter Book assumed a cultural situation in which Anglo-Saxon was still very much studied by readers, who could therefore be expected to appreciate the work of historical reconstruction implicit in his version of the poem.

The symptomatic reading is an historicist approach to the study of translations that aims to situate canons of accuracy in their specific cultural moments. Critical categories like "fluency" and "resistancy," "domesticating" and "foreignizing," can only be defined by referring to the formation of cultural discourses in which the translation is produced, and in which certain translation theories and practices are valued over others. At the same time, however, applying these critical categories in the study of translations is anachronistic: they are fundamentally determined by a cultural political agenda in the present, an opposition to the contemporary dominance of transparent discourse, to the privileg-ing of a fluent domesticating method that masks both the translator's work and the asymmetrical relations – cultural, economic, political – between English-language nations and their others worldwide. Although a humanist theory and practice of translation is equally anachronistic, inscribing the foreign-language text with current domestic values, it is also dehistoriciz-ing: the various conditions of translated texts and of their reception are concealed beneath concepts of transcendental subjectivity and transparent communication. A symptomatic reading, in contrast, is historicizing: it assumes a concept of determinate subjectivity that exposes both the ethnocentric violence of translating and the interested nature of its own historicist approach.

III

The project of the present book is to combat the translator's invisibility with a history of – and in opposition to – contemporary English-language translation. Insofar as it is a cultural history with a professed political agenda, it follows the genealogical method developed by Nietzsche and Foucault and abandons the two principles that govern much conventional historiography: teleology and objectivity. Genealogy is a form of historical representation that depicts, not a continuous progression from a unified origin, an inevitable development in which the past fixes the meaning of the present, but a discontinuous succession of division and hierarchy, domination and exclusion, which destabilize the seeming unity of the present by constituting a past with plural, heterogeneous meanings. In a genealogical analysis, writes Foucault, "what is found at the historical beginnings of things is not the inviolable identity of their origin; it is the dissension of other things. It is disparity" (Foucault 1977:142). The possibility of recuperating these "other" meanings explodes the pretense of objectivity in conventional historiography: its teleological emphasis betrays a complicity with the continuance of past domination and exclusion into the present. Thus, history is shown to be a cultural political practice, a partial (i.e., at once selective and evaluative) representation of the past that actively intervenes into the present, even if the interests served by that intervention are not always made explicit or perhaps remain unconscious. For Foucault, a genealogical analysis is unique in affirming the interested nature of its historical representation, in taking a stand vis-à-vis the political struggles of its situation. And by locating what has been dominated or excluded in the past and repressed by conventional historiography, such an analysis can not only challenge the cultural and social conditions in which it is performed, but propose different conditions to be established in the future. History informed by genealogy, Foucault suggests, "should become a differential knowledge of energies and failings, heights and degenerations, poisons and antidotes. Its task is to become a curative science" (ibid.: 156). By constructing a differential representation of the past, genealogy both engages in present cultural debates and social conflicts and develops resolutions that project utopian images.

The Translator's Invisibility intervenes against the translator's situation and activity in contemporary Anglo-American culture by offering a series of genealogies that write the history of present. It traces the rise of transparent discourse in English-language translation from the seventeenth century onward, while searching the past for exits, alternative theories and practices in British, American, and several foreign-language cultures – German, French, Italian.[12] The chapters form an argument pursued chronologically, showing that the origins of fluent translating lie in various kinds of cultural domination and exclusion, but also that translation can serve a more democratic agenda in which excluded theories and practices are recovered and the prevailing fluency is revised. The acts of recovery and revision that constitute this argument rest on extensive archival research, bringing to light forgotten or neglected translations and establishing an alternative tradition that somewhat overlaps with, but mostly differs from, the current canon of British and American literature.

This book is motivated by a strong impulse to *document* the history of English-language translation, to uncover long-obscure translators and translations, to reconstruct their publication and reception, and to articulate significant controversies. The documentary impulse, however, serves the skepticism of symptomatic readings that interrogate the process of domestication in translated texts, both canonical and marginal, and reassess their usefulness in contemporary Anglo-American culture. The historical narratives in each chapter, grounded as they are on a diagnosis of current translation theory and practice, address key questions. What domestic values has transparent discourse at once inscribed and masked in foreign texts during its long domination? How has transparency shaped the canon of foreign literatures in English and the cultural identities of English-language nations? Why has transparency prevailed over other translation strategies in English, like Victorian archaism (Francis Newman, William Morris) and modernist experiments with heterogeneous discourses (Pound, Celia and Louis Zukofsky, Paul Blackburn)? What would happen if a translator tried to redirect the process of domestication by choosing foreign texts that deviated from transparent discourse and by translating them so as to signal their linguistic and cultural differences? Would this effort establish more democratic cultural exchanges? Would it change domestic values? Or would it mean banishment to the fringes of Anglo-American culture?

Throughout, the emphasis is on "literary" translation in a broad sense (mainly poetry and fiction, but also including biography, history, and philosophy, among other genres and disciplines in the human sciences), as opposed to "technical" translation (scientific, legal, diplomatic, commercial). This emphasis is not due to the fact that literary translators today are any more invisible or exploited than their technical counterparts, who, whether freelance or employed by translation agencies, are not permitted to sign or copyright their work, let alone receive royalties (Fischbach 1992:3). Rather, literary translation is emphasized because it has long set the standard applied in technical translation (viz. fluency), and, most importantly for present purposes, it has traditionally been the field where innovative theories and practices emerge. As Schleiermacher realized long ago, the choice of whether to domesticate or foreignize a foreign text has been allowed only to translators of literary texts, not to translators of technical materials. Technical translation is fundamentally constrained by the exigencies of communication: during the postwar period, it has supported scientific research, geopolitical negotiation, and economic exchange, especially as multinational corporations seek to expand foreign markets and thus increasingly require fluent, immediately intelligible translations of international treaties, legal contracts, technical information, and instruction manuals (Levy 1991:F5). Although in sheer volume and financial worth technical translation far exceeds the translation of literary texts (a recent estimate values the corporate and government translation industry at $10 billion), literary translation remains a discursive practice where the translator can experiment in the choice of foreign texts and in the development of translation methods, constrained primarily by the current situation in the target-language culture.

The ultimate aim of the book is to force translators and their readers to reflect on the ethnocentric violence of translation and hence to write and read translated texts in ways that seek to recognize the linguistic and cultural difference of foreign texts. What I am advocating is not an indiscriminate valorization of every foreign culture or a metaphysical concept of foreignness as an essential value; indeed, the foreign text is privileged in a foreign-izing translation only insofar as it enables a disruption of target-language cultural codes, so that its value is always strategic, depending on the cultural formation into which it is translated. The point is rather to elaborate the theoretical, critical, and textual means by which translation can be studied and practiced as a locus of difference, instead of the homogeneity that widely characterizes it today.

Chapter 2

Canon

Words in One Language Elegantly us'd
Will hardly in another be excus'd,
And some that *Rome* admir'd in *Caesars* Time
May neither suit *Our Genius* nor our *Clime*.
The *Genuine Sence, intelligibly* Told,
Shews a *Translator* both *Discreet* and *Bold*.

Earl of Roscommon

Fluency emerges in English-language translation during the early modern period, a feature of aristocratic literary culture in seventeenth-century England, and over the next two hundred years it is valued for diverse reasons, cultural and social, in accordance with the vicissitudes of the hegemonic classes. At the same time, the illusion of transparency produced in fluent translation enacts a thoroughgoing domestication that masks the manifold conditions of the translated text, its exclusionary impact on foreign cultural values, but also on those at home, eliminating translation strategies that resist transparent discourse, closing off any thinking about cultural and social alternatives that do not favor English social elites. The dominance of fluency in English-language translation until today has led to the forgetting of these conditions and exclusions, requiring their recovery to intervene against the contemporary phase of this dominance. The following genealogy aims to trace the rise of fluency as a canon of English-language translation, showing how it achieved canonical status, interrogating its exclusionary effects on the canon of foreign literatures in English, and reconsidering the cultural and social values that it excludes at home.

I

In 1656, Sir John Denham published a translation with the running title, *The Destruction of Troy, An Essay upon the Second Book of Virgils Æneis. Written in the year, 1636*. The title page is one among many remarkable things about this book: it omits any sign of authorship in favor of a bold reference to the gap between the dates of composition and publication. Most early seventeenth-century translations of classical texts are published with a signature, if not a full name (John Ashmore, John Ogilby, Robert Stapylton, John Vicars), then at least initials and some indication of social position, "Sir T: H:," "W.L., Gent." Denham's omission of his name may be taken as the self-effacing gesture of a courtly amateur, presenting himself as not seriously pursuing a literary career, not asserting any individualistic concept of authorship (the title page presents the translation as no more than an "essay") and thus implying that his text is the fruit of hours idle, not spent in the employ of royal authority, in political office or military service.[1] Denham's title page presented his text as a distinctively aristocratic gesture in literary translation, typical of court culture in the Tudor and Stuart periods, and this is clear even in the imprint, *For Humphrey Moseley*, one of the most active publishers of elite literature during the seventeenth century and a staunch royalist who advertised his political views in the prefaces to his publications. Once the social conditions of Denham's book are recognized, the temporal gap indicated by the dates on the title page fills with significance from his own activities in support of the royalist cause, both in the royal government and army during the civil wars and for the exiled royal family and court during the Interregnum. Perhaps the omission of his name should also be taken as an effort to *conceal* his identity, a precaution taken by royalist writers who intended their work to be critical of the Commonwealth (Potter 1989:23–24).

"Written in 1636" proclaimed a continuity between Denham's translation and the years when court poetry and drama were setting the dominant literary trends in England, when the Caroline experiment in absolutism reached its apex, and when Denham himself, the twenty-year-old son of a baron of the Exchequer, was preparing for a legal career at Lincoln's Inn, dabbling in literary pursuits like translating the *Aeneid*. *The Destruction of Troy* was revised and published much later, in *1656* – after Denham returned from several years of exile with the Caroline court in

France, soon after he was arrested in the Commonwealth's campaign to suppress royalist insurgency, a suspect in a military counterplot, and just a year after the second edition of the text by which he is best remembered today, *Coopers Hill* (1642), a topographical poem that offers a politically tendentious evocation of English history on the eve of the civil wars (O'Hehir 1968; Underdown 1960). At this later juncture, Denham's translation assumes the role of a cultural political practice: "Written in 1636" it functions partly as a nostalgic glance back toward less troubled times for royal hegemony and partly as a strategic cultural move in the present, wherein Denham plans to develop a royalist aesthetic in translation to be implemented now and for the future, when hegemony is regained. "The hope of doing [Virgil] more right," Denham asserted in his preface, "is the only scope of this Essay, by opening this new way of translating this Author, to those whom youth, leisure, and better fortune makes fitter for such undertakings" (Denham 1656:A2ᵛ). Denham saw his audience as the coming generations of English aristocracy, who, unlike him, would have the "better fortune" of escaping social displacement in civil wars.

The aristocratic affiliation would have also been perceived by contemporary readers, from various classes and with differing political tendencies. The translation was cited in "An Advertisement of Books newly published" that appeared in *Mercurius Politicus*, the widely circulated newsweekly licensed by Parliament to present a propagandistic survey of current events (Frank 1961:205–210, 223–226). The notice revealed the translator's identity and used the title "Esquire," indicating not only his status as a gentleman, but perhaps his legal education as well: "*The Destruction of Troy*; an Essay upon the second Book of *Virgils Æneis*. Written by JOHN DENHAM, Esquire" (*Mercurius Politicus*: 6921).

The social functioning of Denham's translation becomes clear when his preface is considered in a broader context of translation theory and practice during the seventeenth century. The first point to observe is that Denham's "way of translating" was hardly "new" in 1656. He was following Horace's dictum in *Ars Poetica* that the poet should avoid any word-for-word rendering: "For, being a Poet, thou maist feigne, create,/Not care, as thou wouldst faithfully translate,/To render word for word" – in Ben Jonson's un-Horatian, line-by-line version from 1605 (Jonson 1968:287). But where Horace took translation as one practice of the poet, Denham took poetry as the goal of translation, especially poetry translation: "I conceive it a vulgar error in translating Poets, to affect being *Fides Interpres*," he wrote, because poetic discourse requires more latitude to capture its "spirit" than a close adherence to the foreign text would allow (Denham 1656:A2^v–A3^r). Denham's term "fides interpres" refers to translations of classical poetry that aim for such an adherence, made not by poets, but by scholars, including scholarly poets (Jonson's Horace) and teachers who translate to produce school textbooks. John Brinsley described his 1633 prose version of Virgil's *Eclogues* as

> Translated Grammatically, and also according to the proprietie of our English tongue, so farre as Grammar and the verse will well permit. Written chiefly for the good of schooles, to be used according to the directions in the Preface to the painfull Schoolemaster.

Denham's slur against this method is tellingly couched in class terms: "I conceive it a vulgar error."

Still, in recommending greater freedom against the grammarians, Denham was advocating a classical translation method that reemerged in England decades before he published his version of Virgil (Amos 1920). Thomas Phaer, whose translations of the *Aeneid* date back to 1558, asserted that he "followed the counsell of *Horace*, teaching the duty of a good interpretour, *Qui quae desperat nitescere possit, relinquit*, by which occasion, somewhat, I haue in places omitted, somewhat altered" (Phaer 1620:V2^r). A freer translation method was advocated with greater frequency from the 1620s onward, especially in aristocratic and court circles. Sir Thomas Hawkins, a Catholic who was knighted by James I and whose translations of Jesuit tracts were dedicated to Queen Henrietta Maria, prefaced his 1625 selection of Horace's odes by fending off complaints that he did not imitate classical meters:

> many (no doubt) will say, *Horace* is by mee forsaken, his *Lyrick* softnesse, and emphaticall *Muse* maymed: That in all there is a generall defection from his genuine Harmony. Those I must tell, I haue in this translation, rather sought his *Spirit*, then *Numbers*; yet the *Musique* of Verse not neglected neither.
>
> (Hawkins 1625: A^r–A^v; *DNB*)

In a 1628 version of Virgil's eclogues that imposed a courtly aesthetic on the Latin text, "W.L., Gent." felt compelled to justify his departures with a similar apology:

> Some Readers I make no doubt they wil meet with in these
> dainty mouth'd times, that will taxe them, for not comming
> resolved word for word, and line for line with the Author [...]
> I used the freedome of a Translator, not tying myselfe to the
> tyranny of a Grammatical construction, but breaking the shell
> into many peeces, was only carefull to preserve the Kernell safe
> and whole, from the violence of a wrong, or wrested
> Interpretation.
>
> (Latham 1628:6^r; Patterson 1987:164–168)

As early as 1616, Barten Holyday, who became chaplain to Charles
I and was created doctor of divinity at the king's order, introduced
his translation of Persius by announcing that "I haue not herein
bound my selfe with a ferularie superstition to the letter: but with
the ancient libertie of a Translator, haue vsed a moderate paraphrase, where the obscuritie did more require it" (Holyday
1635:A5^r–A5^v; *DNB*). Holyday articulated the opposition to the
grammarians that Denham would later join, and with a similarly
Latinate tag, calling close translation "a ferularie superstition,"
belief propagated with the rod (*ferula*), school discipline – a joke
designed especially for a grammarian.

In 1620, Sir Thomas Wroth, a member of the Somerset gentry
who affected the literary pursuits of a courtly amateur (he called
his epigrams *The Abortive of an Idle Houre*), anticipated Denham in
several respects (*DNB*). Wroth likewise chose to translate the
second book of the *Aeneid* and to call it *The Destruction of Troy*, but
he also defined his translatorly "freedome" in "A Reqvest to the
Reader":

> Giue not vp your casting verdict rashly, though you find mee
> sometimes wandring (which I purposely do) out of the visible
> bounds, but deliberately take notice that I stray not from the
> scope and intent of the Author, iustified by the best Commen-
> taries: and so I leaue you to reade, to vnderstand, and to
> encrease.
>
> (Wroth 1620:A2^v)

Wroth's freer method ultimately rested on a scholarly rationale
("Commentaries") reminiscent of Jonson's neoclassicism. And
indeed Wroth's farewell to the reader ("to reade, to vnderstand,
and to encrease") echoed the exhortation with which Jonson

opened his *Epigrammes* (1616): "Pray thee, take care, that tak'st my booke in hand,/To reade it well: that is, to understand" (Jonson 1968:4). In 1634, Sir Robert Stapylton, a gentleman in ordinary of the privy chamber to the Prince of Wales, published a version of Book Four of the *Aeneid* in which he anticipated Denham both by questioning any close translation of poetry and by assigning the freer method the same class affiliation:

> It is true that wit distilled in one Language, cannot be transfused into another without losse of spirits: yet I presume such graces are retained, as those of the Noblest quality will favour this Translation, from an Original, that was sometimes the unenvied Favourite of the greatest Roman Emperour
> (Stapylton 1634: A4ᵛ; *DNB*)

Denham consolidated the several-decades-long emergence of a neoclassical translation method in aristocratic literary culture. It may have seemed "new" to him, not because it did not have any previous advocates, but because it did: it was a modern revival of an ancient cultural practice, making Denham's translation a simulacral "Copy" of Virgil's true "Original," rationalized with a Platonic theory of translation as the copy of a copy of the truth: "I have made it my principal care to follow him, as he made it his to follow Nature in all his proportions" (Denham 1656:A3ᵛ). But Denham's sense of his own modernity was less philosophical than political, linked to a specific class and nation. Coming back from exile in France, he may have found his translation method "new" in the sense of foreign, in fact French. French translation in the 1640s was characterized by theories and practices advocating free translation of classical texts, and Denham, among such other exiled royalist writers as Abraham Cowley and Sir Richard Fanshawe, was no doubt acquainted with the work of its leading French proponent, Nicolas Perrot d'Ablancourt, a prolific translator of Greek and Latin.[2] D'Ablancourt's freedom with Tacitus set the standard. In his preface to his version of the *Annals*, he wrote that

> la diversité qui se trouve dans les langues est si grande, tant pour la construction et la forme des périodes, que pour les figures et les autres ornemens, qu'il faut à tous coups changer d'air et de visage, si l'on ne veut faire un corps monstreux, tel que celuy des traductions ordinaires, qui sont ou mortes et languissantes, ou confuses, et embroüillées, sans aucun ordre ny agréement.

the diversity that one finds among languages is so great, in the arrangement and shape of the periods, as in the figures and other ornaments, that it is always necessary to change the air and appearance, unless one wishes to create a monstrous body, like those in ordinary translations, which are either dead or languishing, or obscure, and muddled, without any order or gracefulness.

(D'Ablancourt 1640)

Compare Denham's preface: "Poesie is of so subtle a spirit, that in pouring out of one Language into another, it will all evaporate; and if a new spirit be not added in the transfusion, there will remain nothing but a *Caput mortuum*" (Denham 1656:A3^r). Denham echoed D'Ablancourt's body/soul metaphor, although following Stapylton's example ("wit distilled in one Language, cannot be transfused into another without losse of spirits") he imagined translation alchemically, as a distillation in which the residue was termed a *caput mortuum* (*OED*; Hermans 1985:122). The alchemical image indicated that a free translation effected a radical change, in which what "was borne a Forraigner" can now be "esteeme[d] as a Native" – or, in this case, English (Stapylton 1634:A2^r).

The "new spirit" that is "added" with this translation method involves a process of domestication, in which the foreign text is imprinted with values specific to the target-language culture. D'Ablancourt called it "changer d'air et de visage." The elliptical, discontinuous discourse of Tacitus must be translated

> sans choquer les delicatesses de nostre langue & la justesse du raisonnement. [...] Souvent on est contraint d'adjoûter quelque chose à sa pensée pour l'éclaircir; quelquefois il en faut retrancher une partie pour donner jour à tout le reste.

> without offending the delicacy of our language and the correctness of reason. [...] Often one is forced to add something to the thought in order to clarify it; sometimes it is necessary to retrench one part so as to give birth to all the rest.

(D'Ablancourt 1640)

Henry Rider reverted to a clothing metaphor in the preface of his 1638 translation of Horace:

> Translations of Authors from one language to another, are like

old garments turn'd into new fashions; in which though the
stuffe be still the same, yet the die and trimming are altered, and
in the making, here something added, there something cut
away.

(Rider 1638:A3^{r})

Denham's formulation used a similar metaphor while nodding
toward the classical author with whom D'Ablancourt pioneered the
free method:

as speech is the apparel of our thoughts, so are there certain
Garbs and Modes of speaking, which vary with the times [...]
and this I think *Tacitus* means, by that which he calls *Sermonem
temporis istius auribus accommodatum* [...] and therefore if *Virgil*
must needs speak English, it were fit he should speak not only
as a man of this Nation, but as a man of this age.

(Denham 1656:A3^{r})

Denham's advocacy of free translation was laden with a nationalism that, even if expressed with courtly self-effacement, ultimately
led to a contradictory repression of the method's parallels and
influences, foreign as well as English:

if this disguise I have put upon him (I wish I could give it a better
name) fit not naturally and easily on so grave a person, yet it may
become him better than that Fools-Coat wherein the French and
Italian have of late presented him.

(Denham 1656:A3^{v})

Denham sought to distinguish his translation from burlesque
versions of the *Aeneid* that were fashionable on the Continent, Paul
Scarron's *Virgile Travesti* (1648–1649) and Giovanni Battista Lalli's
Eneide Travestita (1633) (Scarron 1988:10). He, like other translators associated with the exiled Caroline court, was following
another French fashion in translation, although one linked closer
to a monarchy whose absolutist experiment proved effective:
D'Ablancourt's version of the *Annals* was dedicated to the powerful
royal minister Cardinal Richelieu. Denham's translation of Virgil
in fact reflects the strong resemblance between English and French
translation methods during the period. But the deep nationalism
of this method works to conceal its origins in another national
culture – a contradiction that occurs in Denham's case because the
method answers so specifically to an English problem: the need for

a "new" cultural practice that will enable the defeated royalist segment of the Caroline aristocracy to regain its hegemonic status in English culture. In his commendatory verses "To Sir Richard Fanshawe upon his Translation of Pastor Fido" (1648), Denham calls free translation "a new and nobler way" (Steiner 1975:63). Given the political significance of this method, it is important for Denham to translate a text in a genre that treats nobility, the epic, and refuse the French burlesques that debased Virgil's aristocratic theme by treating social inferiors in the epic manner.

Denham's intention to enlist translation in a royalist cultural politics at home is visible both in his selection of the foreign text and in the discursive strategies he adopted in his version. The choice to translate Virgil's *Aeneid* in early modern England could easily evoke Geoffrey of Monmouth's legend that Brute, the grandson of Aeneas, founded Britain and became the first in a succession of British monarchs. Although this like the Arthurian legends was losing credibility among historians and antiquarians, the matter of Troy continued to be the cultural support of a strong nationalism, and it was repeatedly revised from different and often conflicting ideological standpoints in a wide range of texts – from William Camden's *Britannia* (1586) to Jonson's *Speeches at Prince Henry's Barriers* (1609) to Thomas Heywood's *Life of Merlin* (1641).[3] The early Stuart kings were often given a Trojan genealogy. Anthony Munday's contribution to the royal progress through London, *The Triumphs of Re-united Britannia* (1605), referred to James I as "our second Brute"; Heywood described his narrative as "a Chronographicall History of all the Kings and memorable passages of this kingdom, from Brute to the Reigne of our Royall Soveraigne King Charles" (Parsons 1929:403, 407). In the political debates during the Interregnum, a Trojan genealogy could be used to justify both representative government and absolute monarchy. In 1655, the parliamentarian polemicist William Prynne interpreted the significance of the legend as "1. A Warre to shake off *Slavery*, and recover publick Liberty. 2. A kinde of *Generall Parliamentary Councell* summoned by *Brute*"; whereas in a legal commentary published in 1663 Edward Waterhouse argued that Brute "by his consent to reward the valour and fidelity of his Companions" instituted laws "both touching his Royal Prerogative, and their civil Security in life, member, goods and Lawes" (Jones 1944:401, 403).

Denham's own appropriation of the Brute legend in *Coopers Hill* swells with patriotic fervor, but it also possesses the awareness that

the Trojan genealogy is a legend, increasingly under attack yet able
to function in cultural political struggles, and even, somewhat
contradictorily, true. In a passage that reflects on the vista of
London and environs, Denham writes that "The Gods great
Mother," Cybele,

> cannot boast
> Amongst that numerous, and Celestiall hoast,
> More *Hero's* than can *Windsor,* nor doth Fames
> Immortall booke record more noble names.
> Not to look back so far, to whom this Ile
> Owes the first Glory of so brave a pile,
> Whether to *Caesar, Albanact,* or *Brute,*
> The Brittish *Arthur,* or the Danish *Knute,*
> (Though this of old no lesse contest did move,
> Than when for *Homers* birth seven Cities strove)
> [. . .]
> But whosoere it was, Nature design'd
> First a brave place, and then as brave a minde.
> (Denham 1969:67)

The mention of "contest" in the parenthetical remark seems at first
to question the credibility of heroic genealogies for English kings,
whether historical or literary: "contest" as a reference to the
historiographical "controversy" or "debate." But the couplet
quickly shifts the issue from credibility to social effectivity: even if
of questionable authenticity, poetic genealogies ("*Homers* birth")
are cultural capital and can motivate political and military conflict.
In England's case, however, the heroic genealogies are metaphys-
ically validated, by "Nature design'd." For Denham, the Brute
legend constituted a strategic move in an ideological cultural
practice, poetry in the service of a specific political agenda. But,
like many of his contemporaries, he was apt to mask these material
conditions with providentialist claims and appeals to natural law
that underwrite a notion of racial superiority.

Denham's choice of Virgil's *Aeneid* was uniquely suited to the
nationalistic leanings of his domesticating translation method. And
in line with the recurrent Trojan genealogies of English kings, his
choice of an excerpt he entitled *The Destruction of Troy* allowed him
to suggest, more directly, the defeat of the Caroline government
and his support for monarchy in England. Denham's political
designs can be seen, first, in his decision to prepare Book II for

publication. In 1636, he had written a version of the *Aeneid* II–VI, and in 1668, he revised and published part of IV under the title, *The Passion of Dido for Aeneas*. In 1656, he chose to issue the excerpt whose "argument," the fall of Troy, better lent itself to topicality. The topical resonance of his version becomes strikingly evident when it is juxtaposed to the Latin text and previous English versions. Book II had already been done in several complete translations of the *Aeneid*, and it had been singled out twice by previous translators, Henry Howard, Earl of Surrey, and Sir Thomas Wroth. Yet both of them had rendered the entire book (some eight hundred lines of Latin text). Denham, in contrast, published an abbreviated translation (some 550 lines) that ended climactically with Priam's death.

> haec finis Priami fatorum, hic exitus illum
> sorte tulit Troiam incensam et prolapsa uidentem
> Pergama, tot quodam populis terrisque superbum
> regnatorem Asiae. iacet ingens litore truncus,
> auulsumque umeris caput et sine nomine corpus.
> (Mynors 1969:ll. 554–558)

> Thus fell the King, who yet surviv'd the State,
> With such a signal and peculiar Fate.
> Under so vast a ruine not a Grave,
> Nor in such flames a funeral fire to have:
> He, whom such Titles swell'd, such Power made proud
> To whom the Scepters of all *Asia* bow'd,
> On the cold earth lies th'unregarded King,
> A headless Carkass, and a nameless Thing.
> (Denham 1656:ll. 542-549)

By removing the character and place names in the Latin text ("Priami," "Troiam," and "Pergama," the citadel at Troy) and referring only to "the King," Denham generalizes the import of the passage, enabling Priam's "headless Carkass" to metamorphose into a British descendant's, at least for a moment, inviting the contemporary English reader to recall the civil wars – although from a decidedly royalist point of view. Denham's translation shared the same impulse toward political allegory that characterized, not only the various revisions of *Coopers Hill*, but also royalist writing generally during the years after Charles's defeat, including Fanshawe's translation of Guarini's *Il Pastor Fido* (1647) and Christopher Wase's translation of Sophocles' *Electra* (1649).[4]

The one place name Denham includes in his version of Priam's death, "Asia," may be taken as an allusion to the Orientalism in Caroline court culture. Denham had himself contributed to this trend with *The Sophy* (1642), a play intended for court production and set in Persia. But the allusiveness of the translation is more specific. "The Scepters of all *Asia* bow'd" to Charles in court masques where the king and queen enacted a moral conquest of foreign rulers by converting their nations to Platonic love. In Aurelian Townshend's *Tempe Restor'd* (1632), the royal couple preside over the reformation of Circe's sensual reign, figured in "all the Antimasques, consisting of Indians and Barbarians, who naturally are bestiall, and others which are voluntaries, but halfe transformed into beastes" (Townshend 1983:97).

Yet more striking is Denham's curious addition to the Latin text: "Thus fell the King, who yet survived the State,/With such a signal and peculiar Fate." Virgil's omission of any reference to the dead king's afterlife reveals Denham's own belief in the continuing vitality of the Stuart monarchy after the regicide. Although Charles I was executed, the monarchy "survived the State" instituted by Parliament, initially a Commonwealth governed by a Council of State, which was later redefined to function as an advisor to a Lord Protector; this was a "signal and peculiar" survival for the king because it took the form of a court in exile and royalist conspiracy at home, because, in other words, the king lived on but not in his kingdom. In the political climate of the 1650s, with the Protectorate resorting to oppressive measures to quell royalist insurgency, it would be difficult for a Caroline sympathizer not to see any parallel between the decapitations of Priam and Charles. But in this climate it would also be necessary for a royalist writer like Denham to use such an oblique mode of reference as an allusion in an anonymous translation. Translation was particularly useful in royalist cultural politics, Lois Potter suggests, because it was viewed as "transcendence, the healing wholeness that removes controversy and contradiction" (Potter 1989:52–53). In Denham's translation, the monarchy "survived" its destruction.

The fact that Denham intended his translation to serve a royalist function is borne out by a comparison with his predecessors, which highlights the subtle changes he introduced to bring the Latin text closer to his political concerns:

Of Priamus this was the fatal fine,
The wofull end that was alotted him.
When he had seen his palace all on flame,
With the ruine of his Troyan turrets eke,
That royal prince of Asie, which of late
Reignd over so many peoples and realmes,
Like a great stock now lieth on the shore:
His hed and shoulders parted ben in twaine:
A body now without renome, and fame.
                                    (Howard 1557:cii^v)

See here King Priams end of all the troubles he had knowne,
Behold the period of his days, which fortune did impone.
When he had seene his Citie raz'd, his Pallace, Temples fir'd,
And he who to th'Imperiall rule of Asia had aspir'd,
Proud of his Territories, and his people heeretofore,
Was then vnto the sea side brought, and headlesse in his gore:
Without respect his body lay in publike view of all.
                                    (Wroth 1620:E3^r)

This was king *Priams* end, this his hard fate,
To live to see *Troy* fir'd, quite ruinate:
Even he, who once was *Asia's Keisar* great,
Mightiest in men, and spacious regall seat:
A despicable trunk (now) dead on ground,
His head cut off, his carcasse no name found.
                                    (Vicars 1632:48)

So finish'd *Priams* Fates, and thus he dy'd,
Seeing *Troy* burn, whose proud commands did sway
So many powerful Realms in *Asia*;
Now on the strand his sacred body lyes
Headless, without a Name or Obsequies.
                                    (Ogilby 1654:217, 219)[5]

Denham clearly exceeds his predecessors in the liberties he takes
with the Latin text. His addition about the "signal and peculiar
Fate" becomes more conspicuous and historically charged in such
a comparison, as does his deletion of local markers, including the
Latin "litore" (l.557), a word that situates Priam's fall near the sea
and is rendered by most of the other translators ("shore," "sea
side," "strand"). Denham's translation not only allows the death to
be shifted inland, but throughout he makes a noticeable effort to

domesticate architectural terms, likening the Trojan structures to
the royal buildings in England. Consider this passage where the
Greeks are forcing their way into Priam's palace:

> *Automedon*
> And *Periphas* who drove the winged steeds,
> Enter the Court; whom all the youth succeeds
> Of *Scyros* Isle, who flaming firebrands flung
> Up to the roof, *Pyrrhus* himself among
> The foremost with an Axe an entrance hews
> Through beams of solid Oak, then freely views
> The Chambers, Galleries, and Rooms of State,
> Where *Priam* and the ancient Monarchs sate.
> At the first Gate an Armed Guard appears;
> But th'Inner Court with horror, noise and tears
> Confus'dly fill'd, the womens shrieks and cries
> The Arched Vaults re-echo to the skies;
> Sad Matrons wandring through the spacious Rooms
> Embrace and kiss the Posts: Then *Pyrrhus* comes
> Full of his Father, neither Men nor Walls
> His force sustain, the torn Port-cullis falls,
> Then from the hinge, their strokes the Gates divorce:
> [...]
> Then they the secret Cabinets invade,
> (Denham 1656: ll. 453-480, 491)

Denham's "Chambers, Galleries, and Rooms of State," "Inner
Court," "Arched Vaults," "secret Cabinets" render various Latin
terms, but the Latin is much less defined, and it noticeably refers
to a different architecture: "domus intus," "domus interior" ("the
house within"), "atria longa" ("long halls"), "penetralia" ("interior"), "cauae" ("hollow places"), "thalami" ("the women's bed-
rooms") (ibid.: ll. 484–7, 503). Although the renderings used by
Denham's predecessors display a degree of domestication as well,
they do not match the extremity of his: "the house, the court, and
secret chambers eke," "the palace within," "the hollow halles"
(Howard 1557:ci^v); "the roomes, and all that was within," "the
spacious pallace" (Wroth 1620:E^r); "the rooms within, great halls
and parlours faire," "the rooms within" (Vicars 1632:45); "the
house within," "long halls," "*Priams* bed-chamber," "arched Siel-
ings" (Ogilby 1654:215). And Denham is alone in using "Port-
cullis" for the Latin "postes" ("door-posts"), refusing such previous

and likely renderings as "pillars," "gates," and "posts" for a word that conjures up the architectural structure most closely associated with aristocracy and monarchy, the castle. Denham's architectural lexicon permits the description of the Greek attack to evoke other, more recently besieged castles, like Windsor Castle stormed by the parliamentary armies, or perhaps Farnham Castle, where in 1642 Denham was forced to surrender the royal garrison he commanded there. Denham's domesticating translation casts the destruction of Troy in a form that resonates with certain moments in English history, those when aristocratic rule was dominant (the medieval past) or allied, however tenuously, with the monarchy (the absolutist experiment of the 1630s), or decisively defeated and displaced (the civil wars and Interregnum).

There are other senses in which Denham's decision to translate Book II of the *Aeneid* addressed the displaced royalist segment of the Caroline aristocracy. By choosing this book, he situated himself in a line of aristocratic translators that stretched back to Surrey, a courtly amateur whose literary activity was instrumental in developing the elite court cultures of the Tudor and Stuart monarchs. From Tottel's *Miscellany* (1557) on, Surrey was recognized as an important innovator of the sonnet and love lyric, but his work as a translator also possessed a cultural significance that would not have been lost on Denham: Surrey's translation of Virgil proved to be a key text in the emergence of blank verse as a prevalent poetic form in the period. Following Surrey's example, Denham turned to Book II to invent a method of poetry translation that would likewise prove culturally significant for his class. His aim was not only to reformulate the free method practiced in Caroline aristocratic culture at its height, during the 1620s and 1630s, but to devise a discursive strategy for translation that would reestablish the cultural dominance of this class: this strategy can be called *fluency*.

A free translation of poetry requires the cultivation of a fluent strategy in which linear syntax, univocal meaning, and varied meter produce an illusionistic effect of transparency: the translation seems as if it were not in fact a translation, but a text originally written in English.[6] In the preface to his 1632 *Aeneid*, John Vicars described "the manner, wherein I have aimed at these three things, Perspicuity of the matter, Fidelity to the authour, and Facility or smoothnes to recreate thee my reader" (Vicars 1632: A3[r]). In Denham's words, the translation should "fit" the foreign text "naturally and easily." Fluency is impossible to achieve with close or "verbal" translation, which inhibits the effect of transparency, making the translator's language seem foreign: "whosoever offers at Verbal Translation," wrote Denham,

> shall have the misfortune of that young Traveller, who lost his own language abroad, and brought home no other instead of it: for the grace of Latine will be lost by being turned into English words; and the grace of the English, by being turned into the Latin Phrase.

(Denham 1656:A3^r)

Denham's privileging of fluency in his own translation practice becomes clear when his two versions of *Aeneid* II are compared. The 1636 version is preserved in the commonplace book of Lucy Hutchinson, wife of the parliamentary colonel, John Hutchinson, with whom Denham attended Lincoln's Inn between 1636 and 1638 (O'Hehir 1968:12–13). The book contains Denham's translation of *Aeneid* II–VI – complete versions of IV–VI, partial ones of II and III. Book II is clearly a rough draft: not only does it omit large portions of the Latin text, but some passages do not give full renderings, omitting individual Latin words. There is also a tendency to follow the Latin word order, in some cases quite closely. The example cited by Theodore Banks is the often quoted line "timeo Danaos et dona ferentes," which Denham rendered word for word as "The Grecians most when bringing gifts I feare" (Denham 1969:43–44). The convoluted syntax and the pronounced metrical regularity make the line read awkwardly, without "grace." In the 1656 version, Denham translated this line more freely and strove for greater fluency, following a recognizably English word-order and using metrical variations to smooth out the rhythm: "Their swords less danger carry than their gifts" (Denham 1656: l. 48).

Denham's fluent strategy is most evident in his handling of the verse form, the heroic couplet. The revision improved both the coherence and the continuity of the couplets, avoiding metrical irregularities and knotty constructions, placing the caesura to reinforce syntactical connections, using enjambment and closure to subordinate the rhyme to the meaning, sound to sense:

1636
While all intent with heedfull silence stand
Æneas spake O queene by your command

My countries fate our dangers & our feares
While I repeate I must repeate my feares

1656
While all with silence & attention wait,
Thus speaks *Æneas* from the bed of State:
Madam, when you command us to review
Our Fate, you make our old wounds bleed anew

(ll. 1–4)

1636
We gave them gon & to Micenas sayld
from her long sorrow Troy herselfe unvaild
The ports throwne open all with ioy resort
To see ye Dorick tents ye vacant port

1656
We gave them gone, and to *Mycenae* sail'd,
And *Troy* reviv'd, her mourning face unvail'd;
All through th'unguarded Gates with joy resort
To see the slighted Camp, the vacant Port;

(ll. 26–29)

1636
Guilt lent him rage & first possesst
The credulous rout with vaine reports nor ceast
But into his designes ye prophett drew
But why doe I these thanklesse truths persue

1656
Old guilt fresh malice gives; The peoples ears
He fills with rumors, and their hearts with fears,
And them the Prophet to his party drew.
But why do I these thankless truths pursue;

(ll. 95–98)

1636
While Laocoon on Neptunes sacred day
By lot designed a mighty bull did slay
Twixt Tenedos & Troy the seas smooth face
Two serpents with their horrid folds embrace
Above the deepe they rayse their scaly crests
And stem ye flood wth their erected brests

Then making towards the shore their tayles they wind
In circling curles to strike ye waves behind

1656
Laocoon, Neptunes Priest, upon the day
Devoted to that God, a Bull did slay,
When two prodigious serpents were descride,
Whose circling stroaks the Seas smooth face divide;
Above the deep they raise their scaly Crests,
And stem the floud with their erected brests,
Their winding tails advance and steer their course,
And 'gainst the shore the breaking Billow force.

(ll. 196–203)

Denham's fluent strategy allowed the 1656 version to read more "naturally and easily" so as to produce the illusion that Virgil wrote in English, or that Denham succeeded in "doing him more right," making available in the most transparent way the foreign writer's intention or the essential meaning of the foreign text. Yet Denham made available, not so much Virgil, as a translation that signified a peculiarly English meaning, and the revisions provide further evidence for this domestication. Thus, the 1636 version translated "Teucri" (l. 251) and "urbs" (l. 363) as "Trojans" and "Asias empresse," whereas the 1656 version used just "The City" (ll. 243, 351), suggesting at once Troy and London. And whereas the 1636 version translated "sedes Priami" (l. 437) as "Priams pallace" and "domus interior" (l. 486) as "roome," the 1656 version used "the Court" and "th'Inner Court" at these and other points (ll. 425, 438, 465, 473). Even "Apollinis infula" (l. 430), a reference to a headband worn by Roman priests, was more localized, turned into a reference to the episcopacy: in 1636, Denham rendered the phrase as "Apollos mitre," in 1656 simply as "consecrated Mitre" (l. 416). The increased fluency of Denham's revision may have made his translation seem "more right," but this effect actually concealed a rewriting of the Latin text that endowed it with subtle allusions to English settings and institutions, strengthening the historical analogy between the fall of Troy and the defeat of the royalist party.

Fluency assumes a theory of language as communication that, in practice, manifests itself as a stress on immediate intelligibility and an avoidance of polysemy, or indeed any play of the signifier that erodes the coherence of the signified. Language is conceived as a transparent medium of personal expression, an individualism that construes translation as the recovery of the foreign writer's intended meaning. As Denham's preface asserted, "Speech is the apparel of our thoughts" (Denham 1656:A3^r). Now it will be worthwhile to recall the recurrent metaphors used in the translators' prefaces, the analogy of translation as clothing in which the foreign author is dressed, or the translated text as the body animated by the foreign writer's soul. The assumption is that meaning is a timeless and universal essence, easily transmittable between languages and cultures regardless of the change of signifiers, the construction of a different semantic context out of different cultural discourses, the inscription of target-language codes and values in every interpretation of the foreign text. "W.L., Gent." noted that his versions of Virgil's eclogues involved their own violence against the foreign texts, "breaking the shell into many peeces," but he was nonetheless "carefull to preserve the Kernell safe and whole, from the violence of a wrong, or wrested Interpretation." Some translators gave more of a sense that they faced a welter of competing "Commentaries" (Wroth 1620) from which they selected to rationalize their translation strategy. But none was sufficiently aware of the domestication enacted by fluent translation to demystify the effect of transparency, to suspect that the translated text is irredeemably partial in its interpretation. Denham admitted that he was presenting a naturalized English Virgil, but he also insisted that "neither have I anywhere offered such violence to his sense, as to make it seem mine, and not his" (Denham 1656:A4^r).

Fluency can be seen as a discursive strategy ideally suited to domesticating translation, capable not only of executing the ethnocentric violence of domestication, but also of concealing this violence by producing the effect of transparency, the illusion that this is not a translation, but the foreign text, in fact, the living thoughts of the foreign author, "there being certain Graces and Happinesses peculiar to every Language, which gives life and energy to the words" (Denham 1656:A3^r). Transparency results in a concealment of the cultural and social conditions of the translation – the aesthetic, class, and national ideologies linked to Denham's translation theory and practice. And this is what makes fluent translation particularly effective in Denham's bid to restore aristocratic culture to its dominant position: the effect of transparency is so powerful in domesticating cultural forms because it presents them as true, right, beautiful, natural. Denham's great achievement, in his translations as well as his poems, was to make the heroic couplet seem natural to his successors, thus developing a form that would dominate English poetry and poetry translation for more than a century.

Later writers like John Dryden and Samuel Johnson recognized that the truly "new" thing in Denham was the stylistic refinement of his verse. They were fond of quoting Denham's lines on the Thames in *Coopers Hill* and commenting on their beauty, always formulated as prosodic smoothness, what Dryden in the "Dedication of the *Æneis*" (1697) called their "sweetness" (Dryden 1958:1047).[7] And both Dryden and Johnson saw Denham as an innovator in translation: they were fond of quoting his commendatory verses to Fanshawe's *Il Pastor Fido*, singling out for praise the lines where Denham advocated the free method:

> That servile path, thou nobly do'st decline,
> Of tracing word by word and Line by Line;
> A new and nobler way thou do'st pursue,
> To make Translations, and Translators too:
> They but preserve the Ashes, thou the Flame,
> True to his Sence, but truer to his Fame.
> (Denham 1969: ll. 15–16, 21–24)

Dryden joined Denham in opposing "a servile, literal Translation" because, he noted in his preface to *Ovid's Epistles* (1680), such translation is not fluent: "either perspicuity or gracefulness will frequently be wanting" (Dryden 1956:116).

Dryden also followed Denham, most importantly, in seeing the couplet as an appropriate vehicle for transparent discourse. In the preface to his play *The Rival Ladies* (1664), Dryden asserted that *Coopers Hill*, "for the majesty of the style is and ever will be, the exact standard of good writing" and then proceeded to argue that rhyme does not necessarily inject a note of artificiality to impede transparency (Dryden 1962:7). Any noticeably artificial use of rhyme rather shows the writer's lack of skill:

> This is that which makes them say rhyme is not natural, it being only so when the poet either makes a vicious choice of words, or places them for rhyme sake, so unnaturally as no man would in ordinary speaking; but when 'tis so judiciously ordered that the first word in the verse seems to beget the second, and that the next [...] it must then be granted, rhyme has all the advantages

of prose besides its own. [...] where the poet commonly confines his sense to his couplet, [he] must contrive that sense into such words that the rhyme shall naturally follow them, not they the rhyme.

(Dryden 1962:8)

Denham's work was canonized by later writers because his use of the couplet made his poetry and poetry translations read "naturally and easily" and therefore seem "majestic," in an appropriately royal metaphor, or "more right," more accurate or faithful as translations – but only because the illusion of transparency concealed the process of naturalizing the foreign text in an English cultural and social situation. The ascendancy of the heroic couplet from the late seventeenth century on has frequently been explained in political terms, wherein the couplet is viewed as a cultural form whose marked sense of antithesis and closure reflects a political conservatism, support for the restored monarchy and for aristocratic domination – despite the continuing class divisions that had erupted in civil wars and fragmented the aristocracy into factions, some more accepting of bourgeois social practices than others. Robin Grove is particularly sensitive to the social implications of the discursive "flow" sought by the writers who championed the couplet: "The urbanity of the style," he observed,

> incorporates the reader as a member of the urbanely-responsive class. [...] literature announces itself as a social act, even as the 'society' it conjures around it is an increasingly specialized/ stratified fiction: a fiction which indeed relates to historical fact (provided we don't just coagulate the two), but for whose purposes the ideas of Sense, Ease, Naturalness (cf. *An Essay on Criticism*, 68–140) contained a rich alluvial deposit of aspirations and meanings largely hidden from view.
>
> (Grove 1984:54)[8]

The fact that for us today no form better than the couplet epitomizes the artificial use of language bears witness, not just to how deeply transparency was engrained in aristocratic literary culture, but also to how much it could conceal.

It is Dryden in particular who found Denham's translation of Virgil so important for the rise of this cultural discourse. In the "Dedication of the *Æneis*," he stated that "'tis the utmost of my Ambition to be thought [the] Equal" of Caroline translators like

"Sir *John Denham*, Mr. *Waller*, and Mr. *Cowley*" (Dryden 1958:1051). He admired Denham's version of Book II so much that he absorbed no fewer than eighty lines of it in his own version of the *Aeneid*. A typical example is his rendering of the account of Priam's death, where, as Dryden acknowledged in a footnote, Denham's climactic line is repeated:

> Thus *Priam* fell: and shar'd one common Fate
> With *Troy* in Ashes, and his ruin'd State:
> He, who the Scepter of all *Asia* sway'd,
> Whom monarchs like domestick Slaves obey'd.
> On the bleak Shoar now lies th'abandon'd King,
> A headless Carcass, and a nameless thing.
>   (Dryden 1958: ll. 758–763)

Dryden's dedicatory essay makes clear his advocacy of Denham's free translation method, which he similarly asserts with nationalistic pronouncements ("I will boldly own, that this *English* Translation has more of *Virgil's* Spirit in it, than either the *French*, or the *Italian*" (ibid.:1051)) while finally confessing its likeness to French models:

> I may presume to say, and I hope with as much reason as the *French* Translator, that taking all the Materials of this divine Author, I have endeavour'd to make *Virgil* speak such *English*, as he wou'd himself have spoken, if he had been born in England, and in this present Age. I acknowledge, with Segrais, that I have not succeeded in this attempt, according to my desire: yet I shall not be wholly without praise, if in some sort I may be allow'd to have copied the Clearness, the Purity, the Easiness and the Magnificence of his Stile.
>   (ibid.:1055)

As with Denham, the domestication of Dryden's translation method is so complete that fluency is seen to be a feature of Virgil's poetry instead of the discursive strategy implemented by the translator to make the heroic couplet seem transparent, indistinguishable from "the Clearness, the Purity, the Easiness and the Magnificence of his Stile." And, much more explicitly than Denham, Dryden links his fluent, domesticating translation to aristocratic culture. Thus, he explains his avoidance of specialized terminology in his version of the *Aeneid* – "the proper terms of

Navigation, Land-Service, or [...] the Cant of any Profession" – by arguing that

> *Virgil* has avoided those proprieties, because he Writ not to Mariners, Souldiers, Astronomers, Gardners, Peasants, &c. but to all in general, and in particular to Men and Ladies of the first Quality: who have been better Bred than to be too nicely knowing in the Terms. In such cases, 'tis enough for a Poet to write so plainly, that he may be understood by his Readers.
>
> (ibid.:1061)

Dryden's remark is a reminder that the free translation method was modelled on poetry, that Denham was using translation to distinguish a literary elite from "them who deal in matters of Fact, or matters of Faith" (Denham 1656: A3^r), and that this valorization of the literary contributed to the concealment of the cultural and social conditions of translation, including Dryden's own. For, as Steven Zwicker has shown, Dryden also designed his Virgil to intervene into a specific political struggle: it "is a meditation on the language and culture of Virgil's poetry, but it is also a set of reflections on English politics in the aftermath of the Glorious Revolution," argued Zwicker, "a time when William III's reign was not fixed with the certainty it assumed late in the decade, a time when Stuart restoration might still be contemplated, and not wholly as fantasy" (Zwicker 1984:177). The triumph of the heroic couplet in late seventeenth-century poetic discourse depends to some extent on the triumph of a neoclassical translation method in aristocratic literary culture, a method whose greatest triumph is perhaps the discursive sleight of hand that masks the political interests it serves.

II

In Dryden's wake, from Alexander Pope's multi-volume Homer (1715–1726) to Alexander Tytler's systematic *Essay on the Principles of Translation* (1791), domestication dominated the theory and practice of English-language translation in every genre, prose as well as poetry. It was allied to different social tendencies and made to support varying cultural and political functions. Pope's Homer continued the refinement of a transparent poetic discourse in the heroic couplet, still a literary elitism among the hegemonic classes, dependent less on court patronage than on publishers with subscription lists that were now increasingly bourgeois as well as aristocratic. It became fashionable to subscribe to Pope's translation: over 40 percent of the names on the lists for his *Iliad* were titled, and the MPs included both Tories and Whigs.[9] Fluent translating remained affiliated with the British cultural elite, and its authority was so powerful that it could cross party lines. Pope described the privileged discourse in his preface:

> It only remains to speak of the *Versification*. *Homer* (as has been said) is perpetually applying the Sound to the Sense, and varying it on every new Subject. This is indeed one of the most exquisite Beauties of Poetry, and attainable by very few: I know only of *Homer* eminent for it in the *Greek*, and *Virgil* in *Latine*. I am sensible it is what may sometimes happen by Chance, when a Writer is warm, and fully possest of his Image: however it may be reasonably believed they design'd this, in whose Verse it so manifestly appears in a superior degree to all others. Few Readers have the Ear to be Judges of it, but those who have will see I have endeavour'd at this Beauty.
>
> (Pope 1967:20–21)

Pope manifests the distinctive blind spot of domesticating translation, confusing, under the illusion of transparency, the interpretation/translation with the foreign text, even with the foreign writer's intention, canonizing classical writing on the basis of Enlightenment concepts of poetic discourse, a metrical facility designed to reduce the signifier to a coherent signified, "perpetually applying the Sound to the Sense." The fluency of Pope's Homer set the standard for verse translations of classical poetry, so that, as Penelope Wilson notes,

> we find the ancient poets emerging from the mill of decorum in more or less undifferentiated batches of smooth rhyme, or blank verse, and elegant diction. They are generally met by reviewers with correspondingly vague commendations such as 'not less faithful than elegant'; and when they are condemned, they are more often condemned on stylistic grounds than on those of accuracy.
>
> (Wilson 1982:80)

In the eighteenth century, stylistic elegance in a translation can already be seen as symptomatic of domestication, bringing the ancient text in line with literary standards prevailing in Hanoverian Britain.

During this crucial moment in its cultural rise, domesticating translation was sometimes taken to extremes that look at once oddly comical and rather familiar in their logic, practices a translator might use today in the continuing dominion of fluency. William Guthrie, for instance, in the preface to his version of *The Orations of Marcus Tullius Cicero* (1741), argued that "it is *living Manners* alone that can communicate the Spirit of an Original" and so it is sufficient if the translator has made

> it his Business to be as conversant as he cou'd in that Study and Manner which comes the nearest to what we may suppose his Author, were he now to live, wou'd pursue, and in which he wou'd shine.
>
> (Steiner 1975:98)

This was Guthrie's reason for casting his Cicero as a member of Parliament, "where," he says, "by a constant Attendance, in which I was indulg'd for several Years, I endeavour'd to possess my self of the Language most proper for this translation" (ibid.:99). Guthrie's translation naturalized the Latin text with the transparent discourse he developed as a reporter of parliamentary debates for the *Gentleman's Magazine*.

It is important not to view such instances of domestication as simply inaccurate translations. Canons of accuracy and fidelity are always locally defined, specific to different cultural formations at different historical moments. Both Denham and Dryden recognized that a ratio of loss and gain inevitably occurs in the translation process and situates the translation in an equivocal relationship to the foreign text, never quite faithful, always somewhat free, never establishing an identity, always a lack and a supplement. Yet they also viewed their domesticating method as the most effective way to control this equivocal relationship and produce versions adequate to the Latin text. As a result, they castigated methods that either rigorously adhered to source-language textual features or played fast and loose with them in ways that they were unwilling to license, that insufficiently adhered to the canon of fluency in translation. Dryden "thought it fit to steer betwixt the two Extreams, of Paraphrase, and literal Translation" (Dryden 1958:1055), i.e., between the aim of reproducing primarily the meanings of the Latin text, usually at the cost of its phonological and syntactical features, and the aim of rendering it word for word, respecting syntax and line break. And he distinguished his method from Abraham Cowley's "imitations" of Pindar, partial translations that revised and, in effect, abandoned the foreign text. Dryden felt it was Denham "who advis'd more Liberty than he took himself" (Dryden 1956:117), permitting Denham's substantial liberties – the editing of the Latin text, the domestic lexicon – to pass unnoticed, refined out of existence, naturalized by the majesty of the style. The ethnocentric violence performed by domesticating translation rested on a double fidelity, to the source-language text as well as to the target-language culture, and especially to its valorization of transparent discourse. But this was clearly impossible and knowingly duplicitous, accompanied by the rationale that a gain in domestic intelligibility and cultural force outweighed the loss suffered by the foreign text and culture.

This trend in English-language translation gets pushed to a new extreme at the end of the eighteenth century, in Alexander Fraser Tytler's *Essay on the Principles of Translation* (1791). Tytler's influential treatise is a key document in the canonization of fluency, a digest of its "principles," "laws," and "precepts" which offers a plethora of illustrative examples. His decisive consolidation of earlier statements, French as well as English, constituted a theoretical refinement, visible in the precision of his distinctions and in the philosophical sophistication of his assumptions: domestication is now recommended on the basis of a general human nature that is repeatedly contradicted by an aesthetic individualism.

For Tytler, the aim of translation is the production of an equivalent effect that transcends linguistic and cultural differences:

> I would therefore describe a good translation to be, *That, in which the merit of the original work is so completely transfused into another language, as to be as distinctly apprehended, and as strongly felt, by a native of the country to which that language belongs, as it is by those who speak the language of the original work.*
>
> (Tytler 1978:15)

The "merit" of the foreign text, and the "excellencies and defects" of attempts to reproduce it in translation, are accessible to all, because, in so far as reason and good sense afford a criterion, the opinion of all intelligent readers will probably be uniform. But, as it is not to be denied, that in many of the examples adduced in this Essay, the appeal lies not so much to any settled canons of criticism, as to individual taste; it will not be surprising, if in such instances, a diversity of opinion should take place: and the Author having exercised with great freedom his own judgment in such points, it would ill become him to blame others for using the same freedom in dissenting from his opinions. The chief benefit to be derived from all such discussions in matters of taste, does not so much arise from any certainty we can obtain of the rectitude of our critical decisions, as from the pleasing and useful exercise which they give to the finest powers of the mind, and those which most distinguish us from the inferior animals.

(ibid.:vii–viii)

For Tytler, it is possible both to translate successfully and to evaluate translations because he assumes that linguistic and cultural differences do not exist at a fundamental level, invoking a universal "reason and good sense" that distinguishes a public sphere of cultural consensus ("readers") but extends to the species, "intelligent" human beings.[10] Yet he subsequently narrows this sphere, first excluding consensus ("settled canons of criticism") and then appealing to the "freedom" of "individual taste." Tytler's "common sense" approach to translation rests on a liberal humanism that is stated with a fugitive democratic gesture (a public sphere of cultural debate), but lapses ultimately into an individualist aesthetics with skeptical consequences: "in matters where the ultimate appeal is to Taste, it is almost impossible to be secure of the solidity of our opinions, when the criterion of their truth is so very uncertain" (ibid.:11).

The strain of individualism in Tytler's treatise is so powerful, however "uncertain" the contours of subjectivity may seem, that he never shows the slightest skepticism about aesthetic judgment and in fact constructs a concept of "correct taste" based on "exquisite feeling." The translator's every choice should be governed by it – even to the point of violating the "laws" for good translation. These include, first, "That the Translation should give a complete transcript of the ideas of the original work," and, second, "That the style and manner of writing should be of the same character with that of the original" (Tytler 1978:16). The "man of exquisite feeling," however, is invested with the "liberty" of "adding to or retrenching the ideas of the original," as well as the "privilege" of "correcting what appears to him a careless or inaccurate expression of the original, where that inaccuracy seems materially to affect the sense" (ibid.:54). Of course, what is "correct" is always a domestic value, including the discursive effect that dominates English culture at that moment, transparency. Hence, Tytler's third and final "law" is "That the Translation should have all the ease of original composition" (ibid.:15).

Good translators implement fluent strategies: they avoid syntactical fragmentation, polysemy ("which, by the bye, is always a defect in composition" (Tytler 1978:28)), sudden shifts in discursive registers. Tytler praises Henry Steuart, "Esq.," "the ingenious translator of Sallust," for his "version of a most difficult author, into easy, pure, correct, and often most eloquent language"; Steuart recognized "the fruitlessness of any attempt to imitate the abrupt and sententious manner" of the Latin text (ibid.:188–189). Of Arthur Murphy's Tacitus, Tytler remarks, "We most admire the judgment of the translator in forbearing all attempt to rival the brevity of the original, since he knew it could not be attained but with the sacrifice both of ease and perspicuity" (ibid.:186–187). "To imitate the obscurity or ambiguity of the original, is a fault; and it is still a greater, to give more than one meaning" (ibid.:28–29). Thomas May and George Sandys "manifested a better taste in poetical translation" because they "have given to their versions [of Lucan and Ovid] both an ease of expression and a harmony of numbers, which make them approach very near to original composition," masking both the second-order status of the translation and its domestication of the foreign text. For these translators who produced the sense of originality "have everywhere adapted their expression to the idiom of the language in which they wrote" (ibid.:68). The governing "precept," Tytler states, is "That the translator ought always to figure to himself, in what manner the original author would have expressed himself, if he had written in the language of the translation" (ibid.:201). But the translator must also conceal the figural status of the translation, indeed confuse the domesticated figure with the foreign writer.

Tytler's recommendations of fluency lead to the inscription of the foreign text with a rather conservative set of social representations. These include a squeamishness about physical references that enables his concept of "correct taste" to function as a cultural discourse by which the bourgeoisie and a bourgeois aristocracy express their superiority to lower classes. As Peter Stallybrass and Allon White have shown,

> within the symbolic discourse of the bourgeoisie, illness, disease, poverty, sexuality, blasphemy and the lower classes were inextricably connected. The control of the boundaries of the body (in breathing, eating, defecating) secured an identity which was constantly played out in terms of class difference.
>
> (Stallybrass and White 1986:167)

Thus, Tytler finds that Homer betrays a tendency "to offend, by introducing low images and puerile allusions. Yet how admirably is this defect veiled over, or altogether removed, by his translator Pope" (Tytler 1978:79). Pope is praised for omitting "an impropriety," Homer's "compliment to the nurse's waist" – in Tytler's translation her "waist was elegantly girt" – as well as "one circumstance extremely mean, and even disgusting," a "nauseous image" of Achilles as a child: in Tytler's translation, "When I placed you on my knees, I filled you full with meat minced down, and gave you wine, which you vomited upon my bosom" (ibid.:49–50, 89–90). At other points, the process of domestication is explicitly class-coded, with the translator advised to inscribe the foreign text with elite literary discourses while excluding discourses that circulate among an urban proletariat:

> If we are thus justly offended at hearing Virgil speak in the style of the Evening Post or the Daily Advertiser, what must we think of the translator, who makes the solemn and sententious Tacitus express himself in the low cant of the streets, or in the dialect of the waiters of a tavern?
>
> (ibid.:119)

Transparency, the "ease of original composition" in translation, was a genteel literary effect that avoided the "licentiousness" of popular oral genres:

> The most correct taste is requisite to prevent that ease from degenerating into licentiousness. [...] The most licentious of all translators was Mr Thomas Brown, of facetious memory, in whose translations from Lucian we have the most perfect ease;

but it is the ease of Billingsgate and of Wapping.

(ibid.:220–221)

Ultimately, Tytler's bourgeois valorization of transparent discourse to the exclusion of what Mikhail Bakhtin called the "carnivalesque" reveals a class anxiety about the simulacral status of the translated text and the threat it poses to an individualistic concept of authorship (Bakhtin 1984). Stallybrass and White facilitate this critique of Tytler's translation theory with their Bakhtinian history of the construction of authorship in England:

> Jonson, Dryden, Pope and Wordsworth, each sought to legitimate his claim to the vocation of master-poet by disengaging himself from the carnivalesque scene so as to stand above it, taking up a singular position of transcendence. The traces of this labour, of this act of discursive rejection, are marked out by nothing so much as the poet's attempt to found an illusory unity above and beyond the carnival. In each case, however, this apparently simple gesture of social superiority and disdain could not be effectively accomplished without revealing the very labour of suppression and sublimation involved.
>
> (Stallybrass and White 1986:123–124)

Translation threatens the transcendental author because it submits his text to the infiltration of other discourses that are not bourgeois, individualistic, transparent. In Tytler's case, there is a special concern that classical texts should not be carnivalized and degraded by translation strategies that do not implement canonical readings of those texts – colloquializing "the solemn and sententious Tacitus," for example, or trashing the "strength united with simplicity" that is "characteristic of the language of Homer" by rendering his vulgarities. The very labour of suppression and sublimation involved in Tytler's theory can be glimpsed in his willingness to risk compromising the canonicity of classical texts, admitting that they must be edited to fit his chastening, bourgeois readings of them. Insofar as Tytler's neoclassicism comprehends a free translation method, it at once expresses and declares impossible a nostalgic dream of originality, the ancients' proximity to "Nature," representation and expression free of its discursive conditions.

For Tytler, the threat posed by translation to the author's transcendence is answered by liberal humanism, the contradiction between a general human nature and the individualist aesthetics embodied in the concept of "correct taste." His explicit intention is to address "the subject of translation considered as an *art*, depending on fixed principles" (Tytler 1978:4, my italics). The translator with "correct taste" is in fact an artist, an author: "none but a poet can translate a poet" (ibid.:208); "an ordinary translator sinks under the energy of his original; the man of genius frequently rises above it" (ibid.:42). And it is transparency that signifies the translator's authorship in the text: the ease of originality occurs in "specimens of perfect translation, where the authors have entered with exquisite taste into the manner of their originals" (ibid.:142). The translator's authorship hinges on a sympathetic identification with the foreign author – "to use a bold expression, [the translator] must adopt the very soul of his author, which must speak through his own organs" (ibid.:212) – but in the translation what gets expressed is less the foreign author's "soul" than the translator's: "With what superior taste has the translator heightened this simile, and exchanged the offending circumstance for a beauty"; "in such instances, the good taste of the translator invariably covers the defect of the original" (ibid.:89, 88). The anxiety that translation complicates authorial self-expression by mediating the foreign text with "low" discourses is allayed by Tytler's erasure of the distinction between translator and author, largely on the basis of an illusionistic effect of textuality, now the sign of "correct taste."

Tytler (1747–1813), a Scottish lord who practiced law and pursued various historical, literary, and philosophical interests, published his treatise anonymously in 1791 and then issued two more editions, in 1797 and 1813, expanding the book to more than three times its initial size by adding many, many examples, driven by the empiricist conviction that they would make his concept of "taste" seem true, right, obvious. The treatise was very favorably received by reviewers and readers, confirming Tytler's sense that he was addressing a public sphere of cultural consensus, even if that sphere was limited to a like-minded bourgeois literary elite.[11] The *European Magazine*, which announced itself as "a general Vehicle, by which the literati of the Whole Kingdom may converse with each other and communicate their Knowledge to the World," concluded its review "with wonder at the variety of our Author's reading, with praise of the justness of his judgment and the elegance of his taste" (*European Magazine* 1793:282). Tytler's treatise prompted the *Monthly Review* to reflect on "the gradual progress of taste among our English writers" as evidenced in the rise of fluent translation (*Monthly Review* 1792:361). The anonymous reviewer asserted that "the author's observations are, for the most part, so evidently dictated by good sense, and so consonant to correct taste, as to admit of little dispute; and the examples, by which they are illustrated, are very judiciously selected and properly applied," "sufficient to convince every reader of good taste, that the volume will repay the trouble of a diligent perusal of the whole" (ibid.:363, 366).

Although both of these reviewers expressed some doubts about Tytler's recommendation that the translator edit or "improve" the foreign text, neither found this editing questionable because of the domestication it involved. On the contrary, the question was the specific nature of the domestication, with both offering reasons firmly grounded in domestic translation agendas. The reviewer for the *Monthly Review* suggested that Tytler's "improvements" of the foreign text might interfere with the improvement of taste performed by translation, "the great end of which undoubtedly is to give the unlearned reader a correct idea of the merit of the original" (*Monthly Review* 1792:363). The reviewer for the *European Magazine* was less didactic but equally snobbish in his wish to preserve the classical text in a pure, unmediated state: "Such ornaments appear to us like modern gilding laid upon one of the finest statues of antiquity" (*European Magazine* 1792:188). This antiquarianism, although based on an idealized concept of the past, was actually serving contemporary social interests, labouring, somewhat contradictorily, under the valorization of transparent discourse in elite literary culture, recommending translations that seem to reproduce the foreign text perfectly: "the sober sense of criticism [...] bids a translator to be the faithful mirror of his original" (ibid.:189).

Tytler's importance in the canonization of fluent translation is perhaps most clearly indicated by George Campbell's adherence to the same "principles" in his two-volume version of the Gospels. Campbell's was undoubtedly one of the most popular English translations of its time: between 1789, when it was first issued, and 1834, fifteen editions appeared in Britain and the United States. The massive first volume contained Campbell's "Preliminary Dissertations" on such issues as "The chief Things to be attended to in translating" ("Dissertation the Tenth," 445–519). The closeness to Tytler's recommendations is remarkable:

> The first thing, without doubt, which claims [the translator's] attention, is to give a just representation of the sense of the original. This, it must be acknowledged, is the most essential of all. The second thing is, to convey into his version, as much as possible, in a consistency with the genius of the language which he writes, the author's spirit and manner, and, if I may so express myself, the very character of his style. The third and last thing is, to take care, that the version have at least, so far the quality of an original performance, as to appear natural and easy, such as shall give no handle to the critic to charge the translator with applying words improperly, or in a meaning not warranted by use, or combining them in a way which renders the sense obscure, and the construction ungrammatical, or even harsh.
>
> (Campbell 1789:445–446)

To recommend transparency as the most suitable discourse for the Gospels was indeed to canonize fluent translation. Tytler, who claimed not to know of Campbell's work before publishing his own, made use of it in later editions of the *Essay*, drawing on the "Preliminary Dissertations" for additional examples and joining Campbell in rejecting translations that were either too literal or too free, that deviated too far from fluency and from dominant interpretations of the sacred text. "Dr. Campbell has justly remarked, that the Hebrew is a simple tongue," observed Tytler, agreeing with the Bible translator's rejection of Sebastianus Castalio's version for its "elegant Latinity," for "substituting the complex and florid composition to the simple and unadorned" (Tytler 1978:111, 112). Campbell's description of his own discursive strategy recommended fluency: "As to the Language, particularly of the version itself, simplicity, propriety, and perspicuity, are the principal qualities at which I have aimed. I have endeavoured to keep equally clear of the frippery of Arias, and the finery of Castalio" (Campbell 1789:xx). In Campbell's view, Arias Montanus erred because his Latin version "appears to have been servilely literal," offering obscure etymological renderings and "preserving uniformity, rendering the same word in the original, wherever it occurs, or however it is connected, by the same word in the version" without "attending to the scope of the author, as discovered by the context" (ibid.:449, 450, 451). Fluency requires the translator's lexicon to be varied enough not to call attention to itself as a lexicon, to the artificiality of the translation, or ultimately to the fact that the translator has created a target-language "context" to support his estimation of "the scope of the author."

Campbell's condemnation of close translation is a sharp reminder that any advocacy of transparent discourse conceals an investment in domestic cultural values – in his case, a Christian dogmatism with anti-Semitic overtones:

> A slavish attachment to the letter, in translating, is originally the offspring of the superstition, not of the Church, but of the synagogue, where it would have been more suitable in Christian interpreters, the ministers, not of the letter, but of the spirit, to have allowed it to remain.
>
> (Campbell 1789:456–457)

Like Tytler, however, Campbell also assumed the existence of a public sphere governed by universal reason. In an exchange of letters, Campbell took the self-congratulary view that the similarity of their ideas constituted "evidence" for "a concurrence in sentiment upon critical subjects with persons of distinguished ingenuity and erudition" (Alison 1818:27). Yet the elite and exclusionary nature of this cultural consensus becomes evident, not merely in Campbell's Christian dogmatism, but also in his initial reaction to Tytler's treatise: Campbell wrote to the publisher to learn the author's name because, although he was "flattered not a little to think, that he had in these points the concurrence in judgment of a writer so ingenious," he nonetheless voiced "his suspicion, that the author might have borrowed from his Dissertation, without acknowledging the obligation" (Alison 1818:27; Tytler 1978:xxxii). Campbell too was a translator with a sense of authorship – at once Christian and individualistic – that could be ruffled by other translations and translation discourses, provoking him to reactions that ran counter to his humanist assumptions.

By the turn of the nineteenth century, a translation method of eliding the linguistic and cultural difference of the foreign text was firmly entrenched as a canon in English-language translation, always linked to a valorization of transparent discourse. The canonicity of domesticating translation was so far beyond question that it survived the disintegration of the bourgeois public sphere, "now much less one of bland consensus than of ferocious contention," in which English literary periodicals constituted cultural factions with explicit political positions (Eagleton 1984:37). In 1820, John Hookham Frere, who would later publish his own translations of Aristophanes, unfavorably reviewed Thomas Mitchell's versions of *The Acharnians* and *The Knights* in the staunchly conservative *Quarterly Review*, Tory defender of neoclassical literary theory and the traditional authority of aristocracy and the Anglican Church (Sullivan 1983b:359–367). For Frere, the principal "defect" of Mitchell's translation was that it cultivated an archaic dramatic discourse, "the style of our ancient comedy in the beginning of the 16th century," whereas

> the language of translation ought, we think, as far as possible, to be a pure, impalpable and invisible element, the medium of thought and feeling, and nothing more; it ought never to attract attention to itself; hence all phrases that are remarkable in themselves, either as old or new; all importations from foreign languages and quotations, are as far as possible to be avoided. [...] such phrases as [Mitchell] has sometimes admitted, 'solus cum solo,' for instance, 'petits pates,' &c. have the immediate effect of reminding the reader, that he is reading a translation, and [...] the illusion of originality, which the spirited or natural turn of a sentence immediately preceding might have excited, is instantly dissipated by it.
>
> (Frere 1820:481)

Frere advocated the now familiar fluent strategy, in which the language of the translation is made to read with a "spirited or natural turn," so that the absence of any syntactical and lexical peculiarities produces the "illusion" that the translation is not a translation, but the foreign text, reflecting the foreign writer's intention: "It is the office, we presume, of the Translator to represent the forms of language according to the intention with which they are employed" (ibid.:482). The reviewer for the *Edinburgh Review*, a magazine whose liberal, Whiggish politics called the *Quarterly Review* into existence, nonetheless agreed that Mitchell's Aristophanes was defective, and for the same reason: he "devoted too much time to working in the mines of our early dramatists, instead of undergoing the greater trouble it would have cost him to form a style of his own more suited to the exigency" (*Edinburgh Review* 1820:306).[12] The reviewer defined

this "exigency" in terms of the stylistic feature repeatedly attributed to classical texts throughout the eighteenth century, asserting
that "simplicity should never be forgotten in a translation of
Aristophanes" (ibid.:307). Yet the reviewer also suggested that the
simplicity should be considered a feature of Mitchell's style as well
("a style of his own"), showing unwittingly that fluent translation
domesticates the foreign text, making it intelligible in an English-
language culture that values easy readability, transparent discourse, the illusion of authorial presence.

Once again, the domestication enacted by a fluent strategy was
not seen as producing an inaccurate translation. The usually
contentious periodicals agreed that William Stewart Rose's 1823
version of Ariosto's *Orlando Furioso* was both fluent and faithful.
Blackwood's, a magazine that pursued Tory conservatism to
reactionary extremes, called Rose's translation "a work which, *of
necessity,* addresses itself to the more refined classes," since "never
was such scrupulous fidelity of rendering associated with such light
dancing elegance of language" (*Blackwood's* 1823:30).[13] The
London Magazine, which sought to maintain an independent
neutrality amid its politically factious competitors, similarly found
that Rose "generally combined the garrulous ease and unpremedi-
tated manner of the original with a terse and equable flow of
numbers" (*London Magazine* 1824:626; Sullivan 1983b:288–296).
The *Quarterly Review* took Rose's version as an opportunity to
restate the canons of fluent translation:

> the two characteristics of a good translation are, that it should
> be *faithful,* and that it should be *unconstrained.* Faithful, as well
> in rendering correctly the meaning of the original, as in
> exhibiting the general spirit which pervades it: unconstrained,
> so as not to betray by its phraseology, by the collocation of its
> words, or construction of its sentences that it is only a copy.
>
> (*Quarterly Review* 1823:53)

A fluent strategy can be associated with fidelity because the effect
of transparency conceals the translator's interpretation of the
foreign text, the semantic context he has constructed in the
translation according to target-language cultural values. Rose's
fluent translation was praised for "rendering correctly the meaning of the original" because it assimilated the Italian text to
English values, not only the valorization of "unconstrained"
language, but also the interpretation of Ariosto's poem that

currently prevailed in the target culture. And, once again, the dominion of fluency entailed that canonical texts, the ancient and modern texts in which the sense of original authorship was felt to be most pronounced, would possess stylistic simplicity. The reviewer for the *London Magazine* declared that *Orlando Furioso* is characterized by "this exquisite simplicity, which bears the distinctive mark of a superior genius" (*London Magazine* 1824:626).

In Frere's case, fluency meant a linguistic homogenization that avoided, not merely archaism, but "associations exclusively belonging to modern manners," generalizing the foreign text by removing as many of the historically specific markers as possible. The translator must,

> if he is capable of executing his task upon a philosophic principle, endeavour to resolve the personal and local allusions into the genera, of which the local or personal variety employed by the original author, is merely the accidental type; and to reproduce them in one of those permanent forms which are connected with the universal and immutable habits of mankind.
>
> (Frere 1820:482)

Frere rationalized these admitted "liberties" by appealing to a "philosophic principle":

> The proper domain of the Translator is, we conceive, to be found in that vast mass of feeling, passion, interest, action and habit which is common to mankind in all countries and in all ages; and which, in all languages, is invested with its appropriate forms of expression, capable of representing it in all its infinite varieties, in all the permanent distinctions of age, profession and temperament.
>
> (ibid.:481)

In Frere's view, a fluent strategy enables the translation to be a transparent representation of the eternal human verities expressed by the foreign author.

The principle on which Frere's theory rests is the principle that can now be recognized as central to the history of fluent translation: liberal humanism, subjectivity seen as at once self-determining and determined by human nature, individualistic yet generic, transcending cultural difference, social conflict, and historical change to represent "every shade of the human character" (Frere 1820:481). And, like preceding versions of this principle, Frere's may appear to be democratic in its appeal to what is "common to mankind," to a timeless and universal human essence, but it actually involved an insidious domestication that allowed him to imprint the foreign text with his conservative sexual morality and cultural elitism. He made plain his squeamishness about the physical coarseness of Aristophanic humor, its grotesque realism, and felt the need to explain it away as inconsistent with the author's intention: the "lines of extreme grossness" were "forced compromises," "which have evidently been inserted, for the purpose of pacifying the vulgar part of the audience, during passages in which their anger, or impatience, or disappointment, was likely to break out" (ibid.:491). Hence, "in discarding such passages," Frere asserted, "the translator is merely doing that for his author, which he would willingly have done for himself" – were he not "often under the necessity of addressing himself exclusively to the lower class" (ibid.:491). Frere's advocacy of a fluent strategy was premised on a bourgeois snobbery, in which the moral and political conservatism now ascendant in English culture resulted in a call for a bowdlerized Aristophanes that represented the "permanent" class divisions of humanity, what Frere described as "that true comic humour which he was directing to the more refined and intelligent part of his audience" (ibid.:491). For Frere, "the persons of taste and judgment, to whom the author occasionally appeals, form, in modern times, the tribunal to which his translator must address himself" (ibid.:491).

The *Edinburgh Review* criticized Mitchell's Aristophanes on the basis of similar philosophical and political assumptions, although formulated with an explicitly "liberal" difference. The reviewer's Aristophanes approached his audience with a democratic inclusiveness – "The smiles of the polite few were not enough for the comedian, – he must join them to the shouts of the million" – and since "for all tastes he had to cater," the playwright came to assume several social functions, "Public Satirist," "State Journalist," "Periodical Critic" (*Edinburgh Review* 1820:280) – an Aristophanes modelled on the *Edinburgh*'s own self-image as a liberal magazine. Unlike Frere, this reviewer sighs with relief that Mitchell "does not mean to publish a Family Aristophanes," alluding to the title of Thomas Bowdler's expurgated edition of Shakespeare (Bowdler 1818), and no offense was taken at Mitchell's language. The problem for the *Edinburgh* reviewer was rather Mitchell's description of Aristophanes' "audience as usually made up of a mere 'rabble,' ripe for nothing but 'the nonsense of holiday revelry,' and totally unfit to appreciate merit of an higher order" (*Edinburgh Review* 1820:275). Here the reviewer's "liberal" stance reveals the same contradiction between humanism and cultural elitism that emerged in Frere: Aristophanic comedy "could not be altogether without attractions for the philosophic mind, that explores the principles of human nature, or the cultivated taste, that delights in the triumph of genius" (ibid.:277). Not unexpectedly, the "qualities" that distinguish Aristophanes as "somewhat above the coarse apprehension of a mere mob, and fit to gain applause more precious than the unintellectual roar of plebeian acclamation," are characteristic of transparent discourse: "both clear and perspicuous, – terse and yet magnificent, – powerful and ethical," "that unfailing fluency and copiousness" (ibid.:278, 282).

III

The canonization of fluency in English-language translation during the early modern period limited the translator's options and defined their cultural and political stakes. A translator could choose the now traditional domesticating method, an ethnocentric reduction of the foreign text to dominant cultural values in English; or a translator could choose a foreignizing method, an ethnodeviant pressure on those values to register the linguistic and cultural differences of the foreign text. Around the turn of the nineteenth century, the values in question, although stated somewhat contradictorily in various treatises, translators' prefaces, and reviews, were decidedly bourgeois – liberal and humanist, individualistic and elitist, morally conservative and physically squeamish. The ways in which they constrained the translator's activity, the forms of submission and resistance that a translator might adopt under their domination, become strikingly evident with the first book-length translations of Catullus into English, the versions of Dr. John Nott (1795) and the Honourable George Lamb (1821).

Before these translations appeared, Catullus had long occupied a foothold in the canon of classical literature in English. Editions of the Latin text were available on the Continent after the fifteenth century, and even though two more centuries passed before it was published in England, Catullus had already been imitated by a wide range of English poets – Thomas Campion, Ben Jonson, Edmund Waller, Robert Herrick, among many others (McPeek 1939;

Wiseman 1985:chap. VII). Still, Catullus's place in English literary culture, even if supported by such culturally prominent writers, was rather minor. There were few translations, usually of the same small group of kiss and sparrow poems, showing quite clearly that he was virtually neglected by English translators in favor of Homer, Virgil, Ovid, Horace: these were the major figures, translated in the service of diverse aesthetic, moral, and political interests. Catullus's marginality was partly an issue of genre, with epic privileged over lyric in English poetry translation during this period. But there was also the issue of morality, with English writers at once attracted and disturbed by the pagan sexuality and the physically coarse language, entertaining a guilty fixation on the poet's scandalous affair with "Lesbia."

The first substantial selected translation, the anonymous *Adventures of Catullus, and History of His Amours with Lesbia* (1707), was itself a translation from the French, Jean de la Chapelle's *Les Amours de Catulle*. It consisted of several narrative sections, some in the voices of Catullus and Lesbia, punctuated by versions of the Latin texts, all arranged to support "a train of Historical Conjectures [which] have so great a foundation in the poet's own Verses" (*The Adventures of Catullus* 1707:A2ʳ). For the English editor, the book was didactic, "one of the severest Lessons against our Passions and Vices"; but since it was described as "a just Representation of the Nobility of Antient *Rome*, in a private Life, in their Friendships, Conversation, and Manners within Doors," the editor was also assimilating Roman aristocratic culture to bourgeois values like emotional intimacy and moral propriety and perhaps questioning the "private life" of the British aristocracy: the book was dedicated to the earl of Thomond (ibid.:A2ᵛ–A3ᵛ). In his *Lives of the Roman Poets* (1733), Lewis Crusius, anxiously feeling the need for a "justification of this Writer [who] has been very much censured for the Lewdness of some of his Pieces," asked the English reader to respect the historical and cultural difference of Catullus's poetry, its different sexual morality:

> We would not be understood by any means to vindicate this conduct in our Author, but barely to shew, that Obscenity, according to the Antients, was not only allowable in these sorts of Compositions, but when artfully drest up, was esteemed one of its greatest beauties.
>
> (Crusius 1733:28)

In the end, however, Crusius bared only his moral refinement, concluding that the Latin texts should continue to be censored:

> Many things more might be brought to shew the allowableness of this practice among the *Greeks* as well as *Romans*; but as we think it in the highest degree criminal and offensive in itself, and of most pernicious consequence to the Readers, especially the youth of both sexes, into whose hands such pieces may happen to fall, we shall say no more on this Head.

(ibid.:29)

The appearance of two complete translations of Catullus's poetry within roughly a generation signalled a revision of the classical canon in English, the emergence of a new taste for short poems, mainly epigrams and lyrics, and especially those of an erotic nature. The cultural and social factors that made this revision possible included, not any relaxation of bourgeois moral norms, but the canonization of transparency in English poetry and poetry translation. Crusius had sounded this note early when he praised the "easy unaffected elegance and pleasantry that enlivens this Poet's Style" (Crusius 1733:28). By the beginning of the nineteenth century, Catullus's poetry was routinely assimilated to transparent discourse, considered to offer an especially strong effect of authorial presence, and this occasionally weakened the critics' prudery, leading them to mitigate the coarse language they found so offensive. The work of rehabilitation was evident in Charles Abraham Elton's *Specimens of the Classic Poets* (1814), a three-volume anthology of verse translations from Greek and Latin. Elton felt that Catullus's poetry was rather thin – "pieces of gallantry or satirical epigrams, with a few poems of a more elevated cast" – but he excused this defect by assuming that "much of the poetry of Catullus appears to have been lost" (Elton 1814:I, 30–31). What recommends the extant texts is their "ease" and "simplicity":

> They, who turn with disgust from the coarse impurities that sully his pages, may be inclined to wonder, that the term of *delicacy* should ever have been coupled with the name of Catullus. But to many of his effusions, distinguished both by fancy and feeling, this praise is justly due. Many of his amatory trifles are quite unrivalled in the elegancy of their playfulness; and no author has excelled him in the purity and neatness of his style, the delightful ease and racy simplicity of his manner, and his

graceful turns of thought and happinesses of expression. Some of his pieces, which breathe the higher enthusiasm of the art, and are coloured with a singular picturesqueness of imagery, increase our regret at the manifest mutilation of his works.

(ibid.:II: 31)

In 1818, *Blackwood's* published an essay that remarked on the fluency of Catullus's verse, finding it a mirror of the poet: "This language is uniformly unlaboured.[...] His versification is careless, but graceful. His feeling is weak, but always true. The poet has no inclination to appear any thing but what he is" (*Blackwood's* 1818:487). The essayist then ventured to connect Catullus to a canonical English figure, suggesting that the "obscenity is seldom introduced altogether for its own sake. Like that of Swift, it is only the weapon of satire" (ibid.:488). The final verdict, however, was

that it is quite impossible to read his verses without regretting that he happened to be an idler, a man of fashion, and a debauchee.[...] he might have bequeathed to posterity works fitted to inspire sentiments of virtue and morality, instead of a book, the greater part of which must for ever remain sealed to all those who have any principle of human delicacy in their composition.

(ibid.:489)

The translators of the first book-length versions of Catullus, Nott and Lamb, shared the prevailing assessment of the Latin poet, but it shaped their work very differently. Nott too thought that "strength and simplicity, elegance and perspicuity mark the stile of Catullus" (Nott 1795:I, xxiii), while Lamb wrote of "the poet's natural felicity of expression," "the same natural tone which Catullus rarely or rather never lost" (Lamb 1821:I, xl, xlii). The most remarkable difference between the translators occurred on the question of morality: Nott sought to reproduce the pagan sexuality and physically coarse language of the Latin text, whereas Lamb minimized or just omitted them.

Nott was aware that "Those indecencies occurring so frequently in our poet, which I have constantly preserved in the original, and ventured in some way to translate, may be thought to require apology" (Nott 1795:I, x). His initial reason – to satisfy "the inquisitive scholar [who] might wish to be acquainted with the ribaldry, and gross lampoon of Roman times" (ibid.) – would not

be persuasive to his contemporaries, since such a reader already
had access to the Latin text; perhaps the claim should be viewed
less as a rationale than as a reflection of Nott's own scholarly bent,
his wish to address an academic audience. His main concern seems
to have been twofold: to ward against an ethnocentric response to
the Latin text and preserve its historical and cultural difference:

> When an ancient classic is translated, and explained, the work
> may be considered as forming a link in the chain of history:
> history should not be falsified, we ought therefore to translate
> him fairly; and when he gives us the manners of his own day,
> however disgusting to our sensations, and repugnant to our
> natures they may sometimes prove, we must not endeavour to
> conceal, or gloss them over, through a fastidious regard to
> delicacy.
>
> (ibid.:x–xi)

Nott's sense of historical accuracy assumed a mimetic concept of
translation as a representation adequate to the foreign text. In
1795, this mimetic assumption was beginning to seem dated in
English poetic theory, a throwback to an older empiricism,
challenged now by expressive theories of poetry and original
genius.[14] And yet Nott's adherence to a residual theoretical
assumption enabled him to resist the pressure of bourgeois moral
values on his translation.

In 1821, Lamb possessed a more contemporary, romantic sense
of authorial authenticity that projected an expressive concept of
translation as adequately communicating the foreign author's
psychological state. Catullus's "compositions, few as they are,
probably express his feelings upon every important event of his
short career," Lamb believed, and this led him to conclude that the
Latin poet "seems to have been as little sullied by the grossness of
the age, as was possible [. . .] pure indeed must that mind naturally
have been, which, amidst such coarseness of manners, could
preserve so much expressive delicacy and elevated refinement"
(Lamb 1821: I, xlii–xliii). Lamb's expressive poetics underwrote
not only his belief in the poet's purity, both moral and stylistic, but
also his advocacy of a free translation method that effected the
illusion of transparency while domesticating the Latin text. Explicitly situating himself in the main tradition of fluent translation
from Denham to Johnson, Lamb stated that "the natural course of
translation is, first to secure its fidelity, and then to attempt the

polish of elegance and freedom" (ibid.: lviii). Hence, he handled the "objectionable expressions" by developing strategies of "omission and amplification," recognizing "the necessity of making every attempt to veil and soften before entire omission could be justified," revising on the assumption that Catullus was "a genius orignally pure, however polluted by the immorality of its era" (ibid.: lix, xli).

Lamb's translation submitted to the bourgeois values that dominated English culture, inscribing the Latin text with a conservative morality and a fetish for transparent poetic discourse. Nott worked under the same cultural regime, but he rather chose to resist those values in the name of preserving the difference of the Latin text. Nott foreignized Catullus, although foreignization does not mean that he somehow transcended his own historical moment to reproduce the foreign, unmediated by the domestic. On the contrary, if Nott's translation presented any element of Roman culture during the late Republic, it could only be in English-language cultural terms, making the foreign here not so much "Roman" as a marked deviation from current English values.

The various aspects of Nott's foreignized Catullus stand out conspicuously against Lamb's domestication. Nott's bilingual edition, intended to give "the whole of Catullus without reserve" (Nott 1795: I, x), consisted of 115 poems attributed to the Latin poet; Lamb's English-only edition included 84 (Lamb 1821). Nott translated texts that referred to adulterous affairs and homosexual relationships, as well as texts that contained descriptions of sexual acts, especially anal and oral intercourse. Lamb either omitted or bowdlerized them, preferring more refined expressions of heterosexual love that glanced fleetingly at sexual activity. Catullus's satiric epigram on the "Verbenni," for instance, is a poem that Lamb excluded. Here is the Latin text with Nott's translation:

O furum optime balneariorum
Vibenni pater et cineade fili,
(nam dextra pater inquinatiore,
culo filius est voraciore)
cur non exilium malasque in oras
itis? quandoquidem patris rapinae
notae sunt populo, et natis pilosas,
fili, non potes asse venditare.

Old Vibennius of all your bath-rogues is the first;

Nor less noted his boy for unnatural lust:
The hands of the former are ever rapacious,
The latter's posterior is full as voracious:
Then, o why don't ye both into banishment go,
And deservedly wander in deserts of woe?
Not a soul but the father's mean rapines must tell;
And thou, son, canst no longer thy hairy breech sell.

(Nott 1795: I, 90–91)

Nott's translation deviated from English literary and moral values
in several ways. Not only did he choose to include the Latin text
and translate the sexual references, but his choices ("unnatural
lust," "posterior," "breech") render the Latin quite closely
("cinaede," "culo," "natis"), refusing the traditional free method
and thus minimizing the risk of euphemism and expurgation.
Nott's translation is equally un-English in being no more than
intermittently fluent. The text opens with a false rhyme ("first"/
"lust"). The twelve-syllable line, a departure from the pentameter
standard, is metrically irregular and rather cumbersome, handled
effectively only in the second couplet. And the syntax is elliptical,
inverted, or convoluted in fully half of the lines.

Nott's violations against moral and stylistic propriety are also
apparent when his translations are juxtaposed to Lamb's. Both
translated Catullus's apology for his love poetry, but their treat-
ments of the opening lines are significantly different:

Pedicabo ego vos et irrumabo,
Aureli pathice et cinaede Furi,
qui me ex versiculis meis putastis,
quod sunt molliculi, parum pudicum.

I'll treat you as 'tis meet, I swear,
Notorious pathics as ye are!
Aurelius, Furius! who arraign
And judge me by my wanton strain.

(Nott 1795: I, 51)

And dare ye, Profligates, arraign
The ardour of my sprightly strain,
And e'en myself asperse?

(Lamb 1821: I, 35)

Neither version went as far as the Latin text in specifying the nature of the sexual acts: Catullus's "pedicabo" and "irrumabo" indicate anal and oral intercourse. But Nott's "pathics" was obviously much closer to the Latin than Lamb's "profligates." The word "pathics" was a term of abuse used since the seventeenth century to mean "a man or boy upon whom sodomy is practised; a catamite" (*OED*). Hence, its abusiveness (even if homophobic by late twentieth-century standards) conveyed Catullus's Roman assumption that a male who submitted to anal and oral intercourse – whether willingly or not – was humiliated whereas, "the penetrator himself was neither demeaned nor disgraced" (Wiseman 1985:11). Lamb's choice of "profligates" effectively expurgated the Latin text, but his bourgeois sense of propriety was so intense that he felt compelled to mention the expurgation in a footnote, where he also sought to excuse the coarseness of Catullus's language: it was seen as expressing the intensity of his hurt feelings:

> This poem is a very free imitation of the original, which could not be tolerated if translated literally. Pezay says, this poem being addressed by Catullus to his two great friends, should be looked upon "comme une petite gaité." The tone is rather of serious indignation at the comments on his poems; and he may have been the more exasperated at such treatment from those whom he had considered his friends and defenders.
>
> *The sacred bard, to Muses dear,*
> *Himself should pass a chaste career.*
>
> This assertion of the purity of character which a loose poet should and may preserve has been brought forward both by Ovid, Martial, and Ausonius, in their own defence.
>
> (Lamb 1821:II, 141)

Lamb's version was a paragon, not just of propriety, but of fluency too. Nott used another false rhyme ("swear"/"ye are") and created a somewhat ungainly movement from one couplet to the next, abruptly shifting from declarative statement to epithet to apostrophe. Lamb evidently borrowed Nott's one true rhyme in the passage, but he put it to much more elegant use by making the syntax more continuous and varying the meter more subtly.

There is perhaps no better illustration of the translators' different methods than their versions of *Carmen* V, the object of innumerable English translations and imitations since the sixteenth century:

Vivamus, mea Lesbia, atque amemus,
rumoresque senum severiorum
omnes unius aestimemus assis.
soles occidere et redire possunt:
nobis cum semel occidit brevis lux,
nox est perpetua una dormienda.
da mi basia mille, deinde centum,
dein mille altera, dein secunda centum,
deinde usque altera mille, deinde centum.
dein, cum milia multa fecerimus,
conturbabimus illa, nc sciamus,
aut ne quis malus invidere possit,
cum tantum sciat esse basiorum.

Let's live, and love, my darling fair!
And not a single farthing care
    For age's babbling spite;
Yon suns that set again shall rise;
But, when our transient meteor dies,
    We sleep in endless night:

Then first a thousand kisses give,
An hundred let me next receive,
    Another thousand yet;
To these a second hundred join,
Still be another thousand mine,
    An hundred then repcat:

Such countless thousands let there be,
Sweetly confus'd; that even we
    May know not the amount;
That envy, so immense a store
Beholding, may not have the pow'r
    Each various kiss to count.
                    (Nott 1795: I, 17)

Nott's first stanza possesses considerable fluency, with its continuous syntax woven through a moderately intricate rhyme scheme,
but in the second stanza the false rhymes proliferate, and the third
fairly creaks with syntactical inversions and suspensions and the
jarring rhyme on "store"/"pow'r." Nott's suggestive revisions of the
Latin text stress the opposition between the morality of age ("bab-
bling spite") and the passion of youth ("transient meteor") and

include a couple of mildly sexual references, the erotic pleasure signified by "sweetly confus'd" and the experienced sexuality hinted in "various" kinds of "kisses." Nott's second stanza also revises the Latin (by shifting from "give" to "receive"), creating the rakish image of the male lover passively receiving Lesbia's kisses and thus exaggerating, somewhat comically, the male fantasy of female sexual aggressiveness in Catullus's text. Nott's masculinist translation is a humorous, slightly prurient, and not entirely felicitous celebration of the lovers' youth and sexuality against age and moral strictness. Its sexual frankness conflicts with Lamb's more decorous version, in which the lovers are given to shameful "blushing":

> Love, my Lesbia, while we live;
>   Value all the cross advice
> That the surly greybeards give
>   At a single farthing's price.
>
> Suns that set again may rise;
>   We, when once our fleeting light,
> Once our day in darkness dies,
>   Sleep in one eternal night.
>
> Give me kisses thousand-fold,
>   Add to them a hundred more;
> Other thousands still be told
>   Other hundreds o'er and o'er.
>
> But, with thousands when we burn,
>   Mix, confuse the sums at last,
> That we may not blushing learn
>   All that have between us past.
>
> None shall know to what amount
>   Envy's due for so much bliss;
> None – for none shall ever count
>   All the kisses we will kiss.
>   (Lamb 1821: I, 12–13)

Compared to Nott's, Lamb's translation is distinguished by an extreme fluency: the quatrains unwind quickly, driven by a smoothly varied trochaic meter, and they parcel out the meaning in precise syntactical units, recurring with a regularity that threatens to call attention to its artificial quality, but remains unobtrusive, easy, light. Lamb's additions to the Latin text at once make more explicit the sexual nature of the theme ("burn") and point to the lovers' modesty ("blushing"), a contradiction that is symptomatic of the translator's labor of domestication. Lamb's version, unlike Nott's, is cast as a seduction ("Love, my Lesbia") and thus follows the traditional English treatment of the Latin text: in Jonson's *Volpone* (1605), for instance, an imitation of Catullus's poem is used by Volpone to seduce the chaste Celia. And since Lamb's "grey-beards," unlike Nott's "age," reproduces the male gender that Catullus assigns to the voice of morality, the relationship between the lovers takes on the form of a family romance, with the male lover locked in an oedipal struggle against the patriarchs for control over Lesbia's sexuality. Lamb's final stanza borrows another of Nott's rhymes ("amount"/"count"), and once again this borrowing reveals the different values shaping their translations: in Nott's, the kissing is seen by the envious ("beholding"), the affair treated as public knowledge, whereas in Lamb's the kissing seems to be shielded by privacy ("none shall know," "none shall ever count"). Both versions domesticate the Latin text to some degree, most obviously in their choice of verse form and their use of "farthing" to render the Latin for a bronze coin ("assis"); but Lamb's is traced by various bourgeois values – fluency, moral propriety, the patriarchal family, privacy – whereas Nott's con-stitutes a significant deviation, if not simply a violation of them.

This is in fact the reading that emerges in a survey of contempo-rary responses to the translations. In the late 1790s, Nott's seemed so foreign to English tastes, it provided such an uncomfortably alien reading experience, that it was repeatedly damned on moral and stylistic grounds. The reviewer for the *Gentleman's Magazine* made clear how moral offense could be a bourgeois gesture of social superiority by linking Nott's translation to the popular taste for the Gothic novel, its sensationalized sexuality: "How any man could have presumed to debauch the minds of his countrymen by translating 'indecencies so frequent in this lascivious poet, which the chaste reader must think best omitted,' [...] is a problem which only those who have read such novels as 'The Monk' can solve" (*Gentleman's Magazine* 1798:408).

The disapproval of Nott's "lascivious" translation was general in the literary periodicals, crossing factional lines and thus revealing their common bourgeois assumptions. The *British Critic*, a Tory magazine started by Anglican clergymen who opposed parliamen-tary reform, asserted that "We object, from moral principles, to the translator's plan" and insisted that the translation "should be sedulously removed from youth and from females" (*British Critic* 1798:672); whereas the liberal *Monthly Review* added a carefully worded comment that at once admitted the possibility of another reading of Catullus and refused to sanction it: "though we may appear fastidious to the present translator, we confess that in our opinion a judicious selection of his poems would have been more acceptable to the public" (*Monthly Review* 1797:278).[15]

Nott's translation was neglected by the periodicals, with the first reviews appearing several years after publication and in very small number. Lamb's translation was widely reviewed as soon as it was published; and even though judgments were mixed, they were stated in the same bourgeois terms and tended to be much more favorable than Nott's. The usually contentious reviewers turned not so much nonpartisan, as class-conscious in their embrace of Lamb's version. The liberal *Monthly Magazine*, which announced itself in its first number as "an enterprise on behalf of intellectual liberty against the forces of panic conservatism" (Sullivan 1983b:314–319), praised Lamb's expurgation of Catullus's text:

> the more correct moral feeling of modern times, would never permit a complete version of many of those objectionable passages in which he abounds. This portion of his task Mr. Lamb has executed with considerable judgment, and we need not fear that our delicacy may be wounded in perusing the pages of his translation.
>
> (*Monthly Magazine* 1821:34)

The reactionary *Anti-Jacobin Review* enlisted Lamb in its struggle against the opponents of church, state, and nation:

> The extreme impropriety of many Poems written by Catullus, has obliged Mr. Lamb to omit them, and had he turned his attention wholly to some purer author, it would have honoured his powers of selection. At this hour of contest between the good and evil principle among us, when so many are professedly Atheists, and blasphemy is encouraged by subscription, and sedition supported by charities, no patriot and christian would assist vice by palliating its excesses, or render them less offensive by a decent veil. [...] Mr. Lamb is entitled to both the above characters of patriot and christian.
>
> (*Anti-Jacobin Review* 1821:14)

Reviewers also faulted Nott's translation for lacking fluency. The *Monthly Review* remarked that "we would praise this translator for his general correctness with respect to the English version, yet his inattention to rhime is too gross and too frequent not to incur censure" (*Monthly Review* 1797:278). The *British Critic* complained of "great irregularities both with regard to the spirit, correctness, and harmony" (*British Critic* 1798:671–672). Lamb's prosody was apparently not spirited enough for several reviewers – his versions of the "minor pieces" get described as "languid," or devoid of "poetical ease and beauty" – but at least one magazine, the *Monthly Review,* found that he "preserved no small portion of the spirit and dignity of the original," singling out Lamb's rendering of *Carmen* V for special praise as "the best which we have seen, with the exception only of Ben Jonson's," recognizing Lamb's Catullus as a peculiarly English phenomenon, indicative of the dominance of fluency in poetry translation (*Monthly Review* 1822:11, 9).

We can more fully understand the translators' different motives and methods by considering their translations in the context of their other work, their lives, and their different historical moments. A practicing physician who was constantly engaged in literary projects, Nott (1751–1825) published a number of books that drew impressively on the tradition of the love lyric in classical, European, and Oriental languages (*Gentleman's Magazine* 1825:565–566; *DNB*). Late in his career, he wrote a prose romance entitled *Sappho* (1803), made a selection from Robert Herrick's *Hesperides* (1810), and edited a miscellany of sixteenth-century English poetry beginning with Sir Thomas Wyatt (1812). The bulk of his work, however, was translation, and over a thirty-year period he produced book-length translations of Johannes Secundus Nicolaius (1775), Petrarch (1777), Propertius (1782), Hafiz (1787), Bonefonius (1797), Lucretius (1799), and Horace (1803). The Catullus translation (1795) was an obvious choice for a translator with Nott's interests and energies.

He was so prolific because he felt that more was at stake in translating than literary appreciation, even though aesthetic values always guided his choices as well. The mimetic concept of translation that made him choose a foreignizing method to preserve the difference of the foreign text also made him think of his work as an act of cultural restoration. This was the rationale he often gave in his prefatory statements. His "Attempt to transfer unblemished into the English language the numberless Beauties with which the Basia of Secundus abound" was intended to draw "a deserving Author from that Oblivion in which he has been so long buried" (Nott 1778:vii). Finding it "astonishing, considering his merit," that Propertius had never been translated into English, Nott intended his version "to repair this neglect" (Nott 1782: iii–iv). For Nott, translation performed the work of cultural restoration by revising the canon of foreign literature in English, supporting the admission of some marginalized texts and occasionally questioning the canonicity of others. In his preface to his selection from the Persian poet Hafiz, Nott boldly challenged the English veneration of classical antiquity by suggesting that western European culture originated in the east:

> we lament, whilst years are bestowed in acquiring an insight into the Greek and Roman authors, that those very writers should have been neglected, from whom the Greeks evidently derived both the richness of their mythology, and the peculiar tenderness of their expressions.
>
> (Nott 1787:v–vi)

Nott attacked any Anglocentric dismissal of Oriental poets like Hafiz, arguing the importance of "not judging of the glow of Eastern dialogue by the standard of our colder feelings and ideas," and he went so far as to suggest that "the more exact rules of English criticism and taste" were complicit in English imperialism:

> Was it not probable to suppose, when a fatal ambition had determined us to possess a country, our distance from which made the attempt unnatural; and when, under the pretence of commerce, we became the cruel invaders of another's right; that we should at least have made ourselves acquainted with the language of the conquered? This was necessary, whether to distribute justice, or to exercise compassion. But private avarice and extortion shut up the gates of public virtue.
>
> (ibid.:vii)

Of course Nott's foreignizing translation method could never be entirely free of domestic values and agendas, including the development of a national culture: he felt, for example, that the failure to translate Propertius caused "some degradation to English literature" (Nott 1782:iv). But he was sufficiently sensitive to the ethnocentric violence involved in any encounter with a cultural other to question the imposition of bourgeois canons and interests, whether at home, in translations of foreign literary texts, or abroad, in economic and political relations with foreign countries.

Nott's frequent travel, including a stint on a colonial expedition, no doubt increased his willingness to resist domestic values. After studying medicine in Paris as well as London, he spent years on the Continent as physician to English travellers (1775–1777, 1786–1788, 1789–1793) and made a trip to China as surgeon on a vessel of the East India Company (1783–1786). The class in which Nott travelled must also be included among the conditions of his cultural work: the aristocracy. His father held an appointment in the household of George III, and Nott's patients were generally aristocrats. This class affiliation is important because it indicates a domestic motive for his interest in foreignizing translation. As a physician, Nott was on intimate terms with a group whose sexual practices, far from exhibiting any bourgeois sense of moral propriety, rivalled those of Catullus's Rome in their variousness and sheer frequency, even if they were discussed less openly and with greater refinement – "gallantry" often served as a euphemism for adultery during this period. Lawrence Stone has referred to "plenty of evidence that there was a great deal of extramarital sexual activity among many aristocratic husbands and some aristocratic wives at least as late as the first decade of the nineteenth century" (Stone 1977:534; Perkin 1989:89–96).

In Nott's case, we can be more specific. A confirmed bachelor himself, he served as physician to Georgiana Cavendish, Duchess of Devonshire, when she travelled on the Continent between 1789 and 1793 (Posonby 1955; *DNB*). The fashionable, trend-setting Duchess had been banished abroad by her husband William, the fifth Duke, because gambling losses had driven her deep into debt. In 1792, the Duchess gave birth to a daughter who was assumed to be the offspring of her adultery with Charles Grey, an aggressive young politician who led the Whig party and later became Prime Minister. The Duke himself fathered three illegitimate children, one by a woman with whom he had an affair at the time of his marriage, two by Lady Elizabeth Foster, who separated from her own husband in 1782 and was befriended by the Duke and Duchess. Nott's interest in erotic literature, his refusal to expurgate Catullus's poetry, even the sexual frankness of his translations, were due in some part to the casual sexual morality that characterized his aristocratic milieu during the late eighteenth century. His foreignization of the Latin text did in fact answer to domestic values, however different from those that influenced the periodical reviewers and Lamb.

George Lamb (1784–1834) was born into the same aristocratic milieu as Nott, but thirty years later. The fourth and youngest son of Penniston, Viscount Melbourne, he practiced law for a short while, but left it to pursue various literary and theatrical interests, reviewing for the *Edinburgh*, contributing prologues to revivals at the Drury Lane, and writing a comic opera that was staged at Covent Garden (*Gentleman's Magazine* 1834:437–438; *DNB*). He eventually entered politics, first as an MP in the Duke of Devonshire's interest and then, on the accession of the Whig ministry, as Under Secretary of State to his brother William, Lord Melbourne. In 1809, George married Caroline St. Jules, one of the Duke of Devonshire's illegitimate children with Lady Foster; George's own birth was illegitimate, the result of Lady Melbourne's adultery with the Prince of Wales. Everyone concerned knew of these relations.[16] It was Lamb who informed Caroline of her father's identity a few years before their marriage. The Duke gave her a dowry of £30,000; Lamb's response was that "I can only thank him by devoting my future life to Caroline's happiness" (Posonby 1955:4). The knowledge of these relations extended past the family. In the obituary on Lamb in the *Gentleman's Magazine*, Caroline was described as "a relation of the Duke of the Devonshire" (*Gentleman's Magazine* 1834:438). Still, everything was treated very discreetly. Lady Foster concocted a genealogy to explain Caroline's unusual name, "a certain obscure Comte de St. Jules being the supposed father" (Posonby 1955:4). The most public scandal in Lamb's family did not involve him: in 1812, Lady Caroline Lamb, his brother William's wife, was engaged in a notorious affair with Byron. George himself seems to have been happily married. His obituary referred to "the tranquillity of his domestic life," stating that with the "estimable" Caroline, "of a character entirely assorting with his own, he enjoyed the truest domestic felicity" (*Gentleman's Magazine* 1834: 438).

Lamb's life attests to the fact that the increasing moral conservatism of English society during this period was affecting not only the middle and working classes, but the aristocracy as well. This bourgeois cultural movement toward moral reform, spurred by the rise of Evangelical Christianity and accompanied by the institution of various philanthropic "societies," led to the proliferation of moral and religious tracts and continued the bowdlerization of literary texts that characterized English poetry translation at

least since Pope (Quinlan 1941; Perkin 1989:90, 120–121, 240).[17]
Lamb's first-hand knowledge of the casual sexual morality among
the Whig aristocracy may have made him more receptive to the
emergent conservatism in English culture, since there can be no
doubt that he contributed to it. His work in the theatre included
an adaptation of Shakespeare's *Timon of Athens* (Lamb 1816),
whose goal, he announced in an "Advertisement," was "to restore
Shakespeare to the stage, with no other omissions than such as the
refinement of manners has rendered necessary." Lamb omitted
this dialogue, for example, between Timon and "the churlish
Philosopher" Apemantus:

> *Tim.*   Wilt thou dine with me, Apemantus?
> *Apem.* No; I eat not lords.
> *Tim.*   And thou shouldst, thou'dst anger ladies.
> *Apem.* O they eat lords; so they come by great bellies.
> *Tim.*   That's a lascivious apprehension.
> *Apem.* So thou apprehend'st it; take it for thy labour.
>
> (Shakespeare 1959: I.i.203–208)

Lamb treated Shakespeare just as he did Catullus, expurgating the
text of any coarse language, and his like-minded contemporaries
approved of his work, with one commentator observing that "much
is omitted in the dialogue, and generally with propriety" (Genest
1832:584). Lamb saw no contradiction between professing liberalism as a Whig politician and censoring canonical literary texts. He
followed what David Cecil has called the "canons of Whig ortho-
doxy. All believed in ordered liberty, low taxation and the enclo-
sure of land; all disbelieved in despotism and democracy" (Cecil
1965:7).[18]

Lamb's calculated omission of the carnivalesque in his literary
projects must be taken as another gesture of social superiority by
a member of the hegemonic class. Lamb's elitism, however, was
couched in terms that were belletristic instead of social: he viewed
a poetry translation or a theatrical adaptation as a refined form of
entertainment, an exercise in aesthetic appreciation performed
during periods of leisure, often in private. He prefaced his Catullus
translation with a poem entitled "Reflections before Publication,"
wherein he presented his work, not as an engaged act of cultural
restoration or canon revision, but as the "pleasing" diversion of an
amateur who is now contemplating whether to share it with others:

The pleasing task, which oft a calm has lent
To lull disease and soften discontent;
Has still made busy life's vacations gay,
And saved from idleness the leisure day:
In many a musing walk and lone retreat,
That task is done; – I may not say complete.
Now, have I heart to see the flames devour
The work of many a pleasurable hour?
Deep in some chest must I my offspring thrust,
To know no resurrection from the dust;
Or shall I, printing in this age of paper,
Add to th'unnumber'd stars another taper?
                              (Lamb 1821: I, ix–x)

Lamb was one of those future aristocrats for whom Sir John Denham developed the domesticating method of translating classical poetry, shrinking from the prospect of publication because poetry translation was not the serious work of politics or government service. And with an appropriateness that Denham would have appreciated, Lamb's courtly self-effacement was cast in fluent heroic couplets.

In the thirty years that separated Nott's Catullus from Lamb's, the Whiggish aristocratic milieu in which they lived and worked underwent a substantial change that influenced the fate of their translations and translation methods. Fluent, domesticating translation was valorized in accordance with bourgeois moral and literary values, and a notable effort of resistance through a foreignizing method was decisively displaced. Nott's translation foreignized Catullus by assimilating the Latin text to cultural values that were residual in the 1790s and marginal by the 1820s: a mimetic concept of translation grounded in the paradigm of representation was yielding to a communicative concept of translation grounded in the paradigm of expression; and the casual sexual morality of the aristocracy was challenged by a movement toward moral reform that affected both aristocrat and bourgeois. Nott and Lamb exemplify the two options available to translators at a specific moment in the canonization of fluency. Perhaps most importantly, they show that in foreignizing translation, the difference of the foreign text can only ever be figured by domestic values that differ from those in dominance.

Chapter 3

Nation

> The translator who attaches himself closely to his original more or less abandons the originality of his nation, and so a third comes into existence, and the taste of the multitude must first be shaped towards it.
>
> Johann Wolfgang von Goethe (trans. André Lefevere)

The search for alternatives to fluent translation leads to theories and practices that aim to signify the foreignness of the foreign text. At the turn of the nineteenth century, foreignizing translation lacked cultural capital in English, but it was very active in the formation of another national culture – German. In 1813, during the Napoleonic wars, Friedrich Schleiermacher's lecture *Ueber die verschiedenen Methoden des Uebersetzens* ("On the Different Methods of Translating") viewed translation as an important practice in the Prussian nationalist movement: it could enrich the German language by developing an elite literature and thus enable German culture to realize its historical destiny of global domination. And yet, surprisingly, Schleiermacher proposed this nationalist agenda by theorizing translation as the locus of cultural difference, not the homogeneity that his ideological configuration might imply, and that, in various, historically specific forms, has long prevailed in English-language translation, British and American. Schleiermacher's translation theory rested on a chauvinistic condescension toward foreign cultures, a sense of their ultimate inferiority to German-language culture, but also on an antichauvinistic respect for their differences, a sense that German-language culture is inferior and therefore must attend to them if it is to develop.

These contradictory tendencies are peculiar to the vernacular nationalist movements that swept through Europe during the early nineteenth century, and they indicate that Schleiermacher's translation theory can be detached from the ideological purpose it was intended to serve and be put to other uses. The central contradiction of vernacular nationalist movements is that they are at once made possible and vulnerable by language. As Benedict Anderson has observed, "seen as both a *historical* fatality and as a community imagined through language, the nation presents itself as simultaneously open and closed" because "language is not an instrument of exclusion: in principle, anyone can learn any language" (Anderson 1991:134, 146). Language forms the particular solidarity that is the basis of the nation, but the openness of any language to new uses allows nationalist narratives to be rewritten – especially when this language is the target of translations that are foreignizing, most interested in the cultural difference of the foreign text.

If, as Schleiermacher believed, a foreignizing translation method can be useful in building a national culture, forging a foreign-based cultural identity for a linguistic community about to achieve political autonomy, it can also undermine any concept of nation by challenging cultural canons, disciplinary boundaries, and national values in the target language. This is borne out by the English translation controversy that pitted Francis Newman's foreignized *Iliad* (Newman 1856) against Matthew Arnold's Oxford lectures *On Translating Homer* (1860): Newman's theory of foreignization requires the development of translation strategies that deviate from Victorian standards of transparent discourse, but also from an Arnoldian concept of the national culture that favors an academic elite. The following genealogy reconstructs a foreignizing translation tradition, partly German, partly English, examines the specific cultural situations in which this tradition took shape, and evaluates its usefulness in combating domesticating translation in the present.

I

For Schleiermacher, "the genuine translator" is a writer

> who wants to bring those two completely separated persons, his author and his reader, truly together, and who would like to bring the latter to an understanding and enjoyment of the former as correct and complete as possible without inviting him to leave the sphere of his mother tongue.
>
> (Lefevere 1977:74)[1]

Antoine Berman has called attention to the hermeneutical para-digm introduced here, the emphasis on translation as an object of textual interpretation and a means of interpersonal communica-tion, "a method of intersubjective encounter" ("un processus de rencontre intersubjectif") (Berman 1984:235). And this makes communication the criterion by which methodological choices are validated and authentic translation distinguished from inauthen-tic. Schleiermacher in fact finds only two methods of effecting the domestic reader's understanding of the foreign author: "Either the translator leaves the author in peace, as much as possible, and moves the reader towards him; or he leaves the reader in peace, as much as possible, and moves the author towards him" (74). Schleiermacher privileges the first method, making the target-language reader travel abroad, and he describes the authentic translator's "aim" in social terms, with translation offering an understanding of the foreign text that is not merely ethnocentric, but relative to a specific social group:

> the translator must therefore take as his aim to give his reader the same image and the same delight which the reading of the work in the original language would afford any reader educated in such a way that we call him, in the better sense of the word, the lover and the expert ("Leibhaber und Kenner/amateur et connaisseur"), the type of reader who is familiar with the foreign language while it yet always remains foreign to him: he no longer has to think every single part in his mother tongue, as schoolboys do, before he can grasp the whole, but he is still conscious of the difference between that language and his mother tongue, even where he enjoys the beauty of the foreign work in total peace.
>
> (Lefevere 1977:76)

The translator aims to preserve the linguistic and cultural difference of the foreign text, but only as it is perceived in the translation by a limited readership, an educated elite. This means, first, that translation is always ethnocentric: even when a translated text contains discursive peculiarities designed to imitate a foreign text, even when the translation seems, in Schleiermacher's (Eng-lish translator's) words, "bent towards a foreign likeness" (78–79; "zu einer fremden Aehnlichkeit hinübergebogen" (227)), it never escapes the hierarchy of cultural values inscribed in the target language. These values mediate every move in the translation and every target-language reader's response to it, including the perception of what is domestic or foreign: André Lefevere's English version – "bent toward a foreign likeness" – domesticates Schleiermacher's German by submitting its syntax to the dominant fluent strategy, whereas "toward a foreign likeness bent," a discursive peculiarity that resists fluency by marking the English translation as archaic for the contemporary Anglo-American reader, foreignizes English by bending it toward the German syntax. Interestingly, to imitate the German this closely is not to be more faithful to it, but to be more English, that is, consistent with an English syntactical inversion that is now archaic.

Schleiermacher's theory anticipates these observations. He was keenly aware that translation strategies are situated in specific cultural formations where discourses are canonized or marginalized, circulating in relations of domination and exclusion. Thus, the translation method that cultivates discursive peculiarities to imitate the foreignness of the foreign text "cannot thrive equally well in all languages, but only in those which are not the captives of too strict a bond of classical expression outside of which all is reprehensible"; the ideal site for this method is "languages which are freer, in which innovations and deviations are tolerated to a greater extent, in such a way that their accumulation may, under certain circumstances, generate a certain characteristic mode of expression" (79–80). This linguistic and cultural freedom is complexly determined: not only is it defined against the "bonded languages" of other national cultures, but the "innovations and deviations" of foreignizing translation are defined against the norm set by other translation discourses in the target-language culture. And since Schleiermacher's advocacy of the foreignizing method was also an advocacy of discourses specific to an educated elite, he was investing this limited social group with considerable cultural authority, going so far as to assign it a precise social function – to "generate a certain characteristic mode of expression," developing a national language, "influencing the whole evolution of a culture" (80–81; "die gesammte Geistesentwikkelung" (231)). Here it becomes clear that Schleiermacher was enlisting his privileged translation method in a cultural political agenda: an educated elite controls the formation of a national culture by refining its language through foreignizing translations.

Schleiermacher's lecture permits a much more detailed social and historical specification of this agenda. He concludes with some explicit references to "we Germans," remarking that "our nation," "because of its respect for what is foreign and its mediating nature" (88; "seiner vermittelnden Natur" (243)), uniquely satisfies the "two conditions" necessary for foreignizing translation to thrive, namely "that understanding foreign works should be a thing known and desired and that the native language should be allowed a certain flexibility" (81). This is the understanding of foreign works sought by educated "Germans" like Schleiermacher, a university professor and minister in the Reformed church, who feels that the German language possesses the "flexibility" to support foreignizing translation since it is undeveloped, lacking a definite "mode of expression," not yet "bonded" to the "classical," a "partial mother tongue": "our language, because we exercise it less owing to our Nordic sluggishness, can thrive in all its freshness and completely develop its own power only through the most many-sided contacts with what is foreign" (88). Since the category "foreign" here is determined by the educated, Schleiermacher is using translation to mark out a dominant space for a bourgeois minority in early nineteenth-century German culture.

As Albert Ward observes of this period,

> literature was [...] a predominantly bourgeois art, but it was only a small part of this section of the community that responded most readily to the classical writers of the great age of German literature. [...] Writers like Goethe and Schiller found their public in the *Honoratioren* of the large towns, in the university-trained professional men, the ministers of religion, teachers, doctors, and lawyers, in what might be termed the elite of middle-class society. "High literature" was then even more than now a thing for a small group of scholars.
>
> (Ward 1974:128)[2]

Ward demonstrates the cultural and economic marginality of German "literature," both classical and romantic, by referring to sizes of editions and sales figures amid some striking testimonies from contemporaries in the publishing industry:

> Karl Preusker, who came to Leipzig as a bookseller's apprentice in 1805, names in his autobiography the authors most in demand at that time; the most classical (as we understand the term today) of the authors on his list is Zschokke, "whereas the

works of Schiller and Goethe were sold in only meagre quantities."

(ibid.:132)

Schleiermacher, who associated with the leading German romantics, briefly shared a Berlin apartment with Friedrich Schlegel, and contributed to the Schlegel brothers' small-circulation journal, the *Athenaeum*, was entirely in agreement with Goethe when developing his theory of foreignizing translation. In an essay on "Wieland's brotherly memory" published in February of 1813, four months before Schleiermacher's lecture, Goethe wrote:

> there are two maxims in translation: one requires that the author of a foreign nation be brought across to us in such a way that we can look on him as ours; the other requires that we should go across to what is foreign and adapt ourselves to its conditions, its use of language, its peculiarities. The advantages of both are sufficiently known to educated people through perfect examples. Our friend, who looked for the middle way in this, too, tried to reconcile both, but as a man of feeling and taste he preferred the first maxim when in doubt.

(Lefevere 1977:39)

In siding with this "feeling and taste" for "what is foreign," Schleiermacher was valorizing an elite bourgeois cultural discourse of literary refinement against the larger, more heterogeneous culture of the middle and working classes. "The average middle-class reader," Ward points out, "wanted works which were within his own experience and range of emotion, reflecting his own interests and not conflicting with the demands of his morality" (Ward 1974:133). Whereas Schleiermacher's lecture on translation is quite scholarly in citing only Greek and Latin writing (Plato, Cicero, Tacitus, Grotius, and Leibniz), the wider middle-class readership favored Gothic tales, chivalric romances, realistic novels both sentimental and didactic, biographies of exemplary men, travel literature. This audience was reading translations as well, but the greatest percentage consisted of translations from French and English novels, including the work of Choderlos de Laclos and Richardson. Schleiermacher himself had translated Plato, while other romantics – Voss, August Wilhelm Schlegel, Hölderlin – translated Homer, Sophocles, Dante, and Shakespeare. They were very much aware that they were translating for a relatively narrow

audience, even a coterie, and like Schleiermacher, they saw this
social fact as a value that improved their "literature" and endowed
it with cultural authority. Friedrich Schlegel boasted that "[read-
ers] are forever complaining that German authors write for such a
small circle, often in fact for themselves as a group. I find this a
good thing. German literature gains more and more in spirit and
character because of it" (Ward 1974:191 n.46).

Schlegel's comment shows that this is not only a bourgeois, but
a nationalist concept of literature – "German." And Schleiermacher's theory of foreignizing translation reveals a similar ideological
configuration: it is also pitched against a German nobility that was
not literary and had long lain under French cultural domination.
Aristocratic culture eschewed scholarly research and wide reading
in past and contemporary literature; "the few courts which did take
an active interest in literary affairs," Ward notes, "were characterized by a predominantly bourgeois atmosphere" (Ward
1974:128). In aristocratic education, "the accent was on languages,
particularly French, and often to such an extent that many
noblemen could express themselves better in that language than in
their mother tongue" (ibid.:123). In a letter from 1757, the
aesthetician and dramatist Johann Christoph Gottsched described
an audience with Frederick II, during which he informed the
Prussian king of the serious threat to literary culture posed by the
Gallicized nobility:

> When I said that German writers did not receive sufficient
> encouragement, as the aristocracy and the courts spoke too
> much French and understood too little German to be able to
> grasp and appreciate fully anything written in German, he said:
> that is true, for I haven't read no German book since my youth,
> and je parle comme un cocher, but I am an old fellow of forty-six
> and have no time for such things.
>
> (ibid.:190n.)

Some fifty years later, Schleiermacher's lecture on translation
engages in the cultural struggle for a German literature with an
equally bold criticism of Frederick II. Schleiermacher represents
the king, however, not as Gottsched's anti-intellectual oaf, but as a
German intellect limited by his utter dependence on French:

> Our great king received all his finer and higher thoughts in
> a foreign language, which he had most intimately appropriated

for this field. He was incapable of producing in German the literature and philosophy he produced in French. It is to be deplored that the great preference for England which dominated a part of the family could not have taken the direction of familiarizing him from childhood on with the English language, whose last golden age was then in bloom, and which is so much closer to German. But we may hope that he would have preferred to produce literature and philosophy in Latin, rather than in French, if he had enjoyed a strict scholarly education.

(Lefevere 1977:83)

Here the vernacular nationalism in Schleiermacher's cultural politics becomes more evident: the king is taken to task not so much because he is not "scholarly" (he is in fact portrayed as being genuinely interested in "literature and philosophy"), but because he doesn't write in German, or in a language "closer to German" than French. Whereas Gottsched seems to be lamenting the dearth of literary patronage ("sufficient encouragement") because the Prussian aristocracy is Francophone, Schleiermacher is more concerned about the unequal cultural production in German and French: "He was incapable of producing in German."

Schleiermacher's criticism of the king is a nationalist protest against French domination in Germany, and it is consistent with his intense activity in the Prussian movement for German unification during the Napoleonic wars. As Jerry Dawson makes clear,

the war between France and Prussia in 1806, with the resulting collapse of the Prussian armies and the humiliating peace terms dictated to Prussia by Napoleon, proved to be the final factor needed to turn [Schleiermacher] to nationalism with a complete and almost reckless abandon.

(Dawson 1966:51)[3]

"Germany" did not actually exist at this time: west of the Rhine were several petty principalities, which, after 1806, Napoleon organized into a "confederation"; east was the dominant German-speaking monarchy, Prussia, now dominated by the French. The Prussian defeat caused Schleiermacher to lose his appointment at the University of Halle, and he fled to Berlin, the Prussian capital, where he lectured at the university and preached at various churches. His sermons urged political and military resistance against the French armies, developing a cultural concept of nationality based on the German language and legitimized with Protestant theology. In 1813, three months before his lecture on translation at the Berlin Akademie der Wissenschaften and eight months before Napoleon was finally defeated at the Battle of Leipzig, Schleiermacher delivered a sermon entitled "A Nation's Duty in a War for Freedom," in which he represented the war with France as a struggle against cultural and political domination. If victorious, he exhorted the congregation, "we shall be able to preserve for ourselves our own distinctive character, our laws, our constitution and our culture" (Schleiermacher 1890:73).

In June, the month of his lecture, Schleiermacher wrote a letter to Friedrich Schlegel in which his nationalism turned utopian:

> My greatest wish after liberation, is for one true German Empire, powerfully representing the entire German folk and territory to the outside world, while internally allowing the various *Länder* and their princes a great deal of freedom to develop and rule according to their own particular needs.
>
> (Sheehan 1989:379)

This vision of Germany as a union of relatively autonomous principalities was partly a compensation for the then prevailing international conflict, and it is somewhat backward-looking, traced with a nostalgia for the domestic political organization that prevailed before the French occupation. Napoleon had introduced social innovations achieved by the revolution, abolishing feudalism in Prussia and promoting "enlightened" despotism. Schleiermacher himself was a member of a bourgeois cultural elite, but his nationalist ideology is such that it admits aristocracy, monarchy, even an imperialist tendency – but only when they constitute a national unity resistant to foreign domination.

Presented to the Prussian academic establishment on 24 June 1813, at the height of the conflict with France, Schleiermacher's lecture constructs a role for translation in a nationalist cultural politics. His theory of foreignizing translation should be seen as anti-French because it opposes the translation method that dominated France since neoclassicism, viz. domestication, making the foreign author travel abroad to the target-language reader. When surveying the limited acceptance of foreignizing translation in Western culture, Schleiermacher reserves his most withering sarcasm for France:

The ancients obviously translated little in that most real sense and most moderns, deterred by the difficulties of true translation, also seem to be satisfied with imitation and paraphrase. Who would want to contend that nothing has ever been translated into French from the classical languages or from the Germanic languages! But even though we Germans are perfectly willing to listen to this advice, we should not follow it.

(Lefevere 1977:88)

French exemplifies those languages that are "captives of too strict a bond of classical expression outside of which all is reprehensible," especially the innovations and deviations introduced by foreignizing translation. In a satiric dialogue from 1798, A. W. Schlegel had already made explicit the nationalist ideology at work in identifying French culture with a domesticating translation method:

Frenchman: The Germans translate every literary Tom, Dick, and Harry. We either do not translate at all, or else we translate according to our own taste.
German: Which is to say, you paraphrase and you disguise.
Frenchman: We look on a foreign author as a stranger in our company, who has to dress and behave according to our customs, if he desires to please.
German: How narrow-minded of you to be pleased only by what is native.
Frenchman: Such is our nature and our education. Did the Greeks not hellenize everything as well?
German: In your case it goes back to a narrow-minded nature and a conventional education. In ours education is our nature.

(ibid.:50)[4]

Schlegel's dialogue indicates the metaphysical underpinnings of German nationalism, its assumption of a biological or racial essence from which the national culture issues: "education is our nature." This agrees both with Schleiermacher's view that "our nation" possesses a "mediating nature" and with the organic metaphor he uses to describe the effect of foreignizing translation on German:

Just as our soil itself has no doubt become richer and more

fertile and our climate milder and more pleasant only after much transplantation of foreign flora, just so we sense that our language, because we exercise it less owing to our Nordic sluggishness, can thrive in all its freshness and completely develop its own power only through the most many-sided contacts with what is foreign.

(ibid.:88)

Schleiermacher's nationalist theory of foreignizing translation aims to challenge French hegemony not only by enriching German culture, but by contributing to the formation of a liberal public sphere, an area of social life in which private individuals exchange rational discourse and exercise political influence:

If ever the time should come in which we have a public life out of which develops a sociability of greater merit and truer to language, and in which free space is gained for the talent of the orator, we shall be less in need of translation for the development of language.

(ibid.:89)

Yet Schleiermacher's public sphere manifests the contradiction that characterized the concept from its emergence in eighteenth-century aesthetics. As Peter Uwe Hohendahl puts it, "although in principle the capacity to form an accurate opinion is considered present in everyone, in practice it is limited to the educated" (Hohendahl 1982:51). So in Schleiermacher: although the work of foreignizing translation on the German language is seen as creating a national culture free of French political domination, this public space is open explicitly for "the talent of the orator," a literary elite.

Because this is a strongly nationalist elite, it employs foreignizing translation in a remarkable project of German cultural imperialism, through which the linguistic community "destined" for global domination achieves it. Here nationalism is equivalent to universalism:

An inner necessity, in which a peculiar calling of our people expresses itself clearly enough, has driven us to translating en masse; we cannot go back and we must go on. [...] And coincidentally our nation may be destined, because of its respect for what is foreign and its mediating nature, to carry all the treasures of foreign arts and scholarship, together with its own, in its language, to unite them into a great historical whole, so to speak, which would be preserved in the centre and heart of Europe, so that with the help of our language, whatever beauty the most different times have brought forth can be enjoyed by all people, as purely and perfectly as is possible for a foreigner. This appears indeed to be the real historical aim of translation in general, as we are used to it now.

(Lefevere 1977:88)

Thus, readers of the canon of world literature would experience the linguistic and cultural difference of foreign texts, but only as a difference that is Eurocentric, mediated by a German bourgeois elite. Ultimately, it would seem that foreignizing translation does not so much introduce the foreign into German culture as use the foreign to confirm and develop a sameness, a process of fashioning an ideal cultural self on the basis of an other, a cultural narcissism, which is endowed, moreover, with historical necessity. This method of translation "makes sense and is of value only to a nation that has the definite inclination to appropriate what is foreign" (ibid.:80).

The ideological ensemble in Schleiermacher's cultural politics precipitates contradictory permutations (elite literature/national culture, bourgeois minority/"Germany," foreignizing/Germaniz-ing), so we should not be surprised to find him speaking for and against foreign imports in German culture – in that same turbulent year, 1813. His bourgeois nationalism shapes both his advocacy of "many-sided contacts with the foreign" in the translation lecture and his xenophobic condescension in the patriotic sermon: "Every nation, my dear friends, which has developed a particular, or clearly defined height is degraded also by receiving into it a foreign ele-ment" (Schleiermacher 1890:73–74). This assumes, contrary to the lecture, that German culture has already attained a significant level of development, presumably in classical and romantic literature, which must be protected from foreign contamination and imposed universally, through a specifically German foreignization of world lit-erature. Schleiermacher's translation theory intervenes in "die gesammte Geistesentwikkelung," a phrase that may seem restricted nationally in Lefevere's English, "the whole evolution of a culture" (Lefevere 1977:81), but is shown to have worldwide application in Berman's French: "le processus global de la formation de l'esprit" (Berman 1985:333). And only Berman discloses the idealist meta-physics at work in the German text by choosing "esprit" for "Geist."

Schleiermacher's theory is shaky ground on which to build a
translation ethics to combat ethnocentrism: his lecture does not
recognize any contradiction in asserting that "our nation" is
distinguished by "respect for what is foreign" while envisioning the
geopolitical domination of a German bourgeois cultural elite. It
also does not recognize antinomies in its thinking about language
and human subjectivity which are likewise determined by a
bourgeois nationalism. Schleiermacher evinces an extraordinarily
clear sense of the constitutive properties of language, those that
make representation always an appropriative activity, never transparent or merely adequate to its object, active in the construction
of subjectivity by establishing forms for consciousness. The "proper
field" of the translator, Schleiermacher states, consists of

> those mental products of scholarship and art in which the free
> idiosyncratic combinatory powers of the author and the spirit of
> the language which is the repository of a system of observations
> and shades of moods are everything, in which the object no
> longer dominates in any way, but is dominated by thoughts and
> emotions, in which, indeed, the object has become object only
> through speech and is present only in conjunction with speech.
>
> (Lefevere 1977:69–70)

At the same time, however, Schleiermacher's concept of "free
idiosyncratic combinatory powers" signals a move toward an
autonomous subject whose "thoughts and emotions" transcend
linguistic determinations. "On the one hand," Schleiermacher
asserts,

> every man is in the power of the language he speaks, and all his
> thinking is a product thereof. [...] Yet on the other hand every
> freely thinking, mentally self-employed human being shapes his
> own language. [...] Therefore each free and higher speech
> needs to be understood twice, once out of the spirit of the
> language of whose elements it is composed, as a living
> representation bound and defined by that spirit and conceived
> out of it in the speaker, and once out of the speaker's emotions,
> as his action, as produced and explicable only out of his own
> being.
>
> (ibid.:71)

The "spirit of the language" determines every speech act, is
binding on every subject, but part of that action nevertheless

answers only to an individual "being." At one point, the priority of language over subject is tellingly reversed, with the author becoming the sole origin of the "spirit": the readers of a foreignizing translation are said to "understand" when they "perceive the spirit of the language which was the author's own and [are] able to see his peculiar way of thinking and feeling" (ibid.:72). As Berman points out, Schleiermacher's lecture manifests the late eighteenth-century shift from representation to expression as the conceptual paradigm for language, and hence subject displaces object as the basis of interpretation (Berman 1984:233). Schleiermacher's thinking about language is informed by romantic expressive theory, grounded in the concept of free, unified consciousness that characterizes bourgeois individualism.

As his exposition proceeds, it turns to metaphor and illustration, defining the "spirit of the language" in ethnic terms, yet without abandoning the transcendental subject:

> We understand the spoken word as an act of the speaker only when we feel at the same time where and how the power of language has taken hold of him, where in its current the lightning of thought has uncoiled, snake-like, where and how the roving imagination has been held firm in its forms. We understand the spoken word as a product of language and as an expression of its spirit only when we feel that only a Greek, for instance, could think and speak in that way, that only this particular language could operate in a human mind this way, and when we feel at the same time that only this man could think and speak in the Greek fashion in this way, that only he could seize and shape the language in this manner, that only his living possession of the riches of language reveals itself like this, an alert sense for measure and euphony which belongs to him alone, a power of thinking and shaping which is peculiarly his.
> (Lefevere 1977:72)

The metaphors – "lightning," "snake-like," "roving" – continue the individualistic strain by depicting the subject as a coherent essence, radically independent of language, given to serpentine, potentially subversive "thought," possessing a free "imagination" that takes on various accidental "forms" (obviously, "lightning" and "snake-like" also resonate with mythological and theological allusions, especially in a lecture by a classical scholar and Protestant minister – but these possibilities will not be pursued here). The most striking move in this passage may well be Schleiermacher's example, which initiates a discontinuous series of specifications and revisions, putting the individual in command, first, of a national culture with a literary canon ("the riches of language"; cf. the international "treasures of foreign arts and scholarship" [ibid.:88]), then a specifically literary, even scholarly appreciation of the Greek language ("measure and euphony"), and finally a cognitive "power" that is "peculiarly his," self-expressive and fundamentally self-determining.

The passage is a reminder that Schleiermacher is setting up the understanding of language associated with a particular national cultural elite as the standard by which language use is made intelligible and judged. Hence, in the case of foreignizing translation, "the reader of the translation will become the equal of the better reader of the original only when he is able first to acquire an impression of the particular spirit of the author as well as that of the language in the work" (Lefevere 1977:80). Yet the author-orientation in Schleiermacher's theory, his anthropomorphosis of translation from an intertextual to an intersubjective relationship, psychologizes the translated text and thus masks its cultural and social determinations. This is the much criticized move in Schleiermacher's hermeneutics: he tends to evaporate the determinate nature of the text by articulating a two-fold interpretive process, both "grammatical" and "technical or psychological."[5] A grammatical explanation of the objective "connection between the work and the language" combines with a psychological explanation of the subjective "connection between the work and the thought involved in it" (Szondi 1986:103). Schleiermacher, however, sometimes collapses this distinction, as in his aphorisms on hermeneutics from 1809–1810, which refer to "combining the objective and subjective so that the interpreter can put himself 'inside' the author" (Schleiermacher 1977:64). In the case of German foreignizing translation, then, the translator enables the German-language reader to understand the individuality of the foreign author so as to identify with him, thereby concealing the transindividual, German-language ideologies – cultural (literary elitism), class (bourgeois minority), national ("German") – that mediate the foreignized representation of the foreign author. Such thinking about language and subjectivity is clearly more consistent with domesticating translation, oriented toward conformity with target-language cultural values, and so can do little to question the dominance of transparent discourse in translation today. On the contrary, Schleiermacher's psychologization of the text assumes transparency, the illusory presence of the foreign author in the translation.

There is another kind of thinking in his lecture that runs counter to this idealist strain, even if impossibly caught in its tangles: a recognition of the cultural and social conditions of language and a projection of a translation practice that takes them into account instead of working to conceal them. Schleiermacher sees translation as an everyday fact of life, not merely an activity performed on literary and philosophical texts, but necessary for intersubjective understanding, active in the very process of communication, because language is determined by various differences – cultural, social, historical:

> For not only are the dialects spoken by different tribes belonging to the same nation, and the different stages of the same language or dialect in different centuries, different languages in the strict sense of the word; moreover even contemporaries who are not separated by dialects, but merely belong to different classes, which are not often linked through social intercourse and are far apart in education, often can understand each other only by means of a similar mediation.
>
> (Lefevere 1977:68)

This observation clearly requires Schleiermacher to revise his nationalist concept of "the spirit of the language": he understands it as "the repository of a system of observations and shades of mood," but this is too monolithic and too psychologistic to admit the concept of "different classes," a social hierarchy of cultural discourses, each so distinctively class-coded as to impede communication. Schleiermacher even finds it "inevitable that different opinions should develop as to" foreignizing translation strategies, "different schools, so to speak, will arise among the masters, and different parties among the audience as followers of those schools," but he ultimately individualizes the "different points of view," reducing them to the translator's consciousness, transforming cultural practices with social implications into self-centered eccentricities: "each one in itself will always be of relative and subjective value only" (ibid.:81).

It is cultural difference, however, that guides Schleiermacher's prescriptions for the foreignizing translator, for the invention of discursive peculiarities to signify the foreignness of the foreign text. The translator must reject the discourse that is used most widely in the target-language culture, what he calls the "colloquial" (78; "alltäglich" (227)), refusing "the most universally appealing beauty each genre is capable of" in the language and instead risking the compassionate smile of "the greatest experts and masters who could not understand his laborious and ill-considered German if they did not supplement it with their Greek and Latin" (79). Once again, the cultural difference marked by Schleiermacher's foreignizing translator runs between an educated elite and the uneducated majority: when the translator bends his language to a foreign likeness, he is not doing it with "each genre," "universally," but with literary and scholarly texts in Greek and Latin, so that only "experts and masters" will be able to "understand" his deviant use of language. Schleiermacher's translator avoids the "colloquial," unlearned language use, popular literary forms.

And yet, despite the questionable ideological determinations of Schleiermacher's lecture – its bourgeois individualism and cultural elitism, its Prussian nationalism and German universalism – it does contain the (inadvertent) suggestion that foreignizing translation can alter the social divisions figured in these ideologies, can promote cultural change through its work on the target language:

> every freely thinking, mentally self-employed human being shapes his own language. For in what other way – except precisely by means of these influences – would it have developed and grown from its first raw state to its more perfect elaboration in scholarship and art? In this sense, therefore, it is the living power of the individual which creates new forms by means of the plastic material of language, at first only for the immediate purpose of communicating a passing consciousness; yet now more, now less of it remains behind in the language, is taken up by others, and reaches out, a shaping force.
>
> (Lefevere 1977:71)

This passage reverses its logic. At first language is taken to exist in an unmediated "raw state," worked by a transcendental subject who "shapes his own language," who is the origin of linguistic and cultural innovation and development. By the end, however, the determinate nature of language emerges as the "shaping force" of subjects. In the interval, the materiality of language is socialized: no longer "raw," it contains "new forms" invented by "the individual," but exceeding the function they were intended to serve, the communication of "consciousness," because they have been derived from pre-existing forms used by "others." This indicates that subjectivity is neither self-originating nor the origin of language and culture, that its cultural values (e.g. "scholarship and art") are pre-given and constantly reworked ("elaboration"), and that therefore the subject can be considered self-determining only insofar as it ranks these values – or revises them and alters an established ranking. The discursive innovations and deviations introduced by foreignizing translation are thus a potential threat to target-language cultural values, but they perform their revisionary work only from within, developing translation strategies from the diverse discourses that circulate in the target language.

Schleiermacher's concept of foreignizing translation constitutes a resistance to dominant cultural values in German at the turn of the nineteenth century. The foreign in foreignizing translation then meant a specific selection of foreign texts (literary, philosophical, scholarly) and a development of discursive peculiarities that opposed both French cultural hegemony, especially among the aristocracy, and the literary discourses favored by the largest segment of readers, both middle- and working-class. Schleiermacher's translation project depends on an idealist concept of literature that is at once elitist and nationalist, individualistic yet socially determinate, defined in opposition to capitalist economic practices: "the interpreter plies his trade in the field of commerce; the translator proper operates mainly in the fields of art and scholarship" (Lefevere 1977:68).

It is this ideological ensemble that must be jettisoned in any revival of foreignizing translation to intervene against the contemporary ascendancy of transparent discourse. Today, transparency is the dominant discourse in poetry and prose, fiction and nonfiction, bestsellers and print journalism. Even if the electronic media have weakened the economic, political, and cultural hegemony of print in the post-World War II period, the idealist concept of literature that underwrites that discourse continues to enjoys considerable institutional power, housed not only in the academy and in the literary cultures of various educated elites, but in the publishing industry and the mass-audience periodical press. The distinction that Schleiermacher perceived between the field of commerce and the fields of art and scholarship has been eroded – if it ever existed as more than a fiction designed to consolidate literature as a transcendental cultural concept. Transparent discourse is eminently consumable in the contemporary cultural marketplace, which in turn influences publishing decisions to exclude foreign texts that preempt transparency.

Schleiermacher shows that the first opportunity to foreignize translation occurs in the choice of foreign text, wherein the translator can resist the dominant discourse in Anglo-American culture by restoring excluded texts and possibly reforming the canon of foreign literatures in English. Schleiermacher also suggests that foreignizing translation puts to work a specific discursive strategy. He opposes the foregrounding of the signified by which fluent translation produces the effect of transparency; for him a translation can be foreignized only by approximating the play of signifiers in the foreign text: "the more closely the translation follows the turns taken by the original, the more foreign it will seem to the reader" (Lefevere 1977:78).

Schleiermacher's lecture provides the tools for conceptualizing a revolt against the dominance of transparent discourse in current English-language translation. Yet the effects of this dominance have included, not only the widespread implementation of fluent strategies, but the marginalization of texts in the history of translation that can yield alternative theories and practices – like Schleiermacher's lecture. With rare exceptions, English-language theorists and practitioners of English-language translation have neglected Schleiermacher. His lecture has been recognized as a key "modern" statement in translation theory only recently, and it was not translated into English until 1977.[6] And even its translator, André Lefevere, felt compelled to question Schleiermacher's value: "his requirement that the translation should 'give the feel' of the source language must [...] strike us increasingly as odd" (Lefevere 1977:67). Lefevere argued that translation should be domesticating, as "most theoreticians" recommended, and he specifically referred to Eugene Nida's version of this theory, quoting Nida to criticize Schleiermacher:

> In effect, we are faced here with a not-illogical and very spirited defence of what we know now as "translationese" or, with another phrase: "static equivalence," and which is still very much with us, in spite of the fact that most theoreticians would now subscribe to the concept of dynamic equivalence, which "aims at complete naturalness of expression and tries to relate the

receptor to modes of behavior relevant within the context of his own culture."

(Lefevere 1981:11)[7]

Schleiermacher's concept of foreignizing translation seems odd to Lefevere only because the latter prefers to submit to the contemporary regime of fluency – in Nida's words, "complete naturalness of expression." The canonicity of fluent translation during the post-World War II period coincides with the emergence of the term "translationese" to designate unidiomatic language in a translated text (*OED*). Lefevere approves of Nida's "dynamic equivalence," a concept that now, with the increasing recognition of Schleiermacher's contemporary importance, must be viewed as an egregious euphemism for the domesticating translation method and the cultural political agendas it conceals. Because this method is so entrenched in English-language translation, Lefevere is unable to see that the detection of unidiomatic language, especially in literary texts, is culturally specific: what is unidiomatic in one cultural formation can be aesthetically effective in another. Any dismissive treatment of Schleiermacher maintains the forms of domestication in English-language translation today, hindering reflection on how different methods of translating can resist the questionable values that dominate Anglo-American culture. Schleiermacher can indeed offer a way out.

II

With Schleiermacher's lecture untranslated, however, this way was open to few English-language translators during the nineteenth century. A translator could of course formulate a theory of foreignizing translation, whether or not inspired by the German tradition, but the theory would be a response to a peculiarly English situation, motivated by different cultural and political interests. Such was the case with Francis Newman (1805–1897), the accomplished brother of the Cardinal. In the 1850s, Newman challenged the main line of English-language translation, arguing that "Cowper's attempt to translate Homer had proved as great a failure as Pope's" and suggesting that "a sensible change is taking place, from our recent acquaintance with the extent to which the Germans have carried poetical translation" (Newman 1851:371).[8] This "acquaintance" with the German tradition apparently made

Newman the first in a small group of Victorian translators who developed foreignizing strategies and opposed the English regime of fluent domestication.

A classical scholar who taught for many years, first at Manchester New College, then University College, London, Newman was a prolific writer on a variety of topics, some scholarly, others religious, many of urgent social concern. He produced commentaries on classical texts (Aeschylus, Euripides) and dictionaries and vocabularies for oriental languages and dialects (Arabic, Libyan). He wrote a spiritual autobiography and many religious treatises that reflected his own wavering belief in Christianity and the heterodox nature of that belief (e.g. *Hebrew Theism: The Common Basic of Judaism, Christianity and Mohammedanism*). And he issued a steady stream of lectures, essays, and pamphlets that demonstrated his intense involvement in a wide range of political issues. Newman argued for decentralized government, land nationalization, women's suffrage, the abolition of slavery. He criticized English colonialism, recommending government reforms that would allow the colonized to enter the political process. His *Essays on Diet* advocated vegetarianism, and on several occasions he supported state enforcement of sobriety, partly as a means of curbing prostitution.

The ideological configuration of Newman's writing uneasily combined liberalism with a paternalistic investment in bourgeois moral values, and this also played into his translation projects, which were fundamentally pedagogical and populist. He published Latin versions of the popular literature he assigned his students for class translation exercises: Henry Wadsworth Longfellow's narrative poem *Hiawatha* (1862) and Daniel Defoe's novel *Robinson Crusoe* (1884). The readership he imagined for his translations of Horace (1853) and the *Iliad* (1856) did not know Latin and Greek or were too busy or bored to maintain languages they learned at university – in Newman's words, "the *unlearned* English reader," "those who seek solely for amusement," including "men of business," "commercial England," but also the socially diverse audience of "Dickens and Thackeray" (Newman 1853:iii–v). Compared to Schleiermacher, Newman enlisted translation in a more democratic cultural politics, assigned a pedagogical function but pitched deliberately against an academic elite. For Newman, the aim of education was to foster liberal democracy. In his lecture *On the Relations of Free Knowledge to Moral Sentiment*, he argued that the study of "political economy" teaches a respect for cultural differences that militates against imperialism, nationalism, and class domination:

> political economy has demonstrated that the laws which morality would dictate as just are also the laws of physical well being for nations and for classes; that no cunning regulations will enable a State to prosper at the expense of foreigners; and that the interests of classes and of nations are so knit up, that one cannot permanently be depressed without injury to others. It rescues the patriot from the temptation of being unjust to the foreigner, by proving that that does not conduce to the welfare of his own people.
>
> (Newman 1847b:18–19)

Newman similarly urged the study of history, literary as well as political, because it can "deepen our knowledge of mankind, and our insight into social and political interests" (ibid.:8). Here too the "practical uses" of this knowledge required the recognition of cultural differences. In *Four Lectures on the Contrasts of Ancient and Modern History,* Newman granted the central metaphysical assumption of Enlightenment humanism – "The whole interest of History depends upon the eternal likeness of human nature to itself" – but only to give it a more materialist revision, mindful of historical change: "it is equally needful to be aware of the points at which similarity ceases, and *contrast* begins; otherwise our applications of history to practical uses will be mere delusive pedantry" (Newman 1847a:5–6).

Newman's "practical" concept of education led him to criticize academic specialization because it decreased the social value of knowledge. In his *Introductory Lecture to the Classical Course* at Manchester New College, he asserted that

> we do not advocate *any* thing exclusive. A one-sided cultivation may appear at first like carrying out the principle of division of labour, yet in fact it does not tend even to the general benefit and progress of truth, much less to the advantage of the individual.
>
> (Newman 1841:7)

Although intended to justify the place of classics in an academic curriculum, Newman's lecture attacked the scholarly disdain of translation, describing it as mere snobbery that ironically degraded classical literature by limiting its audience: "It would be no honor to the venerable productions of antiquity, to imagine that all their excellencies vanish with translation, and only a mean exclusiveness of spirit could grudge to impart as much as possible of their instruction to the unlearned" (ibid.:9). To Newman, "exclusive" meant specialized, but also elitist.

It seems clear that only foreignizing translation could answer to Newman's concept of liberal education, to his concern with the recognition of cultural differences. His introductory lecture argued that literary texts were particularly important in staging this recognition because "literature is special, peculiar; it witnesses, and it tends to uphold, national diversity" (Newman 1841:10). In the preface to his version of the *Iliad*, he offered a concise account of his translation method by contrasting it with the "principles which I regard to be utterly false and ruinous to translation." The principles Newman opposed belonged to the fluent, domesticating method that dominated English translation since the seventeenth century:

> One of these is, that the reader ought, if possible, to forget that it is a translation at all, and be lulled into the illusion that he is reading an original work. Of course a necessary inference from such a dogma is, that whatever has a foreign colour is undesirable and is even a grave defect. The translator, it seems, must carefully obliterate all that is characteristic of the original, unless it happens to be identical in spirit to something already familiar in English. From such a notion I cannot too strongly express my intense dissent. I am at precisely the opposite; – to retain every peculiarity of the original, so far as I am able, *with the greater care, the more foreign it may happen to be*, – whether it be a matter of taste, of intellect, or of morals. [...] the English translator should desire the reader always to remember that his work is an imitation, and moreover is in a different material; that the original is foreign, and in many respects extremely unlike our native compositions.
>
> (Newman 1856:xv–xvi)

For Newman, the "illusion" of originality that confused the translation with the foreign text was domesticating, assimilating what was foreign "to something already familiar in English." He recommended a translation method that signified the many differences between the translation and the foreign text, their relative autonomy from one another, their composition in different languages for different cultures. Yet rejecting the illusion of originality meant opposing the discourse that shapes most of "our native compositions" – fluency. Newman felt that his translations were resisting a contemporary standardization of English enforced by the publishing industry:

> In the present day, so intensely mechanical is the apparatus of prose-composition, – when editors and correctors of the press desire the uniform observance of some one rule (never mind what, so that you find it in the "standard" grammar), – every deviation is resented as a vexatious eccentricity; and in general it would appear, that dry perspicuity is the only excellence for which the grammarian has struggled. Every expression which does not stand the logical test, however transparent the meaning, however justified by analogies, is apt to be condemned; and every difference of mind and mind, showing itself in the style, is deprecated.
>
> (ibid.:xvii–xviii)

Since Newman developed his foreignizing method in the translation of classical texts, for him foreignizing necessarily involved a discourse that signified historical remoteness – archaism. In the preface to his selection from Horace, he faulted previous English versions because they modernized the Latin text: "Hitherto our poetical translators have failed in general, not so much from want of talent or learning, but from aiming to produce poems *in modern style*, through an excessive fear that a modern reader will endure nothing else" (Newman 1853:iv). In the preface to his *Iliad*, Newman defined more precisely the sort of archaism Homer required. Partly it was an effort to suggest an historical analogy between earlier forms of Greek and English: "The entire dialect of Homer being essentially archaic, that of a translation ought to be as much Saxo-Norman as possible, and owe as little as possible to the elements thrown into our language by classical learning" (Newman 1856:vi). Homer's "style" required a like solution: "it is similar to the old English ballad, and is in sharp contrast to the polished style of Pope, Sotheby, and Cowper, the best known English translators of Homer" (ibid.:iv).

Yet Newman also made clear that he was "not concerned with the *historical* problem, of writing in a style which actually existed at an earlier period in our language; but with the artistic problem of attaining a plausible aspect of moderate antiquity, while remaining easily intelligible" (Newman 1856:x). Hence, he advocated an artificially constructed archaism, patched together without an excessive regard for historical accuracy or consistency, producing an effect that he called "quaint" as opposed to "grotesque." And he cultivated this discourse on various levels, in the lexicon, syntax, and prosody of his translations. He explained his use of syntactical "inversions," for example, as "not mere metrical expedients, but necessities of the style; partly, to attain *antiquity* and elevation, partly for *emphasis* or for variety" (ibid.:xi).

Newman's translations could only be foreignizing in a culturally specific sense, in relation to concepts of "domestic" and "foreign" that distinguished English literary culture in the Victorian period. Thus, he saw nothing inconsistent in faulting the modernizing tendencies of previous Horace translators while he himself expurgated the Latin text, inscribing it with an English sense of moral propriety. This is where Newman's bourgeois paternalism contradicts the democratic tendencies of his populism:

> I have striven to make this book admissable to the purest-minded English lady, and could never consent to add adornment to a single line of corrupting tendency. It exhibits, no doubt, mournful facts concerning the relations of the sexes in Augustan Rome, – facts not in themselves so shocking, as many which oppress the heart in the cities of Christendom; and this, I think, it is instructive to perceive. Only in a few instances, where the immorality is too ugly to be instructive have I abruptly cut away the difficulty. In general, Horace aimed at a higher beauty than did Catullus or Propertius or Ovid, and the result of a purer taste is closely akin to that of a sounder morality.
>
> (Newman 1853:vi)

What was foreignizing about Newman's translations was not their morality, but their literary discourse, the strangeness of the archaism. This too was homegrown, a rich stew drawn from various periods of English, but it deviated from current usage and cut across various literary discourses, poetry and the novel, elite and popular, English and Scottish. Newman's Horace translation contained "viands," for example, a word that surfaced at the beginning of the fifteenth century and was used extensively in the early modern period in various kinds of writing, literary (Shakespeare's plays) and nonliterary (Edward Hall's historical chronicles). Yet it was also used later as a distinctly poetic form, a poeticism, in widely read Victorian writers like Tennyson and Dickens.[9] Newman's archaic lexicon crossed, not only historical periods, but contemporary reading constituencies. The word "eld" appeared in his Horace translation after a succession of different uses – in Byron's *Childe Harold's Pilgrimage* (1812), Sir Walter Scott's *The Monastery* (1820), Longfellow's *Evangeline* (1847).

Newman's version of the *Iliad* increased the density of the archaism, so that what may have been a recognizable poeticism now risked opacity and reader incomprehension. As if anticipating this risk, Newman appended a two-page "glossary" to the translation that provided his definitions for the archaic words. The glossary was a scholarly gesture that indicated the sheer heterogeneity of his lexicon, its diverse literary origins, and his readers no doubt found it useful when they took up other books, in various genres, periods, dialects. Newman used "callant" ("a young man"), an eighteenth-century word that appeared in Scott's *Waverley* (1814), and "gride" ("to cut gratingly"), a Spenserianism that appeared in Shelley's *Prometheus Bound* (1821) and Tennyson's *In Memoriam* (1850). A brief catalogue suggests the inventiveness of Newman's lexicon, its historical and cultural breadth, but also its occasional impenetrability: "behight," "bragly" ("braw, proudly fine"), "bulkin" ("calf"), "choler," "emprize," "fain," "gramsome" ("direful"), "hie," "lief," "noisome," "ravin," "sith," "whilom," "wight," "wend." There were even some Scottish words drawn from Burns and Scott, like "skirl," meaning "to cry shrilly," and "syne," as in "lang syne" ("long ago").

The foreignizing discourse of Newman's translations definitely registered on contemporary readers. The *London Quarterly Review* included Newman's Horace in two review essays that surveyed English versions of the odes, past and present. Although these essays were published more than fifteen years apart (1858 and 1874), they both disapproved of Newman's strategies and expressed a preference for a modernized Horace, rendered fluently, in immediately intelligible English:

It is an all-prevading and persistent fault in this translation, that obscure and antiquated forms of expression are used, instead of simple and modern English. Thus we find, in the very first Ode, such expressions as "Lydian eld," "quirital mob." Elsewhere we find such phrases as "*tangled* fields" (whatever this means), "the sage *thrice-aged*."

(London Quarterly Review 1874:17)

This was a criticism that crossed political lines, appearing not only in the Tory *London Quarterly*, but the liberal *National Review*, to which Newman was a contributor (Sullivan 1984:237–242). The reviewer of Newman's *Iliad* for the *National* expressed some agreement with him, admitting that "a style in some sort archaic is no doubt desirable, and even necessary, to represent a poet such as Homer" (*National Review* 1860: 292). But Newman's archaism was attacked for deviating too far from the familiar, the transparent:

> we cannot but consider that Mr. Newman's diction is needlessly antiquated and uncouth; and that, although he has not admitted any expressions which are unintelligible from their antiquity, he has omitted to observe the further caution, that archaism should not appear plainly to be constrained or assumed, lest a laboured, artificial style of English should suggest the idea of a laboured, artificial style of Greek, than which nothing can be more opposite to Homer.

(ibid.:292)

The reviewer preferred a reading experience that allowed the English version to pass as a true equivalent of "Homer" while repressing the status of Newman's text as a translation, the sense that the archaism was calculated by the translator, "assumed."

As this passage suggests, however, Newman's translations seemed foreign, not only because their "strained archaic quaintness" preempted the illusion of transparency, but also because they constituted a reading of the foreign text that revised prevailing critical opinion. Newman's decision to translate Horace into unrhymed verse with various accentual meters ignored what the *London Quarterly Review* called "the dignity and the music of the Latin," "the grace and sweetness of the original" (*London Quarterly Review* 1858:192; 1874:18). As a result, Newman's version appeared "somewhat quaint and harsh," whereas "the rhymed versions of Lord Ravensworth and of Mr. Theodore Martin" possessed "the qualities of easy elegance, of sweetness of cadence" (*London Quarterly Review* 1858:192–3; 1874:16, 19). The reviewers looked for a fluent, iconic meter, sound imitating sense to produce a transparent poem, but they also assumed that Horace would have agreed:

Now and then Professor Newman surprises us with a grateful [*sic*] flow of verse: –

> "Me not the enduring Sparta
> Nor fertile-soil'd Larissa's plain
>   So to the heart has smitten
>   As Anio headlong tumbling,
> Loud-brawling Albuneia's grot,
>   Tiburnus' groves and orchards
>   With restless rivulets streaming."

There is something of the rush of cool waters here. But what would Horace say, if he could come to life, and find himself singing the two stanzas subjoined? –

> "Well of Bandusia, as crystal bright,
> Luscious wine to thee with flowers is due;
>   To-morrow shall a kid
> Thine become, who with horny front
>
> Budding new, designs amours and war.
> Vainly: since this imp o' the frisky herd
>   With life-blood's scarlet gush
> Soon shall curdle thy icy pool."

This is hard to read, while the Latin is as pleasant to the ear as the fountain which it brings before us to the imagination.

(*London Quarterly Review* 1858:193)

The reviewers' negative evaluations rested on a contradiction that revealed quite clearly the domestic cultural values they privileged. In calling for a rhymed version, they inscribed the *unrhymed* Latin text with the verse form that dominated current English poetry while insisting that rhyme made the translation closer to Horace. The reviewers were articulating a hegemonic position in English literary culture, definitely slanted toward an academic elite: Horace's text can be "pleasant to the ear" only for readers of Latin. Yet this academic reading was also presented in national cultural terms, with the reviewers assimilating Horace to traditional English prosody:

> To discard the old machinery of recurrent rhymes, which has
> grown with the growth and strengthened with the strength of
> our poetical language, to set aside the thousand familiar and

expected effects of beat, and pause, and repetition, and of the modulation of measure-sound that makes the everchanging charm of lyrical verse – to set aside all this for the disappointing, unfamiliar machinery of verses, each with a different ending, unrelieved by any new grace of expression, any new harmony of sound, is simply the work of a visionary, working not for the enjoyment of his readers, but the gratification of a crotchety and perverted taste.

(*London Quarterly Review* 1874:15)

This call for a domesticated Horace was motivated by a nationalist investment in "the strength of our poetical language." Newman's version was "perverted" because it was un-English: "to have to break up all our English traditions for something utterly novel and yet mediocre, is a severe demand to make from the great public which reads for pleasure" (*London Quarterly Review* 1858:193). Newman tested the reviewers' assumption that the English reading audience wanted every foreign text to be rewritten according to dominant literary values. Yet the very heterogeneity of his translations, their borrowings from various literary discourses, gave the lie to this assumption by pointing to the equally heterogeneous nature of the audience. Newman's foreignized texts were challenging an elitist concept of a national English culture.

The cultural force of his challenge can be gauged from the reception of his *Iliad*. Newman's foreignizing strategy led him to choose the ballad as the archaic English form most suitable to Homeric verse. And this choice embroiled him in a midcentury controversy over the prosody of Homeric translations, played out both in numerous reviews and essays and in a spate of English versions with the most different verse forms: rhymed and unrhymed, ballad meter and Spenserian stanza, hendecasyllabics and hexameters. Here too the stakes were at once cultural – competing readings of the Greek texts – and political – competing concepts of the English nation.

Newman used ballad meter for his *Iliad* because he sought "a poetry which aims to be antiquated and popular" (Newman 1856:xii). "The style of Homer," he argued, "is direct, popular, forcible, quaint, flowing, garrulous, abounding with formulas, redundant in particles and affirmatory interjections, as also in grammatical connectives of time, place, and argument" (ibid.:iv). He defined the "popular" aspect of the Greek text historically, as the product of an oral archaic culture at a rudimentary level of literary development, "a stage of the national mind in which divisions of literature were not recognized[,] even the distinction of prose and poetry" (ibid.:iv). But he also located contemporary "popular" analogues, English as well as Greek. In choosing the ballad, Newman recalled, "I found with pleasure that I had exactly alighted on the metre which the modern Greeks adopt for the Homeric hexameter" in what he called "the modern Greek epic" (ibid.:vii–viii). The texts in question were actually ballads sung by nineteenth-century mountain brigands in the Peloponnese, "Klephts," who fought in the Greek resistance against the Turkish Empire.[10]

The English analogues Newman cited were equally "modern" – contemporary versions of archaic forms. He argued that "our real old ballad-writers are too poor and mean to repesent Homer, and are too remote in diction from our times to be popularly intelligible" (Newman 1856:x). To secure this "popular" intelligibility, his translation reflected the archaism in the English historical novel and narrative poem: he thought Scott would have been an ideal translator of Homer. Yet Newman's discourse was also explicitly oral, unlearned, and English. His syntactical inversions approximated current English speech:

> in all lively conversation we use far more inversion than in the style of essay-writing; putting the accusative before the verb, beginning a sentence with a predicate or with a negative, and in other ways approaching to the old style, which is truly native to every genuine Englishman.
>
> (ibid.:xi)

This was a concept of "the old style" that was nationalist as well as populist. Newman's "Saxo-Norman" lexicon "owe[d] as little as possible to the elements thrown into our language by classical learning" (ibid.:vi). And the "several old-fashioned formulas" he used opposed academic prescriptions for English usage:

> In modern style, our classical scholars at an early period introduced from Latin a principle which seems to me essentially unpopular, viz., to end a clause with *than he, than thou, than she,* &c., where they think a nominative is needed. [...] I cannot listen to unsophisticated English talk, without being convinced that in old English the words *me, thee, him,* &c., are not merely

accusatives, but are also the isolated form of the pronoun, like *moi, toi, lui.* In reply to the question, "Who is there?" every English boy or girl answers *Me,* until he or she is scolded into saying *I.* In modern prose the Latinists have prevailed; but in a poetry which aims to be antiquated and popular, I must rebel.

(ibid.:xi–xii)

The "popular" in Newman's translation was a contemporary construction of an archaic form that carried various ideological implications. It drew on an analogous Greek form affiliated with a nationalist movement to win political autonomy from foreign domination (or, more precisely, a criminal fringe of this movement, the Klepht resistance). And it assumed an English culture that was national yet characterized by social divisions, in which cultural values were ranged hierarchically among various groups, academic and nonacademic. Newman's archaism constituted the democratic tendency in his concept of the English nation because it was populist, assigning popular cultural forms a priority over the academic elite that sought to suppress them. He thought of the ballad as "our Common Metre" (Newman 1856:vii).

Newman's *Iliad* received little attention in the periodicals – until, several years later, Matthew Arnold decided to attack it in a lecture series published as *On Translating Homer* (1861). Arnold, then Professor of Poetry at Oxford, described the lectures as an effort "to lay down the true principles on which a translation of Homer should be founded," and these were principles diametrically opposed to Newman's (Arnold 1960:238). Arnold wanted translation to transcend, rather than signify, linguistic and cultural differences, and so he prized the illusionism of transparent discourse, using the "strange language" of mystical transcendence to describe the process of domestication:

> Coleridge says, in his strange language, speaking of the union of the human soul with the divine essence, that this takes place
>
>> Whene'er the mist, which stands 'twixt God and thee,
>> Defecates to a pure transparency;
>
> and so, too, it may be said of that union of the translator with his original, which alone can produce a good translation, that it takes place when the mist which stands between them – the mist of alien modes of thinking, speaking, and feeling on the

translator's part – "defecates to a pure transparency," and disappears.

(ibid.:103)

In this remarkable analogy, Arnold's translation "principles" assumed a Christian Platonic metaphysics of true semantic equivalence, whereby he demonized (or fecalized) the material conditions of translation, the target-language values that define the translator's work and inevitably mark the source-language text. Current English "modes of thinking, speaking, and feeling" must be repressed, like a bodily function; they are "alien" excrement soiling the classical text. This is an antiquarianism that canonized the Greek past while approaching the English present with a physical squeamishness. Arnold didn't demonize all domestic values, however, since he was in fact upholding the canonical tradition of English literary translation: following Denham, Dryden, Tytler, Frere, he recommended a free, domesticating method to produce fluent, familiar verse that respected bourgeois moral values. The difference between the foreign text and English culture "disappears" in this tradition because the translator removes it – while invisibly inscribing a reading that reflects English literary canons, a specific interpretation of "Homer." In Arnold's case,

> So essentially characteristic of Homer is his plainness and naturalness of thought, that to the preservation of this in his own version the translator must without scruple sacrifice, where it is necessary, verbal fidelity to his original, rather than run any risk of producing, by literalness, an odd and unnatural effect.
>
> (Arnold 1960:157–158)

For Arnold, what determined familiarity of effect was not merely transparent discourse, fluency as opposed to "literalness," but the prevailing academic reading of Homer, validated by scholars at Eton, Cambridge, and Oxford. Indeed, Arnold's main contention – and the point on which he differed most from Newman – was that only readers of the Greek text were qualified to evaluate English versions of it: "a competent scholar's judgment whether the translation more or less reproduces for him the effect of the original" (Arnold 1960:201). Throughout the lectures Arnold repeatedly set forth this "effect" in authoritative statements: "Homer is rapid in his movement, Homer is plain in his words and

style, Homer is simple in his ideas, Homer is noble in manner"
(ibid.:141). Using this explicitly academic reading, Arnold argued
that various translators, past and present, "have failed in rendering
him": George Chapman, because of "the fancifulness of the
Elizabethan age, entirely alien to the plain directness of Homer's
thought and feeling"; Pope, because of his "literary artificial
manner, entirely alien to the plain naturalness of Homer"; William
Cowper, because of his "elaborate Miltonic manner, entirely alien
to the flowing rapidity of Homer"; and, finally, Newman, whose
"manner" was "eminently ignoble, while Homer's manner is
eminently noble" (ibid.:103). Here it becomes clear that Newman's
translation was foreignizing because his archaism deviated from
the academic reading of Homer:

> Why are Mr. Newman's lines faulty? They are faulty, first,
> because, as a matter of diction, the expressions "O gentle
> friend," "eld," "in sooth," "liefly," "advance," "man-ennobling,"
> "sith," "any-gait," and "sly of foot," are all bad; some of them
> worse than others, but all bad: that is, they all of them as here
> used excite in the scholar, their sole judge, – excite, I will boldly
> affirm, in Professor Thompson or Professor Jowett, – a feeling
> totally different from that excited in them by the words of
> Homer which these expressions profess to render.
>
> (ibid.:133)

Arnold's critique of Newman's translation was informed by a
concept of English culture that was nationalist as well as elitist. To
demonstrate the effect of familiarity that a scholar experiences
before the Greek text, Arnold gave examples of English "expressions" that he called "simple," transparently intelligible, but that
also constituted Anglocentric stereotypes of foreign cultures,
implicitly racist:

> [Greek] expressions seem no more odd to [the scholar] than
> the simplest expressions in English. He is not more checked by
> any feeling of strangeness, strong or weak, when he reads them,
> than when he reads in an English book "the painted savage," or,
> "the phlegmatic Dutchman."
>
> (ibid.:123)

In Arnold's view, Newman's translation demonstrated the need for
an academic elite to establish national cultural values:

I think that in England, partly from the want of an Academy,
partly from a national habit of intellect to which that want of an
Academy is itself due, there exists too little of what I may call a
public force of correct literary opinion, possessing within
certain limits a clear sense of what is right and wrong, sound and
unsound, and sharply recalling men of ability and learning from
any flagrant misdirection of these their advantages. I think,
even, that in our country a powerful misdirection of this kind is
often more likely to subjugate and pervert opinion than to be
checked and corrected by it.

(ibid.:171–172)

The social function Arnold assigned translators like Newman was
to "correct" English cultural values by bringing them in line with
scholarly "opinion." Translation for Arnold was a means to
empower an academic elite, to endow it with national cultural
authority, but this empowerment involved an imposition of scholarly values on other cultural constituencies – including the diverse
English-reading audience that Newman hoped to reach. The
elitism in Arnold's concept of a national English culture assumed
an unbridgeable social division: "These two impressions – that of
the scholar, and that of the unlearned reader – can, practically,
never be accurately compared" (ibid.:201). Translation bridges this
division, but only by eliminating the nonscholarly.

Arnold's attack on Newman's translation was an academic
repression of popular cultural forms that was grounded in a
competing reading of Homer. Where Arnold's Homer was elitist,
possessing "nobility," "a great master" of "the grand style," Newman's was populist and, to Arnold, "ignoble." Hence, Arnold
insisted that

the ballad-style and the ballad-measure are eminently inappropriate to render Homer. Homer's manner and movement
are always both noble and powerful: the ballad-manner and
movement are often either jaunty and smart, so not noble; or
jog-trot and humdrum, so not powerful.

(Arnold 1960:128)

Arnold rejected the use of the "ballad-manner" in various English
translations – Chapman's Homer, Dr. William Maginn's *Homeric
Ballads and Comedies of Lucian* (1850), Newman's *Iliad* – because he
found it "over-familiar," "commonplace," "pitched sensibly lower

than Homer's" verse (ibid.:117, 124, 155). Newman's archaism in particular degraded the canonical Greek text by resorting to colloquial Shakespearean expressions, like "To grunt and sweat under a weary load" – a judgment that again revealed the strain of bourgeois squeamishness in Arnold's academic elitism:

> if the translator of Homer [. . .] were to employ, when he has to speak of one of Homer's heroes under the load of calamity, this figure of "grunting" and "sweating," we should say, *He Newmanises*, and his diction would offend us. For he is to be noble; and no plea of wishing to be plain and natural can get him excused from being this.
>
> (ibid.:155)

Arnold's notion of Homer's "nobility" assimilated the Greek text to the scholarly while excluding the popular. He noted that for an American reader the ballad "has a disadvantage in being like the rhythm of the American national air *Yankee Doodle*, and thus provoking ludicrous associations" (ibid.:132). And although Arnold recommended the hexameter as the most suitable verse form for Homeric translation, he was careful to add that he didn't have in mind the hexameters in Longfellow's "pleasing and popular poem of *Evangeline*," but rather those of "the accomplished Provost of Eton, Dr. Hawtrey," who was not only "one of the natural judges of a translation of Homer," but the author of the 1847 volume *English Hexameter Translations* (ibid.:149, 151). Any translation was likely to be offensive to Arnold, given his scholarly adulation of the Greek text. Newman's mixture of homely colloquialism, archaism, and close rendering proved positively alienating:

> The end of the nineteenth book, the answer of Achilles to his horse Xanthus, Mr. Newman gives thus: –
>
> > "Chestnut! why bodest death to me? from thee this was not needed.
> > Myself right surely know also, that 't is my doom to perish,
> > From mother and from father dear apart, in Troy; but never
> > Pause will I make of war, until the Trojans be glutted."
> > He spake, and yelling, held afront the single-hoofed horses
>
> Here Mr. Newman calls Xanthus *Chestnut*, indeed, as he calls Balius *Spotted*, and Podarga *Spry-foot*; which is as if a Frenchman

were to call Miss Nightingale *Mdlle. Rossignol,* or Mr. Bright *M. Clair.* And several other expressions, too, – "yelling," "held afront," "single-hoofed," – leave, to say the very least, much to be desired.

(ibid.:134)

It is in fact Arnold's habit of saying "the very least" that is most symptomatic of the anti-democratic tendency in his critique. Arnold refused to define his concept of "nobleness," the one Homeric quality that distinguished the academic reading and justified his call for a national academy: "I do not attempt to lay down any rules for obtaining this effect of nobleness, – the effect, too, of all others the most impalpable, the most irreducible to rule, and which most depends on the individual personality of the artist" (Arnold 1960:159). Like Alexander Tytler, Arnold valued a public sphere of cultural consensus that would underwrite the "correct" translation discourse for Homer, but any democratic tendency in this national agenda foundered on an individualist aesthetics that was fundamentally impressionistic: "the presence or absence of the grand style can only be spiritually discerned" (ibid.:136). Unlike Tytler, Arnold could not easily accept a humanist assumption of universal "reason and good sense" because the English reading audience had become too culturally and socially diverse; hence Arnold's turn to an academic elite to enforce its cultural agenda on the nation. As Terry Eagleton puts it, "Arnold's academy is not the public sphere, but a means of defense against the actual Victorian public" (Eagleton 1984:64; see also Baldick 1983:29–31).

The "grand style" was so important to Arnold because it was active in the construction of human subjects, capable of imprinting other social groups with academic cultural values: "it can form the character, it is edifying. [...] the few artists in the grand style [...] can refine the raw natural man, they can transmute him" (Arnold 1960:138–139). Yet because Homeric nobleness depended on the individual personality of the writer or reader and could only be experienced, not described, it was autocratic and irrational. The individualism at the root of Arnold's critique finally undermines the cultural authority he assigned to the academy by issuing into contradiction: he vaguely linked nobility to the individual personality, but he also faulted Newman's translation precisely because of its individualism. For Arnold, Newman indulged "some individual fancy," exemplifying a deplorable national trait, "the great defect of

English intellect, the great blemish of English literature" – "eccentricity and arbitrariness" (ibid.:140).

Newman was stung by Arnold's lectures, and by the end of the
year he published a book-length reply that allowed him to develop
more fully the translation rationale he sketched in his preface. At
the outset he made quite clear that his "sole object is, to bring
Homer before the unlearned public" (Newman 1861:6). Newman
questioned the authority Arnold assigned to the academy in the
formation of a national culture. He pointed out that England was
multicultural, a site of different values, and although an academic
himself he sided with the nonacademic:

> Scholars are the tribunal of Erudition, but of Taste the educated
> but unlearned public is the only rightful judge; and to it I wish
> to appeal. Even scholars collectively have no right, and much
> less have single scholars, to pronounce a final sentence on
> questions of taste in their court.
>
> (ibid.:2)

Because Newman translated for a different audience, he refused
such scholarly verse forms as the hexameters Arnold proposed:

> The unlearned look on all, even the best hexameters, whether
> from Southey, Lockhart or Longfellow, as odd and disagreeable
> prose. Mr. Arnold deprecates appeal to popular taste: well he
> may! Yet if the unlearned are to be our audience, we cannot defy
> them. I myself, before venturing to print, sought to ascertain
> how unlearned women and children would accept my verses. I
> could boast how children and half-educated women have
> extolled them; how greedily a working man has inquired for
> them, without knowing who was the translator.
>
> (ibid.:12–13)

Newman's assessment of "popular taste" led him to write his
translation in the ballad form, which he described in terms that
obviously sought to challenge Arnold's: "*It is essentially a noble metre,
a popular metre*, a metre of great capacity. It is essentially the national
ballad metre" (ibid.:22). Newman's reply emphasized the peculiar
ideological significance of his project. His aim to produce a
translation that was at once populist and nationalist was realized in
an archaic literary discourse that resisted any scholarly domestication of the foreign text, any assimilation of it to the regime of
transparent discourse in English:

Classical scholars ought to set their faces against the double heresy, of trying to enforce, that foreign poetry, however various, shall all be rendered in one English dialect, and that this shall, in order of words and in diction, closely approximate to polished prose.

(ibid.:88)

Newman's reply showed that translation could permit other, popular literary discourses to emerge in English only if it was foreignizing, or, in the case of classical literature, historicizing, only if it abandoned fluency to signify "the archaic, the rugged, the boisterous element in Homer" (Newman 1861:22). Because Newman's historiography was essentially Whiggish, assuming a teleological model of human development, a liberal concept of progress, he felt that Homer "not only was antiquated, relatively to Pericles, but is also absolutely antique, being a poet of a barbarian age" (ibid.:48).[11] Newman admitted that it was difficult to avoid judging past foreign cultures according to the cultural values – both academic and bourgeois – that distinguished Victorian elites from their social inferiors in England and elsewhere. He believed that

if the living Homer could sing his lines to us, they would at first move in us the same pleasing interest as an elegant and simple melody from an African of the Gold Coast; but that, after hearing twenty lines, we should complain of meagreness, sameness, and *loss of moral expression*; and should judge the style to be as inferior to our own oratorical metres, as the music of Pindar to our third-rate modern music.

(ibid.:14)

Yet Newman nonetheless insisted that such Anglocentric judgments must be minimized or avoided altogether: "to expect refinement and universal delicacy of expression in that stage of civilization is quite anachronistic and unreasonable" (ibid.:73). In arguing for a historicist approach to translation, Newman demonstrated that scholarly English critics like Arnold violated their own principle of universal reason by using it to justify an abridgement of the Greek text:

Homer never sees things *in the same proportions* as we see them. To omit his digressions, and what I may call his "impertinences," in order to give his argument that which Mr. Arnold is pleased to call the proper "balance," is to value our own logical minds, more than his picturesque but illogical mind.

(ibid.:56)

As such statements suggest, the Whig historiography that informed Newman's concept of classical culture inevitably privileged Victorian social elites as exemplars of the most advanced stage of human development. As a result, it implicitly drew an analogy among their inferiors – the "barbarian," the "savage," the colonized ("Gold Coast"), and the popular English audience – exposing a patronizing and potentially racist side to Newman's translation populism (and edging his position closer to Arnold's). Yet Newman's Whig historiography also enabled him to refine his sense of literary history and develop a translation project that both preserved the cultural difference of the foreign text and acknowledged the diversity of English literary discourses: "Every sentence of Homer was more or less antiquated to Sophocles, who could no more help feeling at every instant the foreign and antiquated character of the poetry, than an Englishman can help feeling the same in reading Burns's poems" (Newman 1861:35–36). Newman's skepticism toward dominant cultural values in English even made him criticize Arnold's admitted "Bibliolatry," his reliance on "the authority of the Bible" in developing a lexicon for Homeric translations (Arnold 1960:165–166). Newman didn't want the Bible's cultural authority to exclude other archaic literary discourses, which he considered equally "sacred": "Words which have come to us in a sacred connection, no doubt, gain a sacred hue, but they must not be allowed to desecrate other old and excellent words" (Newman 1861:89).

The publication of Arnold's lectures made Homeric translation an important topic of debate in Anglo-American culture, provoking not only a reply from Newman and a coda from Arnold, but many reviews and articles in a wide range of British and American periodicals. The reception was mixed. Reviewers were especially divided on the question of whether the ballad or the hexameter was the acceptable verse form for Homeric translation.[12] Yet Arnold was definitely favored over Newman, no matter what ideological standpoint the periodical may have established in previous reviewing. The Edinburgh-based *North British Review*, although "consistently Whiggish in politics," possessed a religious and moral conservatism that led to an evangelical approach in literary reviews – and an endorsement of Arnold's call for an academy with national cultural authority (*North British Review* 1862:348; Sullivan 1984:276). In an article that discussed recent Homeric translations and the Arnold/Newman controversy, the reviewer accepted Arnold's diagnosis of English culture as well as his dismissal of Newman's archaism: "at present we have nothing but eccentricity, and arbitrary likings and dislikings. Our literature shows no regard for dignity, no reverence for law. [...] The present ballad-mania is among the results of this licentiousness" (*North British Review* 1862:348).

Arnold's case against Newman was persuasive even to *The Westminster Review*, which abandoned its characteristically militant liberalism to advocate a cultural elite (Sullivan 1983b:424–433). The reviewer remarked that lecturing in English instead of Latin gave Arnold "the further privilege and responsibility of addressing himself not to the few, but to the many, not to a select clique of scholars, but to the entire reading public" (*Westminster Review* 1862:151). Yet it was precisely the literary values of a select scholarly clique that the reviewer wanted to be imposed on the entire reading public, since he accepted Arnold's "proposed test of a thoroughly good translation – that it ought to produce on the scholar the same effect as the original poem" (ibid.:151). Hence, Arnold's academic reading of the Greek text was recommended over Newman's populist "view that Homer can be rendered adequately into any form of ballad-metre. All ballad-metre alike is pitched in too low a key; it may be rapid, and direct, and spirit-stirring, but is incapable of sustained nobility" (ibid.:165).

Not every reviewer agreed with Arnold on the need for an academic elite to establish a national English culture. But most explicitly shared his academic reading of Homer and therefore his criticism of Newman's archaic translation. *The Saturday Review*, advocate of a conservative liberalism opposed to democratic reform (the labor union movement, women's suffrage, socialism), affected a condescending air of impartiality by criticizing both Arnold and Newman (Bevington 1941). Yet the criteria were mostly Arnoldian. The reviewer assumed the cultural superiority of the academy by chastising Arnold for violating scholarly decorum, for devoting Oxford lectures to a "bitterly contemptuous" attack on a contemporary writer like Newman, "who, whatever his aberrations in other ways, has certainly, as a scholar, a very much higher reputation than Mr. Arnold himself" (*Saturday*

Review 1861:95). Yet Newman's "aberrations" were the same ones that Arnold noticed, especially the archaism, which the reviewer described as "a consistent, though we think mistaken theory" (ibid.:96). The *Saturday Review*'s distaste for Newman's translation was in turn consistent with its other literary judgments: it tended to ridicule literary experiments that deviated from transparent discourse, like Robert Browning's "obscure" poetry, and to attack literary forms that were populist as well as popular, like Dickens's novels (Bevington 1941:208–209, 155–167).

The liberal *British Quarterly Review*, a nonconformist religious periodical edited by a Congregationalist minister, questioned Arnold's desire "to imitate in England the French Academy" (*British Quarterly Review* 1865:292; Houghton *et al.* 1987:IV, 114–125). This was considered "an intellectual foppery" since the fundamental individualism of English culture resisted any notion of a national academy: "Mr. Arnold seems determined to ignore the fact that an academic style is impossible among the English, who are by nature original" (*British Quarterly Review* 1865:292). Yet the reviewer agreed "that Homeric translation demands a noble simplicity," adding that

> unquestionably Mr. Arnold is right in placing Homer in a very different class from the ballad-poets with whom he has frequently been compared. The ballad, in its most perfect form, belongs to a rude state of society – to a time when ideas were few. This cannot be said of Homer. His very existence is sufficient proof of a social development quite equal to that of Shakespeare's time, though far simpler in its form.
>
> (ibid.:293)

The reviewer assumed both Newman's historicist concept of the ballad and the Whig historiography on which it was based. But Newman's populist reading of Homer was rejected in favor of Arnoldian nobility. This move made a liberal periodical like the *British Quarterly Review* no different from the Tory *Dublin University Magazine*, in which a review of two hexameter translations inspired by Arnold's lectures singled out Newman's version for special criticism: "his unrhymed ballad metre, his quaint flat diction, and his laughtermoving epithets" amounted to an "unlucky burlesque" (*Dublin University Magazine* 1862:644; Sullivan 1983b:119–123). Newman's verse form was described as "the mongrel ballad measure of modern Greece," a particularly inappropriate choice for Homer's pure nobility.

Arnold can be said to have won this debate, even if his recommendation of hexameters for Homeric translation took almost a century to gain widespread acceptance – in the "free six-beat line" of Richmond Lattimore's immensely popular version (Lattimore 1951:55).[13] The fate of Newman's project was marginalization in his own time and since, with critiques giving way to virtual oblivion. This can be seen, first, in the publishing histories of the controversial documents. Between 1861 and 1924 British and American publishers brought out seventeen single-volume editions of Arnold's lectures; between 1905 and 1954 fourteen different editions of Arnold's selected essays contained the lectures – not to mention their inclusion in several complete editions of Arnold's writing. Newman's *Iliad* was reprinted only once, in 1871, and thereafter known primarily through quotations in Arnold's lectures. Newman's reply too was printed only once in the nineteenth century. During the first half of the twentieth, it was reprinted frequently, but only in selections of Arnold's essays, presented as a supporting document subordinated to Arnold's more important lectures, a minor text included to provide cultural background for the major author (see, for example, Arnold 1914). In 1960, the editor of Arnold's *Complete Prose Works*, R. H. Super, believed that Newman's reply wasn't worth reprinting:

> His essay has achieved undeserved immortality only by being printed in several modern editions of Arnold's essays (e.g. Oxford Standard Authors and Everyman's Library); readers who wish to see what provoked the best of Arnold's Homeric lectures may find it in one of those volumes.
>
> (Arnold 1960:249)

Super saw Arnold's lectures as valuable in themselves, transcending the cultural moment that called them forth, independent of Newman's translation, of the entire international controversy, unquestionably superior to the other positions in the debate. Arnold's domesticating translation theory, as well as the academic cultural values that informed it, had by this point achieved canonical status in Anglo-American literary culture.

Arnold's ascendancy over Newman has taken other forms since the 1860s. Arnold's lectures coined a satiric neologism for Newman's translation discourse – to "Newmanize" – and for the next twenty-five years this word was part of the lexicon of critical terms in the literary periodicals. In 1886, for example, *The Athenaeum* ran a favorable review of Arthur Way's translation of the *Iliad*, but the reviewer nonetheless complained that "Mr. Way, in fact, is a little inclined to 'Newmanize'" because he "sometimes falls" into a "mongrel vocabulary," deviating from current English usage: "Pure English of the simple sort is amply sufficient for the translating of Homer" (*Athenaeum* 1886:482–483).

A foreignizing translation method similar to Newman's was adopted by another socially engaged Victorian translator, William Morris. In this case, it was Morris's socialist investment in medievalism that led him to cultivate an archaic lexicon drawn from various literary forms, elite and popular (cf. Chandler 1970:209–230). Morris's experiments received much more appreciative reviews than Newman's, but they were also attacked, and for some of the same reasons. In 1888, the *Quarterly Review* ran an adulatory assessment of Arnold's writing that extended his critique of Homeric translations to Morris's *Odyssey* (1887–8): "By this travesty of an archaic diction, Mr. William Morris [...] has overlaid Homer with all the grotesqueness, the conceits, the irrationality of the Middle Ages, as Mr. Arnold justly says that Chapman overlaid him" (*Quarterly Review* 1888:407–408).

In the same year, *Longman's Magazine*, a monthly devoted to bringing "literature of a high standard" to a mass audience, ran an article in which Morris's translations were cited as prime examples of "Wardour-Street Early English – a perfectly modern article with a sham appearance of the real antique about it" (Ballantyne 1888:589; Sullivan 1984:209–213). This reference to the shops in Wardour Street that sold antique furniture, both authentic and imitation, questioned the authenticity of Morris's archaism while linking it to nonstandard English dialects and marginal literary forms. The reviewer's elitism was recognizably Arnoldian:

> Poems in which guests go bedward to beds that are arrayed right meet, poems in which thrall-folk seek to the feast-hall a-winter, do not belong to any literary centre. They are provincial; they are utterly without distinction; they are unspeakably absurd.
>
> (Ballantyne 1888:593)

The "literary centre" was fluent translation. In 1889, the *Quarterly Review* likewise attacked Morris's *Aeneid* (1875) because of "the sense of incongruity inspired by such Wardour-Street English as *eyen* and *clepe*" (Faulkner 1973:28, n. 81). Here the "centre" is also identified as standard English, the language of contemporary political insitutions, leading politicians. The *Longman's* article on "Wardour-Street English" observed that

> if the Lord Chancellor or Mr. Speaker were to deliver one of these solemn pronouncements in any cockney or county dialect, he would leave upon his hearers the same sense of the grotesque and the undignified which a reader carries away from an author who, instead of using his own language in its richest and truest literary form, takes up a linguistic fad, and, in pursuit of it, makes his work provincial instead of literary.
> (Ballantyne 1888:593–594)

Morris's translations did no more than "pretend to be literature," because literary texts were written in a dialect of English that was educated and official and thus excluded popular linguistic and literary forms.

"Wardour-Street English" eventually came to be used as a term of abuse for archaic diction in any kind of writing – applied to widely read historical novels, particularly imitations of Scott, but also to nonfiction prose, including an eccentric volume like *The Gate of Remembrance* (1918). Produced by the director of the excavations at Glastonbury Abbey, F. Bligh Bond, this was an attempt to enlist "psychical research" in the "work of architectural exploration" (*Spectator* 1918:422). Bligh's volume presented the "automatic writing" of one "J.A.," in which the historical associations of the abbey were personified and given voice in various languages: Latin ("William the Monk"), Anglo-Saxon ("Awfwold ye Saxon"), and a mixture of Middle and Early Modern English ("Johannes, Lapidator or Stone-Mason," "defunctus anno 1533"). The reviewer for the *Spectator* judged this linguistic experiment favorably, but got more pleasure from the Latin, which, he felt, "is much to be preferred to the Wardour Street English" assigned to the stonemason (ibid.:422). Interestingly, the passage of automatic writing quoted by the reviewer links English archaism once again to the unlearned, the subordinate: it shows the stonemason resisting the use of Latin architectural terms imposed on him by monkish treatises:

Ye names of builded things are very hard in Latin tongue –

transome, fanne tracery, and the like. My son, thou canst not understande. Wee wold speak in the Englyshe tongue. Ye saide that ye volte was multipartite yt was fannes olde style in ye este ende of ye choire and ye newe volt in Edgares chappel.... Glosterfannes (*repeated*). Fannes ... (*again*) yclept fanne ... Johannes lap ... mason.   (ibid.:422)

To the reviewer, such language was "thoroughly bad," and it marred even a "very curious and attractive passage" about "the tomb of Arthur" by suggesting popular literary forms: "there are obvious reminiscences of Sir Walter Scott and *Ivanhoe* in this piece of most unblushing but rather vivid Wardour Street" (ibid.).

The stigma attached to archaism involved an exclusion of the popular that is also evident in prescriptive stylistic manuals, like H. W. Fowler's *Dictionary of Modern English Usage* (1926). Fowler included an entry on archaism that treated it as

> dangerous except in the hands of an experienced writer who can trust his sense of congruity. Even when used to give colour to conversation in historical romances, what Stevenson called tushery is more likely to irritate the reader than to please him.
>
> (Fowler 1965:34)

Fowler's "experienced writer" was apparently not the author of popular historical romances. And the reader he had in mind obviously preferred transparent discourse.

In the academy, where Arnold the apologist for an academic elite was ensconced as a canonical writer, the historicizing translations of Newman and Morris have repeatedly been subjected to Arnoldian thrashings. T. S. Osmond's 1912 study of the Arnold/Newman controversy agreed with Arnold's "protests against the use of ridiculous or too uncommon words" in translations because they preempt the illusion of transparency: "One's attention is held by the words, instead of by the thing that is being told" (Osmond 1912:82). In 1956, Basil Willey's attempt to rehabilitate Newman's reputation focused mainly on his religious treatises, particularly *The Soul* (1849), which Willey felt should be admitted to the Victorian canon, assigned "a much higher rank in devotional literature" (Willey 1956:45). Yet although Willey gave a generally balanced account of the translation controversy, he finally agreed with Arnold that Newman lacked the "individual personality" to render Homer's "grand style": "Newman, with all his great merits, was not a poet" because "his spirit was not sufficiently "free, flexible and elastic'" (ibid.; see also Annan 1944:191).

In 1962, J. M. Cohen, the translator of canonical writers like Rabelais and Cervantes, published a history of English-language translation in which he approvingly described the dominant domesticating method and the "complete reversal of taste" that made Victorian archaism "unreadable" (although, as we have seen, it was definitely unreadable to many Victorians as well): "In contrast to the Victorians and Edwardians [...] craftsmen in the last twenty years have aimed principally at interpretation in current language" (Cohen 1962:65). Cohen himself followed this dominant tendency toward transparent discourse, asserting that "the theory of Victorian translation appears from our point of view to have been founded on a fundamental error" and faulting Morris in particular for the density of his archaism: "Even the meaning has become obscure" (ibid.:24, 25). Cohen agreed with Arnold in attributing what he considered the defects of Victorian translation to its historicism. The experiments developed by translators like Newman, Morris, Robert Browning, Dante Gabriel Rossetti, and Edward Fitzgerald were misguided, Cohen felt, because the translators had "adapted their authors' styles to their more or less erroneous pictures of the age in which these authors lived and worked" (ibid.:29). Yet Cohen was himself making the anachronistic assumption that the correct historical "pictures" were in "current language," respectful of the modern canon of "plain prose uniformity" in translation (ibid.:33).

Finally, there is perhaps no clearer sign of Arnold's continuing power in Anglo-American literary culture than Robert Fagles' 1990 version of the *Iliad*, winner of the Harold Morton Landon Award for poetry translation from the Academy of American Poets. Fagles' preface begins by acknowledging the oral quality of Homeric verse, but then reverts to Arnold's reading of Homer:

> Homer's work is a performance, even in part a musical event. Perhaps that is the source of his speed, directness and simplicity that Matthew Arnold heard – and his nobility too, elusive yet undeniable, that Arnold chased but never really caught.
>
> (Fagles 1990:ix)

A classics translator who edited Pope's Homer and is currently professor of Comparative Literature at Princeton, Fagles demonstrates not just that Arnold's reading still prevails today, but that it continues to be affiliated with the academy and with the dominant tradition of English-language translation, fluent domestication. Fagles aimed for a version that was "literate" in an academic (i.e., Arnoldian) sense, negotiating between the "literal" and the "literary" in a way that implemented Dryden's notion of "paraphrase," producing in the end a modernized Homer:

> Not a line-for-line translation, my version of the *Iliad* is, I hope, neither so literal in rendering Homer's language as to cramp and distort my own – though I want to convey as much of what he says as possible – nor so literary as to brake his energy, his forward drive – though I want my work to be literate, with any luck. For the more literal approach seems too little English, and the more literary seems too little Greek. I have tried to find a cross between the two, a modern English Homer.
>
> (ibid.:x)

Fagles also follows – even if in a flexible way – Arnold's recommendation of hexameters for Homeric translation: "Working from a loose five- or six-beat line but inclining more to six, I expand at times to seven beats [...] or contract at times to three" (ibid.:xi).

III

The Victorian controversy offers several lessons that can be brought to bear on contemporary English-language translation. Perhaps most importantly, the controversy shows that domesticating translation can be resisted without necessarily privileging a cultural elite. Newman advocated Schleiermacher's foreignizing method, but he detached it from the cultural and political interests of a German literary coterie, at once elitist and nationalist. Newman instead assumed a more democratic concept of an English national culture, acknowledging its diversity and refusing to allow a cultural minority like the academy to dominate the nation. Newman was a scholar who truly believed that an English translator could address diverse cultural constituencies, satisfying scholarly canons of translation equivalence while appealing to popular taste: "While I profess to write for the *unlearned* English reader, yet I must necessarily be judged by classical scholars on the question of fidelity and correctness" (Newman 1853:vi).

Yet the "foreign" in Newman's foreignizing translations was defined precisely by his resistance to academic literary values, by his aim to encompass rather than exclude popular forms affiliated with various social groups. Foreignizing translation is based on the assumption that literacy is not universal, that communication is complicated by cultural differences between and within linguistic communities. But foreignizing is also an attempt to recognize and allow those differences to shape cultural discourses in the target language. Arnold's advocacy of domesticating translation also did not assume a homogeneous national culture – indeed, for him the diversity of English literature meant chaos. Arnold's response to cultural differences was to repress them, hewing to the dominant tradition in English-language translation and empowering an academic elite to maintain it. Newman demonstrated, however, that foreignizing translation can be a form of resistance in a democratic cultural politics.

The Victorian controversy also offers a practical lesson for contemporary English-language translators. It shows that close translation, what Arnold called Newman's "literalness," does not necessarily lead to unidiomatic, unintelligible English. Schleiermacher suggested that "the more closely the translation follows the turns taken by the original, the more foreign it will seem to the reader" (Lefevere 1977:78), and Newman likewise argued that "in many passages it is of much value to render the original line by line" (Newman 1856:viii–ix), incurring Arnold's satire for verbatim renderings of Homeric epithets – "ashen-speared," "brazen-cloaked" (Arnold 1960:165). But Newman's close adherence to the lineation and word-order of the Greek text was matched by an equally close attention to a distinctly English lexicon, syntax, and range of literary forms. Close translation certainly risks obscure diction, awkward constructions, and hybrid forms, but these vary in degree from one foreign text to another and from one domestic situation to another. Detections of "translationese" assume an investment in specific linguistic and cultural values to the exclusion of others. Hence, close translation is foreignizing only because its approximation of the foreign text entails deviating from dominant domestic values – like transparent discourse.

What is "literal" about this method is that it focuses on the letter of the translation as well as the foreign text, emphasizing the signifier, the signifying play that routinely gets fixed in English-language translation, reduced to a relatively coherent signified.

Newman's foreignizing translation released this play, adding a surplus of domestic meanings to the foreign text by encompassing various English-language cultural discourses, past and present, elite and popular, poetic and novelistic, English and Scottish. In foreignizing translation, the ethnocentric violence that every act of translating wreaks on a foreign text is matched by a violent disruption of domestic values that challenges cultural forms of domination, whether nationalist or elitist. Foreignizing undermines the very concept of nation by invoking the diverse constituencies that any such concept tends to elide.

Chapter 4

Dissidence

> The fundamental error of the translator is that he stabilizes the state in which his own language happens to find itself instead of allowing his language to be powerfully jolted by the foreign language.
>
> Rudolf Pannwitz (trans. Richard Sieburth)

The search for alternatives to the domesticating tradition in English-language translation leads to various foreignizing practices, both in the choice of foreign texts and in the invention of translation discourses. A translator can signal the foreignness of the foreign text, not only by using a discursive strategy that deviates from the prevailing hierarchy of domestic discourses (e.g. dense archaism as opposed to fluent transparency), but also by choosing to translate a text that challenges the contemporary canon of foreign literature in the target language. Foreignizing translation is a dissident cultural practice, maintaining a refusal of the dominant by developing affiliations with marginal linguistic and literary values at home, including foreign cultures that have been excluded because of their own resistance to dominant values.[1] On the one hand, foreignizing translation enacts an ethnocentric appropriation of the foreign text by enlisting it in a domestic cultural political agenda, like dissidence; on the other hand, it is precisely this dissident stance that enables foreignizing translation to signal the linguistic and cultural difference of the foreign text and perform a work of cultural restoration, admitting the ethnodeviant and potentially revising domestic literary canons.

The translation projects of the Italian writer Iginio Ugo Tarchetti (1839–1869) offer a provocative way to explore these issues. Tarchetti belonged to the Milanese movement known as the *scapigliatura*, a loosely associated group of artists, composers, and writers who contested bourgeois values in their bohemianism (*scapigliato* means "dishevelled") and in their formal innovations. The literary members of this dissident group were at variance with the highly conservative realism that dominated Italian fiction since Alessandro Manzoni's *I promessi sposi* (*The Betrothed*) (1827, rev. 1840). And some of them abandoned Manzoni's sentimental Christian providentialism for a democratically oriented representation of class divisions, realistic but also romantic, historically detailed yet melodramatic, often with a topical engagement in events surrounding the Italian Unification, like the Austrian presence or the Italian conscript army (Carsaniga 1974).

Tarchetti's first novel, *Paolina* (1865), followed a seamstress who is persecuted by an aristocrat and ultimately raped and murdered. His second novel, *Una nobile follia* (*A Noble Madness*) (1866–1867), a protest against the new standing army, focused on a military officer moved to desertion by distracted, pacifistic musings. The book caused an uproar in the press, and copies were openly burned at many barracks. Tarchetti's later narratives took more experimental forms. *Fosca* (1869), a semi-autobiographical novel about a pathological love affair, mixed several fictional discourses – romantic, fantastic, realistic, naturalistic – to counter the notion of character as a unified subjectivity (Caesar 1987). In a number of short narratives, some of which were posthumously published in 1869 as *Racconti fantastici* (*Fantastic Tales*), Tarchetti deployed the conventions and motifs of nineteenth-century fantasy to issue a fundamental challenge to realist representation and its ideological grounding in bourgeois individualism.

The appropriation of foreign texts was a crucial component of Tarchetti's dissident cultural politics. He was the first practitioner of the Gothic tale in Italy, and most of his fantastic narratives are based on specific texts by writers like E.T.A. Hoffmann, Edgar Allan Poe, Gérard Nerval, Théophile Gautier, and the collaboration of Émile Erckmann and Louis-Alexandre Chatrian (Mariani 1967; Rossi 1959). Tarchetti adapted fantastic motifs, reproduced scenes, translated, even plagiarized – yet each discursive practice served the political function of interrogating ideologies and addressing hierarchical social relations in Italy. His fantastic narratives mobilized foreign texts to question the hegemony of realist discourse in Italian fiction, and yet this mobilization, insofar as it entailed transforming foreign texts to function in a different cultural formation, simultaneously critiqued them from a different ideological standpoint. Tarchetti's Gothic tales were foreignizing in their appropriation of foreign texts that deviated from Italian cultural values, initiating a reformation of the Italian literary canon that admitted fictional discourses other than realism, whether domestic or foreign. For the English-language translator who would implement a foreignizing method under the regime of fluency Tarchetti's practices show how translation can revise domestic cultural values by casting strategically chosen foreign texts in the dominant language, the standard dialect.

I

Tarchetti's first foreignizing move was his decision to appropriate the fantastic, a foreign discourse opposed to the bourgeois realism that prevailed in Italian fiction. The fantastic proves to be subversive of bourgeois ideology because it negates the formal conventions of realism and the individualistic concept of subjectivity on which they rest. The realist representation of chronological time, three-dimensional space, and personal identity is based on an empiricist epistemology that privileges a single, perceiving subject: the key assumption is that human consciousness is the origin of meaning, knowledge, and action, transcending discursive and ideological determinations (Watt 1957). The unity of time and space in realism points to a unified consciousness, usually a narrator or character taken to be authorial, and this subject-position establishes intelligibility in the narrative, making a specific meaning seem real or true, repressing the fact that it is an illusory effect of discourse, and thus suturing the reading consciousness into an ideological position, an interested ensemble of values, beliefs, and social representations. The truth-effect of realism, the illusion of transparency whereby language disappears and the world or the author seems present, shows that the form itself reproduces the transcendental concept of subjectivity in bourgeois individualism: as Catherine Belsey indicates,

> Through the presentation of an intelligible history which effaces its own status as discourse, classic realism proposes a model in which author and reader are subjects who are the source of shared meanings, the origin of which is mysteriously extra-discursive. [...] This model of intersubjective understanding, of

shared understanding of a text which re-presents the world, is the guarantee not only of the truth of the text but of the reader's existence as an autonomous and knowing subject in a world of knowing subjects. In this way, classic realism constitutes an ideological practice in addressing itself to readers as subjects, interpellating them in order that they freely accept their subjectivity and their subjection.

(Belsey 1980:72, 69)

The fantastic undermines the transcendental subject in realist discourse by creating an uncertainty about the metaphysical status of the narrative. Often this uncertainty is provoked by using the formal conventions of realism to represent a fantastic disorder of time, space, and character and thereby to suspend the reader between two discursive registers, the mimetic and the marvelous. Confronted with the fantastic, the reader experiences what Tzvetan Todorov calls a "hesitation" between natural and supernatural explanations: "The fantastic [...] lasts only as long as a certain hesitation: a hesitation common to reader and character, who must decide whether or not what they perceive derives from 'reality' as it exists in the common opinion" (Todorov 1975:41; cf. Jackson 1981:26–37). The unified consciousness of realism is thus split between opposing alternatives, intelligibility gives way to doubt, and the reader is released from the ideological positioning in the text, invited to perceive that "the common opinion" of reality encodes moral values and serves political interests, that subjectivity is not transcendental but determinate, a site of confused meanings, ideological contradictions, social conflicts. The fantastic explodes the formal conventions of realism in order to reveal their individualistic assumptions; but by introducing an epistemological confusion, a fantastic narrative can also interrogate the ideological positions it puts to work, expose their concealment of various relations of domination, and encourage thinking about social change. In the fantastic, Hélène Cixous observes, "the subject flounders in the exploded multiplicity of its states, shattering the homogeneity of the ego of unawareness, spreading out in every possible direction, into every possible contradiction, transegoistically"; and it is this discursive strategy that distinguishes nineteenth-century writers like Hoffmann as opponents of "logocentrism, idealism, theologism, all the props of society, the scaffolding of political and subjective economy, the pillars of society" (Cixous 1974:389).

Tarchetti's thinking on the relations between fictional discourse and ideology can be glimpsed in an essay from the very start of his career, "Idee minime sul romanzo" ("Minimum Ideas on the Novel"), published in the periodical *Rivista minima* on 31 October 1865. This early statement shows him slipping uneasily between various positions, advocating different kinds of fictional discourse, assuming different concepts of subjectivity, imagining different forms of social organization. He initially asserts a realist view of the novel, likening it to history:

> Dalle prime confidenze, dalle prime rivelazioni che gli uomini fecero agli uomini, dal primo affetto, dal primo dolore, dalla prima speranza, nacque il romanzo che è la storia del cuore umano e della famiglia, come la storia propriamente detta è il romanzo della società e della vita pubblica.

> From the first confidences, from the first revelations men make to men, from the first emotion, the first pain, the first hope, is born the novel, which is the history of the human heart and the family, just as history is properly called the novel of society and public life.
>
> (Tarchetti 1967, II:523)

But then Tarchetti proceeds to argue for the priority of fictional over historical representation by putting the truth-effect of realism into question, characterizing the novel as an imaginary resolution to social contradictions, a genre that fictively compensates for the "terribile odissea di delitti" ("terrible odyssey of crimes") in history and makes possible a renewal of social life:

> ebbi tra le mani un romanzo, e per poco io fui tentato di riconciliarmi [agli uomini]; non dirò quanto mi apparissero diversi da quelli conosciuti nelle storie, non accennerò a quel mondo meraviglioso che mi si aperse allo sguardo: nel romanzo conobbi l'uomo libero, nella storia aveva conosciuto l'uomo sottoposto all'uomo.

> I held a novel in my hands, and in a little while I was tempted to reconcile myself [to men]; I shall not say how different they appeared to me from those I encountered in histories, I shall not note the marvelous world that opened to me at a glance: in

the novel I knew man free, in history I knew man subjected to man.

(ibid.)

Discourse produces concrete social effects; the novel can alter subjectivity and motor social change, even for a literary bohemian like Tarchetti, whose *scapigliato* refusal to conform to the canons of bourgeois respectability situated him in the margins of Italian society. For the novel to have this social function, however, it would seem that realism must be rejected: a realist discourse like history can represent social life only as an "odyssey," a wandering, an atomization in which agents victimize one another; the novel can contribute to a social homecoming, the reconstruction of a collective, only by representing a "marvelous world" wherein hierarchical social relations are resolved.

Tarchetti's distinction between the freedom of the novel and the subjection of history at first appears a romantic retreat from society to culture, a transcendental aesthetic realm where the subject can regain its self-possession, its autonomy, although at the expense of a withdrawal from political engagement.[2] Tarchetti does in fact revert to romantic expressive theory at various points in the essay, validating an individualistic program of authorial self-expression, transparent discourse, illusionistic response: he favors writers whose

vita intima [...] rimane in un'armonia così perfetta colle loro opere, che il lettore non è tentato di dire a se stesso: la mia commozione è intempestiva, quell'uomo scriveva per ragionamento; buttiamo il libro che non nacque che dall'ingegno.

inner life [...] remains in such perfect harmony with their works, that the reader is not tempted to say to himself: my emotion is inappropriate, that man wrote to argue a position; we toss away any book that issues only from ingenuity.

(Tarchetti 1967, II:531)

At other points, however, Tarchetti views the novel not as a window onto the author, "le onde trasparenti di quei laghi che nella loro calma lasciano scorgere il letto che le contiene"/"the transparent waves of those lakes which in their calmness allow a glimpse of the bed containing them" (ibid.), but rather as a historically specific "forma di letteratura"/"form of literature" (ibid.:522), a genre of literary discourse with a social significance that exceeds authorial psychology:

> L'Italia composta di tanti piccoli stati, diversi tutti per leggi, per usi, per dialetto, per abitudini sociali, e direi quasi per suolo, doveva creare dei grandi e svariatissimi romanzi.

> Italy, composed of many small states, with entirely different laws, customs, dialects, social practices, and I dare say, soils, should create great and extremely varied novels.

> (ibid.:526)

And when Tarchetti describes the value of a long tradition in the novel, he assumes that fictional discourse can never be free of social determinations:

> Se il romanzo fosse così antico quanto la storia, e avesse avuto in tutti i tempi e in tutte le nazioni quella popolarità di cui ora fruisce in Europa, quante tenebre sarebbero diradate, quanta luce sarebbe fatta sopra molti punti ignorati, sopra le arti, le costumanze, le leggi e le abitudini e la vita domestica di molti popoli, cui la storia non si riferisce che per i rapporti politici con altri popoli. Quale felicità, quale esuberanza di vita morale nel rivivere in un passato così remoto, quanti insegnamenti per l'età presente, quale sviluppo nelle nostre facoltà immaginative, e direi quasi quante illusioni nella potenza della nostra fede e delle nostre memorie, e quale rassegnazione maggiore nel nostro destino! S'egli è vero che l'umanità progredisca lentamente, ma in modo sicura, e che nulla possa arrestare e far retrocedere il genio nel suo cammino, i nostri posteri, fra migliaia di anni, vivranno moralmente della nostra vita attuale: le lettere avranno raggiunto per essi quello scopo sublime e generale, che è di moltiplicare ed accrescere ed invigorire nello spirito quelle mille ed infinite sensazioni per le quali si manifesta il sentimento gigantesco della vita.

> If the novel were as ancient as history, and at all times and in all nations had the popularity which it now enjoys in Europe, how many shadows would have been cleared away, how much light would have been cast on many neglected points, on the arts, the customs, the laws and habits and domestic life of many countries whose history refers only to political relations with other countries. What happiness there would be, what exuberance of

moral life in reliving such a remote past, what lessons for the present age, what development of our imaginative faculties, and I dare say how many illusions in the power of our faith and our memories, and what greater resignation to our fate! If it is true that humanity progresses slowly, but steadily, and that nothing can stop or drive genius backward in its path, our posterity, in thousands of years, will live our current moral life: for them letters will have reached that sublime and general goal, which is to multiply and increase and invigorate in the spirit the thousands and infinite sensations by which the gigantic senti-ment of life is manifested.

(ibid.: 523–4)

The beginning of this remarkably discontinuous passage has Tarchetti optimistically treating fictional discourse as a liberating source of knowledge and utopian imagining, assuming a liberal humanism in which the novel restores to subjectivity its freedom and unity ("development of our imaginative faculties"). Yet Tar-chetti's sudden reference to "illusions" sceptically revises this view: the novel now becomes a source of collective mystifications ("illusions in the power of our faith and our memories") and imaginary compensations for frustrated desire ("greater resigna-tion to our fate"), whereby the passage shifts to the assumption that subjectivity is always situated in transindividual conditions of which it can never be fully conscious or free. In the end, the "progresses" of "humanity" seem measured not by a liberal model of social life which guarantees personal identity and autonomy, but a demo-cratic collective characterized by subjective difference and cultural heterogeneity ("the gigantic sentiment of life"). Hence, the "let-ters" which represent and sustain this democracy aim "to multiply and increase and invigorate in the spirit [...] thousands and infinite sensations." The kind of fictional discourse suggested by this aim seems less a panoramic representation of social groups which adheres to the unities of realism, than a social delirium which proliferates psychological states and confounds temporal and spatial coordinates, representing that "marvelous world" where the reader is freed from social isolation.

In evaluating the current situation of the Italian novel, Tarch-etti's constant theme is the moral and political failure of realism. He laments Italy's lack of a strong tradition in the novel in contrast to other countries. Amid much praise for English, American,

German and French writers, Manzoni is degraded as second-rate:

> Non vi ha luogo a dubitare che *I promessi sposi* sieno finora il migliore romanzo italiano, ma non occorre dimostrare come esso non sia che un mediocre romanzo in confronto dei capolavori delle altre nazioni.

> There is no room to doubt that *I promessi sposi* has so far been the best Italian novel, but it is unnecessary to demonstrate that it is a mediocre novel compared to the masterpieces of other nations.

(Tarchetti 1967, II: 528)

Tarchetti repeats a list of defects in Manzoni's novel and attributes them to its realist discourse:

> in quanto all'accusa mossagli da taluno, che in quel libro via sia poco cuore, che quell'eterno episodio (quantunque bellissimo) della monaca, nuoccia più che altro al romanzo, e desti nel lettore tanto interesse senza appagarlo, che quel Don Abbondio si faccia piu disprezzare per la sua viltà che amare per l'amenità del suo carattere, che quel Renzo e quella Lucia sieno due amanti terribilmente apati e freddi, giova in parte osservare che il Manzoni volle dipingere gli uomini quali sono, non quali dovrebbero essere, e in ciò fu scrittore profondo e accurato.

> As for the charge moved by someone, that the book contains little heart, that the eternal episode of the nun (although very beautiful) damages the novel more than anything else, and arouses in the reader such interest as is not satisfied, that Don Abbondio becomes more disparaged for his cowardice than loved for the agreeableness of his character, that Renzo and Lucia are two terribly apathetic and cold lovers, it is worth in part observing that Manzoni wanted to paint men as they are, not as they should be, and in that he was a profound and accurate writer.

(ibid.:528-9)

Tarchetti's laconic defense comes off weakly against his detailed statement of the charge, and realism appears very unattractive indeed: it is incapable of representing extreme emotional states and contains ideological contradictions in its representation of the priest Don Abbondio which are symptomatic of its Christian conservatism and bourgeois sentimentality.

Tarchetti recognizes that the canonization of *I promessi sposi* and the numerous translations of contemporary French novels made realism the dominant fictional discourse in Italy, but he concludes that Italian culture is suffering from a "decadenza" ("decadence") partly maintained by the translation patterns of Italian publishers (Tarchetti 1967, II:535). He argues that the French novels

> che vengono tradotti e pubblicati dai nostri editori, sono generalmente tali libri che godono di nessuna o pochissima reputazione in Francia [e] tranne alcune poche eccezioni, la loro speculazione si è tuttor rivolta alla diffusione di romanzi osceni.

> which are translated and issued by our publishers, are generally such books as enjoy no or little reputation in France [and] with very few exceptions, their investment is always aimed at the circulation of obscene novels.

> (ibid.:532)

Tarchetti singles out French novelists like the prolific Charles-Paul de Kock (1794–1871), whose sentimental, titillating realism enjoyed enormous popularity in Italy. Italian translations of over sixty novels by de Kock were published between 1840 and 1865, bearing titles like *La moglie, il marito e l'amante* (*The Wife, The Husband and The Lover*, 1853) and *Il cornuto* (*The Cuckold*, 1854); some of these novels appeared in different translations a few years apart from various publishers, showing that the Italian publishing industry was scrambling to exploit de Kock's marketability (Costa and Vigini 1991). Tarchetti was most concerned about the social and political implications of these cultural developments, which he finally brands retrograde:

> Non si voglia dimenticare che l'Italia, unica al mondo, possiede una guida per le case di tolleranza, che i nostri romanzi licenziosi sono riprodotti e popolari anche in Francia, che gli uomini che li scrissero godono di tutti i diritti civili e dell'ammirazione pubblica, e che apparatengono in gran parte alla stampa periodica [mentre] ogni scritto politico avverso ai principi del governo, ma conforme a quelli dell'umanità e del progresso, è tosto impedito nella sua diffusione.

> It must not be forgotten that Italy, unique in the world, possesses a guide to brothels, that our licentious novels are reproduced

and popular in France as well, that the men who write them enjoy every civil right and public admiration, and belong for the most part to the periodical press [whereas] the circulation of every political text opposed to the principles of the government, but consistent with those of humanity and progress, is immediately obstructed.

(Tarchetti 1967, II:534–5)

Tarchetti's experiments with the fantastic can be seen as an intervention into this cultural situation: they were developed to resolve the crisis he diagnosed in Italian fictional discourse, the inadequacy of realism to serve a democratic cultural politics. The fantastic answered Tarchetti's call for a fiction to represent that "marvelous world" of "sensations" which he saw as a remedy for hierarchical social relations and his own social isolation; the freeing of subjectivity in fantastic discourse was a freedom from subjection. Because, in Tarchetti's view, realism dominated Italian fiction to no politically progressive end, his intervention took the form of writing in a foreign genre opposed to realism, the Gothic tale. Tarchetti's effort to write against the Manzonian grain in fact projected a revision of the history of fiction, in which the novel didn't originate in Europe, but in "l'oriente da cui si diffuse dapprima la civiltà per tutto il mondo"/"the Orient, from which civilization spread through all the world" (Tarchetti 1967, II:524). The prototype of the novel became, not epic or any form of realist discourse, but fantasy, and not the Bible or the *Iliad,* but *The Arabian Nights*:

I Persiani e gli Arabi attinsero dalla varietà della loro vita nomade, e dalla loro vergine natura, e dal loro cielo infuocato le prime narrazioni romanzesche, onde le leggi e le abitudini di comunanza sociale e domestica degli Arabi ci sono note e famigliari da gran tempo, e Strabone si doleva che l'amore del meraviglioso rendesse incerte le storie di queste nazioni.

The Persians and the Arabs drew from the variety of their nomad life, and from their virgin nature, and from their burning sky the first novelistic narratives, hence the laws and customs of the Arabs' social and domestic community have been well-known and familiar to us for a long time, and Strabo lamented that love for the marvelous rendered uncertain the histories of these nations.

(ibid.)

Tarchetti's Orientalist literary history clarifies the political agenda in his use of the fantastic, but simultaneously discloses an ideological contradiction which runs counter to that agenda. The passage shows him actively rewriting his cultural materials so as to transform the Orient into a vehicle for his democratic social vision. Whereas the Arabian tales actually offer glimpses of despotic monarchies, and the geographer Strabo describes the nomadic Arabs as "a tribe of brigands and shepherds" who are less "civilised" than the Syrians because their "government" is not as well "organised" (Strabo 1930:VII, 233, 255), Tarchetti drew on Rousseau's notion of natural human innocence and perceived only a utopian "comunanza," a community or fellowship, close to "virgin nature" and not corrupted by the hierarchical social organization of Europe. Tarchetti also represented the Orient as exotic and phantasmagorical ("their burning sky," "love for the marvelous"), setting his concept of fiction apart from the realist discourse that dominated Italy by identifying with its other, the fantastic. Both these representations of the Orient, however, are clearly Eurocentric: they aim to make Persia and Arabia perform a European function, the regeneration of Italian fiction and society, and they never escape the racist opposition between Western rationality and Eastern irrationality. Tarchetti's literary history assumed the range of meanings which, as Edward Said has observed, were typical of romantic representations of the Orient: "sensuality, promise, terror, sublimity, idyllic pleasure, intense energy" (Said 1978:118).

This racial ideology, obviously in conflict with Tarchetti's democratic politics, becomes more explicitly damaging to his project in his closing reference to Strabo, which abruptly reverses the logic of his argument. Tarchetti initially treated Arabian narratives as a mirror of the Arabian social order, a reliable representation of its "laws and customs," but he concluded in apparent agreement with Strabo's complaint that these texts reflect little more than an overheated imagination. Tarchetti's typically romantic Orientalism seems to result in an uncritical acceptance of Strabo's equation of the East with "love for the marvelous." Yet Strabo's point that the "histories" of Eastern countries lack a firm basis in reality renders "uncertain," not only Arabian narratives, but the democratic images that Tarchetti found in them, questioning his earlier treatment of the novel as figuring a "marvelous world" without social hierarchies. Tarchetti's citation of Strabo suggests that the utopian world of the novel may be no more than a misrepresentation of its social situation, especially in the case of the Eastern prototypes of the genre. It is worth noting that Tarchetti in effect reiterated this view at the end of his brief tale, "La fortuna di capitano Gubart" ("Captain Gubart's Fortune"), published the same year as his essay on the novel. After demonstrating the arbitrariness of class distinctions by relating how a poor street musician is mistakenly awarded a royal military commission, the narrator concluded: "Questo fatto comunque abbia una decisa analogia con quelli famosi delle novelle arabe, è incontrastabilmente vero e conosciuto"/"This incident, despite its decided resemblance to those famous ones of the Arabian tales, is indisputably true and well-known" (Tarchetti 1967, I:79). This reference to *The Arabian Nights* seems designed to satirize Italian social relations as fantastic and therefore irrational, but it can make this satiric point only by assuming the irrationality of Eastern culture and by distinguishing Tarchetti's narrative as "true." Tarchetti sought to enlist foreign fantastic texts in the democratic cultural politics he conducted in Italy, but his Orientalism was implicated in the key binary opposition by which Europe subordinated, and justified its colonization of, the same foreign countries whose texts he considered politically useful.

Given the diverse linguistic, cultural, and ideological materials that constituted Tarchetti's project, it can be seen as what Gilles Deleuze and Félix Guattari call a minor utilization of a major language:

> Even when it is unique a language remains a mixture, a schizophrenic mélange, a Harlequin costume in which very different functions of language and distinct centers of power are played out, blurring what can be said and what can't be said; one function will be played off against the other, all the degrees of territoriality and relative deterritorialization will be played out. Even when major, a language is open to an intensive utilization that makes it take flight along creative lines of escape which, no matter how slowly, no matter how cautiously, can now form an absolute deterritorialization.
>
> (Deleuze and Guattari 1986:26)

The major language that Tarchetti confronted was the Tuscan dialect of Italian, the linguistic standard for Italian literature since the Renaissance. In 1840, after more than a decade of research into the question of a national language, Manzoni published an extensive revision of the first version of *I promessi sposi* which recast it in the Tuscan dialect, undertaking the nationalistic project of unifying Italy through its language and literature, at once situating his text in the Italian literary canon and establishing a linguistic model for fiction which could be understood by most Italian readers (Reynolds 1950). Because Tarchetti's fantastic narratives were written in the Tuscan dialect, they took the major language on a line of escape that deterritorialized the dominant fictional discourse. He used the Italian literary standard to produce Gothic tales, a genre that was not merely marginal in relation to realism, but that existed in Italian culture primarily as sporadic translations of a few foreign writers, namely Hoffmann, Poe, and Adelbert von Chamisso.[3] Traced with German, English, French, even Arabic texts, Tarchetti's tales foregrounded what realism repressed, the discursive and ideological determinations of subjectivity. In his foreign-derived, fantastic narratives, the standard dialect was turned into a political arena where the bourgeois individualism of realist discourse was contested in order to interrogate various class, gender, and racial ideologies. Nevertheless, Tarchetti's Orientalism shows that he did not have his cultural politics entirely under control: his interrogations were democratically directed, but they sometimes repressed the ideological contradictions precipitated by their own materials and methods of appropriating them.

II

Methods of cultural appropriation like translation would clearly be useful to Tarchetti's project of putting the major language to minor uses. And the deterritorializing effect of this project would clearly make his translations foreignizing in their impact on dominant cultural values in Italian. His most intensive utilization of the standard dialect did in fact occur in his translation of a foreign fantastic narrative, an English Gothic tale written by Mary Wollstonecraft Shelley. The political significance of Tarchetti's translation, however, is complicated by the fact that it is a plagiarism of the English text.

In 1865, Tarchetti published a tale entitled "Il mortale immortale (dall'inglese)" ("The Immortal Mortal (From the English)") in the *Rivista minima* in two installments, on 21 June and 31 August. The first installment was unsigned; the second bore his name. These appearances indicate Tarchetti's authorship, and so Italian readers have always assumed, none venturing beyond the supposition that he adapted the fantastic motif of his tale, the elixir of immortality, from two French texts. What Tarchetti actually published, however, is his Italian translation of Shelley's tale "The Mortal Immortal," which was first published in the English literary annual *The Keepsake* in 1833. In 1868, Tarchetti had another opportunity to acknowledge his translation, but he did not: while serving as the editor of the periodical *Emporio pittoresco*, he reprinted it under his name with a different title, "L'elixir dell'immortalità (imitazione dall'inglese)" ("The Elixir of Immortality (An Imitation from the English)").

Tarchetti's use of parenthetical subtitles ("From the English," "An Imitation from the English") appears to glance at the actual nature of his text, but this is misleading: they offer only the vaguest indication of the relationship between his Italian version and Shelley's tale. Tarchetti did introduce some significant changes: he altered a date, used different names for two main characters, omitted a few phrases and sentences, and added some of his own, all of which amount to a strong transformation of the English text. Nevertheless, in sentence after sentence, paragraph after paragraph, his Italian version is governed by the aim of reproduction: it adheres so closely to the syntactical and lexical features of Shelley's English as to be less an "imitation" than an interlingual translation. By failing to acknowledge his text as a translation, Tarchetti asserted his authorship of Shelley's material and therefore committed plagiarism. And it seems certain that he was fully aware of this fact. In 1865, he began a brief but intense period of activity in the burgeoning Milanese publishing industry, first printing his short fiction and serializing his novels in the periodical press, and then issuing them in book form with several large publishers. He was also employed to write book-length translations. In 1869, he published his Italian versions of two English novels, one of which was Dickens's *Our Mutual Friend* (1865). In both cases, he was credited as the translator.

Tarchetti's financial difficulties no doubt figured into his motives to plagiarize Shelley's tale. The frenzied pace of his writing during the last four years of his life demonstrates that he was producing for immediate publication and payment. A memoir by his friend and collaborator Salvatore Farina shows Tarchetti drifting from one address to another, writing for several periodicals and publishers at once, but constantly poor, shabbily dressed, ill – he died of typhus and tuberculosis. In a letter dated 31 January 1867, Tarchetti complained to Farina about

> le mie solite complicazioni economiche [...] che ho nulla al mondo, che devo pensare da oggi a domani come pranzare, come vestirmi, come ricoverarmi.

> my usual economic complications [...] that I have nothing in the world, that from one day to the next I must find some way to dine, to dress, to house myself.
>
> (Farina 1913:37, 38)

The letter referred to Tarchetti's antimilitaristic novel *Una nobile follia*, which was currently being serialized in the periodical *Il sole* (November 1866 to March 1867): "aspetto sempre la completazione di quei drammi dai quali posso avere un po' di danaro"/ "every day I expect to finish these dramas [from the military life] which should yield me a little money" (ibid.:39).

Farina's memoir suggests a financial motive for Tarchetti's plagiarism by relating an incident in which his knowledge of English becomes the pretext of a fraudulent scheme. Living for some weeks in a hotel in Parma, but unable to pay the bill, Tarchetti "s'improvvisò professore di lingua inglese"/"posed as a professor of English" and

> annunziò per la via delle gazzette e alle cantonate di tutte le vie di Parma che, trovandosi di passaggio in quella città, avrebbe dato un corso completo di quaranta lezioni per insegnare la lingua inglese con un suo metodo spicciativo.

> announced in the newspapers and on every street corner of Parma that since he was travelling through the city, he would give a complete, forty-lesson course in the English language with his rapid method.
>
> (Farina 1913:34, 35)

Farina's rather melodramatic memoir seems to be unduly minimizing Tarchetti's proficiency in English by limiting it to "pochissimo, appena il tanto da intendere alla meglio Shakespeare e Byron e tradurre ad orecchio Dyckens"/"very little, just enough to attain a rudimentary understanding of Shakespeare and Byron and to translate Dickens by ear" (ibid.:34). Tarchetti's translation of Shelley's tale confirms, on the contrary, that he had an excellent reading knowledge of English. All the same, this does not necessarily disprove Farina's assertion that "non parlava inglese affatto e sarebbe stato imbarazzato a sostenere una conversazione"/"he did not speak English at all and would have been embarrassed to sustain a conversation" (ibid.). Farina notes that the registration for the course netted "una retata magnifica"/"a magnificent haul" (ibid.:35), but Tarchetti gave much fewer than forty lessons:

> quando il professore non seppe più che cosa insegnare ai suoi scolari, lessero insieme Shakespeare e Byron e fumarono le sigarette che Iginio preparava sul tavolino all'ora della lezione.

> when the professor no longer knew what to teach his pupils, together they read Shakespeare and Byron and smoked the cigarettes Iginio put out on the desk when the lesson began.
>
> (ibid.:36)

This teaching scam was probably more profitable than Tarchetti's plagiarism. Yet since translation was poorly remunerated in nineteenth-century Italy, with payment usually taking the form of books as well as money, his implicit claim that his text was his creation would have earned him a higher fee than if he had published it as a translation (Berengo 1980:340–346). A financial motive may also explain the curious retitling and reprinting of the text when he took over the editorship of the *Emporio pittoresco*. The different title and his signature claimed that it was his original tale being published for the first time.

Because the legal status of translation was just beginning to be defined in 1865, Tarchetti's plagiarism did not in fact constitute a copyright infringement which resulted in a financial loss for Shelley's estate and her English publisher. By the early nineteenth century, many countries had developed copyright statutes which gave the author exclusive control over the reproduction of her text for life and beyond. But international copyright conventions were slow to emerge, and translation rights were not always reserved for the author. In 1853, for example, a federal court in the United States held that a German translation of *Uncle Tom's Cabin* (1852) which had not been licensed by Harriet Beecher Stowe did not infringe her copyright for the English-language text (Kaplan 1967:29). Although England instituted the first important copyright statute at the beginning of the eighteenth century, in 1851, the year of Shelley's death, English law did not give the author translation rights. It was not until 1852 that the right of authors to license translations of their published texts was recognized by statute, which limited it to five years from the date of publication (Sterling and Carpenter 1986:103). A general copyright law was not formulated in Italy until the Unification: on 25 June 1865, four days after Tarchetti published the first installment of his translation as his tale, the Italian government gave authors the right to "publish, reproduce, and translate" their texts, although the translation rights were limited to ten years from the date of publication (Piola-Caselli 1927:22, 24, 26).

Tarchetti's plagiarism was not so much copyright infringement as a violation of the individualistic notion of authorship on which copyright is based. As Martha Woodmansee shows, copyright laws recognize the writer's ownership of a text insofar as he is its author or originator – "that is, insofar as his work is new and original, an intellectual creation which owes its individuality solely and exclusively to him" (Woodmansee 1984:446). This notion of authorship assumes romantic expressive theory: the text is seen as expressing the unique thoughts and feelings of the writer, a free, unified consciousness which is not divided by determinations that exceed and possibly conflict with his intention. The author is assigned the sole and exclusive copyright because his subjectivity is taken to be a metaphysical essence which is present in his text and all its copies, but which transcends any difference or change introduced by formal determinations, like printing and binding, language and genre, and by economic and political conditions, like the publishing industry and government censorship. The very idea of authorial copyright, however, confesses the possibility of change because it is designed to control the form and marketing of the book by licensing reproduction and repressing change that is not authorized. Copyright opens up a contradiction in the individualistic notion of authorship by demonstrating that such law is suspended between metaphysics and materialism, acknowledging the material contingencies of form, the possibility of its difference from the author, but enacting its transparency with the metaphysical assumption of authorial presence.

Tarchetti's plagiarism violated this notion of authorship not by merely copying Shelley's tale, but by translating it. Because his plagiarism was a translation, it introduced a decisive change in the form of the original, specifically in its language; his assertion of authorship simultaneously masked this change and indicated that it was decisive enough to mark the creation of a new text which originated with him. Tarchetti's plagiarism covertly collapsed the distinction that an individualistic notion of authorship draws between author and translator, creator and imitator. Yet because his plagiarism remained undiscovered and unrationalized – at least until today – it continued to support this distinction; it did not reflect or contribute to any revision of nineteenth-century Italian opinion concerning the aesthetic and legal status of translation. All the same, the fact that Tarchetti's plagiarism was covert did not in any way mitigate its violation of authorship – nor its effect as an eminently foreignizing translation practice. Because his Italian translation was a plagiarism, it was especially subversive of bourgeois values in the major language. On the one hand, Tarchetti's text flouted bourgeois propriety and property by fraudulently exploiting the process of literary commodification in the Italian publishing industry; in this way, his plagiarism exemplified the nonconformist tendency of the *scapigliatura* to identify with socially subordinate groups, particularly the worker, the poor, and the criminal, professing a dissident refusal of the dominant by affiliating with the subcultural (Mariani 1967). On the other hand, Tarchetti's text deterritorialized the bourgeois fictional discourse that dominated Italian culture precisely because it was a plagiarism in the standard dialect, because it passed itself off not just as an original Gothic tale, but as one written originally in the Italian of Manzonian realism and therefore foreignizing in its impact on the Italian literary scene.

Yet Shelley's authorship comes back to worry the ideological standpoint of Tarchetti's intervention by raising the issue of gender. To be effective as a subversion of bourgeois values that deterritorialized the Italian literary standard, his text was required to maintain the fiction of his authorship, referring to Shelley's tale only in the vaguest way ("imitation"). At the same time, however, this fiction suppressed an instance of female authorship, so that the theft of Shelley's literary creation had the patriarchal effect of female disempowerment, of limiting a woman's social agency. This would seem to be a consequence which Tarchetti did not anticipate: some of his other fiction explicitly addressed male domination of women and the social construction of gender, whether in the graphic depiction of Paolina's oppression or in the gender dislocations of his fantastic experiments (Caesar 1987). Most importantly, the tale he chose to plagiarize interrogates patriarchal images of male power and female weakness. Grounded in an antifeminist suppression of Shelley's authorship, Tarchetti's plagiarism nonetheless circulated her feminist fictional project in Italian culture. This ideological contradiction is further complicated by the fact that Tarchetti's text is a translation. In order for Shelley's tale to perform its political function in a different culture, it underwent a radical transformation that was simultaneously faithful and abusive, that both reproduced and supplemented the English text. The clearest indication of this uneven relationship appears in the subtle differences introduced by the Italian version: they questioned the class and racial ideologies which informed Shelley's tale.

III

Shelley's "The Mortal Immortal" is a first-person narrative in which an assistant to the sixteenth-century alchemist Cornelius Agrippa laments drinking the elixir of immortality. The opening sentence provokes the distinctive hesitation of the fantastic by citing a date that glanced at the English reader's reality before suddenly establishing an unreal chronology: "July 16, 1833. – This is a memorable anniversary for me; on it I complete my three hundred and twenty-third year!" (Shelley 1976:219). The text aims to suspend the reader between the two registers of fantastic discourse, the mimetic and the marvelous, by representing the circumstances surrounding the assistant's fateful action, particularly his relationship with the woman he loves and ultimately marries. The fantastic premise of immortality leads to a number of satirical exaggerations by which patriarchal gender representations are thrown into confusion.

By assigning the immortality to a male narrator, Shelley's text turns it into a fantastic trope for male power, initiating a critique of patriarchy which resembles Mary Wollstonecraft's. In *A Vindication of the Rights of Woman* (1792), Wollstonecraft argues that the "bodily strength [which] seems to give man a natural superiority over woman [...] is the only solid basis on which the superiority of the sex can be built" (Wollstonecraft 1975:124). Shelley's fantastic narrative questions male physical superiority by setting up the assistant as the unstable position from which the action becomes intelligible. There is doubt about whether he is in fact physically superior. His "story" is framed by the fundamental question, "Am I immortal?" (Shelley 1976:219, 229), and interrupted by several inconclusive meditations on the authenticity and effectiveness of Cornelius's elixir. The value of male physical superiority is unsettled by the assistant's contradictory representation of the alchemical science that may have made him immortal. At first, alchemy is stigmatized as unnatural and heretical. We hear the "report" of the "accident" involving Cornelius's "scholar, who, unawares, raised the foul fiend during his master's absence and was destroyed," with the result that "all his scholars at once deserted him," and "the dark spirits laughed at him for not being able to retain a single mortal in his service" (ibid.:219–220). The assistant seems to accept this association of alchemy with witchcraft: "when Cornelius came and offered me a purse of gold if I would remain under his roof, I felt as if Satan himself tempted me" (ibid.:220). In the midst of this passage, however, he drops the suggestion that the "report" may be "true or false" (ibid.:219); and later in the narrative, after Cornelius dies, this skepticism reappears to exculpate the alchemist – and reinforce the doubt concerning the assistant's immortality:

> I derided the notion that he could command the powers of darkness, and laughed at the superstitious fears with which he was regarded by the vulgar. He was a wise philosopher, but had no acquaintance with any spirits but those clad in flesh and blood.
>
> (ibid.:226)

The uncertainty which Shelley's text generates about male physical superiority is maintained by the characterization of the assistant. He is a weak, vacillating figure, dominated by the woman he loves, at times ridiculous, a most unlikely candidate for immortality. His name is "Winzy," which, as Charles Robinson observes, is related to "winze," the Scottish word for curse, but which also "might suggest that the protagonist of this story is a comic character" (Shelley 1976:390). After listening to his friends' "dire tale" of the "accident," Winzy's reaction to Cornelius's offer of employment is sheer slapstick: "My teeth chattered – my hair stood on end: – I ran off as fast as my trembling knees would permit" (ibid.:220). Winzy's characterization satirizes the ideological basis of patriarchy in biological determinism because his physical superiority is not innate, but an error: he drinks the elixir of immortality only because Cornelius has deceptively told him that it is a philter to cure love. Since part of the comedy in Winzy's character derives from his utter lack of psychological control, the satire also extends to a distinctively bourgeois version of patriarchal ideology, the link between male power and the individualistic concept of the free, unified subject. Winzy's fearful retreat from Cornelius's workshop leaves him with so little presence of mind that he lapses into poverty and must be browbeaten by his love Bertha in order to return to work: "Thus encouraged – shamed by her – led on by love and hope, laughing at my late fears, with quick steps and a light heart, I returned to accept the offers of the alchymist, and was instantly installed in my office" (ibid.:220–221). Because Winzy is so submissive to Bertha, so cowered by the fear of her rejection, he endures her "inconstancy" and can gain the "courage and resolution" to act only when he is deceived that the potion he drinks cures him of his unhappy love (ibid.:221, 224). Winzy never possesses the inner autonomy of male power; he is in fact a man who does not want any power, who by the end of his narrative deeply regrets his longevity.

Shelley's tale follows Wollstonecraft's feminist critique most closely in the characterization of Bertha. Just as Wollstonecraft finds male domination most oppresssive of women in the affluent classes because "the education of the rich tends to render them vain and helpless" (Wollstonecraft 1975:81), so Shelley's text marks an unfortunate change in Bertha when her parents die and she is adopted by "the old lady of the near castle, rich, childless, and solitary" (Shelley 1976:220). Living in the aristocratic splendor of a "marble palace" and "surrounded by silk-clad youths – the rich and gay," Bertha becomes "somewhat of a coquette in manner," and her relationship with the poor Winzy is endangered (ibid.:220–221). Women develop "coquettish arts," Wollstonecraft argues, because they assimilate the patriarchal image of themselves as the passive object of male desire: "only taught to please, women are always on the watch to please, and with true heroic ardour endeavor to gain hearts merely to resign or spurn them when the victory is decided and conspicuous" (Wollstonecraft 1975:115, 147). Hence, Bertha's change is manifested in her devious and perverse manipulation of Winzy:

> Bertha fancied that love and security were enemies, and her pleasure was to divide them in my bosom. [...] She slighted me in a thousand ways, yet would never acknowledge herself to be

in the wrong. She would drive me mad with anger, and then force me to beg her pardon. Sometimes she fancied that I was not sufficiently submissive, and then she had some story of a rival, favoured by her protectress.

(Shelley 1976:221)

As this catalogue of abuse suggests, Shelley's tale satirizes the patriarchal image of woman that shapes Bertha's characterization by transforming it into caricature. The fantastic premise of immortality results in an exaggeration of her vanity: as Winzy remains twenty years old and she becomes a "faded beauty" of fifty, "she sought to decrease the apparent disparity of our ages by a thousand feminine arts – rouge, youthful dress, and assumed juvenility of manner" (ibid.:226, 228). The constant concern with beauty that patriarchy forces on women in Wollstonecraft's critique is magnified into Bertha's ludicrous, maddening obsession: "Her jealousy never slept," Winzy relates,

Her chief occupation was to discover that, in spite of outward appearances, I was myself growing old. [...] She would discern wrinkles in my face and decrepitude in my walk, while I bounded along in youthful vigour, the youngest looking of twenty youths. I never dared address another woman: on one occasion, fancying that the belle of the village regarded me with favouring eyes, she bought me a gray wig.

(ibid.:228)

Unable to maintain her attractive appearance, Bertha even goes so far as to disparage youth and beauty:

she described how much more comely gray hairs were than my chestnut locks; she descanted on the reverence and respect due to age – how preferable to the slight regard paid to children: could I imagine that the despicable gifts of youth and good looks outweighed disgrace, hatred, and scorn?

(ibid.:227)

Tarchetti's "L'elixir dell'immortalità" is a rather close translation which perfectly catches the humor of Shelley's feminist satire, but he also made revisions which go beyond the English text. Some of the revisions suggest a strategy of amplification designed to increase the epistemological confusion of the fantastic for the Italian reader (the italicized words in the Italian quotations below indicate Tarchetti's additions to the English text). Thus, the translation heightens the marvelous register of Shelley's fantastic discourse by adding a strong tendency toward sensationalism. Tarchetti followed the English by initiating the fantastic hesitation in the first sentence, with a date that glanced at the Italian reader's reality, yet he inserted slight changes that intensify the narrator's amazement:

> Dicembre 16, 1867. – È questo per me un anniversario *assai* memorabile. Io compio oggi il mio trecentoventinovesimo anno *di vita.*

> December 16, 1867. – This is a *very* memorable anniversary for me. Today I complete my three hundred and twenty-ninth year *of life.*
>
> (Tarchetti 1967, I:114)

Winzy's first expression of doubt about his physical superiority is the simple question, "Am I, then, immortal?" (Shelley 1976:219), whereas the Italian version resorts to a more emphatic restatement: "*Ma non invecchierò io dunque?* Sono io dunque *realmente* immortale?"/"*But shall I not age, then?* Am I, then, *really* immortal?" (Tarchetti 1967, I:114). Sometimes the amplification produces a melodramatic effect: "belief" and "thought" (226) are inflated into the more stagy "illusione" and "dubbio"/"dream" and "suspicion" (I:126); "sad" (224) is rendered by "pazza"/"mad" (I:124), "fondly" – as in "my Bertha, whom I had loved so fondly" (228) – by "pazzamente"/"madly" (I:129). And sometimes the melodrama tips into the marvelous. When the aged Bertha tries to salve her wounded vanity by telling Winzy that "though I looked so young, there was ruin at work within my frame," the Italian version turns the "ruin" into a preternaturally abrupt process: "quantunque io apparissi così giovane, eravi qualche cosa in me che m'avrebbe fatto *invecchiare repentimente*"/"although I looked so young, there was something in me which would make me age *all of sudden*" (I:130).

At other points, Tarchetti's translation increases the Italian reader's epistemological confusion by strengthening the mimetic register of Shelley's fantastic discourse. The main characters are rechristened Vincenzo and Ortensia, two quite ordinary Italian names which remove the comic improbability suggested by an

immortal called Winzy. Tarchetti's strategy of mimetic amplification works by accumulating verisimilar details and explanations.
When Vincenzo recounts the tragedy of Cornelius's "allievo che
avendo inavvertentemente evocato durante l'assenza del maestro,
uno spirito maligno, ne fu ucciso"/"pupil who having inadvertently
raised a malign spirit in his master's absence was killed by it,"
Tarchetti added another detail to the English passage to make the
incident more plausible: "senza che alcuno avesse potuto soccor-
rerlo"/"before anyone could come to his aid" (I:115). The Italian
version similarly enhances the psychological realism of the English
text. When Winzy and Bertha part after their first falling out, he
tersely states that "we met now after an absence, and she had been
sorely beset while I was away" (220). In the translation, however, the
meeting is much more histrionic, with Vincenzo physically expressing his passion for Ortensia and emphasizing the distress caused by
their separation:

> Io la *riabbracciava* ora dopo un'assenza *assai dolorosa; il bisogno di
> confidenza e di conforti mi aveva ricondotto presso di lei.* La fanciulla
> non aveva sofferto meno di me durante la mia lontananza.

> I embraced her again now after a *very painful* absence; *the need
> for intimacy and comfort led me back to her.* The girl had not suffered
> less than me during my distance.

> (I:117)

Because the translation tends to favor extreme emotional states,
this sort of mimetic amplification easily turns a relatively realistic
English passage into overwrought fantasy. When Winzy fearfully
runs away from the allegedly satanic Cornelius, he turns to Bertha
for consolation: "My failing steps were directed whither for two
years they had every evening been attracted, – a gently bubbling
spring of pure living waters, beside which lingered a dark-haired
girl" (220). The Italian version infuses the landscape and the girl
with Gothic overtones:

> I miei passi si diressero anche quella volta a quel luogo, a cui pel
> giro di due anni erano stati diretti ogni sera, – *un luogo pieno
> d'incanti, una sterminata latitudine di praterie,* con una sorgente
> d'acqua viva che scaturiva gorgogliando *malinconicamente,* e
> presso la quale sedeva *con abbandono* una fanciulla.

> My steps were directed that time as well toward that place,

where for a period of two years they had been directed every evening, – *a place full of enchantments, a boundless expanse of grassland*, with a fountain of living water which gushed with a *melancholy* gurgling, and beside which sat a girl *with abandon*.

(I:116)

Tarchetti's strategy of amplification effectively reproduces Shelley's feminist critique by further exaggerating the patriarchal gender images which shape the characters. When Winzy drinks what he mistakenly assumes is a remedy for his frustrated love of Bertha, he experiences a sudden fit of self-esteem and daring which comically confirms his psychological weakness, thus continuing the satire of male power: "methought my good looks had wonderfully improved. I hurried beyond the precincts of the town, joy in my soul, the beauty of heaven and earth around me" (223). The Italian version turns Vincenzo into a parody of the romantic individual, narcissistic, chest-thumping, Byronic:

parvemi che *i miei occhi, già così ingenui, avessero acquistata una sorprendente espressione*. Mi cacciai fuori del recinto della città colla gioia nell'anima, *con quella orgogliosa soddisfazione che mi dava il pensiero di essere presto vendicato*.

it seemed to me that *my eyes, previously so ingenuous, had acquired a striking expression*. I dashed beyond the city limit with joy in my heart, *with that proud satisfaction which made me think that I would soon be avenged*.

(I:122)

The translation likewise accentuates the caricature of female vanity. Whereas Winzy observes that his youthfulness drove Bertha to find "compensation for her misfortunes in a variety of little ridiculous circumstances" (228), Ortensia is said to revert to "puerili e ridicole circostanze"/"*childish* and ridiculous circumstances" (I:129). And whereas Winzy states that Bertha "would discern wrinkles in my face and decrepitude in my walk" (228), Vincenzo complains that Ortensia "*struggeasi* di scoprire delle grinze sul mio viso, e qualche cosa di *esitante*, di decrepito nel mio incesso"/"was *consumed* with discovering wrinkles in my face, and something *hesitant*, decrepit in my gait" (I:130).

Tarchetti's first decisive departure from the ideological determinations of Shelley's tale occurs on the issue of class. Shelley challenges the patriarchal assumption that gender identity is

biologically fixed by indicating that Bertha's transformation into a
coquette is socially determined, an effect of her upward mobility.
Bertha's class position is evidently bourgeois: "her parents, like
mine," states Winzy, "were of humble life, yet respectable" (220).
This "life" should be seen as bourgeois even though "humble," not
only because it is labelled "respectable," but because it enables
Winzy to be apprenticed to an alchemist with whom he earns "no
insignificant sum of money" (221). Bertha and Winzy are
"humble" in relation to her protectress, who is an aristocrat, a
"lady" living in a feudal "castle." Shelley's tale thus begins by
associating patriarchy with aristocractic domination, sexual equal-
ity with the bourgeois family. This is most clear in a striking
passage which alludes explicitly to Wollstonecraft's treatise. When
Bertha finally leaves her aristocratic protectress and returns to
Winzy's parents, he asserts that she "escaped from a gilt cage to
nature and liberty" (224), echoing one of Wollstonecraft's
metaphors for the self-oppression to which patriarchal ideology
subjects women: "Taught from their infancy that beauty is woman's
sceptre, the mind shapes itself to the body, and roaming round its
gilt cage, only seeks to adore its prison" (Wollstonecraft 1975:131).

As the narrative unfolds, however, the class logic of Shelley's
feminist critique is undone. Although Winzy's attack on the
aristocratic protectress implicitly equates the bourgeois family with
a natural state free of patriarchal gender representations, his own
marriage to Bertha compels her to live them out in an even more
obsessive way. They continue to be financially independent: Winzy
refers to "my farm" (Shelley 1976:227), and although at one point
"poverty had made itself felt" because his perpetual youthfulness
caused them to be "universally shunned," they are nonetheless
able to sell off their "property" and emigrate to France, having
"realised a sum sufficient, at least, to maintain us while Bertha
lived" (ibid.:228). Thus, whether living with their parents or on
their own, after they are married, they continue to lead a "humble
life, yet respectable." But their relationship can hardly be
considered "nature and liberty" for either of them. Bertha
becomes the passive object of Winzy's desire:

> We had no children; we were all in all to each other; and
> though, as she grew older, her vivacious spirit became a little
> allied to ill-temper, and her beauty sadly diminished, I cher-
> ished her in my heart as the mistress I had idolized, the wife I

had sought with such perfect love.

(ibid.:227)

And when Bertha's vanity drives her to ridiculous, alienating extremes, Winzy helplessly acknowledges the gender hierarchy established by his physical superiority: "this mincing, simpering, jealous old woman. I should have revered her gray locks and withered cheeks; but thus! – It was my work, I knew; but I did not the less deplore this type of human weakness" (ibid.:228). Bertha's return to the bourgeoisie ultimately contradicts Winzy's attack on the protectress: their marriage shows that the bourgeois family is not an egalitarian refuge from aristocratic patriarchy, but a continuation of male dominance.

This ideological contradiction lies at the center of Shelley's feminism. As Anne Mellor has argued,

> Mary Shelley was a feminist in the sense that her mother was, in that she advocated an egalitarian marriage and the education of women. But insofar as she endorsed the continued reproduction of the bourgeois family, her feminism is qualified by the ways in which her affirmation of the bourgeois family entails an acceptance of its intrinsic hierarchy, a hierarchy historically manifested in the doctrine of separate spheres [and] in the domination of the male gender.

(Mellor 1988:217)

Shelley's characteristic valorization of marriage emerges in "The Mortal Immortal" primarily because Winzy is the narrator: he makes his love for Bertha and their marriage the positions from which their actions are intelligible, and hence the bourgeois family, with its patriarchal construction of gender, is established as the standard by which they are judged. What the text imposes as true or obvious is that Winzy is the devoted lover and husband, attending to their material needs, controlling their destiny in the public sphere, whereas Bertha controls their private life, compelled by her vanity to trifle with his affection, envy his youthfulness, even threaten their lives. Reasoning that Winzy's unchanging appearance could get them executed "as a dealer in the black art" and his "accomplice[,] at last she insinuated that I must share my secret with her, and bestow on her like benefits to those I myself enjoyed, or she would denounce me – and then she burst into tears" (Shelley 1976:227).

Tarchetti's translation probes the contradictions of Shelley's feminism by subtly revising the ideologies her tale puts to work. The Italian follows the English in having Vincenzo assert that "io divenni marito di Ortensia"/"I became Ortensia's husband" (Tarchetti 1967, I:123), but it repeatedly omits signs of their marriage. When Bertha becomes aware of Winzy's immortality, he renews his conjugal vows to her: "I will be your true, faithful husband while you are spared to me, and do my duty to you to the last" (228). Tarchetti deletes this entire statement. And where Winzy and Bertha address each other with "my poor wife" and "my husband" (227, 228), Vincenzo and Ortensia say "mia buona compagna" and "mio amico"/"my good companion" and "my friend" (I:128). These changes show an effort to weaken, however slightly, the valorization of marriage in Shelley's tale and perhaps reflect a *scapigliato* rejection of bourgeois respectability. Most significantly, Tarchetti's changes locate the very ideological determination which qualifies Shelley's feminist project, and they do so by emphasizing friendship rather than marriage, hinting at the possibility of an equal relationship between the lovers, questioning the gender hierarchy of the bourgeois family.

At the same time, Tarchetti's translation superimposes another class conflict on the English text. This too requires a diminution of Shelley's bourgeois values. The Italian version reproduces all of those passages which point to the main characters' financial independence – except the most explicit one: the description of Vincenzo's and Ortensia's parents deletes "respectable" and emphasizes "humble," clearly suggesting that they are not bourgeois, but members of the working class: "I suoi parenti erano, come i miei, di *assai* umile condizione"/"Her parents were, like mine, of *very* humble rank" (I:116). Ortensia's adoption by the protectress thus figures patriarchy as aristocratic domination of the working class. The Italian version underscores this representation by encoding Ortensia's vain obsessions with aristocratic attitudes. Whereas Bertha, driven by her envy of Winzy's physical appearance to the paradoxical extreme of disparaging beauty, tells him that "gray hairs" are "much more comely," and that "youth and good looks" are "despicable gifts" (227), Ortensia expresses an aristocratic sense of social superiority: the Italian version replaces "comely" with "gentili" ("fair," but also "polite," "noble") and "despicable" with "volgari" ("common," "unrefined") (I: 127, 128). With these changes, Tarchetti's translation forces Shelley's tale to address the hierarchical relationship between the aristocracy and the working class, an instance of class domination which her bourgeois feminism represses.

This pressure in the translation to expose forms of ideological mystification also makes itself felt in deletions which remove the Orientalism from Shelley's tale. Tarchetti omits Winzy's response to Bertha's coquettish behavior: "I was jealous as a Turk" (221). Because any particularly violent or aggressive show of jealousy would be comically inconsistent with Winzy's submissiveness, his assertion can be seen as contributing to the satire of male power built into his characterization. Yet once the feminist significance of the joke is appreciated, the reader is positioned in an another ideology, European Orientalism: the satire becomes intelligible only when the reader thinks that Winzy's jealousy could never possibly be as excessive as a Turk's, i.e., only when the reader assumes the truth of the cliché and thus accepts an ethnic slur, drawing a racist distinction between the West as rational and the East as irrational. Shelley's use of the cliché to support the feminist satire ridicules a gender hierarchy by introducing one based on race.

The absence of this racial ideology from the Italian version might seem insignificant, were it not that Tarchetti omits another, much more complicated Orientalist reference in the English text: an allusion to *The History of Nourjahad*, an Eastern tale written by the eighteenth-century novelist and playwright Frances Sheridan. Near the beginning of Shelley's text, Winzy wistfully cites "fabled" instances of longevity which proved much more tolerable than his:

> I have heard of enchantments, in which the victims were plunged into a deep sleep to wake, after a hundred years, as fresh as ever: I have heard of the Seven Sleepers – thus to be immortal would not be so burthensome; but, oh! the weight of never-ending time – the tedious passage of the still-succeeding hours! How happy was the fabled Nourjahad!
>
> (Shelley 1976:219)

The extremely elliptical quality of this allusion, especially compared to the explanatory statement that precedes the Seven Sleepers, indicates the enormous popularity of Sheridan's character, even as late as 1833, when Shelley was writing her own tale. Published in 1767, a year after Sheridan's death, *The History of Nourjahad* went through at least eleven British editions by 1830, including an illustrated abridgement for children, and it was twice adapted for the stage, first as a "melodramatic spectacle" in 1802, then as a musical production in 1813 (Todd 1985:282–284). Having already published several tales in *The Keepsake*, Shelley knew that Oriental motifs were in vogue among its readers, she seems even to have assumed that the "fabled Nourjahad" was more familiar to them than the rather learned allusion to the Seven Sleepers, and so she needed merely to have her "mortal immortal" drop the character's name to signify immortality punctuated by "deep sleep."[4] Yet, for readers who know *The History of Nourjahad*, the reference is too abrupt and unqualified to stop resonating, so that it constitutes a disturbing point of indeterminancy in Shelley's text, limited only by the cultural and social conditions under which it is read.

Sheridan's Nourjahad is the favorite of the Persian sultan Schemzeddin, who would like to appoint him as "first minister" but must establish that he is worthy, innocent of the faults imputed to him by court advisors: "youth," "avarice," "love of pleasure," and "irreligion" (Weber 1812:693). Schemzeddin tests Nourjahad by asking him what he would like if his every desire could be satisfied, and Nourjahad's response confirms the advisors' suspicions:

> I should desire to be possessed of inexhaustible riches; and, to enable me to enjoy them to the utmost, to have my life prolonged to eternity, [disregarding] hopes of Paradise [in order to] make a paradise of this earthly globe while it lasted, and take my chance for the other afterwards.
>
> (Weber 1812:694)

Nourjahad elicits the sultan's rebuke, and that night he is visited by his "guardian genius" who fulfills his desire for wealth and immortality, although with the proviso that any vice he commits will be "punished by total privation of [his] faculties," lasting "for months, years, nay for a whole revolution of Saturn at a time, or perhaps for a century" (ibid.:695). Nourjahad forgets this punishment, further alienates Schemzeddin by devoting himself to "nothing but giving loose to his appetites" (ibid.:698), and performs three immoral acts which are each punished by long periods of deep sleep. While indulging himself "with an unbounded freedom in his most voluptuous wishes," Nourjahad, "for the first time, got drunk," whereupon he sleeps over four years (ibid.:700); then he invents a "celestial masquerade" in which he orders "the women of his seraglio to personate the houris," while "he himself would needs represent Mahomet; and one of the mistresses whom he loved best [...] Cadiga, the favourite wife of the great prophet," for which "wild and profane idea" he sleeps forty years (ibid.:705); finally, when his "appetites palled with abundance," he begins to delight in "cruelty" and brutally kills Cadiga, thereafter sleeping twenty years (ibid.:710). Upon waking Nourjahad reforms and embarks on a vast program of philanthropy, so profoundly regretting his wealth and immortality that his guardian genius reappears to take them away. It is subsequently revealed that Nourjahad's "adventure [...] was all a deception" (ibid.:719), he did not actually kill Cadiga, he was never wealthy or immortal, and only fourteen months have passed, not more than sixty years. Schemzeddin had invented everything to bring about his favorite's moral reformation.

Shelley's allusion to Sheridan's tale puts into play several themes dense with ideological significance. Nourjahad appears "happy" to Winzy, most obviously, because the burden of his immortality was eased by long periods of sleep and finally removed. Yet given Winzy's relationship to Bertha, Nourjahad would also be enviable because he was finally reunited and married to his beloved Mandana, "a young maid, so exquisitely charming and accomplished, that he gave her the entire possession of his heart" (Weber 1812:698), but was later deceived that she died in childbirth. What distinguished Nourjahad's relationship to Mandana was that he chose her as his confidant – "longing to unbosom himself to one on whose tenderness and fidelity he could rely, to her he disclosed the marvellous story of his destiny" (ibid.) – thereby exemplifying the eighteenth-century rise of companionate marriage, which stressed domestic friendship, a sharing of affection and interests between the spouses, while maintaining the husband's authority (Stone 1977). It was no doubt this antecedent of Shelley's own concept of egalitarian marriage, in addition to the fantastic premise of immortality, that attracted her to Sheridan's tale, especially since it occurs within a narrative that can be read as a critique of patriarchy. For *The History of Nourjahad*, like "The Mortal Immortal," questions a patriarchal gender image: Nourjahad represents male physical superiority pushed to destructive extremes of violence against women. Hence, when Winzy compares himself to Nourjahad, Shelley's text signals that it will address gender differences and offers any reader of *The Keepsake* who could make the comparison and shared Wollstonecraft's thinking a feminist joke at Winzy's expense: the allusion inevitably points to the discrepancy between his cringing weakness and Nourjahad's potent excess, beginning the satire of male power that is Shelley's theme.

Yet whatever feminist design can be detected in Sheridan's tale is finally skewed by the racial and class ideologies that underwrite it. In interrogating patriarchy, *The History of Nourjahad* is clearly overdetermined by Orientalism: it simultaneously demonstrates and rehabilitates the moral inferiority of the East. Nourjahad's characterization involves the racist procedure of naturalizing ethnic stereotypes, grounding them in biology: "he was not of an active temper," "he was naturally choleric" (Weber 1812:698, 700). And although Islam is treated reverentially, with Nourjahad receiving his most severe punishment for blaspheming the Koran, Sheridan's valorization of marriage is linked to an explicit privileging of the West and to a consistent representation of women as the object of male sexual desire – even in the context of companionate marriage. Thus, Mandana's reciprocation of Nour-jahad's love is described as "a felicity very rare among eastern husbands," and she is revealed to be Schemzeddin's gift to his favorite, freed from her status as the sultan's "slave" because she participated in his "contrivance" by impersonating Nourjahad's guardian genius and later joining his seraglio (ibid.:698, 719–720). Insofar as Schemzeddin is responsible for Nourjahad's reformation, moreover, the narrative affirms a specific political institution, a despotic monarchy that relies on paternalistic interventions. The ideological configuration of Sheridan's tale, what can be called an Orientalist image of patriarchal despotism, jars against the bourgeois feminism that can be read out of Shelley's allusion, forcing Winzy's exclamation to precipitate still more contradictions in her project. "How happy was the fabled Nourjahad" – that he lived under a despot who exercised absolute power over his subjects? That he dominated his wife as well as the women in his seraglio? That he was a Persian who overcame his Oriental propensity to vice? These potential meanings would have been accessible to readers of *The Keepsake*: the audience for these expensive giftbooks was largely aristocratic and bourgeois women, politically conservative, accustomed to prose and poetry that was often Orientalist and filled with patriarchal constructions of gender (Faxon 1973:xxi; Altick 1957:362–363).

Although *The History of Nourjahad* enjoyed some popularity on the continent during the late eighteenth century, when it was translated into French, Russian, and Hungarian, it seems unlikely that Tarchetti knew it. His deletion of any reference to Nourjahad from his translation may have been merely due to his ignorance of Sheridan's tale. He certainly did not remove it because he was aware of and opposed Orientalist stereotypes, since the same racial ideology surfaces elsewhere in his writing, even when he tries to formulate a democratic cultural politics for Italian fiction. Whatever Tarchetti's motive may have been, his deletion necessarily affects both the English text and the Italian translation. The mere absence of the allusion at once isolates a node of ideological contradiction in Shelley's text and erases it, allowing the translation to address class and gender domination in Italy without the burden of racism and despotic monarchy. Yet the absence also points to an antifeminist effect in the translation because of the cultural and social functions that every allusion performs. As Susan Stewart has argued,

> the allusive act always bears reference to and creates tradition, [but] it also always bears reference to and creates the situation at hand, articulating the relation between that situation and tradition, and articulating the varying degrees of access available to tradition[,] levels of readership, levels of accessibility to knowledge.
>
> (Stewart 1980:1146, 1151)

Shelley's allusion to Sheridan's tale not only announces her own project as a feminist critique of patriarchy, but implicitly constructs a tradition of female authorship and feminist ideological critique, even as the revelation of that tradition conceals its contradictory ideological conditions in both writers' texts. Shelley's allusion, furthermore, makes the tradition available to the socially prominent women who read *The Keepsake* and were singled out by Wollstonecraft as most oppressed by patriarchy. Tarchetti's deletion quashes this act of feminist traditionalization, entirely blocking the Italian reader's access to the tradition it constructs.

IV

Tarchetti's translation sets up two discontinuous relationships, one with Shelley's tale, the other with Italian culture, which can best be understood with Philip Lewis's concept of abusive fidelity. In this sort of translation, Lewis states, the translator focuses on the "abuses" of the source-language text, "points or passages that are in some sense forced, that stand out as clusters of textual energy," and attempts to reproduce their abusive quality in the target-language culture (Lewis 1985:43). The translator's attempt at reproduction, however, simultaneously supplements the source-language text in an interrogative way. This concept of fidelity in translation is abusive because it performs what Lewis calls

> a dual function – on the one hand, that of forcing the linguistic and conceptual system of which it is a dependent, and on the other hand, of directing a critical thrust back toward the text that it translates and in relation to which it becomes a kind of unsettling aftermath (it is as if the translation sought to occupy the original's already unsettled home, and thereby, far from 'domesticating' it, to turn it into a place still more foreign to itself).
>
> (ibid.)

Lewis seems to regard abusive fidelity as a strategic choice, at least partly within the translator's control ("partly" because the choices are contingent, varying from one source-language text to another, from one target-language culture to another). Yet the foregoing treatment of Tarchetti's translation requires a revision of Lewis's concept to include translation choices that remain unarticulated and unconscious, and that therefore can support an effect exceeding the translator's intention. Any of the translator's moves, in other words, may both reproduce and supplement the source-language text.

Tarchetti's translation, with its formal techniques of marvelous and mimetic amplification, reproduces the key abuse in Shelley's feminist fictional project, her use of the fantastic to dislocate patriarchal gender representations; and because his translation is a plagiarism written in the standard Italian dialect, it deterritorializes the dominant realist discourse in Italy, where it conducts an ideological cultural practice which is radically democratic, which combats class (aristocratic and bourgeois), gender (patriarchal), and racial (Orientalist) ideologies. Tarchetti's translation moves are such that they exhibit this political agenda even in instances (e.g. the removal of Shelley's Orientalism) where they seem to be uncalculated, or at least to lack a political calculation.

The abusiveness of Tarchetti's translation does not stop with the target-language culture, for it also enacts an "unsettling" ideological critique of Shelley's tale, exposing the political limitations of her feminism, its failure to recognize the gender hierarchy in the bourgeois marriage and its concealment of working-class oppression and European racism. The paradox of Tarchetti's translation strategy is that its abuses issue mostly from its manifold fidelities – to the standard Italian dialect, but not the dominant realism; to the syntactical and lexical features, fantastic discourse, and feminist ideology of the English text, but not its bourgeois values and Orientalism. These lacks in Tarchetti's translation are supplied by another fidelity, to a democratic cultural politics.

More specifically, the attention to class in Tarchetti's translation provides one example of how his use of the fantastic was designed to confront class divisions that were altered but nonetheless maintained after the Italian Unification. This social transformation was ultimately liberalizing, not democratizing: it freed markets from regional restrictions and encouraged the development of professional, manufacturing, and mercantile interests, particularly in the north, yet without markedly improving the lives of the agrarian and industrial workers who composed the largest segment of the population. On the contrary, the economic reorganization, instead of weakening workers' dependence on landowners and employers, added the uncertainties of market conditions, of higher prices and taxes. And the institution of a national government with a standing army faced workers with conscription, while their widespread illiteracy hindered their participation in the political process (Smith 1969). Tarchetti's translation, like his other fantastic tales, intervenes into these social contradictions, not only by criticizing aristocratic and bourgeois domination of the working classes, but by adopting a fictional discourse that overturns the bourgeois assumptions of realism. He made this intervention, moreover, in the highly politicized cultural formation of the 1860s, publishing his tales in Milanese periodicals that were closely allied to the most progressive, democratic groups and thus reaching the northern bourgeoisie who stood to benefit most from the economic and political changes in post-Unification Italy (Portinari 1989:232–240; Castronovo *et al.* 1979).

Yet Tarchetti's reliance on plagiarism to forward his political agenda, as well as his deletion of a literary allusion he probably did not understand, gives a final twist to Lewis's concept of abusive fidelity in translation. Both moves show that the source-language text can cause "a kind of unsettling aftermath" in the target-language text, indicating points where the latter is "foreign" to its own project or where it conflicts with the translator's intention. As soon as Tarchetti's theft is known and his deletion located, Shelley's tale enacts an ideological critique of his translation which reveals that he imported her feminist fiction into Italy with some violence, suppressing her authorship and her construction of a feminist literary tradition. The antifeminist effects of Tarchetti's text constitute an egregious reminder that translation, like every cultural practice, functions under conditions that may to some extent be unacknowledged, but that nonetheless complicate and perhaps compromise the translator's activity – even when it aims to make a strategic political intervention.

For the contemporary English-language translator who seeks forms of resistance against the regime of fluent domestication, Tarchetti exemplifies a foreignizing translation practice that operates on two levels, that of the signified as well as the signifier. His discursive strategy deviated from the dominant realism by releasing the play of the signifier: he amplified the discursive registers of Shelley's fantastic narrative, both mimetic and marvelous, and thus forced an uncertainty over the metaphysical status of the representation (is the elixir "real" or not?), preempting the illusion of transparency. Yet Tarchetti's plagiarism also produced the illusion of his authorship: he effaced the second-order status of his translation by presenting it as the first Gothic tale written in the Italian of the dominant realist discourse, establishing his identity as an oppositional writer, fixing the meaning of his text as dissident. Like the contemporary writer of fluent English-language translations, Tarchetti was invisible to his readers as a *translator*. Yet this very invisibility enabled him to conduct a foreignizing translation practice in his Italian situation because he was visible as an *author*.

Tarchetti's translation practices cannot be imitated today without significant revision. Plagiarism, for example, is largely excluded by copyright laws that bind translators as well as authors, resulting in contracts designed to insure that the translation is in fact a translation, and that it does not involve the unlicensed use of any copyrighted material. Here is a sampling of standard clauses from recent translation contracts,[5] including those wherein the translator is termed the "author" of the translation:

You warrant that your work will be original and that it does not infringe upon the copyright or violate the right of any person or party whatsoever, and you agree to indemnify and hold us and any licensee or seller of the Work harmless against any damages sustained in any claim, action, proceeding or recovery based on an alleged violation of any of the foregoing warranties.

The Author warrants that he has full power to make this agreement; that the Work has not previously been published in book form in the English language; that all rights conveyed to the Publisher hereunder are free of encumbrances or prior agreements; that the Work does not violate any copyright in any way. The Author will hold harmless and defend the Publisher and its licensees against all claims, demands or suits related to these warranties. The Author will compensate the Publisher [...]

Author warrants that he is the sole author of the Work; that he is the sole owner of all the rights granted to the Publisher [...] Author shall hold harmless Publisher, any seller of the Work, and any licensee subsidiary right in the Work, against any damages finally sustained.

The shrewdness and sheer audacity of Tarchetti's plagiarism may make it attractive to dissidents in Anglo-American literary culture – especially dissident translators interested in upsetting current practices in the publishing industry. Yet the fact remains that to publish an unauthorized translation of a copyrighted foreign text is to invite legal proceedings whose cost will far exceed the translator's income from even a bestselling translation.

What the contemporary English-language translator can learn from Tarchetti is not how to plagiarize a foreign text, but how to choose one to translate. Tarchetti shows that foreignizing translation takes the form, not just of deviant translation strategies, but also of foreign texts that deviate from dominant literary canons in the target-language culture. Tarchetti's choice to translate Shelley's Gothic tale was foreignizing in its introduction of a fictional discourse that challenged the dominant realism, and his translation, along with the few other Italian translations of foreign fantasies that had already been published, initiated a change in literary taste that culminated in a significant canon reformation. Other members of the *scapigliatura*, notably Arrigo and Camillo

Boito and Emilio Praga, published Gothic tales in the 1860s, and Italian translations of foreign writers like Poe, Gautier, and Erckmann-Chatrian increased rapidly during the remainder of the nineteenth century. Hoffmann's tales, for example, appeared in eight different Italian editions between 1877 and 1898 (Costa and Vigini 1991; Rossi 1959). It is partly as a result of these trends that the fantastic became a dominant genre in twentieth-century Italian fiction, modernist as well as postmodernist, inspiring such diverse canonical writers as Luigi Pirandello, Massimo Bontempelli, Dino Buzzati, Tommaso Landolfi, and Italo Calvino (Bonifazi 1971 and 1982). The lesson Tarchetti teaches the dissident English-language translator is that the choice of a foreign text for translation can be just as foreignizing in its impact on the target-language culture as the invention of a discursive strategy. At a time when deviations from fluency may limit the circulation of a translation or even prevent it from getting published in the first place, Tarchetti points to the strategic value of discriminating carefully among foreign texts and literatures when a translation project is developed.

Chapter 5

Margin

> The translation of a poem having any depth ends by being one of two things: Either it is the expression of the translator, virtually a new poem, or it is as it were a photograph, as exact as possible, of one side of the statue.
>
> Ezra Pound

The dominance of transparent discourse in English-language translation was decisively challenged at the turn of the twentieth century, when modernism emerged in Anglo-American literary culture. The experimentation that characterized the literature of this period brought with it new translation strategies that avoided fluency by cultivating extremely heterogeneous discourses, principally in poetry translations, but also more widely in poetic composition. Translation now became a key practice in modernist poetics, motivating appropriations of various archaic and foreign poetries to serve modernist cultural agendas in English (see, for example, Hooley 1988). At the same time, English-language translation theory attained a new level of critical sophistication, summoned as it was to rationalize specific modernist texts, poems that were translations as well as translations of poems.

But translation today seems to bear little sign of these developments. The dominance of transparent discourse has remained so secure in English that even though modernist poetry and prose have long been canonized in Anglo-American literary cultures, both in and out of the academy, the innovations that distinguish modernist translation continue to be marginal, seldom actually implemented in an English-language translation, seldom recommended in theoretical statements by translators or others. In the search for exits from the dominance of transparency, it is important to assess the innovations of modernist translation, interrogating the cultural functions it performed with such force at the beginning of the century, but also the conditions of its marginalization from mid-century onward. What alternatives did modernist translation offer in its challenge to transparency? Why were they relegated to the fringes of Anglo-American culture?

I

In a review published in the *Criterion* in 1936, Basil Bunting criticized E. Stuart Bates's study *Modern Translation* for not keeping the promise of its title, for failing, in fact, to present a modern concept of translation. In Bunting's view, Bates couldn't distinguish school "cribs (e.g. Loeb Classics) from translations" that Bunting himself valued, "translations meant to stand by themselves, works in their own language equivalent to their original but not compelled to lean on its authority, claiming the independence and accepting the responsibility inseparable from a life of their own" (Bunting 1936:714). Modernism asserts the "independence" of the translated text, demanding that it be judged on its "own" terms, not merely apart from the foreign text, but against other literary texts in its "own" language, accepting the "responsibility" of distinguishing itself in the literary terms of that language. But as soon as a modernist translation chooses these terms, it can never be an independent work, can never be its "own" insofar as the translation is written in a language coded with cultural values that are fundamentally different from those circulating in the foreign language. Modernism believes that the responsibility of translation is to be independent, but the responsibility assumed in this belief is actually owed to a domestic intelligibility and cultural force that erase, somewhat irresponsibly, the linguistic and cultural difference of the foreign text. For Bunting, this difference wasn't the important thing in translation, partly because the opportunities to experience it in English seemed to him rare, or simply nonexistent. "No one is truly bilingual," he wrote, "but it does not matter" (ibid.:714).

Modernism seeks to establish the cultural autonomy of the translated text by effacing its manifold conditions and exclusions, especially the process of domestication by which the foreign text is rewritten to serve modernist cultural agendas. Bunting was aware of this domestication. He praised Edward Fitzgerald's *Rubáiyát of*

Omar Khayyám (1859) because "Fitzgerald translated a poem that never existed, yet by an unforced, natural expansion of Dryden's aim, made Omar utter such things 'as he would himself have spoken if he had been born in England and in' an age still slightly overshadowed by Byron" (Bunting 1936:715). For Bunting, Fitzgerald embodied the modernist ideal by appearing to translate a poem that "never existed," but paradoxically the translator drew on pre-existing materials: he followed Dryden's domesticating translation method (which made Virgil a Restoration English poet), and his translation was noticeably influenced by Byron, Byronism, the Orientalism in romantic culture. Bunting's awareness of this domesticating process was never sufficiently skeptical to make him question his concept of translation, to doubt the autonomy of the translated text, or to wonder about what happened to the foreignness of the foreign text when it got translated. He was interested only in translation that makes a difference at home, not translation that signifies the linguistic and cultural difference of the foreign text.

In modernist translation, these two kinds of difference get collapsed: the foreign text is inscribed with a modernist cultural agenda and then treated as the absolute value that exposes the inadequacy of translations informed by competing agendas. In a 1928 review of Arthur Symons' translation of Baudelaire, T. S. Eliot acknowledged that a translation constitutes an "interpretation," never entirely adequate to the source-language text because mediated by the target-language culture, tied to a historical moment: "the present volume should perhaps, even in fairness, be read as a document explicatory of the 'nineties, rather than as a current interpretation" (Eliot 1928:92). Eliot assumed the modernist view that translation is a fundamental domestication resulting in an autonomous text: "the work of translation is to make something foreign, or something remote in time, live with our own life" (ibid.:98). But the only "life" Eliot would allow in translation conformed to his peculiar brand of modernism. What made Symons's version "wrong," "a mistranslation," "a smudgy botch" was precisely that he "enveloped Baudelaire in the Swinburnian violet-coloured London fog of the 'nineties," turning the French poet into "a contemporary of Dowson and Wilde" (ibid.:91, 99–100, 102, 103). The "right" version was shaped by what Eliot announced as his "general point of view," "classicist in literature, royalist in politics, and anglo-catholic in religion" (ibid.:vii). Thus, "the important fact about Baudelaire is that he was essentially a Christian, born out of his due time, and a classicist, born out of his due time" (ibid.:103), where the "time" that matters is Eliot's present: "Dowson and Wilde have passed, and Baudelaire remains; he belonged to a generation that preceded them, and yet he is much more our contemporary than they" (ibid.:91).

Pound too privileged foreign texts that he could mobilize in a modernist cultural politics, but his ideological standpoint was different from Eliot's and more than a little inconsistent. Certain medieval poetries, notably the Provençal troubadour lyric and the *dolce stil nuovo*, were to be recovered through interpretation, translation, and imitation because they contained values that had been lost in western culture, but that would now be restored by modernism. Guido Cavalcanti's poetry was assimilated to modernist philosophical and poetic values like positivism and linguistic precision. In Pound's essay "Cavalcanti" (1928), "the difference between Guido's precise interpretive metaphor, and the Petrarchan fustian and ornament" is that Guido's "phrases correspond to definite sensations undergone" (Anderson 1983:xx). This essay also made clear the peculiarly political nature of Pound's cultural restoration, couching his modernist reading of Cavalcanti's poetry in a rabid anti-clericalism and racism:

> We have lost the radiant world where one thought cuts through another with clean edge, a world of moving energies "*mezzo oscuro rade*," "*risplende in sé perpetuale effecto*," magnetisms that take form, that are seen, or that border the visible, the matter of Dante's *Paradiso*, the glass under water, the form that seems a form seen in a mirror, these realities perceptible to the sense, interacting, "*a lui si tiri*" untouched by the two maladies, the Hebrew disease, the Hindoo disease, fanaticisms and excess that produce Savonarola, asceticisms that produce fakirs, St. Clement of Alexandria, with his prohibition of bathing by women.
>
> (Anderson 1983:208)

Elsewhere in the same essay Pound shifted this ideological standpoint by linking his interest in medieval poetry to an anti-commercialism with radical democratic leanings. Cavalcanti's philosophical canzone, "Donna mi prega,"

> shows traces of a tone of thought no longer considered dangerous, but that may have appeared about as soothing to the

Florentine of A.D. 1290 as conversation about Tom Paine, Marx, Lenin and Bucharin would to-day in a Methodist bankers' board meeting in Memphis, Tenn.

(ibid.:203)

Pound, like Bunting and Eliot, concealed his modernist appropriation of foreign texts behind a claim of cultural autonomy for translation. He concluded his 1929 essay "Guido's Relations" by briefly distinguishing between an "interpretive translation," prepared as an "accompaniment" to the foreign text, and "the 'other sort'" of translation, which possesses an aesthetic independence:

> The "other sort," I mean in cases where the "translator" is definitely making a new poem, falls simply in the domain of original writing, or if it does not it must be censured according to equal standards, and praised with some sort of just deduction, assessable only in the particular case.
>
> (Anderson 1983:251)

Pound drew this distinction when he published his own translations. As David Anderson has observed, the 1920 collection *Umbra: The Early Poems of Ezra Pound* ended with a "Main outline of E.P.'s works to date," in which Pound classified "The Seafarer," "Exile's Letter (and *Cathay* in general)," and "Homage to Sextus Propertius" as "Major Personae," whereas his versions of Cavalcanti and Provençal poets like Arnaut Daniel were labelled "Etudes," study guides to the foreign texts (Anderson 1983:xviii xix). Pound saw them all as his "poems," but used the term "Major Personae" to single out translations that deserved to be judged according to the same standards as his "original writing." The appeal to these (unnamed) standards means of course that Pound's translations put foreign texts in the service of a modernist poetics, evident, for example, in his use of free verse and precise language, but also in the selection of foreign texts where a "persona" could be constructed, an independent voice or mask for the poet. Here it is possible to see that the values Pound's autonomous translations inscribed in foreign texts included not only a modernist poetics, but an individualism that was at once romantic and patriarchal. He characterized the translation that is a "new poem" in the individualistic terms of romantic expressive theory ("the expression of the translator"). And what received expression in translations like "The Seafarer" and "The River Merchant's Wife: A Letter" was the psychology of an aggressive male or a submissive female in a male-dominated world.

Yet Pound's translation theory and practice were various enough to qualify and redirect his modernist appropriation of foreign texts, often in contradictory ways. His concept of "interpretive translation," or "translation of accompaniment," shows that for him the ideal of cultural autonomy coincided with a kind of translation that made explicit its dependence on domestic values, not merely to make a cultural difference at home, but to signal the difference of the foreign text. In the introduction to his translation, *Sonnets and Ballate of Guido Cavalcanti* (1912), Pound admitted that "in the matter of these translations and of my knowledge of Tuscan poetry, Rossetti is my father and my mother, but no one man can see everything at once" (Anderson 1983:14). Pound saw Dante Gabriel Rossetti's versions as the resource for an archaic lexicon, which he developed to signify the different language and cultural context of Cavalcanti's poetry:

> It is conceivable the poetry of a far-off time or place requires a translation not only of word and of spirit, but of "accompaniment," that is, that the modern audience must in some measure be made aware of the mental content of the older audience, and of what these others drew from certain fashions of thought and speech. Six centuries of derivative convention and loose usage have obscured the exact significance of such phrases as: "The death of the heart," and "The departure of the soul."
>
> (ibid.:12)

The translation of accompaniment required bilingual publication. It signified the cultural difference of the foreign text by deviating from current English usage and thereby sending the reader across the page to confront the foreign language. "As to the atrocities of my translation," Pound wrote in "Cavalcanti," "all that can be said in excuse is that they are, I hope, for the most part intentional, and committed with the aim of driving the reader's perception further into the original than it would without them have penetrated" (Anderson 1983:221). In a 1927 "Postscript" to his variorum edition of Cavalcanti's poems, Pound criticized his archaizing strategy, but felt it needed further refinement, not abandonment, in order to suggest the generic distinctions in the Italian texts: "the translator might, with profit, have accentuated the differences and used for the occasional pieces a lighter, a more

Browningesque, and less heavy Swinburnian language" (ibid.:5). A couple of years later, in "Guido's Relations," Pound crankily condemned his earlier use of archaism, arguing that he "was obfuscated by the Victorian language," "the crust of dead English, the sediment present in my own available vocabulary" (ibid.:243). But once again he didn't decide to abandon it. On the contrary, his idea was that the discourses in English-language translation should be as heterogeneous as possible: "one can only learn a series of Englishes," he insisted, and so "it is stupid to overlook the lingual inventions of precurrent authors, even when they were fools or flapdoodles or Tennysons" (ibid.:244). When, in this 1929 essay, Pound offered his own translation of Cavalcanti as an example, he described his discourse as "pre-Elizabethan English" (ibid.:250).

Pound's interpretive translations display this increasing heterogeneity, particularly since he revised them repeatedly over the course of several decades. His debt to Rossetti was announced early, in *The Spirit of Romance* (1910), where he quoted often and admiringly from the Victorian poet's versions of the *dolce stil novisti*. When Pound wrote his own first versions of Cavalcanti's poems, they sometimes echoed Rossetti's. Cavalcanti's evocation of the angelic lady –

> Chi è questa che vien, ch'ogni uom la mira,
> Che fa di clarità l'aer tremare!
> E mena seco Amor, sì che parlare
> Null'uom ne puote, ma ciascun sospira?
> Ahi Diu, che sembra quando gli occhi gira!
> Dicalo Amor, ch'io nol saprei contare;
> Cotanto d'umiltà donna mi pare,
> Che ciascun'altra in vêr di lei chiam'ira.
> Non si potria contar la sua piacenza,
> Ch'a lei s'inchina ogni gentil virtute,
> E la beltate per sue Dea la mostra.
> Non fu sì alta gia la mente nostra,
> E non si è posta in noi tanta salute,
> Che propriamente n'abbiam conoscenza.
>   (Anderson 1983:42)

– was translated fluently by Rossetti, who resorted to a relatively unobtrusive archaism in verse form (an Italianate sonnet) and in diction ("thereon," "benison," "ne'er") – relatively unobtrusive, that is, in the context of Victorian poetry:

Who is she coming, whom all gaze upon,
    Who makes the air all tremulous with light,
And at whose side is Love himself? that none
    Dare speak, but each man's sighs are infinite.
    Ah me! how she looks round from left to right,
Let Love discourse: I may not speak thereon.
Lady she seems of such high benison
    As makes all others graceless in men's sight.
The honour which is hers cannot be said;
    To whom are subject all things virtuous,
        While all things beauteous own her deity.
Ne'er was the mind of man so nobly led,
Nor yet was such redemption granted us
    That we should ever know her perfectly.
                            (Rossetti 1981:223)

Some of Rossetti's deviations from the Italian improve the fluency
of the translation by simplifying the syntax. "At whose side is Love
himself," for instance, is a free rendering of "mena seco Amor" that
reads much more easily than a closer version like "she leads Love
with herself." Rossetti also added different nuances to Cavalcanti's
idealization of the lady, making it more moral or spiritual, even
theological, by using "benison" for "umiltà" ("humility," "meek-
ness," "modesty"), "honour" for "piacenza" ("pleasantness"), and
"redemption" for "salute" ("health," "salvation"). Pound's 1910
version quoted Rossetti's, but it adhered more closely to the Italian
text and noticeably increased the archaism. Next to Rossetti's
version, moreover, Pound's offered a more human image of the
lady by referring to her "modesty" and "charm" and suggesting that
she commands the attention of an aristocratic elite ("noble
powers"). The lover meanwhile possesses a knightly "daring" that
"ne'er before did look so high," spiritually or socially:

Who is she coming, whom all gaze upon,
Who makes the whole air tremulous with light,
And leadeth with her Love, so no man hath
Power of speech, but each one sigheth?
Ah God! the thing she's like when her eyes turn,
Let Amor tell! 'Tis past my utterance:
And so she seems mistress of modesty
That every other woman is named "Wrath."
Her charm could never be a thing to tell

For all the noble powers lean toward her.
Beauty displays her for an holy sign.
Our daring ne'er before did look so high;
But ye! there is not in you so much grace
That we can understand her rightfully.

(Anderson 1983:43)

The version Pound published in his 1912 collection, *Sonnets and Ballate*, constituted a substantial revision, but it did not alter his basic archaizing strategy:

Who is she coming, drawing all men's gaze,
Who makes the air one trembling clarity
Till none can speak but each sighs piteously
Where she leads Love adown her trodden ways?

Ah God! The thing she's like when her glance strays,
Let Amor tell. 'Tis no fit speech for me.
Mistress she seems of such great modesty
That every other woman were called "Wrath."

No one could ever tell the charm she hath
For all the noble powers bend toward her,
She being beauty's godhead manifest.

Our daring ne'er before held such high quest;
But ye! There is not in you so much grace
That we can understand her rightfully.

(ibid.:45)

Pound retained some of his borrowings from Rossetti and used additional archaic forms ("adown," "godhead," "quest") that introduced a romantic medievalism traced with misogyny. The opening characterized the lady as a Keatsian "belle dame sans merci," implying that she exploits her commanding beauty ("drawing all men's gaze") to victimize her many admirers ("each sighs piteously") with some frequency ("adown her trodden ways"). There was even a hint of moral imperfection, a potential for infidelity ("her glance strays").

In 1932, Pound published *Guido Cavalcanti Rime*, a critical edition of the Italian texts along with several translations that included a final version of this sonnet. Here the archaism was pushed to an extreme, apparent not just in Pound's lexicon, syntax, and orthography, but also in pseudo-archaic neologism

("herward"). The lady underwent yet another metamorphosis, this
time into a mystical image "that borders the visible":

> Who is she that comes, makying turn every man's eye
> And makyng the air to tremble with a bright clearnesse
> That leadeth with her Love, in such nearness
> No man may proffer of speech more than a sigh?
>
> Ah God, what she is like when her owne eye turneth, is
> Fit for Amor to speake, for I can not at all;
> Such is her modesty, I would call
> Every woman else but an useless uneasiness.
>
> No one could ever tell all of her pleasauntness
> In that every high noble vertu leaneth to herward,
> So Beauty sheweth her forth as her Godhede;
>
> Never before was our mind so high led,
> Nor have we so much of heal as will afford
> That our thought may take her immediate in its embrace.
>
> (Anderson 1983:46)

The lady is portrayed as perceptible to the senses but unattainable
in her spirituality, a neo-Platonic Idea that exceeds even the quasi-
physical "embrace" of human "thought." This representation
certainly pinpoints a central theme in the *dolce stil nuovo*, but it is
also recognizable as Pound's modernist reading of the medieval
poetries he celebrated: "The conception of the body as perfected
instrument of the increasing intelligence pervades" (ibid.:206);
"the central theme of the troubadours, is the dogma that there is
some proportion between the fine thing held in the mind, and the
inferior thing ready for instant consumption" (ibid.:205). Just as in
"Philip Massinger" (1920) Eliot posited a unified "sensibility" in
English literary culture before the late seventeenth century, "a
period when the intellect was immediately at the tips of the senses"
(Eliot 1950:185), Pound discovered a "harmony *of* the sentient" in
Cavalcanti, "where the thought has its demarcation, the substance
its *virtù*, where stupid men have not reduced all 'energy' to
unbounded undistinguished abstraction" (Anderson 1983:209).

On the thematic level, Pound's translations inscribed Cavalcanti's texts with values that differed from Rossetti's in being both
modernist and patriarchal, notably in the representation of the
lady, transformed by his revisions from "the inferior thing ready for

instant consumption" into "the fine thing held in the mind." But Pound's successive versions were also interrogative in their relation to the Italian texts and to Rossetti's translations, showing how the female idealization of the *dolce stil novisti* and the pre-Raphaelites assumed a female degradation, a misogynist suspicion that the lady's value is "inferior," dependent on the male imagination. In fashioning himself as a poet–translator, Pound was competing against two poetic "fathers," Cavalcanti and Rossetti, and this oedipal competition took the form of revising the image of the lady.

On the level of discourse, however, Pound's translations don't easily support the positivist concept of language in his modernist readings. The dense archaism hardly produces the illusionistic effect of transparency that he valued in the *dolce stil novisti*, what he described so rapturously as the virtual invisibility of literary form, "the glass under water" (Anderson 1983:208). The peculiarities of Pound's archaic text preempt any illusionism by calling attention to the language as a specific kind of English, a poetic discourse linked to a specific historical moment that is neither Pound's nor Cavalcanti's nor Rossetti's. The final version of the sonnet, "Who is she that comes," was the text Pound quoted in "Guido's Relations" to illustrate how "pre-Elizabethan English" can be used to translate Cavalcanti. Pound's rationale for this discourse was distinctively modernist: he described the pre-Elizabethan as "a period when the writers were still intent on clarity and explicitness, still preferring them to magniloquence and the thundering phrase" (ibid.:250). But Pound also knew that his archaizing strategy resulted less in clarity and explicitness than in a sense of oddity or unfamiliarity:

> The objections to such a method are: the doubt as to whether one has the right to take a serious poem and turn it into a mere exercise in quaintness; the "misrepresentation" not of the poem's antiquity, but of the proportionate feel of that antiquity, by which I mean that Guido's thirteenth-century language is to twentieth-century Italian sense much less archaic than any fourteenth-, fifteenth-, or early sixteenth-century English is for us.
>
> (ibid.:250)

The archaism did not achieve any greater fidelity to the Italian texts, nor did it establish an analogy between two past cultures, one

Italian, the other English. Despite Pound's modernist pronouncements, the archaism could not overcome "six centuries of derivative convention and loose usage" to communicate "the exact significances of such phrases as: 'The death of the heart,' and 'The departure of the soul'" because it pointed to a different literary culture in a different language at a different historical moment (Anderson 1983:12). Pound's pre-Elizabethan English could do no more than signify the remoteness of Cavalcanti's poetry, along with the impossibility of finding any exact linguistic and literary equivalent. And the archaism did this only because it radically departed from cultural norms that currently prevailed in English. This is perhaps most noticeable in Pound's archaic prosody: as Anderson has observed, he wanted "to free the cadence of his English versions from the Elizabethan and post-Elizabethan iambic pentameter," still the standard for English-language verse at the beginning of the twentieth century (Anderson 1982:13; Easthope 1983).

Pound's comments on his versions of Arnaut Daniel revealed his acute awareness that current cultural norms constrained his work as a translator. These were his most experimental translations, texts where he developed the most heterogeneous discourses. Like the later Cavalcanti translations, they mixed various archaic forms, mainly "Pre-Raphaelite mediaevalism" (Pound's notation for "Rossetti: Italian poets" in *The ABC of Reading* (Pound 1960:133)) and pre-Elizabethan English, culled mainly from Gavin Douglas's 1531 version of the *Aeneid*, but also from such early Tudor poets as Sir Thomas Wyatt (McDougal 1972:114; Anderson 1982:13). And there were occasional traces of twentieth-century American colloquialism and foreign languages, particularly French and Provençal. The following exemplary passages are excerpts from the translations Pound published in his essay, "Arnaut Daniel" (1920):

> When I see leaf, and flower and fruit
>   Come forth upon light lynd and bough,
> And hear the frogs in rillet bruit,
>   And birds quhitter in forest now,
> Love inkirlie doth leaf and flower and bear,
> And trick my night from me, and stealing waste it,
> Whilst other wight in rest and sleep sojourneth.
> (Pound 1953:177)

> So clear the flare
> That first lit me

To seize
Her whom my soul believes;
If cad
Sneaks,
Blabs, slanders, my joy
Counts little fee
Baits
And their hates.
   I scorn their perk
   And preen, at ease.
Disburse
Can she, and wake
Such firm delights, that I
Am hers, froth, lees
Bigod! from toe to earring.
          (ibid.:161, 163)

Flimsy another's joy, false and distort,
No paregale that she springs not above. [. . .]
Her love-touch by none other mensurate.
To have it not? Alas! Though the pains bite
Deep, torture is but galzeardy and dance,
For in my thought my lust hath touched his aim.
God! Shall I get no more! No fact to best it!
          (ibid.: 179, 181)

Pound saw these as interpretive translations that highlighted the
elaborate stanzaic forms of the Provençal texts, mimicking their
rhythms and sound effects. But he also knew that by doing so his
translations ran counter to literary values that prevailed in modern
European languages like English and French. In the essay on
Daniel, he apologized for his deviations:

> in extenuation of the language of my verses, I would point out
> that the Provençals were not constrained by the modern literary
> sense. Their restraints were the tune and rhyme-scheme, they
> were not constrained by a need for certain qualities of writing,
> without which no modern poem is complete or satisfactory.
> They were not competing with De Maupassant's prose.
>   (Pound 1954:115)

The mention of De Maupassant indicates that Pound's translations could signify the difference of Daniel's musical prosody only by challenging the transparent discourse that dominates "the modern literary sense," most conspicuously in realistic fiction. To mimic an archaic verse form, Pound developed a discursive heterogeneity that refused fluency, privileging the signifier over the signified, risking not just the unidiomatic, but the unintelligible. In a 1922 letter to Felix Schelling, a professor at the University of Pennsylvania who taught Pound English literature and unfavorably reviewed his Daniel translations, Pound cited the cultural remoteness of troubadour poetry as "the reason for the archaic dialect": "the Provençal feeling is archaic, we are ages away from it" (Pound 1950:179). And Pound measured this remoteness on a scale of current English-language values:

> I have proved that the Provençal rhyme schemes are not impossible in English. They are probably inadvisable. The troubadour was not worried by our sense of style, our "literary values," so he could shovel in words in any order he liked. [...] The troubadour, fortunately perhaps, was not worried about English order; he got certain musical effects because he cd. concentrate on music without bothering about literary values. He had a kind of freedom which we no longer have.
>
> (ibid.)

Pound's translations signified the foreignness of the foreign text, not because they were faithful or accurate – he admitted that "if I have succeeded in indicating some of the properties [...] I have also let [others] go by the board" (Pound 1954:116) – but because they deviated from domestic literary canons in English.

Pound's first versions of Cavalcanti's poetry did in fact look alien to his contemporaries. In a review of the *Sonnets and Ballate* that appeared in the English *Poetry Review* (1912), professor of Italian Arundel del Re found the translation defective and not entirely comprehensible, including the bilingual title: "The translation of the 'Sonnets and Ballate' – why not Sonetti e Ballate or Sonnets and Ballads? – show the author to be earnestly striving after a vital idea of which one sometimes catches a glimpse amidst the general tangle and disorder" (Homberger 1972:88). Yet Del Re recognized the historicizing effect of Pound's archaism, quoting phrases from Pound's own introduction to describe it: "Notwithstanding its almost overpowering defects this is a sincere if slip-shod attempt to translate into English the 'accompaniment' and 'the mental

content of what the contemporaries of Guido Cavalcanti drew
forth from certain forms of thought and speech'" (ibid.). In John
Bailey's review for the *Times Literary Supplement*, the "strangeness"
of Pound's translation also began with the choice of foreign text:
he felt that "though not belonging to the high universal order,"
Cavalcanti's poetry does possess the "peculiar charm" of "an
escape from all that is contemporary or even actual into [the]
hortus conclusus of art" (Homberger 1972:88). But what Bailey
found unpleasantly strange about Pound's translation was that,
compared to Rossetti's, it was utterly lacking in fluency:

> He is sometimes clumsy, and often obscure, and has no fine tact
> about language, using such words and phrases as "Ballatet,"
> "ridded," "to whomso runs," and others of dubious or unhappy
> formation. A more serious fault still is that he frequently
> absolves himself altogether from the duty of rhyming, and if an
> English blank verse sonnet were ever an endurable thing it
> would not be when it pretends to represent an Italian original.
>
> (ibid.:91)

Bailey praised Rossetti because he "preserves" a great deal "more
of the original rhyme and movement" (ibid.:92). What constituted
fluent translation for Bailey was not just univocal meaning,
recognizable archaism, and prosodic smoothness, but a Victorian
poetic discourse, pre-Raphaelite medievalism, only one among
other archaic forms in Pound's translations. The fact that Pound
was violating a hegemonic cultural norm is clear at the beginning
of Bailey's review, where he allied himself with Matthew Arnold
and claimed to speak for "any rich and public-spirited statesman of
intellectual tastes to-day" (ibid.:89).

Other commentators were more appreciative of Pound's work as
a translator, but their evaluations differed according to which of
his changing rationales they accepted. In a 1920 article for the
North American Review, May Sinclair, the English novelist who was a
friend of Pound's, offered a favorable assessment of his publications to date. Following Pound's sense of the cultural remoteness
of Provençal poetry, Sinclair argued that the archaism in his
translations signalled the absence of any true equivalence in
modern English:

> By every possible device – the use of strange words like
> "gentrice" and "plasmatour" – he throws [Provençal poetry]

seven centuries back in time. It is to sound as different from modern speech as he can make it, because it belongs to a world that by the very nature of its conventions is inconceivably remote, inconceivably different from our own, a world that we can no longer reconstruct in its reality.

(Homberger 1972:183)

In a 1932 review of *Guido Cavalcanti Rime* for *Hound & Horn*, A. Hyatt Mayor followed Pound's modernist reading of the Italian texts, his positivist sense of their precise language, and therefore didn't see the strangeness of the archaism, praising the translations instead for establishing a true equivalence to the "freshness" of the Italian:

> The quaint language is not a pastiche of pre-Shakespearean sonnets, or an attempt to make Cavalcanti talk Elizabethan the way Andrew Lang made Homer try to talk King James. Ezra Pound is matching Cavalcanti's early freshness with a color lifted from the early freshness of English poetry.
>
> (Mayor 1932:471)

Sinclair saw that Pound's translations were interpretive in their use of archaism, meant to indicate the historical distance of the foreign text, whereas Mayor took the translations as independent literary works that could be judged against others in the present or past, and whose value, therefore, was timeless. "The English seems to me as fine as the Italian," he wrote, "In fact, the line *Who were like nothing save her shadow cast* is more beautifully definite than *Ma simigliavan sol la sua ombria*" (ibid.:470).

Pound's theory and practice of interpretive translation reverse the priorities set by modernist commentators on translation like Mayor, Bunting, Eliot, and Pound himself. Interpretive translation contradicts the ideal of autonomy by pointing to the various conditions of the translated text, foreign as well as domestic, and thus makes clear that translation can make a cultural difference at home only by signifying the difference of the foreign text. The discursive heterogeneity of Pound's interpretive translations, especially his use of archaism, was both an innovation of modernist poetics and a deviation from current linguistic and literary values, sufficiently noticeable to seem alien. Pound shows that in translation, the foreignness of the foreign text is available only in cultural forms that already circulate in the target language, some with greater cultural capital than others. In translation, the foreignness of the foreign text can only be what currently appears "foreign" in the target-language culture, in relation to dominant domestic values, and therefore only as values that are marginal in various degrees, whether because they are residual, survivals of previous cultural forms in the target language, or because they are emergent, transformations of previous forms that are recognizably different, or because they are specialized or nonstandard, forms linked to specific groups with varying degrees of social power and prestige. The foreign can only be a disruption of the current hierarchy of values in the target-language culture, an estrangement of them that seeks to establish a cultural difference by drawing on the marginal. Translation, then, always involves a process of domestication, an exchange of source-language intelligibilities for target-language ones. But domestication need not mean assimilation, i.e., a conservative reduction of the foreign text to dominant domestic values. It can also mean resistance, through a recovery of the residual or an affiliation with the emergent or the dominated – choosing to translate a foreign text, for instance, that is excluded by prevalent English-language translation methods or by the current canon of foreign literature in English and thus forcing a methodological revision and a canon reformation.

The remarkable thing about modernist translation is that, even though in theoretical statements it insists on the cultural autonomy of the translated text, it still led to the development of translation practices that drew on a broad range of domestic discourses and repeatedly recovered the excluded and the marginal to challenge the dominant. Pound's translations avoided the transparent discourse that has dominated English-language translation since the seventeenth century. Instead of translating fluently, foregrounding the signified and minimizing any play of the signifier that impeded communication, pursuing linear syntax, univocal meaning, current usage, standard dialects, prosodic smoothness, Pound increased the play of the signifier, cultivating inverted or convoluted syntax, polysemy, archaism, nonstandard dialects, elaborate stanzaic forms and sound effects – textual features that frustrate immediate intelligibility, empathic response, interpretive mastery. And by doing this Pound addressed the problem of domestication that nags not just his own claim of cultural autonomy, but also the transparent discourse dominating English-language translation. Transparency inscribes the foreign text with dominant English values (like transparency) and simultaneously conceals that domestication under the illusion that the translated text is not a translation, but the "original," reflecting the foreign author's personality or intention or the essential meaning of the foreign text; whereas modernist translation, by deviating from transparency and inscribing the foreign text with marginal English values, initiates a foreignizing movement that points to the linguistic and cultural differences between the two texts (admitting, of course, that some of the values inscribed by modernists like Pound are neither marginal nor especially democratic – e.g. patriarchy).

This is not a concept of translation that modernism theorized with any consistency, but rather one that its translation theories and practices make possible. It won't be found in a modernist critic of modernism like Bunting, Eliot, or Hugh Kenner, because such critics accept the claim of cultural autonomy for the translated text. "Ezra Pound never translates 'into' something already existing in English," wrote Kenner, "only Pound has had both the boldness and resource to make a new form, similar in effect to that of the original" (Pound 1953:9). Yet what can now be seen is that a translation is unable to produce an effect equivalent to that of the foreign text because translation is domestication, the inscription of cultural values that differ fundamentally from those in the source language. Pound's effects were aimed only at English-language culture, and so he always translated into preexisting English cultural forms – Anglo-Saxon patterns of accent and alliteration, pre-Elizabethan English, pre-Raphaelite medievalism, modernist precision, American colloquialism. In fact, Pound's reliance on preexisting forms erases his distinction between two kinds of translation: both interpretive translations and translations that are new poems resort to the innovations of modernist poetics, and so both can be said to offer "a photograph, as exact as possible, of one side of the statue" (Anderson 1983:5) – the side selected and framed by English-language modernism. The discursive heterogeneity Pound created may have made the translated texts look "new" – to modernists – but it was also a technique that signalled their difference, both from dominant English values and from those that shaped the foreign text. Modernism enables a postmodernist concept of translation that assumes the impossibility of any autonomous cultural value and views the foreign as at once irredeemably mediated and strategically useful, a culturally variable category that needs to be constructed to guide the translator's intervention into the current target-language scene.

II

By the start of the 1950s, modernist translation had achieved widespread acceptance in Anglo-American literary culture – but only in part, notably the claim of cultural autonomy for the translated text and formal choices that were now familiar enough to insure a domestication of the foreign text, i.e., free verse and precise current language. The most decisive innovations of modernism inspired few translators, no doubt because the translations, essays, and reviews that contained these innovations were difficult to locate, available only in obscure periodicals and rare limited editions, but also because they ran counter to the fluent strategies that continued to dominate English-language poetry translation. The first sign of this marginalization was the reception given to the selected edition of Pound's translations published by the American press New Directions in 1953. This book offered a substantial retrospective, reprinting his latest versions of Cavalcanti and Daniel in bilingual format, as well as "The Seafarer," *Cathay*, Noh plays, a prose text by Rémy de Gourmont, and a miscellany of poetry translations from Latin, Provençal, French, and Italian.

At the time of this publication, Pound was an extremely controversial figure (Stock 1982:423–424, 426–427; Homberger 1972:24–27). His wartime radio broadcasts under Mussolini's government got him tried for treason in the United States and ultimately committed to St. Elizabeth's Hospital for the Criminally Insane in Washington DC (1946). But he was also recognized as a leading contemporary American poet with the award of the Bollingen Prize for *The Pisan Cantos* (1948), an event that prompted fierce attacks and debates in *The New York Times*, *Partisan Review*, and the *Saturday Review of Literature*, among other newspapers and magazines. In this cultural climate, it was inevitable, not just that the translations would be widely reviewed, but that they would provoke a range of conflicting responses. Some recognized the innovative nature of Pound's work, even if they were unsure of its value; others dismissed it as a failed experiment that was now dated, void of cultural power.

The favorable judgments came, once again, from reviewers who shared a modernist cultural agenda. In England, the *Poetry Review* praised the "clever versification" of the Daniel versions, while treating their discursive heterogeneity with the sort of elitism Pound sometimes voiced in his own celebrations of earlier poetries: "It is said that Arnaut was deliberately obscure, so that his songs should not be understood by the vulgar. Rather modern" (Graham 1953:472).[1] In the United States, John Edwards' review for *Poetry* shared the basic assumption of his Berkeley doctoral dissertation on Pound – namely, that this was a canonical American writer – and so the review complained at length that the translations deserved much better editorial treatment than New Directions gave them (Edwards 1954:238). Edwards' sympathy for modernism was apparent in his unacknowledged quotation from Kenner's introduction to the translations (said to represent "an extension of the possibilities of poetic speech in our language" (ibid.:238)), but also in a remarkable description of the Cavalcanti versions that was blind to their dense archaism:

> One need only read Cavalcanti's *Sonnet XVI* in the Rossetti version (*Early Italian Poets*), then in the first Pound attempt (*Sonnets and Ballate of Guido Cavalcanti*, 1912), and finally in the 1931 Pound translation given here, and one can watch the crust falling off and the line grow clean and firm, bringing the original over into English, not only the words but the poetry.
>
> (ibid.:238)

Edwards accepted Pound's modernist rationale for his translations: that Cavalcanti's Italian texts were distinguished by linguistic precision, and that pre-Elizabethan English possessed sufficient "clarity and explicitness" to translate them (Anderson 1983:250). But Edwards lacked Pound's contrary awareness that this strategy made the translations less "clean and firm" than odd or unfamiliar, likely to be taken as "a mere exercise in quaintness" (ibid.).

There were also reviewers who were more astute in understanding the modernist agenda of the translations, but who were nonetheless skeptical of its cultural value. In a review for the *New Statesman and Nation*, the English poet and critic Donald Davie, who has attacked the project of Pound's poetry even while reinforcing its canonical status in academic literary criticism,[2] saw that the interpretive translations came with a peculiarly dogmatic claim of cultural autonomy, most evident in their archaism:

when he translates Cavalcanti, he aspires to give an *absolute* translation – not, of course, in the sense that it is to reproduce in English all the effects of the original, but in the sense that it is to be Cavalcanti in English for good and all, not just for this generation or the next few. Hence the archaic diction, sometimes with olde-Englysshe spelling. [...] Pound believes that English came nearest to accommodating the sort of effects Cavalcanti gets in Italian, in one specific period, late-Chaucerian or early Tudor.

(Davie 1953:264)

But Pound never assumed an "absolute" equivalence between period styles. In fact, in "Guido's Relations," he pointed to the impossibility of finding an exact English-language equivalent: at least one quality of the Italian texts "simply does not occur in English poetry," so "there is no ready-made verbal pigment for its objectification"; using pre-Elizabethan English actually involved "the 'misrepresentation' not of the poem's antiquity, but of the proportionate feel of that antiquity" for Italian readers (Anderson 1983:250). What seemed too absolute for Davie was really Pound's rationale for using archaism: he didn't like the translations because he didn't accept the modernist readings of the foreign texts ("I still ask out of my ignorance if Cavalcanti is worth all the claims Pound has made for him, and all the time he has given him" (Davie 1953:264)). Yet Davie did accept the modernist ideal of aesthetic independence, erasing the distinction between interpretive translation and new poem by evaluating all Pound's translations as literary texts in their own right – and finding the most experimental ones mediocre performances. The Cavalcanti versions "give the impression of not a Wyatt but a Surrey, the graceful virtuoso of a painfully limited and ultimately trivial convention" (ibid.).

George Whicher of Amherst College reviewed Pound's translations twice, and on both occasions the judgments were unfavorable, resting on an informed but critical appreciation of modernist poetics. In the academic journal *American Literature*, Whicher felt that the "evidence contained in this book" did not support Kenner's claim of cultural autonomy: "far from making a new form, Pound was merely producing a clever approximation to an old one" (Whicher 1954:120). In the end, Pound's work as a translator indicated his marginality in the American literary canon, "somewhat apart from the tradition of the truly creative American poets like Whitman, Melville, and Emily Dickinson" (ibid.:121). Whicher measured Pound's translations against his call for linguistic precision and faulted their "pedantic diction": "he had not yet freed himself from the affectation of archaism which marks and mars his 'Ballad of the Goodly Frere'" (ibid.:120).[3] In the *New York Herald Tribune*, Whicher joined Davie in questioning Pound's choice of foreign texts, using the translations as an opportunity to treat modernism as passé, perhaps once seen as "revolutionary," but rather "dull" in 1953:

> It is almost impossible to realize [...] how revolutionary was the publication of "Cavalcanti Poems" in the year 1912. Here was a first conscious blow in the campaign to deflate poetry to its bare essentials. [...] Now, however, we wonder how so excellent a craftsman as Pound could have labored through so many dull poems, even with the help of a minor Italian.
>
> (Whicher 1953:25)

The negative reviews of these and other critics (Leslie Fiedler's, in a glance at Pound's hospital confinement, called his Daniel versions "Dante Gabriel Rossetti gone off his rocker!" (Fiedler 1962:120)) signalled a midcentury reaction against modernism that banished Pound's translations to the fringes of Anglo-American literary culture (Perkins 1987; von Hallberg, 1985). The center in English-language poetry translation was held by fluent strategies that were modern, but not entirely modernist – domesticating in their assimilation of foreign texts to the transparent discourse that prevailed in every form of contemporary print culture; consistent in their refusal of the discursive heterogeneity by which modernist translation sought to signify linguistic and cultural differences. The review of Pound's translations written by the influential Dudley Fitts exemplified this cultural situation in the sharpest terms.

Fitts (1903–1968) was a poet and critic who from the late thirties onward gained a distinguished reputation as a translator of classical texts, for the most part drama by Sophocles and Aristophanes. He translated Greek and Latin epigrams as well and edited a noted anthology of twentieth-century Latin American poetry. As translator and editor of translations, he produced sixteen books, mainly with the large commercial press Harcourt Brace. His reviews of poetry and translations were widely published in various magazines, mass and small circulation, including some linked with modernism: *Atlantic Monthly, The Criterion, Hound & Horn, Poetry, Transition.* The entry on Fitts in *Contemporary Authors* concisely indicates the cultural authority he wielded during the fifties and sixties, while offering a glimpse of the canonical translation strategy his work represented:

> Dudley Fitts was one of the foremost translators from the ancient Greek in this century. Differing from the procedure many scholars follow, Fitts attempted to evoke the inherent character from the work by taking certain liberties with the text. The result, most reviewers agreed, was a version as pertinent and meaningful to the modern reader as it was to the audiences of Sophocles and Aristophanes.
>
> (Locher 1980:152)

The "inherent character" of "the work," "as pertinent and meaningful to the modern reader as" to the Greek "audiences" – the assumption is that appeals to the foreign text can insure a true equivalence in the translation, transcending cultural and historical differences and even the linguistic "liberties" taken by the translator. This anonymous, somewhat contradictory entry makes clear that Fitts's authority as a translator rested on his advocacy of a free, domesticating method that rewrote the foreign text in recognizable terms, like "modern" English.

In the preface to his *One Hundred Poems From the Palatine Anthology* (1938), Fitts described his method in some detail:

> I have not really undertaken translation at all – translation, that is to say, as it is understood in the schools. I have simply tried to restate in my own idiom what the Greek verses have meant to me. The disadvantages of this method are obvious: it has involved cutting, altering, expansion, revision – in short, all the devices of free paraphrase. [...] In general, my purpose has been to compose, first of all, and as simply as possible, an English poem. To this end I have discarded poeticisms, even where (as in Meleagros, for instance) they could have been defended. Except in certain Dedications and in similar pieces where the language is definitely liturgical, I have avoided such archaisms as 'thou' and 'ye' and all their train of attendant ghosts. Less defensibly, I have risked a spurious atmosphere of monotheism by writing 'God' for 'Zeus' (but Mr. Leslie would

have it 'Jupiter'!) whenever the context admitted it without too
perilous a clash.

(Fitts 1956:xvii–xviii)

The first thing worth remarking is how much Fitts's method was
indebted to modernist translation, especially Pound's work. The
assertion of the aesthetic independence of the translation, the
practice of "altering" the foreign text and using contemporary
English, even the swipe at academic translations, presumably too
literal and therefore not literary – all this characterized Pound's
translation theory and practice (but also earlier figures in the
history of English-language translation: some of Pound's views, like
Bunting's, date back to Denham and Dryden). Fitts knew and
reviewed Pound's work, corresponded with him during the thirties,
and, at the Choate School, taught Pound's poetry to James
Laughlin, who launched New Directions and published Fitts's
Palatine Anthology as well as many of Pound's books (Stock
1982:322–323; Carpenter 1988:527–528). Fitts's most significant
departure from Pound in this volume, a departure that was now
determining Pound's reception both in and out of the academy,
was the refusal of different poetic discourses, including archaism.
Preexisting cultural materials fade into "ghosts" with the claim of
cultural autonomy for the translation, which can then carry out a
thoroughgoing domestication that inscribes the foreign text with
target-language values, both linguistic (fluency) and cultural (a
Judeo-Christian monotheism – "writing 'God' for 'Zeus' ").

When Fitts reprinted this translation in 1956, he added a "Note"
that apologized for not revising the texts: "My theories of translation have changed so radically that any attempt to recast the work
of fifteen or twenty years ago could end only in confusion and the
stultification of whatever force the poems may have once had"
(Fitts 1956:xiii). But a few years later, when he published an essay
on translation entitled "The Poetic Nuance," first as a "privately
printed" volume produced by Harcourt "for the friends of the
author and his publishers" (Fitts 1958), then in Reuben Brower's
Harvard University Press anthology *On Translation* (Brower 1959),
it was clear that Fitts's translation theory hadn't changed at all. He
argued the same basic ideas, which continued to be the canons of
English-language poetry translation, made available by both trade
and academic publishers and underwritten by Fitts's prestige as a
translator and reviewer. Thus, the point of "The Poetic Nuance"

was that "The translation of a poem should be a poem, viable as a
poem, and, as a poem, weighable" (Fitts 1958:12). Yet the only kind
of poem Fitts recognized was written in a fairly standard American
English, punctuated by familiar and socially acceptable colloquialisms. To present his argument, Fitts first discussed a poem by the
Mexican Enrique González Martínez that constituted an "attack
upon the spurious elegance of poeticism" (ibid.:13); then he used
his own modern version of an epigram by Martial:

Quod nulli calicem tuum propinas,
humane facis, Horme, non superbc.

You let no one drink from your personal cup, Hormus,
when the toasts go round the table.
Haughtiness?
                Hell, no.
Humanity.

(ibid.:25)

Fitts read the Latin text as Martial's "joke" about Hormus' unsavory
"hygiene," concluding that "his fun depends largely upon the
composure of his form, the apparent decorum of his words"
(ibid.), particularly his use of the word *humane* ("Humanity"). In
Fitts's reading, "Hormus is personally so unclean that even he has
enough hygienic sense not to press upon another a cup that he
himself has been using"; hence, "his bad manners arc really
humanitarianism" (ibid.22). Fitts's translation signified this reading by breaking the "decorum" of his English, shifting from an
extremely prosaic, almost rhythmless colloquialism in the first two
lines to a relatively formal, slightly British abstraction ("Haughtiness") to a staccato slang expression ("Hell, no"). The shift from
elite formality to popular slang inscribed the Latin text with a class
hierarchy, making the joke depend on the reader's acknowledgement that Hormus was violating class distinctions – and
improperly so. Fitts's translation, like his reading, constructed a
socially superior position from which to laugh at the character, but
the fluency of the English made this elitism seem natural.

Fitts evidently felt a deep ambivalence toward modernist translation. He shared Pound's valorization of linguistic precision in
reading and translating earlier poetries. Fitts's enthusiastic fore-
ward to Mary Barnard's 1958 version of Sappho praised her
perception that the Greek texts were written in a "pungent

downright plain style" requiring an appropriately "plain" English:

> Some say a cavalry corps,
> some infantry, some, again,
> will maintain that the swift oars
>
> of our fleet are the finest
> sight on dark earth; but I say
> that whatever one loves, is.

I do not see how that could be bettered. Like the Greek, it is stripped and hard, awkward with the fine awkwardness of truth. Here is no trace of the "sweete slyding, fit for a verse" that one expects to find in renderings of Sappho. It is exact translation; but in its composition, the spacing, the arrangement of stresses, it is also high art. This, one thinks, is what Sappho must have been like.

(Barnard 1958:ix)

Yet Barnard's version was "exact," not so much because she found a true equivalent to the Greek text – she herself later admitted that she used "padding," making the fragments more continuous – but rather because she was influenced by Pound (Barnard 1984:280–284). She corresponded with Pound during the fifties while he was confined at St. Elizabeth's, and she showed him her versions of Sappho, revising them in accordance with his recommendation that she use "the LIVE language" instead of "poetik jarg" (ibid.:282). This recommendation dovetailed with Barnard's reading of Sappho's poetry, which was partly modernist ("It was spare but musical"), partly romantic ("and had, besides, the sound of the speaking voice making a simple but emotionally loaded statement"). Barnard finally developed a fluent strategy that produced the effect of transparency, seeking "a cadence that belongs to the speaking voice" (ibid.:284), and Fitts appreciated this illusionistic effect, taking the English for the Greek text, the poem for the poet: "This, one thinks, is what Sappho must have been like."

But even though both Fitts and Barnard joined in Pound's valorization of linguistic precision, they were unable to share his interest in a more fragmentary and heterogeneous discourse – i.e., in a translation strategy that preempted transparency. Thus, Barnard ignored passages in Pound's letters where he questioned her adherence to standard English grammar ("utility of syntax?

waaal the chink does without a damLot") as well as her cultivation
of a "homogene" language:

> it is now more homogene / it is purrhapz a bit lax /
> whether one emend that occurs wd/ lax it still more ???
> it still reads a bit like a translation /
>
> what is the maximum abruptness you can get it TO ?
>
> Fordie: "40 ways to say anything"
>   I spose real exercise would consist in trying them ALL.
> (Barnard 1984:283)

Fitts, in turn, praised Barnard's Sappho because it *was* "homogene," because it used "exact," current English without any
"spurious poeticism, none of the once so fashionable Swinburne–
Symonds erethism": "What I chiefly admire in Miss Barnard's
translations and reconstructions is the direct purity of diction and
versification" (Barnard 1958:ix).

By the 1950s, Fitts had already reviewed Pound's writing on a few
occasions, gradually distancing himself from his early approval.[4]
His negative review of Pound's translations typified the midcentury reaction against modernism: he attacked the most
experimental versions for the distinctively modernist reason that
they didn't stand on their own as literary texts. "When he fails,"
Fitts wrote, "he fails because he has chosen to invent a
no-language, a bric-a-brac archaizing language, largely (in spite of
his excellent ear) unsayable, and all but unreadable" (Fitts
1954:19). Fitts revealed his knowledge of Pound's rationale for
using archaism – namely, its usefulness in signifying the cultural
and historical remoteness of foreign texts – but he rejected any
translation discourse that did not assimilate them to prevailing
English-language values, that was not sufficiently transparent to
produce the illusion of originality:

> True, Daniel wrote hundreds of years ago, and in Provençal. But
> he was writing a living language, not something dragged out of the
> remoter reaches of Skeat's Etymological Dictionary. He said *autra
> gens*, which is "other men," not "other wight"; he said *el bosc l'auzel*,
> not "birds quhitter in forest"; and so on. Pound [...] may have
> "absorb[ed] the ambience," but he has not written a "poem of his
> own"; he has simply not written a poem.
>
> (ibid.)

Phrases like "living language" and "'poem of his own'" demonstrate that Fitts was very selective in his understanding of Pound's translation theory and practice, that he did not share Pound's interest in signifying what made the foreign text foreign at the moment of translation. On the contrary, the domesticating impulse is so strong in Fitts's review that foreign words (like "autra gens") get reduced to the most familiar contemporary English version, ("other men") as if this version were an exact equivalent, or he merely repeats them, as if repetition had solved the problem of translation ("he said *el bosc l'auzel*, not 'birds quhitter in forest'"). Like Davie, Fitts ignored Pound's concept of interpretive translation, evaluating the Daniel versions as English-language poems, not as study guides meant to indicate the differences of the Provençal texts. And, again, the poems Fitts found acceptable tended to be written either in a fluent, contemporary English that was immediately intelligible or in a poetic language that seemed to him unobtrusive enough not to interfere with the evocation of a coherent speaking voice. Hence, like many other reviewers, Fitts most liked what Pound called his "Major Personae": "We may look upon *The Seafarer*, certain poems in *Cathay*, and the *Noh Plays* as happy accidents" (ibid.). Fitts's work as a translator and as an editor and reviewer makes quite clear that the innovations of modernist translation were the casualty of the transparent discourse that dominated Anglo-American literary culture.

These innovations were generally neglected in the decades after the publication of Pound's translations. British and American poets continued to translate foreign-language poetry, of course, but Pound's experimental strategies attracted relatively few adherents. And those poets who pursued a modernist experimentalism in translation found their work dismissed as an aberration of little or no cultural value. Perhaps no translation project in the post-World War II period better attests to this continuing marginality of modernism than Celia and Louis Zukofsky's remarkable version of Catullus.

Working over roughly a ten-year period (1958–1969), the Zukofskys produced a homophonic translation of the extant canon of Catullus's poetry, 116 texts and a handful of fragments, which they published in a bilingual edition in 1969 (Zukofsky and Zukofsky: 1969).[5] Celia wrote a close English version for every Latin line, marked the quantitative meter of the Latin verse, and parsed every Latin word; using these materials, Louis wrote English-language poems that mimic the sound of the Latin while also attempting to preserve the sense and word order. The Zukofskys' preface, written in 1961, offered a very brief statement of their method: "This translation of Catullus follows the sound, rhythm, and syntax of his Latin – tries, as is said, to breathe the 'literal' meaning with him" (Zukofsky 1991:243). Refusing the free, domesticating method that fixed a recognizable signified in fluent English, the Zukofskys followed Pound's example and stressed the signifier to make a foreignized translation – i.e., a version that deviated from the dominant transparency. This foreignizing process began in their title, where they retained a Latin version that possessed both a scholarly elegance and the promise of a narrow, if not inscrutable, specialization: *Gai Valeri Catulli Veronensis Liber* (in a close rendering, "The Book of Gaius Valerius Catullus from Verona"). One reviewer was moved to write that "their no-English title offers to elucidate nothing" (Braun 1970:30).

Below is one of Catullus's brief satiric poems, done first by Charles Martin, whose fluent translation explicitly adopts Dryden's free method, and then by the Zukofskys, whose discourse is marked by abrupt syntactical shifts, polysemy, discontinuous rhythms:

> Nulli se dicit mulier mea nubere malle
>   quam mihi, non si se Iuppiter ipse petat.
> dicit: sed mulier cupido quod dicit amanti,
>   in uento et rapida scribere oportet aqua.

> My woman says there is no one she'd rather marry
>   than me, not even Jupiter, if he came courting.
> That's what she says – but what a woman says to a passionate
>   lover
> ought to be scribbled on wind, on running water.
> (Martin 1990:xxiv)

> Newly say dickered my love air my own would marry me all
>   whom but one, none see say Jupiter if she petted.
> Dickered: said my love air could be o could dickered a man too
>   in wind o wet rapid a scribble reported in water.
> (Zukofsky 1991, no. 70)

Although both versions could be considered paraphrases that give a fair estimation of the Latin sense, the Zukofskys' homophonic translation is obviously more opaque, frustratingly difficult to read on its own and only slightly easier if juxtaposed to a transparent version like Martin's.

The opacity of the language is due, however, not to the absence of meaning, but to the release of multiple meanings specific to English. Jean-Jacques Lecercle (1990) describes such effects of homophonic translation as the "remainder," what exceeds transparent uses of language geared to communication and reference and may in fact impede them, with varying degrees of violence. As at least one reviewer of the Zukofskys' Catullus realized (the classicist Steele Commager), homophonic translation is an analogue of a modern French cultural practice, *traduscon*, translating according to sound, a method that always results in a proliferation of ambiguities (Commager 1971). In the Zukofskys' version, the Latin word "dicit," from *dicere*, a verb meaning "to say," is rendered homophonically as the English "dickered," which carries some of the sense of "say" if it is taken as "haggled" or "bargained," but which in this erotic context becomes an obscene colloquialism for sexual forms of intercourse. The sequence "my love air" translates "mulier" ("woman"), but the homophonic method adds the English word "air," and this sets going more possibilities, especially in a text that skeptically compares the woman's profession of her love to wind. "Air" also puns on "ere," introducing an archaism into a predominantly modern English lexicon and permitting a construction like "my love, ere my own, would marry me." The pun on "air" bears out Lecercle's observation that the remainder is the persistence of earlier linguistic forms in current usage, "the locus for diachrony-within-synchrony, the place of inscription for past and present linguistic conjunctures" (Lecercle 1990:215). He acknowledges the foreignizing impulse in these effects by comparing the homophonic translator to the speaker for whom

> a foreign language is a treasury of strange but fascinating sounds, and the speaker is caught between the urge to interpret them, the pervasive need to understand language and the fascinated desire to play with words, to listen to their sound, regardless of their meanings.

> (ibid.:73)

The Zukofskys' homophonic translation didn't "interpret" the Latin words by fixing a univocal meaning, easy to recognize. But they did "listen to their sound," and what they heard was a dazzling range of Englishes, dialects and discourses that issued from the foreign roots of English (Greek, Latin, Anglo-Saxon, French) and from different moments in the history of English-language culture.[6]

To signify the foreignness of Catullus's poetry, then, Louis Zukofsky not only sought to bend his English into conformity with the Latin text and the diverse materials Celia provided him; he also cultivated the discursive heterogeneity that distinguishes modernist translation, releasing the remainder in language, recovering marginal cultural forms to challenge the dominant. Many of the English texts are cast into a sixteenth-century poetic language, distinctively Elizabethan, even Shakespearean. This includes isolated words – "hie" (no. 51), "hest" (no. 104), "bonnie" (no. 110) – but also substantial sections that evoke the blank verse of English Renaissance drama:

> Commend to you my cares for the love I love,
> Aurelius, when I'm put to it I'm modest –
> yet if ever desire animated you, quickened
> to keep the innocent unstained, uninjured,
> cherish my boy for me in his purity;
> (Zukofsky 1991, no. 15)

> [. . .] Could he, put to the test,
> not sink then or not devour our patrimonies?
> In whose name, in Rome's or that of base opulence –
> (ibid., no. 29)

> No audacious cavil, precious quaint nostrils,
> or we must cavil, dispute, o my soul's eye,
> no point – as such – Nemesis rebuffs too, is
> the vehement deity: laud her, hang cavil.
> (ibid., no. 50)

There are also strains of an eighteenth-century elegance ("perambulate a bit in all cubicles" (no. 29), "darting his squibs of iambs" (no. 36), "tergiversator" (no. 71), a modernist, Joycean experimentation ("harder than a bean or fob of lapillus" (no. 23), "O quick floss of the Juventii, form" (no. 24), and a scientific terminology taken from biology and physics ("micturition" (no. 39), "glans" and "quantum" (no. 88), "gingival" (no. 97)). Last but not least in effect is a rich assortment of colloquialisms, some British ("a bit more bum" (no. 39)), most American, chosen from different periods in the twentieth century and affiliated with different social groups: "side-kick" (no. 11), "canapes" (no. 13), "don't conk out" (no. 23), "collared" (no. 35), "faggots" (no. 36), "moochers" (no. 37), "hunk" (no. 39), "amigos" (no. 41), "suburban" (no. 44), "con" (no. 86), "bra" (no. 55), "hick" (no. 55), "kid" (no. 56), "mug" (no. 57), "homo" (no. 81). In the homophonic context created by the Zukofskys' translation method, individual words echo, becoming nodes of different dialects and discourses. In no. 70 (quoted on p. 215), "say" can also mean "for the sake of argument," "for example," or even be a clipped form of the archaic "save"; "see" can be an abbreviated form of "you see." These possibilities give a punchy, colloquial turn to the phrasing, gangster lingo with an Elizabethan archness: "Newly, say, dickered"; "none, see, save Jupiter." A line in no. 17 – "your lake's most total paludal puke" – sounds like a 1950s teenage hipster. There is even a trace of black dialect ("pa's true bro" (no. 111), "they quick" (no. 56)), most pronounced in one of the strongest translations:

> O rem ridiculum, Cato, et iocosam,
> dignamque auribus et tuo cachinno.
> ride, quidquid amas, Cato, Catullum:
> res est ridicula et nimis iocosa.
> deprendi modo pupulum puellae
> trusantem: hunc ego, si placet Dionae,
> protelo rigida mea cecidi.

> Cato, it was absurd, just too amusing,
> fit for your ears & fit to make you cackle!
> You'll laugh if you love your Catullus, Cato:
> it was absurd & really *too* amusing!
> Just now I came across a young boy swiving
> his girlfriend, and – don't take offense now, Venus!
> I pinned him to his business with my skewer.
>   (Martin 1990, no. 56)

> O ram ridicule home, Cato, the jokes some
> dig, now cool your ears so the two cock in – no.
> Read: they quick, kid, almost as Cato, Catullus:
> raciest ridicule it may not miss jokes.
> Prehended a mode of pupa, loon boy lay
> crux on to her: and cog I, so placate Dione,
> pro tale, o rig it all, me I cogged kiddie.
>   (Zukofsky 1991, no. 56)

The narrow range of Martin's modern lexicon is highlighted by his use of "swiving," which here seems less the archaism that it is (Chaucerian) than a polite euphemism for sexual activity, comparable to "business" or "skewer." The Zukofskys' homophonic version again shifts abruptly between discursive registers, from contemporary slang ("dig," "cool") to pseudo-archaic construction ("it may not miss jokes") to scientific term ("pupa") to Elizabethanese ("cog") to contemporary colloquialism ("kiddie"). These shifts are foreignizing because, in their deviation from transparency, they force the English-language reader to confront a Catullus that consists of the most extreme linguistic and cultural differences, including self-difference – a self-critical tendency that questions the source of his own amusement (the head-shaking phrase, "the jokes some dig") and points to his own sexual excess, even suggesting a homoerotic relationship between himself and Cato ("they quick, kid, almost as Cato [and] Catullus"). This sort of self-consciousness is so faint as to be absent from both the Latin ("ride, quidquid amas, Cato, Catullum") and Martin's version ("You'll laugh if you love your Catullus, Cato"). Martin's goal was the evocation of "the poet's voice" (Martin 1990:xiii), and this meant a fundamental domestication that fixed a clear, modernized meaning in the Latin text by assigning Catullus the standard English dialect dotted with some slang; the Zukofskys' goal of approximating the sound of the Latin led them to sound the many voices, standard and nonstandard, that constitute English speech and writing.

The discursive heterogeneity of the Zukofskys' Catullus mixes the archaic and the current, the literary and the technical, the elite and the popular, the professional and the working-class, the school and the street. In its recovery of marginal discourses, this translation crosses numerous linguistic and cultural boundaries, staging "the return within language of the contradictions and struggles that make up the social" (Lecercle 1990:182), exposing the network of social affiliations that get masked by the illusionistic effect of transparency. And since the Zukofskys' Catullus calls attention to the social conditions of its own English-language effects, it interrogates the unified appearance that English is given in fluent versions like Martin's, showing instead that

> when we speak of "English," we speak of a multiplicity of dialects, registers, and styles, of the sedimentation of past conjunctures,

of the inscription of social antagonisms as discursive antagonisms, of the coexistence and contradiction of various collective
arrangements of utterance, of the interpellation of subjects
within apparatuses embodied in linguistic practices (schools,
the media).

(ibid.:229)

The recovery of the marginal in the Zukofskys' Catullus challenges
the illusionism of versions like Martin's, whereby a standard
English dialect and the dominant translation discourse (i.e.,
transparency) come to appear the right choices for the Latin text,
the means to establish a true equivalence. The Zukofskys' translation shows, on the contrary, that these English-language cultural
forms are not so much "right" as conservative, engaged in the
maintenance of existing linguistic norms and literary canons and
therefore exclusive of other cultural forms. The Zukofskys' effort
to admit the marginal makes their translation seem strange in
English because it is abusive, not just of transparent discourse, but
of the Latin text as well. For there can be no doubt that their
version, no matter how "close" to the Latin, enacts an ethnocentric
violence in its imposition of translation effects that work only in
English, in an English-language literary culture.

This translation certainly seemed strange to reviewers, who with
rare exceptions criticized it in the most damning terms. And the
sense of strangeness was measured, not surprisingly, against the
canons of fluent translation, which several reviewers formulated so
as to make clear its origins in the late seventeenth and eighteenth
centuries. In the *Grosseteste Review,* an English magazine usually
sympathetic to modernist poetics, Hugh Creighton Hill found fault
with the Zukofskys' Catullus because it violated the domesticating
translation method favored by Johnson: "According to Samuel
Johnson the duty is one of changing one language into another
while retaining the sense, hence the main reason [to translate]
would be to present the meaning of an otherwise incomprehensible writer in recognisable terms" (Hill 1970:21). In *Arion,* an
academic journal devoted to classical literature, Burton Raffel
echoed a string of English translation theorists from Dryden to
Tytler when he suggested that translating Catullus required "(*a*) a
poet, and (*b*) an ability to identify with, to almost *be* Catullus over
a protracted period" (Raffel 1969:444). Raffel praised Peter Whig-
ham's 1966 Catullus for achieving the domestication that Denham

and Dryden recommended: "it is recognizably like what Catullus might have said, had he been alive and well in London" (ibid.:441). Raffel's valorization of transparency permitted him to appreciate only those instances in the Zukofskys' version where the illusionistic effect of authorial presence was the strongest; and again the terms of his praise recalled countless English commentators on translation during the Enlightenment: "Zukofsky's rendering [of 2a] is easy, graceful; it has an air of confidence, and it warms to the touch as you read it over and over" (ibid.:437). In the *Poetry Review*, Nicholas Moore agreed with Raffel – and the humanist assumptions of their Enlightenment forebears: "To really get the spirit of an original postulates a kinship of temperament and even style over and beyond time, language, nationality and milieu" (Moore 1971:182). Moore also judged the Zukofskys' version against the eighteenth-century reception of Catullus's poetry, praising "the essential simplicity" of the Latin texts while inadvertently showing the domestication at work in this reading with a comparison to several English poets: Catullus, Moore felt, is "a sort of mixture of Herrick and Burns with the sharpness of Pope and freedom of the Restoration thrown in here and there" (ibid.:180). These comments demonstrate quite clearly that even in the late 1960s and early 1970s, the centuries-old canons of fluent translation continued to dominate Anglo-American literary culture.

The fact is that the Zukofskys' Catullus posed a cultural threat to unsympathetic reviewers, driving them to make explicit, extreme, and somewhat contradictory statements about the value of transparent discourse. In the literary magazine *Chelsea*, Daniel Coogan, a teacher of foreign languages at the City University of New York, asserted that he "can find little to praise in this translation" because "it is an essential principle of poetry that it be clear" (Coogan 1970:117). In the *New Statesman*, the English poet Alan Brownjohn praised James Michie's recent version of Catullus as "a performance of immense lucidity and pace," while attacking the Zukofskys' as "knotted, clumsy, turgid and ultimately silly" (Brownjohn 1969:151). The demand for immediate intelligibility was so intense in the reviews that words like "gibberish," "unreadable," and "mad" get repeatedly applied to the Zukofskys' translation. For Robert Conquest writing in *Encounter*, to take their project as "seriously" as they did "is to feel the chill wind from the abysses of unreason" (Conquest 1970:57).

But the reviews also bear witness to the unreason of transparency.

After earlier stating that "I am not so naive as to believe that I do not myself have theories of translation, too!" Raffel contradicted himself by concluding that "translation cannot be accomplished under the aegis of a theory, but only under the protection of the Muse, who will tolerate theory, who can make use of madness, but who cannot excuse failure to perform" (Raffel 1969:437, 445). Raffel questioned whether the Zukofskys' translation "theory" had any use at all, whether aesthetic, scholastic or otherwise. Yet instead of rationalizing the use he found most desirable, he reverted to an anti-intellectual assertion of aesthetic value as self-evident, the mystifying Muse that transcends the limitations of time and space, the differences of language and culture. He, like Coogan and Brownjohn, was willing to license only that kind of translation "performance" that conceals its own assumptions and values with the illusionistic effect of transparency. Raffel's anti-intellectualism manifested itself, not merely in his preference for the sweeping judgment to the theoretically nuanced argument, but also in his rather naive assumption that transparent discourse truly represents the foreign text, or, indeed, the foreign author: "no one should have done this book: it does not perform, and it is neither translation nor Catullus" (ibid.:445).

Raffel's concern about the use value of the Zukofskys' work showed that he equated translation with domestication; their Catullus was foreignized, high in abuse value. The English reviewer Nicholas Moore similarly complained that the Zukofskys' translation "doesn't relate to the present in any real way" (Moore 1971:185), ignoring the contemporary lexicons on which it draws and failing to admit his own deep investment in a fairly standard dialect of English tilted toward Britishisms. He exemplified his privileged discourse by translating several of Catullus's poems and publishing his versions with his review. Here is no. 89 done by him and the Zukofskys:

> Gellius est tenuis: quid ni? cui tam bona mater
>   tamque valens uiuat tamque venusta soror
> tamque bonus patruus tamque omnia plena puellis
>   cognatis, quare is desinat esse macer?
> qui ut nihil attingat, nisi quod fas tangere non est,
>   quantumuis quare sit macer invenies

> Coldham is rather run-down, and who wouldn't be!
> With so kindly and sexy a mother,

With a sister so sweet and lovable,
With a kindly uncle and such a large circle of
Girl-friends, why should he cease to look haggard?
If he never touched any body that wasn't taboo,
You'd still find dozens of reasons why he should look haggard!

(Moore 1971)

Gellius is thin why yes: kiddin? quite a bonny mater
    tom queued veil lanced *viva*, tom queued Venus his sister
tom queued bonus pat 'truce unk,' tom queued how many
plenum pullets
    cognate is, query is his destiny *emaciate*?
Kid if he only tingled not seeing what dangler's there, honest
can't he wish where *thin* sit makcr envious.

(Zukofsky 1991)

In effect, Moore was recommending a wholesale Anglicization of
the Latin text, down to using the most current English ("sexy") and
discarding the Latin name for a British-sounding one ("Cold-
ham"). The Zukofskys' version offered their estranging combination of archaism ("bonny"), Britishism ("queued"), American
colloquialism ("bonus," "unk"), and Latinate words, both popular
("viva," as in "Viva Gellius's mother") and scientific ("plenum").
The discursive heterogeneity stops the reader from confusing the
English text with the Latin one, insists, in fact, on their simultaneous independence and interrelatedness (through homophony),
whereas Moore's fluency blurs these distinctions, inviting the
reader to take a domesticated version for the "original" and to
ignore the linguistic and cultural differences at stake here.

The marginality of modernist translation projects like the
Zukofskys' has extended into the present, both in and out of the
academy. Not only do the innovations of modernism inspire few
English-language translators, but the critical commentary these
innovations receive is shaped by the continuing dominance of
transparent discourse – which is to say that they are treated
dismissively, even by the fledgling academic discipline of Translation Studies. This is apparent in Ronnie Apter's *Digging for the
Treasure: Translation after Pound* (Apter 1987).

Apter sought to distinguish Pound's achievement as a poet–
translator from that of his Victorian predecessors and then
measure his influence on later English-language poetry translation, mainly in the United States. But she was not fond of the most

daring modernist experiments. Although her discussion included many translators, well-known as well as obscure (Kenneth Rexroth, Robert Lowell, Paul Blackburn, W. S. Merwin), she totally ignored the Zukofskys' Catullus, preferring instead to comment on the free, colloquial version of Catullus 8 that Louis Zukofsky included in his volume of poems, *Anew* (1946). For Apter, what was valuable about this version was its evocation of a familiar speaking voice, its illusion of transparency: "the effect recreates Catullus's pain as if he were alive today" (Apter 1987:56). In line with many other reviewers and critics, she also professed greater admiration for Pound's "Major Personae" than for the interpretive translations in which he pushed his discourse to heterogeneous extremes. "His translation experiments are interesting," Apter observed, "but not entirely successful" (ibid.:67).

The standard of "success" here is fluent, domesticating translation where discursive shifts are unobtrusive, scarcely noticeable. Thus, Apter praised Blackburn's Provençal translations because "he develops a diction in which both modern colloquialisms and deliberate archaisms seem at home" (Apter 1987:72). But Pound's version of Arnaut Daniel's "L'aura amara" "is marred by pseudo-archaic excursions" and "ludicrous" renderings, making it "sometimes marvelous and sometimes maddeningly awful" (ibid.:70, 71, 68). Apter definitely shared part of the modernist cultural agenda, notably the "emphasis on passion and intellect combined." And she went so far as to inscribe this agenda in Pound's translations, calling his versions of Daniel "Donne-like," using T. S. Eliot's reading of "metaphysical" poetry to describe an English-language translation of a Provençal text and then concluding, somewhat disingenuously, that it was Pound, not she, who "has made a semi-successful comparison of Arnaut Daniel and John Donne" (ibid.:71). The kind of translation Apter preferred, however, was not modernist, but Enlightenment, not historicist, but humanist, lacking the distancing effect of the foreign, transparent. She praised Burton Raffel's version of *Sir Gawain and the Green Knight* because "Raffel has a knack of getting his readers to identify with the emotions of the fourteenth-century characters," who come to "seem all too human" (ibid.:64).[7]

III

The marginalization of modernism in English-language translation during the postwar period limited the translator's options and

defined their cultural and political stakes. Most translators chose a
fluent, domesticating method that reduced the foreign text to
dominant cultural values in English, above all transparent discourse, but also a varied range of concepts, beliefs, and ideologies
that were equally dominant in Anglo-American culture at this time
(Judeo-Christian monotheism, Enlightenment humanism, cultural
elitism). The few translators who chose to resist these values by
developing a foreignizing method, taking up the innovations
pioneered by Pound to signify the linguistic and cultural differences of the foreign text, encountered condemnation and neglect.
The ways in which this cultural situation constrained the translator's activity, the forms of resistance that a modernist translator
might adopt at the margins of English-language literary culture,
are pointedly illustrated by the career of the American poet Paul
Blackburn (1926–1971). The overriding question in this assessment of Blackburn's career is twofold: How did his translation
projects come to negotiate the dominance of transparency and
other values in postwar American culture? And to what extent can
he serve as a model of how to resist this dominance?

Pound played a crucial role in Blackburn's formation as a poet-
translator. It was under Pound's influence that Blackburn began
studying Provençal troubadour poetry in 1949–1950, when he was
an undergraduate student at the University of Wisconsin. Blackburn's account, in an interview given some ten years later, shared
the skepticism toward academic institutions that Pound voiced on
many occasions, particularly the view that existing curricula did
not include earlier poetries validated by a modernist cultural
agenda. Blackburn cast himself as the advocate of modernism
forcing a revision in the university curriculum by reviving older
course offerings:

> What got me started on Provençal was reading squibs of it in *The
> Cantos* and not being able to understand it, which annoyed me.
> It hadn't been taught at Wisconsin since the '30's, so I found
> Professor [Karl] Bottke, the medievalist out there, who offered
> to tutor me in it. I needed the course for credit, and to give
> credit he needed five students. I got him eight and we had a
> very good course.
>
> (Ossman 1963:22)

One of Blackburn's classmates, Sister Bernetta Quinn, who
subsequently devoted several critical studies to Pound's writing,

described the course as an effort "to act upon their master's counsel" in works like *The Spirit of Romance* (Quinn 1972:94). She also noted that Blackburn's imitation of the "master" evolved into a translation project: "Many of our class assignments, refined, appeared in 1953 in Blackburn's *Proensa,* a revelation of the beauty to be found in troubadour song 'made new' and a tribute to the influence of Pound" (ibid.).

Published by the poet Robert Creeley's Mallorca-based Divers Press, *Proensa* was a bilingual translation of eleven texts by seven Provençal poets. It was on the basis of this work that Blackburn received a Fulbright fellowship to continue his Provençal studies at the University of Toulouse during 1954–1955. When the fellowship ended, he stayed in Europe for a couple more years, at first teaching English conversation at Toulouse while researching Provençal manuscripts and editions at French and Italian libraries, then moving through towns in Spain and Mallorca, writing his own poems and translating. By 1958, Blackburn had produced a substantial book-length translation of troubadour poetry. As he put it in a postcard to Pound (dated "IV. 17. 58"),

> I have the anthology of troubadours licked now. 105 pieces (cut fr/150 – and want to bet they'll want to cut it more?). But the *works,* fr. G[uille]m. to Cardenal, Riquier and Pedro de Aragon. (1285). 8 years on this job. I hv. an extra carbon without notes, if you will send it back after a bit. Just say you care to see it.[8]

Perhaps the most decisive moment in Blackburn's apprenticeship as a modernist poet-translator was his correspondence with Pound. Beginning in 1950 and continuing off and on until 1958, Blackburn wrote to Pound at St. Elizabeth's and occasionally visited him after relocating to New York. With these letters Blackburn frequently sent Pound his translations, seeking detailed, word-by-word criticisms as well as answers to specific questions about the Provençal texts. Pound's first response, scrawled over a single sheet of paper, encouraged Blackburn to develop a translation discourse that "modernized off Joyce onto Ford" (10 February 1950). Later Pound explicitly endorsed Blackburn's translations, instructing Dorothy Pound to write that "you have a definite feeling for the Provençal and should stick to it" and then arranging for the publication of one version. In a typescript added to Dorothy's letter, Pound wrote: "[Peire Vidal's]

'Ab l'alen' sufficiently approved for Ez to hv/ forwarded same to
editor that pays WHEN he prints" (12 August 1950).

Most importantly, Pound's letters furthered Blackburn's education in the modernist cultural agenda. Pound's first response
attacked language use in the United States from the standpoint of
modernist poetics:

> The fatigue,
> The   "   , my dear Blackpaul,
> of a country where no
>   exact statements are
> ever made ! !
>   (10 February 1950)

Pound suggested that Blackburn read certain troubadours from
modernist angles: "Pieire Cardinal was not hiding under aestheti-
cism" (undated; 1957?); "Try Sordello" (1 December 1950). He
recommended that Blackburn meet other modernist poets living
in New York, like Louis Dudek and Jackson MacLow (4 July 1950).
And he urged Blackburn to study cultural and economic history
"to set the stuff IN something," to situate his Provençal translations
in a historical context (25 January 1954?). Pound repeatedly
criticized academic institutions for failing to teach a sense of
history and sometimes even quizzed Blackburn on historical
figures:

> Ignorance of history in univ/ grads/   also filthy. blame not
> the pore stewwddent, but the goddam generations of con-
> ditioned profs/   /// thesis fer Sister B/ : absolute decline
> of curiosity re/ every vital problem in U,S. educ/ from 1865
> onward.   whentell did Agassiz die ? anyhow.)
>   (20 March 1950)

The sense of history that Pound taught in these letters avoided any
wholesale reduction of the past to the present, as well as any
reduction of the present to the past. The former led to
"'modernizing'/curricula, i.e. excluding any basic thought from
ALL the goddam univs" (20 March 1950), whereas the latter led to
an antiquarianism without contemporary relevance: "merely retrospective philology LACKS vitality" (1957?). The "vitality" came
from allowing the historical difference of earlier cultures to
challenge the contemporary cultural situation. "BLACKBURN,"
Pound wrote, "might git some life into it IF he/ wd/ extend his

curiosity," and then he provided a reference to the historian Brooks Adams' *Law of Civilization and Decay* (1895): "Vid Brooks Adams/ Civ/ & Dec Knopf reissue/ p. 160" (25 January 1954?).

The fact that Blackburn was learning from this correspondence is clear in his 1953 review of Hugh Kenner's study *The Poetry of Ezra Pound*. Blackburn described Pound's "strongest and most criticized positions": his "case for the honorable intelligence as against the material cunning of usurers" and "his insistence on definition and exactitude as against muddle, the deliberate obscuring of facts and downright mendacity" (Blackburn 1953:217). In this rather negative review, Blackburn affected a cranky tone that sounded remarkably like Pound, questioning Kenner's decision to criticize the critics of *The Cantos*: "He puts a mouthful of teeth in those moth-eaten wolves, journalism and education, and that other pack of elderly puppies who run with what he calls 'the upper-middle-brow literary press,' and then proceeds to beat them off" (ibid.:215). The question Blackburn addressed to Kenner, as well as to every reader of Pound's poetry, was

> why waste time on the dunderheads? Spend your honest effort positively, do the honest work, educate from the top, where there is any. Kung says: "You can't take *all* the dirt out of the ground before you plant seed."
>
> (ibid.:216)

Blackburn seems to be alluding to Pound's Confucianism in *The Cantos* ("Kung says"), an allusion that casts Blackburn as Pound, establishing a process of identification for the reviewer (an aspiring poet–translator), yet in a way that is recognizable to the reader of the review, understood as a pose. The correspondence further complicates the allusion by revealing another, more competitive level of identification: this passage from Blackburn's review is a plagiarism; the tone, the ideas, even the words are actually Pound's. Blackburn was quoting from one of Pound's letters to him, although without acknowledgement:

> Acc/ Kung : not necessary to take all the dirt out of
> the field before yu plant seed.

> Hindoo god of wealth inhabits cow dung. Del Mar : gold mining not
> only ruins the land , it ruins it FOREVER. No reason to
> sleep on a middan.

bombs no kulchurl value.
        IF possible to educate from the top ??
where there is any top. but at least from where one IS.
                                    (12 August 1950)

Pound's adage-like directive to Blackburn – "Acc/Kung" – seems to suggest that preexisting cultural materials are "necessary" for innovations, however regressive those materials might appear ("the dirt"). And indeed this paradox is signified in Pound's fractured language, "Acc/Kung," a pun on "Achtung" ("attention") that made the adage at once Chinese and German, a recovery of Confucianism with a fascistic overtone – the topical resonance of "Achtung" would have been more pronounced, and more ideologically significant, to an English-language reader in the Cold War era. Blackburn's review transformed this passage from Pound's letter into a directive that the critic allow the current cultural situation, however regressive, to determine the "requisite labor," the sort of commentary that will change that situation into one more favorable to Pound's poetry (Blackburn 1953:215). In the case of Kenner, this meant educating the educators ("the top") about Pound's "form or technique or the materials, or what follows from them, what they lead to" (ibid.). Blackburn charged Kenner with "a too-simple discipleship" while he himself presumably exemplified a more complicated one, as we now know, apparent in his plagiarized quotations from Pound's letters.

In this plagiarism, Blackburn at once assumed and qualified Pound's identity, recommending a strategic appropriation of modernism at a moment when it occupied a marginal position in American culture. Blackburn's strategy required an interrogation of Pound's modernist cultural politics, revising it to intervene into a later social situation. He faulted Kenner for an "uncritical" acceptance of Pound's modernism

> without facing the economic and social axes of his criticism, and the conclusions these entail. The poet, this poet, as economic and social reformer, is a dilemma all of us must face eventually. It must be faced before it can be worked. The problem cannot be ignored, nor will any uncritical swallowing of the man's facts and theories do. And it is useless and ignorant to abuse him, simply. There is more than one madhouse in Washington these days.
>
> (Blackburn 1953:217)

The correspondence shows that Blackburn's identity as poet-translator was not only modernist, but masculinist. It was constructed on the basis of an oedipal rivalry with Pound, in which Blackburn sought approval and encouragement from his poetic father in frank, personal letters that linked his writing to sexual relationships with women. The oedipal nature of this rivalry shapes Blackburn's bohemian self-portrait in the correspondence, his deviations from bourgeois respectability, his occasional use of obscenities ("The defense is to not give a fuck"). His letters imitated the gruff colloquialism of Pound's letters, but far exceeded them in shock value (Pound doesn't go beyond "goddam"). After Pound wrote that he submitted Blackburn's version of Peire Vidal's "Ab l'alen" to an editor (12 August 1950), Blackburn's response made clear the oedipal configuration of his authorial identity:

> T H A N K Y O U, P O U N D. And the dry season is over! Have been sitting here trying to divert me by reading. NG. Other diversions physical better for the health et alli. Going to sources like sex and finally getting it relaxed and fine and broke the drought in a shower of somethingorother. Pure peace: to go into a woman relaxed, i.e. in control of the tensions; to sit and write again, i.e. in control of the tensions. So up and about and seeing and doing and feeling.
>
> (early September 1950?)

Although this remarkable passage opens with Blackburn thanking Pound "for the practical encouragement" of submitting the translation, it quickly begins to suggest that Blackburn himself "broke the drought" in his writing through "sex." Blackburn does not challenge Pound in any direct way: one of the striking things about the passage is the conspicuous omission of any first-person pronouns that would indicate Blackburn's agency. This passage constructs only one subject-position, Pound's. Yet an agent appears in the sudden syntactical break at "broke the drought," which assumes an "I," distinct from Pound, and thus hints at the sexual competition underlying Blackburn's identity as poet–translator. This identity is fundamentally a patriarchal construction requiring the female to be an object of male sexuality so that Blackburn might regain his "control" over his writing. A sexual exploitation of "a woman" displaces Blackburn's literary dependence on Pound.

A few months later, on his twenty-fifth birthday, Blackburn wrote
a long letter to Pound that continued this link between writing and
sexuality. This time another canonical writer is invoked, and the
sexual partners multiply:

> A month ago, three weeks, something, I got rid of two girl
> friends, picked fights, having adequate reasons, broke off. A
> month later both grace my bed at intervals, much more secure
> because of the honesty regained in their and my reassessments.
> One doesn't break off relationships. Stories don't end. Shxpr
> knew and killed off all his major characters, ending THEIR
> story: la seule methode effectif.
>
> (24 November 1950)

Blackburn is again "in control," devising his own, sexually
powerful concept of "honesty," writing his own narrative as well as
those of his "girl friends," here likened to Shakespearean
characters as he is to Shakespeare.

This is the double triangle of Blackburn's authorial identity: the
rivalry with Pound is worked out through a sexual dominance over
women and an identification with other canonical writers:

> Funny thing, fear of death. I am twenty-five on this
> date. Seen, faced, lived with, worked with, d e a t h. We
>   are all
> familiars with it, the twenty-five to thirty group. Somewhat,
> someh o w.
> The defensc is to not give a fuck.
> I am defenseless.
> I care about too much.
> Your position too. Why you are where you are.
> Elective affinities. Good title. (G. was afraid of his genius.)
> (Loved many worthy and unworthy women and married – his
> housekeeper.)
>
> (ibid.)

Blackburn's imitation of the discontinuous writing in Pound's
letters resulted in a suggestive free-associating that revealed not
only the height of his poetic ambitions (Goethe), but also their
sexual conditions. The rivalry with Pound, at once literary and
sexual, finally becomes explicit near the end of this letter:

> Would you care to see more [translations]? I'll make copies.

> Reminding me I shall get you some texts of such stuff for xmas.
> I want to give you something. If you need anything I could find
> for you let me know. I am unreliable and faithful. If that makes
> sense to you. I am faithful to two remarkable women at the same
> time.
>
> (ibid.)

Blackburn is "faithful" to Pound in his respect for the elder
writer's literary authority, but "unreliable" in his effort to
challenge that authority through assertions of his sexual potency
(i.e., when he is "faithful to two remarkable women at the same
time").

It is impossible to know what Pound thought of such personal
revelations. None of his letters referred to them. Still, after this last
revealing letter from Blackburn, Pound seems to have broken off
the correspondence, which was not resumed for three years. "Is
anything wrong?" Blackburn suddenly wrote in 1953, "Or is it, on
your part, a cessation of correspondence? And do you object if I
write you from time to time, if the latter shot is the case?" (4 July
1953). The correspondence had become important enough to
Blackburn's sense of himself as a writer that he needed merely to
write to Pound, without getting any response.

Late in the correspondence, Blackburn's rivalry emerges in a
choice to translate an obscene Provençal text that Pound, in an
access of bourgeois squeamishness, refused to translate. This was
"Puois en Raimons e n Trucs Malecs," written by the poet that
inspired Pound's most innovative translations: Arnaut Daniel. In
The Spirit of Romance, Pound had called Daniel's text a "satire too
rank for the modern palate" (Pound 1952:35). Blackburn,
however, translated it, and on 3 January 1957, writing from
Malaga, he sent it to Pound. Here is a strophe:

> Better to have to leave home, better into exile,
> than to have to trumpet, into the funnel between
> the griskin and the p-hole, for from that place there come
> matters better not described (rust-colored). And you'd never
> have the slightest guarantee that she would not leak
> over you altogether, muzzle, eyebrow, cheek.

In a cover letter, Blackburn pronounced his translation successful,
"fair literal and the spirit is there," and he acknowledged Pound's
earlier sense of its obscenity by adding that "it will never be

published." Blackburn viewed obscene language as the prerogative of the modernist poet who uses a colloquial discourse, following William Carlos Williams, and in his interview with David Ossman he treated such language as male:

> if you want to start from the point of view that speech, and that common speech even, is a very fair and valid medium for poetry, you're going to find some people whose common speech is commoner than most. That would include a lot of male members – ladies usually watch their language fairly carefully, and that's only right.
>
> (Ossman 1963:25)

In 1959, soon after Blackburn contracted with Macmillan to publish his Provençal translation, he again wrote to Pound and suggested that obscenity was the prerogative of the male poet–translator:

> Macmillan bringing out the troubadours in a condensed version in spring, if I get the intro. done. I believe I have saved the literal of 'tant las fotei com auziretz' but on the whole, whenever they complained about strong language, I suggested cutting the piece entirely from the book. Marcabru, Guillem VII etc. had no protestant tradition to deal with. Jeanroy cutting, eliminating those stanzas completely in his fr. literal version in the edition. His wife read the proofs?
>
> (5 February 1959)

Blackburn had rendered the Provençal *fotei* as "fucked." The interest in obscenity, expressed in the version of "Truc Malecs" as well as this letter, illustrates how the rivalry with Pound determined Blackburn's translation projects, occasionally in very direct ways.

The most intensely masculinist expression of this rivalry, at once intersubjective and intertextual, involves a text by Bertran de Born, a celebration of feudal militarism on which both Pound and Blackburn worked: "Bem platz lo gais temps de pascor." Pound had done a version of it in *The Spirit of Romance*, partly in verse and partly in prose, to illustrate his claim that "De Born is at his best in the war songs":

> E altresim platz de senhor
> Quant es primiers a l'envazir

En chaval armatz, sens temor,
Qu'aissi fai los seus enardir
   Ab valen vassalatge,
E puois que l'estorns es mesclatz,
Chascus deu esser acesmatz
   E segrel d'agradatge,
Que nuls om non es re prezatz
Tro qu'a maintz colps pres e donatz.

Massas e brans elms de color
E scutz trauchar e desgarnir
Veirem a l'intrar de l'estor
E maintz vassals ensems ferir,
   Dont anaran aratge
Chaval dels mortz e dels nafratz;
E quant er en l'estorn entratz
   Chascus om de paratge,
No pens mas d'asclar chaps e bratz,
Que mais val mortz que vius sobratz.
                    (Thomas 1971:132)

Thus that lord pleaseth me when he is first to attack, fearless, on
his armed charger; and thus he emboldens his folk with valiant
vassalge; and then when stour is mingled, each wight should be
yare, and follow him exulting; for no man is worth a damn till
he has taken and given many a blow.

We shall see battle axes and swords, a-battering colored
haumes and a-hacking through shields at entering melee; and
many vassals smiting together, whence there run free the horses
of the dead and wrecked. And when each man of prowess shall
be come into the fray he thinks no more of (merely) breaking
heads and arms, for a dead man is worth more than one taken
alive.

                    (Pound 1952:35)

Even though this is a fairly close version, Pound develops a
heterogeneous English-language discourse to indicate the historical remoteness of the Provençal text – most obviously, an archaic
lexicon. The word "stour" renders the Provençal *estorn*, *estor*,
meaning "struggle," "conflict" (Levy 1966). Pound's choice is
virtually a homophonic equivalent, a calque, but it is also an
English-language archaism, meaning "armed combat," initially in

Anglo-Saxon, but retained in Middle and Early Modern English as well. It appears in Gavin Douglas's *Aeneid*, among many other literary texts, prose and poetry, "pre-Elizabethan" and Elizabethan. Pound's curious use of "colored haumes" for the Provençal "elms de color" ("painted helmets"), effectively increases the archaism in the translation, but its etymology is uncertain, and it may not strictly be an archaic English word: it seems closer to a variant spelling of the modern French for "helmet," *heaume*, than to any archaic English variants for "helm" (cf. *OED*, s.v. "helm"). What the archaism made seem foreign in this text was the militaristic theme, which Pound at once defined and valorized in a suggestive choice. He translated "chascus om de paratge" as "each man of prowess," rejecting the possibilities of "paratge" that are more genealogical ("lineage," "family," "nobility") and more indicative of class domination, in favor of a choice that stresses a key value of the feudal aristocracy and genders it male: "valour, bravery, gallantry, martial daring; manly courage, active fortitude" (*OED*, s.v. "prowess").

In 1909, a year before the publication of *The Spirit of Romance*, Pound had published a free adaptation of Bertran's text, "Sestina: Altaforte," in which he used the same archaizing strategy. Here, however, Pound celebrated the mere act of aggression, characterized as distinctively aristocratic and masculinist, but devoid of any concept of bravery:

> The man who fears war and squats opposing
> My words for stour, hath no blood of crimson
> But is fit only to rot in womanish peace
> Far from where worth's won and the swords clash
> For the death of such sluts I go rejoicing;
> Yea, I fill all the air with my music.
>   (Pound 1956:8)

As Peter Makin has argued, Pound's appropriations of earlier poets like Bertran serve "as an exemplum, a demonstration of a possible way of living," and they are laden with various cultural and ideological determinations (Makin 1978:42). Makin links the "phallic aggressiveness" of "Sestina: Altaforte" to Pound's esteem for "the 'medieval clean line'" in architecture, as well as to his eulogies of dictators past and present, like Sigismondo Pandolfo Malatesta of Renaissance Rimini and Benito Mussolini, "a male of the species" (Makin 1978:29–35; Pound 1954:83).

Blackburn included a translation of Bertran's poem in the

troubadour anthology he mentioned to Pound in 1958. He followed Pound's example by pursuing a modernist translation strategy, resorting to free verse with the most subtly intricate rhythms and making an inventive selection of archaisms. Blackburn's translation is a strong performance that competes favorably against both of Pound's appropriations of the Provençal text:

> And I love beyond all pleasure, that
> lord who horsed, armed and beyond fear is
> forehead and spearhead in the attack, and there
>   emboldens his men with exploits. When
>   stour proches and comes to quarters
>   may each man pay his quit-rent firmly,
>   follow his lord with joy, willingly,
> for no man's proved his worth a stiver until
>   many the blows
>   he's taken and given.

>   Maces smashing painted helms,
>   glaive-strokes descending, bucklers riven:
>   this to be seen at stour's starting!
> And many valorous vassals pierced and piercing
>   striking together!
> And nickering, wandering lost, through
>   the battle's thick,
>   brast-out blood on broken harness,
> horses of deadmen and wounded.

>   And having once sallied into the stour
>   no boy with a brassard may think of aught, but
>   the swapping of heads, and hacking off arms –
> for here a man is worth more dead
>   than shott-free and caught!

>   (Blackburn 1958:119–120)

"Quit-rent," "vassals," "glaive-strokes" – Blackburn created a lexicon that was obviously medieval, and he occasionally mimicked Anglo-Saxon patterns of rhythm and alliteration ("brast-out blood on broken harness"). Yet his translation discourse was not only historicizing, but foreignizing: some of the archaisms are decidedly unfamiliar, or anachronistic, used in later periods than the Middle Ages. "Stiver," a small coin, is first used in the sixteenth century.

The verb "nicker" is a nineteenth-century usage for "neigh," appearing in such literary texts as Sir Walter Scott's novel *The Monastery* (1820). "Brassard" is French for "armor," but in English it constitutes another nineteenth-century usage, this time Victorian, adding a touch of pre-Raphaelite medievalism to the translation. The word "proches" is also French, at least in spelling; in Blackburn's translation it is a pseudo-archaic neologism, an Anglicized French word that appears to be an archaic variant spelling of "approaches" but actually isn't (no such spelling is recorded in the *OED*).

And of course there is the borrowing from Pound, "stour," one of many such borrowings that recur throughout Blackburn's translations (Apter 1987:76–77; and Apter 1986). Apter has argued that they constitute a "homage" to Pound "as the source of [Blackburn's] interest in and guide to the translation of Provençal lyrics" (1987:77). But insofar as the borrowings insert Pound's language in a different context, their meaning is variable, and they can just as well signify a competition with Pound, even a betrayal. Blackburn's borrowing of "stour" allows his translation to contest Pound's appropriations of Bertran's poem, and the rivalry is figured, interestingly enough, in provocative revisions that interrogate the ideological determinations of Pound's texts. Thus, in striking contrast to Pound, Blackburn rendered "chascus om de paratge" as "no boy with a brassard." The phrase creates dizzying possibilities of meaning. It can be taken as a modern colloquialism, an affectionate expression of male bonding. Blackburn used "boys" in this way at the beginning of Guillem de Poitou's *Companho, faray un vers . . . covinen*:

> I'm going to make a vers, boys . . . good enough,
> But I witless, and it most mad and all
> Mixed up, mesclatz, jumbled from youth and love and joy –

Yet the singular "boy" in the translation can be taken as another sort of colloquialism, a masculinist expression of contempt, usually for another's weakness. Even taken in its most accepted meaning ("male child"), Blackburn's use of "boy" neatly ironizes Bertran's euology of feudal militarism, branding it as childish, unmanly, and deleting the suggestion of aristocratic domination in "paratge". What is interesting here is that Blackburn's oedipal rivalry with Pound, although possessing a masculinist configuration in itself, paradoxically leads to a translation that questions the poetic

father's phallic aggressiveness, his investment in the feudal patriarchy figured in the Provençal texts.

This rivalry drove Blackburn to exceed Pound in the development of a translation discourse that Pound himself had pioneered.
And given the oedipal construction of their relationship, it was
inevitable that the discursive competition would get played out
over the troubadour representations of the lady. Just as Pound
produced his innovative work with Cavalcanti by challenging the
pre-Raphaelite image of the lady in Rossetti's versions (Pound's
poetic "father and mother"), so Blackburn increased the heterogeneity of his translations and questioned Pound's investment in the
patriarchal images of the Provençal love lyric.

Female characters in Provençal poetry are often the objects of
male sexual desire, but their representation varies according to
their class. Aristocratic women undergo a spiritual and physical
idealization, transformed into a passive ornament by the elabo-
rately worked imagery of their lovers, who meet with varying sexual
success; women of lower classes receive a more realistic treatment
involving forms of seduction that range from pleasant cajoling to
brutal intimidation. For *The Spirit of Romance* Pound translated
Marcabru's "L'autrier jost'un sebissa," which he identified as a
"pastorella," a dialogue in which a knight riding through the
country comes upon a farm girl and attempts to seduce her.
Pound's version is written in precise, current English, lightly
archaized:

L'autrier jost'un sebissa
trobei pastora mestissa,
de joi e de sen massissa,
si cum filla de vilana,
cap' e gonel' e pelissa
vest e camiza trelissa,
sotlars e caussas e lana.

Ves lieis vinc per la planissa:
"Toza, fim ieu, res faitissa,
dol ai car lo freitz vos fissa."
"Seigner, som dis la vilana,
merce Dieu e ma noirissa,
pauc m'o pretz sil vens m'erissa,
qu'alegreta sui e sana."

"Toza, fi'm ieu, cauza pia,
destors me sui de la via
per far a vos compaignia;
quar aitals toza vilana
no deu ses pareill paria
pastorgar tanta bestia
en aital terra, soldana."
                    (Dejeanne 1971:33)

The other day beside a hedge
I found a low-born shepherdess,
Full of joy and ready wit,
And she was the daughter of a peasant woman;
Cape and petticoat and jacket, vest and shirt of fustian,
Shoes, and stockings of wool.

I came towards her through the plain,
"Damsel," said I, "pretty one,
I grieve for the cold that pierces you."
"Sir," said the peasant maid,
"Thank God and my nurse
I care little if the wind ruffle me,
For I am happy and sound."

"Damsel," said I, "pleasant one,
I have turned aside from the road
To keep you company.
For such a peasant maid
Should not, without a suitable companion,
Shepherd so many beasts
In such a lonely place."
                    (Pound 1952:62–63)

Pound's version is again rather close, and it is not distinguished by prosodic and lexical invention. His sharpest departure from the Provençal, however, is extremely pointed: he used the archaism "damsel" to render the knight's epithet for the shepherdess, "toza," which Emil Levy defined as "jeune fille" ("young girl") (Levy 1966), yet with an unsavory connotation, "fille de mauvaise vie" ("immoral girl"). (The Provençal text also stigmatizes the girl with "mestissa," a reference to her low birth that likewise carries the sense of "mauvais, vil.") Pound's use of "damsel" at once idealizes and ironizes the image of the girl, sarcastically marking her inferior social position and portraying the knight as a wittily devious seducer, out to overcome her resistance with flattering appeals to her (presumed) class aspirations.

Pound so enjoyed the knight's predatory sexuality that he wistfully imagined the girl yielding at last. After quoting his partial translation of the poem, he added that "The adventure is finally brought to a successful termination" (Pound 1952:63). But the fact is that the girl withstands the knight's advances and concludes the dialogue with some cryptic wit of her own – in Frederick Goldin's rendering,

> "Don, lo cavecs vos ahura,
> que tals bad'en la peintura
> qu'autre n'espera la mana."

> "Master, that owl is making you a prophecy:
> this one stands gaping in front of a painting,
> and that one waits for manna."
>   (Goldin 1973:77)

Blackburn translated Marcabru's entire text, and his version quite clearly borrows lines from Pound's, while just as clearly revising the father's phallic aggressiveness:

> The other day, under a hedge
> I found a low-born shepherdess,
> full of wit and merriment
> and dressed like a peasant's daughter:
> her shift was drill, her socks were wool,
> clogs and a fur-lined jacket on her.

> I went to her across the field:
> — Well, baby! What a pretty thing.
> You must be frozen, the wind stings . . .
> — Sir, said the girl to me,
> thanks to my nurse and God, I care
> little that wind ruffle my hair,
> I'm happy and sound.

> — Look, honey, I said, I turned
> into here and out of my way
> just to keep you company.
> Such a peasant girl ought not

without a proper fellow
pasture so many beasts alone
in such a wild country.
                    (Blackburn 1958:24)

Blackburn worked hard to surpass Pound on every level. His
inventive prosody aimed to mimic the song-like sound effects of
the Provençal text, evoking the music of Christopher Marlowe's
"The Passionate Shepherd to His Love," especially at the end of
the first stanza. And he created a translation discourse that
sampled the most varied lexicons, past ("drill") and present
("honey"), British ("proper fellow") and American ("pretty
thing"), standard usage ("sir") and slang ("baby"). In a later
version, Blackburn coarsened the colloquialism "pretty thing" into
"pretty piece," revealing at the outset the knight's sexual designs
on the girl and treating him (instead of her, as in the Provençal
"toza") in the most unsavoury way, as some sort of sex-crazed '50s
hipster given to pornographic come-ons: "Well, baby! What a
pretty piece" (Blackburn 1986:35). Blackburn continues this
ironic image of the knight by revising the Provençal text at "pareill
paria" (roughly "social equals," "your fellows," "your peers"), which
he translated as "proper fellow," suggesting both the knight's
superior social position and the moral impropriety concealed by
his "proper" accent. Blackburn's mixture of archaism with current
usage juxtaposes the cultural representations from two periods,
allowing them to interrogate one another: the coarse contemporary slang demystifies the more formal rhetorical effects (troubadour and Marlovian) that mystified aristocratic domination (in
medieval Provence and Elizabethan England); and the archaism
defamiliarizes the most recent and familiar sexual terms ("pretty
piece") by exposing their complicity with masculinist images of
women in past aristocratic literary cultures.

    This interrogative effect of Blackburn's mixed lexicons strength-
ens his version of the shepherdess's cryptic conclusion – which
Pound misread and suppressed. In Blackburn's version, she
describes the mystifying rhetoric of feudal patriarchy as an archaic-
sounding "simple show" and then unmasks it as a distraction from
the material conditions of the seduction, not the transcendental
mana in the Provençal text, but the unequal social relations in
which she and the knight are involved, signified here by a
colloquialism, "the lunch basket":

> — Sir, the owl is your bird of omen.
> There's always some who'll stand open-
> mouthed before the simple show,
> while there's others'll wait until
>   the lunch basket comes around.
>   (Blackburn 1958:25)

Given the interrogative effects of its mixed lexicon, Blackburn's translation can be read as a critique of the ideological determinations, both aristocratic and masculinist, that shape Pound's version as well as Marcabru's text.

Blackburn's Provençal translations are the distinguished achievement of a modernist poet–translator. Taking up the innovations that Pound developed in his versions of troubadour poets like Arnaut Daniel, Blackburn cultivated a discursive heterogeneity to signify the linguistic and cultural difference of the Provençal texts. And he did it by recovering various English-language dialects and discourses – residual, dominant, emergent. There is a rich strain of archaism, partly medieval, partly Elizabethan, suggestive of Chaucer, Douglas, Sir Philip Sidney, Shakespeare: "the king's helots," "choler," "her soft mien," "seisin," "cark," "sire," "wench," "harlotry," "puissance," "haulberk," "doublets," "thee," "forfend," "dolors," "gulls," "escutcheon," "villeiny," "beyond measure." And there is an equally rich strain of contemporary colloquialism, occasionally British ("tart"), but mostly American, including slang and obscenity from the 1950s, but cutting across different periods, cultural forms (elite and mass), and social groups: "jay-dee" (for "juvenile delinquent"), "phonies," "push-cart vendor," "budged," "cash," "grouch," "make-up," "goo," "asshole," "cunt," "the doc," "we'll have some lovin'," "all of 'em crapped out," "balls," "this bitch," "hard-up," "shell out," "nymphos," "creeps," "hide-the-salami," "skimpy," "floored," "you sound like some kind of nut," "Mafiosi," "garage," "steam-rolls," "a pain in his backside," "hassle," "keep his eye peeled for them," "shimmy," "90 proof." Blackburn's multiple lexicons are also multilingual, including Provençal ("trobar," "canso," "vers,"), French ("fosse," "targe," "copains," "maistre,"), and even Gallicized pseudo-archaism ("cavalage," drawn from the Provençal *encavalgar*, "to ride a horse").

Blackburn's various discursive strategies included syntactical peculiarities adopted by Pound. Dudley Fitts's review of Pound's translations took exception to their syntax: after quoting a line from Pound's Daniel, "Love inkerlie doth leaf and flower and bear," Fitts complained that "Those, Reader, are verbs, not nouns" (Fitts 1954:19). Blackburn likewise used nouns as verbs, frustrating the reader's grammatical expectations with phrasing that was strange ("I grouch"), but also evocative ("the night they sorcered me").

Blackburn's prosody owes a debt to Pound's recommendations "as to the use of canzoni in English, whether for composition or in translation" (Anderson 1983:217). Pound felt that some English "rhymes are of the wrong timbre and weight" for the intricately rhymed stanza in Provençal and Italian, and to compensate he developed a "rhyme-aesthetic" that differed from the foreign texts, as well as from current stanzaic forms in English-language poetry: "Against which we have our concealed rhymes and our semi-submerged alliteration" (ibid.). Blackburn's acute sense of word placement and timing led to varying patterns of internal and end rhyme that sometimes heightened the anachronism of his lexical mix, the clash of different cultures, different historical periods – like the "okay"/"atelier" rhyme in his version of Guillem de Poitou's *Ben vuelh que sapchon li pluzor*:

> I would like it if people knew this song,
> a lot of them, if it prove to be okay
> when I bring it in from my atelier, all
> fine and shining:
> for I surpass the flower of this business,
> it's the truth, and I'll
> produce the vers as witness
> when I've bound it in rhyme.
>   (Blackburn 1986:12)

Blackburn's attention to the musicality of the Provençal text assumes Pound's discussion of "melopoeia" in the canso and canzone: "the poems of medieval Provence and Tuscany in general, were all made to be sung. Relative estimates of value inside these periods must take count of the cantabile values" of the work, "accounting for its manifest lyric impulse, or for the emotional force in its cadence" (Anderson 1983:216, 230). For Pound, this rhythm-based lyricism produced an effect that was individualistic but also masculinist, constructing a lyrical "I" in the translation that was explicitly male: "I have in my translations tried to bring over the qualities of Guido's rhythm, not line for line, but to embody in the whole of my English some trace of that power which implies the man," what Pound later called "a *robustezza,* a masculinity" (ibid.:19, 242). But Pound's most innovative translations tended to diverge from his modernist critical representations of the foreign texts, principally because his translation discourse was so heterogeneous, full of textual effects that undermined any illusionism, any sense of the foreign author's presence, any coherent "I." In the same way, Blackburn's lyrical prosody definitely constructs a subject-position with which the listener/reader can identify, but the rhythms are always varying, asymmetrical at points, and the lexical and syntactical peculiarities are constantly foregrounding the textuality, weakening the coherence of the speaking voice, splintering the discourse into different cultures and periods, even different genders (depending on the genre), now locked in a mutual interrogation. Here is the opening of Blackburn's version of Cercamon's *Ab lo temps qe refrescar:*

>   With the fine spring weather
> that makes the world seem young again,
> when the meadows come green again
> I want to begin
> with a new song
> on a love that's my cark and desire,
> but is so far I cannot hit her mark
> or my words fire her.

I'm so sad nothing can comfort me,
better off dead, for foul mouths
have separated me from her, God-
damn them – o,
I would have wanted her so much! Now
I grouch and shout, or weep, or sing
or walk about
like any hare-brained golden thing.

And how lovely she I sing is! more
than I know how to tell you here.
Her glance is straight, her color's fresh
and white, white without blemish, no
    she wears no make-up.
They can say no hard word of her, she

is so fine and clear as an emerald.

(Blackburn 1958:17)

Blackburn's odd rhythms and diction destabilize the reader's sympathetic identification with the lyric voice, preventing the translation from being taken as the "original," the transparent expression of the foreign author, and instead insisting on its second-order status, a text that produces effects in English, distinct from the Provençal poem but also departing from contemporary English usage, possessing a powerful self-difference, a sudden shifting from the familiar to the unfamiliar, even to the unintelligible.

Blackburn's translation of Provençal poetry is clearly more accessible than the Zukofskys' Catullus, requiring a less aggressive application to appreciate because of a more inviting lyricism. But it too follows Pound's innovations by developing a translation discourse that is both historicist and foreignizing, that signals the cultural differences of the foreign texts through a linguistic experimentalism. The project is marked by the rivalry with Pound that formed Blackburn's identity as a modernist poet–translator, determining not only the choice of texts and the development of a translation discourse, but also a revisionism that critiques Pound's own appropriations of the same texts, questioning their investment in aristocracy, patriarchy, individualism – ideological determinations that also marked Blackburn's writing in varying degrees and across many different forms (letters, poems, translations, interviews). Blackburn's Provençal project was decisive in his personal formation as a author; but since this formation occurred in writing, the translation could also be conceived as a strategic public intervention, a cultural political practice that was fundamentally modernist, but that was not uncritical in its acceptance of Pound's modernism.

Blackburn's rare comments on his work suggest that he saw it along these or related lines. In a 1969 interview, he responded to the question, "What poets have influenced your work?" by citing Pound, Williams, Creeley, Charles Olson, whose poetry he read because "I wanted to find out who my father was" (Packard 1987:9). Blackburn may not have psychoanalyzed his relationship to Pound, but after translating for some twenty years and spending many years in analysis, he definitely possessed a psychoanalytic view of the translating process, of the relationship between the translation and the foreign text, the translator and the foreign author. This is clear in the interview:

> I don't become the author when I'm translating his prose or poetry, but I'm certainly getting my talents into his hang-ups. Another person's preoccupations are occupying me. They literally own me for that time. You see, it's not just a matter of reading the language and understanding it and putting it into English. It's understanding something that makes the man do it, where he's going. And it's not an entirely objective process. It must be partially subjective; there has to be some kind of projection. How do you know which word to choose when a word may have four or five possible meanings in English? It's not just understanding the text. In a way you live it each time, I mean, *you're there*. Otherwise, you're not holding the poem.
>
> (ibid.:13)

English translation theorists from the seventeenth century onward had recommended a sympathetic identification between the translator and the foreign author. In Alexander Tytler's words, "he must adopt the very soul of his author, which must speak through his own organs" (Tytler 1978:212). Yet this sort of sympathy was used to underwrite the individualism of transparent translation, the illusion of authorial presence produced by fluent discourse: it was Tytler's answer to the question, "How then shall a translator accomplish this difficult union of ease with fidelity?" Blackburn's modernist sense of identification acknowledged that there could never be a perfect sympathy, that the translator developed a "projection," a representation, specific to the target-language culture, that interrogated the foreign author, exposing "his hang-ups." When Blackburn's translator is "there," the sense of immediacy comes, not from any direct apprehension of the foreign text, but from living out an interpretation that enables the translator to "hold the poem," rationalize every step in the translation process, every choice of a word.

In responding to a 1970 questionnaire from the *New York Quarterly*, Blackburn used similar psychological terms to describe the textual effects of translation, observing that the translator's identification changes the foreign author, but also the translator himself, who increasingly becomes the site of multiple sub-jectivities, a deviation from rational norms:

He must be willing (& able) to let another man's life enter his own deeply enough to become some permanent part of his original author. He should be patient, persistent, slightly schizoid, a hard critic, a brilliant editor [...] We are all hundreds, maybe thousands of people, potentially or in fact.

(Blackburn 1985:616)

In both the interview and questionnaire, Blackburn's view of the poet–translator is insistently masculinist: the process of identification or "projection" occurs between men. In the interview, it was part of Blackburn's bohemian self-presentation, where he abruptly segued from a discussion about "writing in a travel situation" to "girl-watching": "To come back to the city, though, the subway is an incredible place for girl-watching. You find one face or a good pair of legs – you can look at them for hours" (Packard 1987:14). And yet if, in Blackburn's account, translation multiplies subjectivities by mediating cultural differences, it can only explode any individualistic concept of identity, masculinist or otherwise. Blackburn felt that the range of different demands made on the translator was extreme, resulting in deviancy, inviting psychiatric terms or allusions to popular cultural forms, like blues and rock-and-roll (or even more specifically the blues-based rock of Bob Dylan's 1965 album *Bringing It All Back Home*), linking the translator to other racial and youth subcultures:

In your view, what is a translator?

A man who brings it *all* back home.
In short, a madman.

(Blackburn 1985:616)

Blackburn was of course aware that the psychological processes he described so facetiously could be figured only in discursive strategies, and these he saw as a challenge to bourgeois values, not just to individualistic concepts of identity, but to a moralistic sense of propriety in conduct and language. As early as 1950, in a letter to Pound, he remarked on "the impossibility of translating poems written in a twelfth century aristocratic vocabulary into MODERN ENGLISH POEMS written in a twentieth century bourgeois vocabulary" (24 November 1950). Twenty years later, in a response to the *New York Quarterly* questionnaire, Blackburn acknowledged that the translator must draw on current English usage, but he also advocated a linguistic experimentalism that recovered marginal discourses, even with the most canonical of literary texts:

> How far should a translator attempt to "modernize" an antiquarian piece?
>
> Try first to find a diction, a modern diction, which will translate as many values as possible of the original. I've seen Latin poetry translated into hip language that works very well for certain pieces. Carried too far, of course, over a whole body of work, it'd be a stunt. Some stunts, however, are brilliantly executed.
>
> (Blackburn 1985:617)

Blackburn's investment in Provençal poetry was partly due to the troubadours' anti-bourgeois themes, present not only in the celebration of feudal aristocratic values, but also in a representation of the troubadours culled partly from the biographical details in the *vidas* and *razos*. Some troubadours were itinerant performers born to commoners – farmers, tradesmen, merchants – but later living and working on the margins of feudal courts; others were landless knights, somewhat migrant, their loyalties drifting among various lords and ladies. In his poem "Sirventes" (1956), a satire "against the city of Toulouse," Blackburn adopts a troubadour persona and invokes Peire Vidal, portraying him as a bohemian poet, a beatnik, intent on offending any bourgeois sense of decency:

> That mad Vidal would spit on it,
> that I as his maddened double
> do – too
> changed, too changed, o
> deranged master of song,
> master of the viol and the lute
> master of those sounds,
> I join you in public madness,
> in the street I piss
> on French politesse
> that has wracked all passion from the sound of speech.
> A leech that sucks the blood is less a lesion. Speech!
> this imposed   imposing   imported   courtliness,   that
> the more you hear it the more it's meaningless
>   & without feeling.
>
> (Blackburn 1985:89–90)

In the Provençal translations, Blackburn sometimes tilts his lexicon heavily toward contemporary English, inscribing the troubadour poem with a satire on capitalist economic practices, on businessmen and lawyers. This occurs with another of Bertran de Born's war songs, *No puosc mudar un chantar non esparga*. In Blackburn's version, the marauding knight becomes more criminal, more gangster-like – "A good war, now, makes a niggardly lord/turn lavish and shell out handsomely" – but the knight is also more business-like, given to financial planning ("expenditures") and living in suburbia:

> have I not taken blows upon my targe?
> And dyed red the white of my gonfalon?
> Yet for this I have to suffer and pinch my purse,
> for Oc-e-No plays with loaded dice.
> I'm hardly lord of Rancon or Lusignan
> that I can war beyond my own garage
>   without an underwriter's check.
> But I'll contribute knowledge and a good strong arm
> with a basin on my head and a buckler on my neck!
> (Blackburn 1958:116)

Blackburn actually addressed the social implications of translation on one occasion: in "The International Word," an article he contributed to a special issue of *The Nation* devoted to culture and politics. Published in 1962, on the eve of the Cuban Missile Crisis, when Blackburn was serving as poetry editor of this left-wing magazine, "The International Word" argues that a modernist cultural politics can effectively intervene in the current global situation: in Blackburn's diagnosis, "the crisis of identity of the individual in a world whose underlying realities are the cold war and the bomb" (Blackburn 1962:358). In a survey of contemporary American poetry, Blackburn found the most politically engaged poets to be modernist: his litany includes Pound, Williams, the Objectivists, Black Mountain, the Beats, the New York School – figures and tendencies that had recently been presented as oppositional in Donald Allen's anthology, *The New American Poetry* (Allen 1960). Blackburn noted Pound's insistence "on the values of bringing across other sensibilities in other languages and from all periods of history and civilization" (Blackburn 1962:357) and assigned translation a key geopolitical role: "the mutual insemination of cultures is an important step in

what our policy makers think of as international understanding"
(ibid.:358). In this politicized rationale for cultural exchange,
modernist translation was summoned to resolve a domestic crisis,
searching foreign cultures to supply the lack of confidence in the
"official values" of Cold War American culture:

> The Cold War and the possibly imminent illumination of the
> world have created another reaction in poets [...] There is an
> affirmation, a reaffirmation, of values, a searching of the older
> cultures, both American and foreign, modern and ancient, for
> values to sustain the individual in a world where all the official
> values have let us down entirely by being in the main
> hypocritical (consider the phrase "business ethics" for a
> moment), the religions attentuated to the point where even the
> monks are screaming from the pinch.
>
> (ibid.:359)

Blackburn's concern about the "identity of the individual" did not
assume a liberal individualism grounded in concepts of personal
freedom, self-determination, psychological coherence; he rather
saw human identity as other-determined, a composite constructed
in relationships to "values" that were transindividual, cultural and
social, housed in institutions like the state, the church, the school.
If translation could change the contours of subjectivity, Blackburn
thought, then it could contribute to a change in values, away from
"the military stance and the profit motive" toward less strained
geopolitical relations, "perhaps breadth of understanding for
other peoples, a greater tolerance for and proficiency in other
languages, combined with political wisdom and expediency over
the next two generations" (ibid.:358).

Some of Blackburn's remarks have come to seem much too
optimistic. He judged from "the current flood of translations in
both prose and poetry" that "The ducts of free exchange are
already open in literature" (Blackburn 1962:357, 358). But
cultural exchange through translation wasn't then (nor ever could
be) "free" of numerous constraints, literary, economic, political,
and English-language translation certainly wasn't free in 1962.
That year the number of translations issued by American
publishers was actually small, approximately 6 percent of the total
books published (*Publishers Weekly* 1963). We now know that
American translation rates reached their apex in the early 1960s,
but they have consistently been quite low in contrast to foreign

publishing trends throughout the postwar period, which show much higher percentages of translating English-language books.

Blackburn's utopianism also has a pro-American slant that seems too uncritical after numerous subsequent developments – the Vietnam War, the political and military interventions in El Salvador and Nicaragua, government skittishness on ecological issues, the emergence of multinational corporations, especially in publishing, where the number of English-language translations has fallen to less than 3 percent of the total books published. In 1962, however, Blackburn imagined that

> Perhaps even nationalism, so living a force today in Africa and the Far East, is beginning to die a little in the affluent West. Except for the political forms, Western Europe is on the threshold of becoming an economic unity. Is it an impossible dream to think of a bilingual America stretching from Tierra del Fuego to the Arctic Ocean, comprised of eighty-three states instead of fifty? Not by conquest but by union. How move more efficiently to raise the standard of living of underdeveloped countries in our own hemisphere than by removing the borders?
>
> (Blackburn 1962:358)

Readers in 1962 no doubt regarded this passage as a utopian flight. Blackburn himself called it "an impossible dream." In the following year, he published a somber article in *Kulchur*, "The Grinding Down," which surveyed the current poetry "scene" and found modernism marginal and fragmented: "the Renaissance," Blackburn wrote, "didn't take"; it was now centered in a few small-circulation magazines, "making a place somewhere between the outer fringe of the academic and the inner sector of the so-called beat" (Blackburn 1963:17, 10). In 1962, Blackburn was more sanguine about the prospects of modernism, but the emphasis on the "West" in his utopianism shows the difficulty of imagining relations between the hemispheres during the Cold War – even for a politically engaged poet–translator like him. The perspective from which he anticipated future global developments was clearly that of North American hegemony, allied with western Europe in a strategic containment of Soviet expansionism, but permitted to indulge in some hemispheric expansion of its own ("eighty-three states").

Blackburn's article is valuable, not as a historical prediction or foreign policy, but rather as a theoretical model, useful in thinking how translation can be enlisted in a democratic cultural politics. Blackburn saw modernist translation as an effective intervention in American culture, based on a social diagnosis that found hegemonic domestic values implicated in unequal or exclusionary social relations. Blackburn's own translations, with their various foreignizing strategies, served a left-wing internationalism, designed to combat the ideological forms of exclusion in Cold War America, perhaps most evident in the hysterical patriotism excited by hardening geopolitical positions (Whitfield 1991). The Provençal translation was especially subversive in this cultural situation because it revealed a broad range of influences, foreign and historical. The clear debt to modernism made the project vulnerable to Leslie Fiedler's politicized attack on Pound's translations for lacking a "center," an allegiance to one national literature, American: "Our Muse is the poet without a Muse, whom quite properly we acquit of treason (what remains to betray?) and consign to Saint Elizabeth's" (Fiedler 1962:459).

Blackburn's Provençal translation was marked, not only by a connection to an un-American poet–translator, but by an affiliation to popular culture through his resonant use of colloquialism. As Andrew Ross has shown, Cold War intellectuals associated popular culture with totalitarianism, mass thinking, brainwashing, but also with commercialism, egalitarianism, radical democracy. As the American government pursued a policy of Soviet containment abroad, at home intellectuals like Fiedler constructed a national culture of consensus that "depended explicitly upon the containment of intellectual radicalism and cultural populism alike" (Ross 1989:47). In Robert von Hallberg's view, "what is important to literary history is not only that this consensus existed but that its maintenance and definition depended somehow upon academic institutions. [...] To the extent that poets looked to universities for an audience, they were addressing [...] the audience that felt greatest responsibility for the refinement of taste and the preservation of a national culture" (Von Hallberg 1985:34). Blackburn's work with Provençal poetry both questioned and resisted this hegemonic domestic tendency. Allied to a modernist poetic movement that defined itself as "a total rejection of all those qualities typical of academic verse" (Allen 1960:xi), Blackburn's translation was radical in its ideological interrogations (of the foreign texts, previous English-language appropriations, contemporary American culture) and populist in its juxtaposition of elite and popular cultural discourses.

The publishing history of Blackburn's manuscript shows without a doubt that the cultural and political values represented by his translation continued to be marginal in the United States late into the 1970s. In Blackburn's case, however, the marginality was not signalled by mixed reviews or bitter attacks or even media neglect; there was never a publication to review. The manuscript Blackburn felt was finished in 1958 did not see print until twenty years later.

In March of 1958, the influential poetry critic M. L. Rosenthal, who had taught Blackburn briefly at New York University (1947), recommended the Provençal manuscript to Macmillan.[9] In 1957, as poetry editor for *The Nation*, Rosenthal had accepted one of Blackburn's translations, his Pound-inspired version of Bertran de Born's *Bem platz lo gais temps pascor.* Rosenthal was now advising Emile Capouya, an editor in Macmillan's Trade Department, on a series of poetry volumes. Blackburn submitted the manuscript, tentatively entitled *Anthology of Troubadours*. It was a translation of sixty-eight texts by thirty poets, considerably reduced from the "105 pieces" that Blackburn mentioned to Pound, "cut fr/150" (17 March 1958). Capouya solicited an outside reader's report and then, despite a highly critical evaluation, accepted it for publication, issuing Blackburn a contract that paid a small advance ($150) against a full author's royalty (10 percent of the cover price, $3.50, with a first printing of 1500 copies), plus all the income from first serial rights (initial publications in magazines and anthologies). Although, by October of 1958, the contracts had been signed and countersigned, the manuscript was not complete: Blackburn needed to submit the introduction he had planned. Capouya scheduled the publication date for the fall of 1959, but Blackburn did not complete the manuscript, and the project languished until 1963, when, a few years after Capouya's departure from Macmillan, another editor decided to cancel the contract. During the 1960s Blackburn tried to get his manuscript accepted by other publishers, like Doubleday, who asked Rosenthal to evaluate the project. But these attempts were sporadic and without success. The translation at last appeared posthumously in 1978 as *Proensa: An Anthology of Troubadour Poetry,* edited by Blackburn's friend, the medievalist and poet George Economou, for the University of California Press.

Why didn't Blackburn complete a project that was certain to be published and under contractual terms that were favorable to the translator (despite the low advance)? Different answers have been offered for this question, ranging from Blackburn's unsettled personal life at the time (his divorce from his first wife, his financial straits) to a psychoanalytic assessment that found his relations with women, particularly his mother, the poet Frances Frost, linked to an "obsession" with "the idealization of woman as expressed by the Troubadours" (Eshleman 1989:19). The Macmillan episode could only be determined by these private investments in a most public form, which here included a harsh reader's report. Sara Golden, Blackburn's second wife (1963–1967), recalled that the report "sent Paul back to an endless spiral of revisions that never ended until his death" (Telephone interview, 23 January 1992). Rosenthal described Blackburn as "appalled" by the report; the poet Robert Kelly, a friend of Blackburn's who edited some of his posthumous books, mentioned that "Paul was both hurt and amused by it" and would sometimes read out the criticisms in a comically exaggerated voice (Telephone interviews, 26 December 1991 and 23 July 1992). Taken aback by these criticisms, after years of encouragement from writers like Pound and Creeley and from editors at magazines like *Hudson Review*, *Origin*, and *The Nation*, Blackburn did not complete the manuscript. On the contrary, he suddenly felt that it needed an enormous amount of work, not just an introduction and annotations, but substantial revisions of the translation. Unfortunately, he also lacked an editor to facilitate his completion of the project and bring it to press.

Capouya sought evaluations from powerful poet–translators and critics. He turned first to a poet and translator of Dante, John Ciardi, then associated with *Saturday Review*, who wrote back "Anthol of Troubadours sounds interesting" but declined because of prior commitments. Capouya then turned to Ramon Guthrie, an American poet who lived in France for many years and was currently professor of French at Dartmouth. Guthrie (1896–1973) published his first books in the 1920s: translations and adaptations of troubadour poetry and a novel based on the texts of Marcabru. Under a pseudonym, Guthrie also published *The Legend of Ermengarde*, what Sally Gall has described as an "exuberantly indecent poem" inspired by troubadour poetry (Gall 1980:184). Capouya planned to publish Guthrie's volume of poems, *Graffitti*, also recommended by Rosenthal, who suggested that Guthrie evaluate Blackburn's translation. Perhaps in an effort to pique Guthrie's interest, or to ward off any expectations of academic fidelity to the Provençal texts, Capouya's letter described Blackburn's project as "a collection of adaptations," not the "anthology" he mentioned to Ciardi. Guthrie, it turned out, was actually the worst possible reader for Blackburn's manuscript.

In the 1920s, his own translations of Provençal texts were cast in current English usage with a slight pre-Raphaelite archaism, in diction and verse form (a rhymed stanza). This is the opening of "Winter-Song," Guthrie's translation from Marcabru:

Since the withered leaves are shredded
From the branches of the trees,
Mauled and tousled and behcaded
By the bitter autumn breeze,
More I prize the sleety rain
Than the summer's mealy guile,
Bearing wantonry and lewdness.
(Guthrie 1927a:68)

Although Guthrie lived in Paris during the 1920s and was fond of evoking that modernist cultural moment in his later poetry, the poetry itself reveals him to be more Wordsworthian than Poundian:

Montparnasse
that I shall never see again, the Montparnasse
of Joyce and Pound, Stein, Stella Bowen,
little Zadkine, Giacometti [. . .] all gone in any case,
and would I might have died, been buried there.
(Guthrie 1970:15)

By the 1950s, Guthrie had also become an academic, even though he lacked a high school diploma and had received the degrees for foreigners offered at the University of Toulouse. And this immersion in academic culture played into his evaluation of Blackburn's manuscript. His response was substantial and detailed, checking individual translations against the Provençal texts, giving what he called "suggestions" in a two-page report and many marginal comments scattered throughout the manuscript. He didn't mind Blackburn's use of obscenity, although in the 1920s he himself was sufficiently prudish to use a French pseudonym for a lewd parody and to bowdlerize his signed translation from Guillem de Poitou: "In which time – here we expurgate ... One hundred times and eighty-eight,/Till heart and back were both in great/Danger of breaking" (Guthrie 1927a:59). Blackburn's version initially read "fucked," but then, apparently in a moment of uncertainty about his male bohemianism, he struck it and added "loved." Guthrie encouraged Blackburn to use the obscenity, which perhaps served to confirm his own sense of masculinity, compensating for his earlier expurgation through another translator's work:

> The word "loved" is too much like sneaking out the back-door. Why not either the original word in English as was, or "f ---- d" or leave it in Occitanian "las fotei?" In as legitimate a cause as this, one ought to be able to get away with *one* 4 letter word.

What did not seem "legitimate" to Guthrie was the modernist experimentalism of Blackburn's translation: the foreignizing strategies deviated too widely from prevailing domestic values in the reception of archaic texts, especially scholarly annotation and fluent discourse.

Guthrie's own work with troubadour poetry in the 1920s had assumed the modernist ideal of translation as an independent literary text: he published his translations as poems in their own right, identifying them as translations only in vague footnotes that omitted any precise identification of the Provençal texts. In 1958, however, Guthrie did not recognize Blackburn's pursuit of this same modernist ideal, his emphasis on the literary qualities of the translation at the expense of annotations, which he limited to the Provençal titles and to the *vidas* and *razos* that accompanied the texts in manuscripts. Guthrie wanted Blackburn's translation to have a more academic cast, even while acknowledging "the general reader":

> There should be a short introduction explaining what, when and where the troubadours were; something of the nature and importance of their work; the formal qualities of their works and the differences between their forms and P.B.'s rendering – also a few words on P.B.'s purpose.
>
> There should also be definitions in the appropriate places (most of which I have marked) of such terms as "alba," "tenson," "sirventes," etc. [...]

A number of poems (see pp. 163, 55, 129) need short introductions badly.

Omitting annotations can of course signal the cultural difference of the foreign texts, insisting on their foreignness with all the discomfort of incomprehension. Most of Blackburn's foreignizing strategies, however, were realized in his translations, and since they constituted notable deviations from fluent discourse, they definitely looked strange to Guthrie. Thus, Blackburn resorted to variant spellings to mimic the absence of standardized orthography and pronunciation in Provençal, but for Guthrie this made the text too resistant to easy readability:

> For the reader's convenience, there should be uniformity in spelling proper nouns. It is confusing to the uninitiate to find (often on the same page) Peitau & Poitou, Caersi & Quercy, Talhafer & Tagliaferro (I'd translate it "Iron-Cutter," since it is a nickname); Ventadorn & Ventadour: Marvoill & Mareuil: Amfos & Alfons. Using the modern names of the towns would help the general reader.

Blackburn's use of variant spellings were a means of archaizing the text, signifying its historical remoteness. Guthrie preferred current English usage ("Iron-Cutter"), even the latest cartography.

Guthrie's criticisms went deep to the heart of Blackburn's project. They touched the texts that figured in the oedipal rivalry with Pound: Guthrie's concern with fluency led to the suggestion that Blackburn *delete* his Pound-inspired version of Bertran de Born's war song. "Maybe I am too harsh," wrote Guthrie, "but from the first line to the last, it seems forced and ineffectual compared with either the original or with E. Pound's Sestina drawn from the same source." When Guthrie reached page 135 in the 187-page manuscript, he scrawled a somewhat exasperated criticism of Blackburn's mixed lexicons:

> P.B.
> No, look, if you are going to call somebody a burgesa in one line and make the poor inhorantes go looking it up in Levy, you can't have the burgesa's husband getting into a (since 1950) hassle nor somebody doing somebuditch dishonor and smoting him on ye hede in the line after.
>
> R.G.

> If one says "copains," one cannot say in the same sentence "had been taken ill." It is as if one said "His buddy" (only in a foreign language) "gave up the ghost."

It is interesting to note that Guthrie repeatedly set himself up as a spokesperson for the nonspecialist, nonacademic audience ("the uninitiate," "the inhorantes"), but simultaneously made the elitist gesture of excluding popular discourses and dialects, especially working-class colloquialisms. Guthrie's investment in the standard dialect came with a sense of social superiority that surfaced in his comment on another translation, Blackburn's version of Bernart de Ventadorn's *Can vei la lauzeta mover*. Blackburn's text is typically heterogeneous:

> Narcissus at the spring, I kill
>   this human self.

> Really, though, without hope, over the ladies;
> never again trust myself to them.
>   I used to defend them
>   but now
> I'm clearing out, leaving town, quit.
> Not one of them helps me against her
> who destroys and confounds me,
> fear and disbelieve all of them,
>   all the same cut.
>   (Blackburn 1958:47)

Guthrie thought the colloquialism degraded the foreign text, which he saw as more lofty in tone, more proper in speech, more aristocratic: "This," he wrote, "gets cheap, a sort of Flatbush parody on Bernart, RG." Blackburn's use of "Hell" similarly departed from Guthrie's elite image of the troubadours: "This isn't in accord with Bernart's mood, but maybe it's more modern than 'Alas.'" For Guthrie, marginal translation discourses trashed canonical texts. The English he preferred was the standard American dialect; if archaism was used, it needed to be unobtrusive and consistent.

Inevitably, Blackburn's more inventive experiments provoked Guthrie to domesticate the translations, revising them for fluency, but also deleting the political satire enabled by the mixed lexicon. When Blackburn edged his version of Bertran de Born closer to contemporary social issues by portraying feudal knights as bourgeois entrepreneurs, "unable to war beyond my own garage/ without an underwriter's check" (Blackburn 1958:125), Guthrie complained about the strange effects produced by the multi-lingual diction:

> Since P.B. uses so many anachronisms on the modern side, why "targe" for "shield." The rime scheme of this sestina aren't [*sic*] followed in the translation anyway and, being spotty, would be better omitted. But if a rime must be had (and God knows the "targe - garage" is nothing to be awfully happy about), why not "shield - field"? [...] The "garage" part is bad from all angles. If "tarja" must be "targe," why not have Bertran too poor to fight "at large"?

Guthrie seemed willing to recognize Blackburn's attention to prosody: free verse that was "spotty," with the concealed rhymes and semi-submerged alliteration that Pound had recommended for the "cantabile values" of the Provençal text. Yet Guthrie remained unwilling to license Blackburn's heterogeneous discourse. By crossing languages, cultures, historical periods, the "targe"/"garage" rhyme preempts transparency, any illusionistic sense of an authorial voice, and calls attention to the multiple codes that make this an English-language translation, with a cultural political agenda. Guthrie's response shows that Blackburn's translation was in part the casualty of literary values that dominated American culture during the Cold War, in and out of the academy, values that were elitist in their exclusion of marginal cultural discourses, and reactionary in their refusal of the democratic politics that animated Blackburn's modernist project.

After the Macmillan episode, Blackburn's writing took various developments. Some responded directly to Guthrie's report; most continued his already significant accomplishments as a modernist poet–translator, but in new directions. Blackburn's relationship to the Provençal translation certainly changed. The depth of Guthrie's impact can be gauged from the final version of the translation: Blackburn incorporated some of Guthrie's suggestions – even when these conflicted with his modernist experimentalism. At several points, Blackburn followed Guthrie's insistence on standard English: he used Guthrie's recommended spelling, "night," instead of his initial choice, the subcultural "nite"; he accepted Guthrie's change of "like" to "as" in the colloquialism, "like/they say" (Blackburn 1958:32; 1986:46, 47). Here Blackburn

was browbeaten by Guthrie's distaste for grammatical impropri-
eties, by his rather ethnocentric assumption that the troubadours
should be held to English-language cultural norms: "That 'like' for
'as' must have Guilhem twirling in his grave," wrote Guthrie, "It
fills me with a creeping horror." Blackburn also abandoned the
much criticized "targe"/"garage" rhyme, adopting Guthrie's
"shield"/"field" (Blackburn 1986:164).

Finally, however, Blackburn did not make numerous revisions in
the lexicon and syntax of the 1958 versions. Instead, he expanded
the selection of Provençal translations, including four more satires
by Marcabru that required a larger variety of obscenities. He also
added annotations that provided some of the information Guthrie
requested and sought to answer his objections. In one note
Blackburn commented on the variant spellings, revealing the
different, somewhat contradictory determinations that shaped his
final version: the historicist impulse apparent in his respect for the
Provençal manuscripts, but also his concern with the prosody of
his translation, and even his partial acceptance of Guthrie's call
for consistent, modern spelling. Blackburn's note specifically
addresses Guthrie's report:

> *Mareuil* (Dordogne): I use the modern French spelling to
> normalize the place name. In the manuscripts you'll find
> Maroill, Maruoill, Marueill, Maruelh, Marvoill, Merueil, Mer-
> uoill, Miroill, and Miroilh. Some of these may be simply
> copyists' mistakes, but they also reflect slight differences in
> pronunciation from area to area. [...] The point I would make
> here is that neither the pronunciation nor the orthography was
> particularly standardized. Especially in the poems, I use the
> version that suits my ear at that point. In the razo here I use
> Anfos for the king of Aragon: the name is also Amfos, Alfons –
> I don't remember using the French Alphonse ever.
>
> (Blackburn 1986:285)

The publishing history that banished Blackburn's Provençal
translations to the margins of American literary culture, available
only in small-circulation magazines and limited-edition books,
inevitably confined the influence of their striking effects. These
inspired, not the work of other translators or translation theorists
and critics, but mainly Blackburn's own poetry (Sturgeon 1990).
Throughout the 1960s, the translations became a field of prosodic
experiment for Blackburn: he explored Charles Olson's perform-

ance-oriented notion of "projective verse," "in which the poet manages to register both the acquisitions of his ear and the pressures of his breath" (Allen 1960:393). Olson argued that this prosody followed the modernist abandonment of the pentameter standard ("the experiments of Cummings, Pound, Williams"), but it was uniquely made possible by the typewriter, which, "due to its rigidity and space precisions," could produce a poem "as a script to its vocalization" (ibid.). Blackburn, in his *New York Quarterly* interview, similarly took the layout of the text as a set of notations for performance: "Punctuation serves much the way that spacing does – that is, to indicate the length of a pause" (Packard 1987:11).

After the Macmillan episode, Blackburn's revisions of the Provençal translations included more attention to their formal qualities – punctuation, line break, spacing. Occasionally the results were dramatic. Blackburn's work on the opening of this text by Marcabru developed the iconic aspect of the prosody, its imitation of the falling leaf:

> When the leaf spins
>   its staying power
> gone,
>   twists off,
>   falls
>   spinning
> down through the branches from top limbs whence
>   wind has torn it,
> I watch.
> It is a sign.
>   The icy storm that's brewing's better
>   than grumbling and meandering summer
>   congesting us with hates and whoring.
>   (Blackburn 1958:30)

> When the leaf spins
> its staying power
>   gone,
> twists off,
>   falls
>   spinning
> down through the branches

from top limbs from
which the wind has
                    torn it, I
watch.
It is a sign.
        The icy storm that's brewing's better
        than grumbling and meandering summer
        congesting us with hates and whoring.
                            (Blackburn 1986:43)

In the later version, Blackburn sacrificed the archaism "whence," but replaced it with a repetitive syntactical turn that is more evocative of the "spinning" leaf ("from top limbs from/which the wind has"). These prosodic experiments culminated in Blackburn's last poems, *The Journals* (1967–1971), where the autobiographical verse is polyrhythmic – lyrical and angular, conversational and iconic, quietly emotional and parodic – but always inventive, attuned to a reflective music, multicoded:

Seaplane going over, going
    somewhere . over
        head, the blue re-
            ally re-
                    flected in this sea .
                        (Blackburn 1985:572)

The end of a distance come
so early in the morning
    where the eye stops,
                    flames
running O their tongues up thru
    along the rooftree of
        down the coping of
            that church in Harlem .
                    (ibid.:555)

The wind blowth
snow fallth
branches whip in the wind
    down, rise, forth and back
        drifts groweth summat

It's going to take us two days at least to
shovel out of this one, off to Buf-fa-lo, o
March, after all, Spring
cometh .

(ibid.:613)

The Journals is essentially an individualistic project, a verse diary of
Blackburn's last years, travelling in Europe and the United States
with his wife Joan and son Carlos, suffering through the final
stages of his illness with cancer. Yet Blackburn's prosodic experiments give all this an anti-individualistic edge by pushing the verse
toward greater heterogeneity, using rhythm, punctuation, typog-
raphy to foreground the textuality and erode the coherence of
the speaking voice, now a site of diverse lexicons, cultural codes,
social affiliations, whose very juxtaposition invites a mutual
questioning.

The Provençal project was also a source of personae and themes
for Blackburn's poems, some of which carry on the social criticism
he occasionally worked into the lexicon of the translations. His
version of Guillem de Poitou's *Ab lo dolchor del temps novel* –

In the new season
when the woods burgeon
and birds
sing out the first stave of new song,
time then that a man take the softest joy of her
    who is most to his liking.

(Blackburn 1958:13)

– gets quoted in a poem contemporary to the 1958 manuscript,
"Meditation on the BMT":

Here, at the beginning of the new season
before the new leaves burgeon,   on
either side of the Eastern Parkway station
    near the Botanical Gardens
they burn trash on the embankment, laying
barer than ever our sad, civilized refuse.

1 coffee can without a lid
1 empty pint of White Star, the label
    faded by rain
1 empty beer-can

2 empty Schenley bottles
1 empty condom, seen from
1 nearly empty train
   empty

(Blackburn 1985:141)

Blackburn's quotation uses the troubadour motif to interrogate consumer capitalism, juxtaposing a lyrical evocation of spring to an itemized list of "trash" visible from a New York subway. The Provençal idealization of human sexuality as a renewing natural pleasure emphasizes the dirty realism of contemporary sexual practices, which come to seem less "civilized," more emotionally impoverished, even as they suggest that troubadour poetry is itself suspect, a mystification of the material conditions and consequences of sexuality.

It is worth noting, finally, that Blackburn's experience with the Provençal translation also bears on his other translation projects. With the 1958 manuscript unpublished, he turned his attentions to Latin American writing, particularly the fiction of the Argentine Julio Cortázar. In 1959, Blackburn entered into a contract with Cortázar that made him the Argentine writer's "exclusive and official literary representative (AGENT) throughout the entire world (except in): France, Germany, Italy and all the Spanish-speaking countries."[10] Blackburn negotiated the publication of the first English-language versions of Cortázar's fiction, which were two novels: *The Winners*, translated by Elaine Kerrigan in 1965, and *Hopscotch*, translated by Gregory Rabassa in 1966. Late in the 1950s, Blackburn began translating Cortázar's poems and short stories, mostly for magazine publication, and in 1967, the stories were issued as *End of the Game*. He then translated another collection of Cortázar's short prose pieces, *Cronopios and Famas* (1969), and was the likely translator for the next volume of Cortázar's stories to appear in English, *All Fires The Fire* (1973), but his failing health prevented him from taking on this project. Blackburn's work with Cortázar served the modernist cultural politics that informed his Provençal translation and his article "The International Word," a left-wing internationalism that viewed translation as a foreignizing intervention in American culture. The Cortázar translations, however, were much more effective in their dissidence, questioning and actually changing literary canons in English.

Blackburn, among the other translators and publishers of Cortázar's writing, was importing the so-called "boom" in twentieth-century Latin American fiction, a body of foreign literature characterized by experimentalist strategies that challenged the realism dominating British and American narrative. The Latin American boom began circulating in English during the 1950s, when translations of writers like Jorge Luis Borges appeared in magazines and anthologies. Among the first book-length translations in this tendency was in fact Borges' *Ficciones* (1962), rendered by various hands, American and British. A few years later, the reviews of the Cortázar translations repeatedly linked him to "his countryman" Borges, and both were inserted in the modernist mainstream of European fiction: Franz Kafka, Italo Svevo, Günter Grass, Alain Robbe-Grillet, Michel Butor, Nathalie Sarraute.[11] Contemporary British and American fiction was for the most part realist at this time, with narrative experimentalism banished to the obscure fringes (Djuna Barnes, Samuel Beckett, Flann O'Brien, William Burroughs, William Gaddis, John Hawkes, Thomas Pynchon) – or to popular forms, like horror and science fiction. This is reflected in *The New York Times* "Best Seller List" for 9 July 1967, the issue in which Blackburn's *End of the Game* was reviewed (see Table 3). The list contains mostly varieties of realism (historical and contemporary); the only deviation is a Gothic fantasy, an archaic popular genre modernized in Ira Levin's novel, *Rosemary's Baby*.

The success of Latin American writers like Borges and Cortázar was both critical and commercial, owing to numerous, mostly favorable reviews, the support of trade publishers like Grove, Pantheon, and New Directions, and publishing subventions issued through the Center for Inter-American Relations, a cultural organization funded by private foundations. The translations were very well received. Rabassa's version of *Hopscotch* won the 1966 National Book Award for Translation. Within the first six months of publication, *The Winners* sold 8195 hardback copies; within five months, *Hopscotch* sold 6965. Both novels were quickly reprinted as paperbacks. Blackburn's *End of the Game* (1967) received some twenty enthusiastic reviews in England and the United States, and selections appeared in *The New Yorker* and *Vogue*. Within three months of publication, 3159 hardback copies were sold, and during the next few years several stories were frequently anthologized. By 1974, there had been four paperback printings. The

Table 3 New York Times "Best Seller List for Fiction," 9 July 1967

	Position		
This week		*Last week*	*Weeks on list*
1	*The Eighth Day* Thornton Wilder	2	13
2	*The Arrangement* Elia Kazan	1	20
3	*Washington, DC* Gore Vidal	3	8
4	*The Chosen* Chaim Potok	4	7
5	*The Plot* Irving Wallace	5	5
6	*Tales of Manhattan* Louis Auchincloss	6	13
7	*The Secret of Santa Vittoria* Robert Crichton	7	43
8	*Rosemary's Baby* Ira Levin	8	4
9	*Fathers* Herbert Gold	10	11
10	*Go to the Widow-Maker* James Jones	—	7

Source: *New York Times Book Review* 9 July 1967, p. 45

paperbacks, ironically enough, were published by Macmillan, who retitled the book *Blow-Up* to capitalize on the publicity from Michelangelo Antonioni's 1967 film, a free adaptation of a Cortázar story.

The cultural intervention that Blackburn failed to make with his Provençal translation came to pass with the Cortázar – in a different genre, in a modern language, and with a contemporary writer. The English-language success of Latin American writing during the 1960s undoubtedly altered the canon of foreign fiction in Anglo-American culture, not only by introducing new texts and writers, but by validating experimentalist strategies that undermined the assumptions of classic realism, both theoretical (individualism, empiricism) and ideological (liberal humanism). The Latin American boom must also be counted among the cultural tendencies that altered the canon of British and American fiction during the 1960s, the proliferation of diverse narrative experiments inspired by modernism: Donald Barthelme, Christine Brooke-Rose, Angela Carter, Robert Coover, Guy Davenport, among many others. Blackburn's work with Cortázar continued the modernist cultural politics that animated his Provençal translation: he recovered a foreign literature that was currently marginal in Anglo-American culture, so that it might make a cultural difference in English, interrogating dominant literary values (realism, bourgeois individualism) and influencing the development of new English-language literatures.

Blackburn's work with Cortázar displayed a foreignizing impulse in choosing to translate marginal texts, but he also produced translations that were foreignized enough to be compellingly strange. The remarkable thing about the translations that supported the canonization of Latin American fiction in English is that they are distinguished by considerable fluency. Blackburn's translations smuggled Cortázar's fiction into Anglo-American culture under the fluent discourse that continues to dominate English-language translation. Translating fluently, insuring the illusion of transparency and the evocation of a coherent voice, positioning the reader in a narrative point of view, ultimately heightens Cortázar's modernist effects, the discontinuities that dislodge the reader from the narrative positioning and encourage a self-consciousness sceptical of the realist illusion. The reviewer for the British magazine *Books and Bookmen* acknowledged the foreignizing impulse in Blackburn's choice of Cortázar, whose "world is a strange one, and to most people, I would think, an unfamiliar one." But the reviewer also felt that the fluency of Blackburn's translation was powerful in delivering this strangeness:

> Ignorant of the experience to come, I opened the violet-jacketed copy of Julio Cortázar's short story collection, and found myself on the other side of the Looking Glass in one minute flat. Where to begin on this dazzling book? Perhaps with Paul Blackburn's translation into splendid, flexible English, whose metaphors carry the savage accuracy of a punch in the stomach.
>
> (Stubbs 1968:26)

The reviewer for *The Nation* described Blackburn's reliance on current English usage, but also pointed to a foreignizing tendency in the lexicon, which, the reviewer suggested, would foster innovations in English-language prose:

> The translation, by Paul Blackburn, is properly colloquial, elegant and eloquent, and is flavored with just enough touches of Spanish and French phrases to spice the narrative. At this point in the development of a freer form for prose writing, Cortázar is indispensable.
>
> (Stern 1967:248)

Yet perhaps this passage should read *"Blackburn's translation of* Cortázar is indispensable" to innovative prose. In the regime of transparent discourse, where fluency routinely makes the translator invisible, even reviewers who praise the translator by name are likely to reduce the translation to the foreign author. Blackburn's translation, although fluent, is inevitably free at points, departing from "Cortázar," inscribing the Spanish texts with different linguistic and cultural values, enabling them to produce effects that work only in English. A closer look at Blackburn's discursive moves will reveal the effectiveness of his Cortázar translations.

"Continuity of Parks" ("Continuidad de los Parques") is a brief but characteristic text from *End of the Game* that seamlessly shifts between two realistic narratives, finally provoking a metaphysical uncertainty about which is the text, which reality. A businessman sitting in an armchair at his estate reads a novel about an unfaithful wife whose lover goes to kill her husband; when the crime is about to be performed, the victim is revealed as the businessman sitting in the armchair at the opening. At the climactic end, the "real" man reading a novel suddenly becomes a character in that novel, just as the characters suddenly become "real" to end the man's life. Cortázar involves the Spanish-language reader in this conundrum by, first, constructing the businessman as the narrative point of view and then, without warning, abruptly shifting to the lovers. The rapid conclusion is a bit jolting, not only because the text ends just before the murder occurs, but because the reader was earlier positioned in the victim's point of view, assuming it to be reality.

Blackburn's fluent translation enables this positioning most obviously by using consistent pronouns. The subject of every sentence at the opening is "he," maintaining the realist distinction between the man's reality and the fictiveness of the novel he is reading:

> He had begun to read the novel a few days before. He had put it down because of some urgent business conferences, opened it again on his way back to the estate by train; he had permitted himself a slowly growing interest in the plot, in the characterizations. That afternoon, after writing a letter giving his power of attorney and discussing a matter of joint ownership with the manager of his estate, he returned to the book in the

tranquillity of his study which looked out upon the park with its oaks. Sprawled in his favorite armchair, its back toward the door – even the possibility of an intrusion would have irritated him, had he thought of it – he let his left hand caress repeatedly the green velvet upholstery and set to reading the final chapters.

(Cortázar 1967:63)

Blackburn's translation has all the hallmarks of fluency – linear syntax, univocal meaning, current usage – easily setting up the "he" as the position from which the narrative is intelligible, the description true, the setting real. The translation is also quite close to the Spanish text, except for one telling deviation: the parenthetical remark in Blackburn's last sentence revises the Spanish. Cortázar's text reads, "de espaldas a la puerta que lo hubiera molestado como una irritante posibilidad de intrusiones" (in a close version, "with his back to the door which annoyed him like an irritating possibility of intrusions"). Blackburn's revision adds the aside, "had he thought of it," which suddenly shifts to a new discursive level, a different narrative point of view, at once omniscient and authorial, identifying the "he" as a character in *Cortázar's* text and briefly undermining the realist illusion established in the previous sentences. Blackburn's fluent translation possesses considerable stylistic refinement, present even in this subtle revision, an addition to the Spanish that is very much in tune with Cortázar's narrative technique.

Blackburn's choices show him strengthening the realist illusion when the narrative suddenly shifts to the description of the novel, positioning the reader in the lovers, erasing the line between fiction and reality. But then – following the Spanish text closely – he momentarily redraws that line by using literary terms to describe the novel ("dialogue/diálogo," "pages/páginas") and by making a tacit reference to the reading businessman ("one felt/se sentía"):

The woman arrived first, apprehensive; now the lover came in, his face cut by the backlash of a branch. Admirably, she stanched the blood with her kisses, but he rebuffed her caresses, he had not come to perform again the ceremonies of a secret passion, protected by a world of dry leaves and furtive paths through the forest. The dagger warmed itself against his chest, and underneath liberty pounded, hidden close. A lustful, panting dialogue raced down the pages like a rivulet of snakes, and one felt it had all been decided from eternity.

(Cortázar 1967:64)

On the one hand, Blackburn increases the verisimilitude of the translation by adding more precise detail, like the phrase "through the forest," which is absent from the Spanish text (in another passage, he similarly adds the phrase "leading in the opposite direction" to "On the path" (ibid.:65)). On the other hand, Blackburn exaggerates the melodramatic aspects of the scene: he uses "lustful, panting" to render one Spanish word, *anhelante* ("craving," "yearning," "panting"), and chooses "raced" for *corría* (instead of the flatter "ran"). Two other additions to the Spanish text produce the same exaggerated effect: "unforeseen," in the sentence, "Nothing had been forgotten: alibis, unforeseen hazards, possible mistakes"/"Nada había sido olvidado: cortadas, azares, posibles errores" (Cortázar 1967:65; and 1964:10)); and "flying," in the sentence, "he turned for a moment to watch her running, her hair loosened and flying"/"él se volvió un instante para verla correr con pelo suelto" (Cortázar 1967:66; and 1964:10). Blackburn's melodramatic lexicon reinforces the realist illusion, making the narrative more suspenseful, suturing the reader more tightly in the lovers' position; yet it also classes the narrative in a popular fictional genre, the steamy romance, encouraging the reader to interrogate the realist illusionism that dominates English-language fiction – most obviously in bestselling novels. Cortázar's text challenges individualistic cultural forms like realism by suggesting that human subjectivity is not self-originating or self-determining, but constructed in narrative, including popular genres. This and the fact that it is a businessman who turns out to be living a fiction dovetail with the critique of bourgeois values, economic and cultural, that recurs in Blackburn's other writing.

Blackburn's work as a translator spanned various languages and periods, and he published several other translation projects, including *The Cid*, a selection of Lorca's poetry, and Picasso's prose poems, *Hunk of Skin*. Still, enough has been said to sketch the main contours of his career – and to judge it a powerful response to his cultural situation. Blackburn followed the modernist innovations that were developed by Pound but marginalized by the regime of fluency in English-language translation. This meant cultivating an extremely heterogeneous discourse (a rich mixture of archaism, colloquialism, quotation, nonstandard punctuation and orthography, and prosodic experiment) that prevented the translation from being taken as the "original" and instead asserted its independence as a literary text in a different language and culture. Blackburn's experimentalist practices were foreignizing: their challenge to fluency, among other domestic values (academic criticism, linguistic elitism, bourgeois propriety, realism, individualism), enabled his translations to signal the linguistic and cultural differences of the foreign texts. Yet Blackburn was also appropriating these texts for domestic cultural agendas: in the construction of his authorial identity through a rivalry with Pound; in the prosodic and thematic development of his own poetry; and in a dissident political intervention designed to foster a left-wing internationalism in American culture during the Cold War, when a foreign policy of containing ideological opponents led to a domestic surge of nationalism that excluded cultural differences.

Blackburn's Provençal translation intervened into this situation, but was also constrained by it, caught between the midcentury reaction against modernism, the academic reception of archaic literary texts, and an elitism that marginalized nonstandard dialects and discourses. Even twenty years later, in 1978, when the manuscript was finally published, the reception reflected the continuing marginality of modernist translation. In *The New York Times Book Review*, the academic critic and translator Robert M. Adams acknowledged Blackburn's development of a translation poetics ("Blackburn was a poet, and he responded to the poetry of his originals"), but faulted his "pronounced stylistic mode (in essence the labored slang of Ezra Pound)" and found George Economou's editing inadequate on largely scholarly grounds: "historical and biographical information is sparse and uncommonly confused in its presentation"; "there is never any indication in the text of where a footnote occurs" (Adams 1979:36).

Blackburn's own response after the Macmillan episode was to develop new translation projects that continued to serve a modernist cultural politics, although with different foreign literatures and different translation discourses. As Cortázar's agent and translator, Blackburn worked to get Latin American fiction admitted to the canon of foreign literature in English; and to achieve this canon reformation, he, like many other English-language translators, resorted to fluency, assimilating marginal experimental narratives to the transparent discourse that distinguished the dominant realism. Blackburn's career as a modernist poet–translator shows quite clearly that translation strategies can be defined as "foreignizing" or "domesticating" only in relation to specific cultural situations, specific moments in the changing reception of a foreign literature, or in the changing hierarchy of domestic values.

Chapter 6

Simpatico

How many people today live in a language that is not their own? Or no longer, or not yet, even know their own and know poorly the major language that they are forced to serve? This is the problem of immigrants, and especially of their children, the problem of minorities, the problem of a minor literature, but also a problem for all of us: how to tear a minor literature away from its own language, allowing it to challenge the language and making it follow a sober revolutionary path? How to become a nomad and an immigrant and a gypsy in relation to one's own language?

Gilles Deleuze and Félix Guattari (trans. Dana Polan)

In 1978, soon after my translations of Italian poetry began appearing in magazines, I met another American translator of Italian, an older, widely published, and very gifted writer who commented on some of my work and gave me advice about literary translation. Among his many shrewd remarks was the recommendation that I translate an Italian author of my own generation, something which he himself had been doing for many years and with much success. He explained that when author and translator live in the same historical moment, they are more likely to share a common sensibility, and this is highly desirable in translation because it increases the fidelity of the translated text to the original. The translator works better when he and the author are *simpatico*, said my friend, and by this he meant not just "agreeable," or "congenial," meanings which this Italian word is often used to signify, but also "possessing an underlying sympathy." The translator should not merely get along with the author, not merely find him likeable; there should also be an identity between them.

The ideal situation occurs, my friend believed, when the translator discovers his author at the start of both their careers. In this instance, the translator can closely follow the author's progress, accumulating exhaustive knowledge of the foreign texts, strengthening and developing the affinity which he already feels with his author's ideas and tastes, becoming, in effect, of the same mind. When *simpatico* is present, the translation process can be seen as a veritable recapitulation of the creative process by which the original came into existence; and when the translator is assumed to participate vicariously in the author's thoughts and feelings, the translated text is read as the transparent expression of authorial psychology or meaning. The voice that the reader hears in any translation made on the basis of *simpatico* is always recognized as the author's, never as a translator's, nor even as some hybrid of the two.

My friend's ideas about translation still prevail today in Anglo-American culture, although they have dominated English-language translation at least since the seventeenth century. The earl of Roscommon's *Essay on Translated Verse* (1684) recommended that the translator

> chuse an *Author* as you chuse a *Friend*:
> United by this *Sympathetick Bond,*
> You grow *Familiar, Intimate,* and *Fond*;
> Your *Thoughts,* your *Words,* your *Stiles,* your *Souls* agree,
> No longer his *Interpreter,* but *He.*
>
> (Steiner 1975:77)

Alexander Tytler's *Essay on the Principles of Translation* (1798) asserted that if the translator's aim is fluency, "he must adopt the very soul of his author" (Tytler 1978:212). John Stuart Blackie's article on the Victorian translation controversy, "Homer and his translators" (1861), argued that "the successful translator of a poet must not only be a poet himself, but he must be a poet of the same class, and of a kindred inspiration," "led by a sure instinct to recognise the author who is kindred to himself in taste and spirit, and whom he therefore has a special vocation to translate" (Blackie 1861:269, 271). Burton Raffel's review of the Zukofskys' modernist Catullus similarly argued that the optimal conditions for translating the Latin texts include "(*a*) a poet, (*b*) an ability to identify with, to almost *be* Catullus over a protracted period, and (*c*) great good luck" (Raffel 1969:444).

From this chorus of theorists, critics, and translators it seems clear that the idea of *simpatico* translation is consistent with ideas about poetry that prevail today in Anglo-American culture, although they too were formulated centuries ago, perhaps most decisively with the emergence of romanticism in England. From William Wordsworth to T. S. Eliot to Robert Lowell and beyond, the dominant aesthetic in English-language poetry has been transparency, the view, as Antony Easthope neatly puts it in his incisive critique, that "poetry expresses experience; experience gives access to personality, and so poetry leads us to personality" (Easthope 1983:4–5). My friend's notion of *simpatico* was in fact a development of these assumptions to characterize the practice of translation (it was transparent) and to define the role of the translator (identification with the foreign author's personality).

I was profoundly attracted by my friend's remarks. No doubt this attraction was partly due to his cultural authority, his command of publishers and his growing list of awards, the sheer success he had achieved with his translations. But he also offered a sophisticated and rather lyrical understanding of what I wanted to do, a position of identification for me as translator, someone I could be when translating – i.e., my successful friend, but also, in the process, the author of a foreign text. I followed this advice, and as chance would have it I came upon an Italian writer who is roughly my own age, the Milanese poet Milo De Angelis.

Born in 1951, De Angelis made his precocious debut in 1975, when he was invited to contribute some of his poems to *L'almanacco dello Specchio*, a prestigious annual magazine centered in Milan and published by one of Italy's largest commercial presses, Arnoldo Mondadori Editore. The title of the anthology, literally "The Almanac of the Mirror," asserts its claim to be a representative literary survey, but the title also connects it with Mondadori's longstanding series of poetry volumes, called *Lo Specchio*, whose editorial policies the anthology seems to share: both print recent work by canonized twentieth-century writers, foreign and Italian, along with a few newcomers. The issue of *L'almanacco* to which De Angelis contributed also included poems by Eugenio Montale and Pier Paolo Pasolini, as well as Italian translations from the poetry of various foreign writers, Russian (Marina Tsvetayeva), German (Paul Celan), and American (Robert Bly). De Angelis's first book of poems, called *Somiglianze* ("Resemblances"), appeared in 1976 from the small commercial press Guanda, noted in the 1970s for its list of innovative contemporary writing. These two titles, the assertive mirror and the tentative resemblances, raised a range of questions about the possibility of *simpatico* translation, questions about representation, canon formation, and literary publishing, which continue to haunt my encounter with De Angelis's poetry.

I

As I followed De Angelis's success in Italy, I quickly saw that he couldn't match it in the United States and England, at least not today. The current canon of twentieth-century Italian poetry in English translation hasn't yet admitted his kind of writing, doesn't find it *simpatico*, and has in fact constrained my attempts to publish my translations. At the center of this canon is Eugenio Montale (1896–1981), flanked by several other Italian poets who exhibit a stylistic affinity with his poetry or who received his admiration in essays and reviews and, in some cases, his recommendation to publishers. At the margins are the successive waves of experimentalism that swept through Italian poetry in the post-World War II period and gave rise to poets like De Angelis. Montale's canonical status in Anglo-American poetry translation, I learned, cast a shadow of neglect over the legions of Italian poets who followed him.

English translation of Montale's poetry began early, with a 1928 appearance in Eliot's *Criterion*, and it has continued to this day in myriad magazines and anthologies. It was only in the late 1950s, however, that book-length translations started to proliferate, so that Montale now rivals Dante in the number of versions by different hands to be found on publishers' lists. Montale brought out seven slim volumes of poetry, all of which have been englished in their entirety or in part, some of them more than once.[1] Individual sequences of poems have frequently been lifted out of these volumes and published as chapbooks. There have been five representative selecteds, a book of autobiographical prose, a slim miscellany of critical prose, and a large selection of essays (some 350 pages). At present, thirteen English-language translations of Montale's writing are in print. They are published by an impressively broad range of trade, academic, and small presses in the United States, England, and Canada: Agenda, Boyars, Ecco, Graywolf, Kentucky, Mosaic, New Directions, Norton, Oberlin, Oxford, Random House. And the numerous translators include talented poets, scholars, and editors, some of whom are internationally known: William Arrowsmith, Jonathan Galassi, Dana Gioia, Alastair Hamilton, Kate Hughes, Antonino Mazza, G. Singh, and Charles Wright. Italian poets linked to Montale by influence, stylistic or otherwise, have also appeared in a number of book-length translations since the late fifties: Guido Gozzano (1883–1916), Giuseppe Ungaretti (1888–1970), Salvatore Quasimodo (1901–1968), Lucio Piccolo (1903–1969), Sandro Penna (1906–1976), Leonardo Sinisgalli (1908–1981), and Vittorio Sereni (1913–1983). Here too the presses are varied and the translators accomplished: Anvil, Carcanet, Cornell, Hamish Hamilton, Minerva, New Directions, Ohio State, Princeton, Red Hill, Red Ozier; Jack Bevan, Patrick Creagh, W. S. Di Piero, Ruth Feldman and Brian Swann, Allen Mandelbaum, J. G. Nichols, Michael Palma, and Paul Vangelisti. Eleven books by poets who can be described, without too much violence, as Montale avatars in English are currently in print, a couple with essays by him.

Compared to the increasing interest that distinguishes Montale's reception in Anglo-American culture, other postwar tendencies in Italian poetry have received limited attention. Among them, experimentalism is remarkably underrepresented, given its importance in Italy. In a conservative estimate, approximately fifty poets writing over four decades can be classed in this category, making it a central movement in contemporary Italian poetry. The first wave, sometimes called "I novissimi" ("The Newest") after the title of an important 1961 anthology, includes its editor Alfredo Giuliani (1924–), Corrado Costa (1929–), Edoardo Sanguineti (1930–), Giulia Niccolai (1934–), Nanni Balestrini (1935–), Antonio Porta (1935–1989), Franco Beltrametti (1937–), and Adriano Spatola (1941–1989). The second wave, which began publishing during the 1970s, includes Nanni Cagnone (1939–), Gregorio Scalise (1939–), Luigi Ballerini (1940–), Angelo Lumelli (1944–), Giuseppe Conte (1945–), Cesare Viviani (1947–), Michelangelo Coviello (1950–), and Milo De Angelis. There are also various other poets whose careers do not coincide with these chronologies, but whose writing is marked by a strong experimental impulse – Andrea Zanzotto (1921–), for instance, and Amelia Rosselli (1930–). The fact that these names are more than likely to be meaningless to English-language readers of poetry is symptomatic of the poets' current marginality (and perhaps that of any other Italian poet but Dante and Montale) in Anglo-American writing.

Book-length English translations of the experimental poetry took much longer to appear (over a decade after the Italian publication) than English versions of Montale's poems (within three years of his first volume). In the 1970s, Ruth Feldman and Brian Swann did a selected Zanzotto with Princeton, and Paul Vangelisti published his chapbook version of Spatola's *Majakovskiiiiiij* with John McBride's Los Angeles-based Red Hill Press. Vangelisti and McBride built a small library of Italian experimentalism, with nine books from Beltrametti, Costa, Niccolai, Porta, and Spatola, as well as an anthology that aims to map the movement, *Italian Poetry, 1960–1980: from Neo to Post Avant-garde*. Porta has been the most translated: five books altogether, including an individual volume from City Lights and a selected from the Canadian press Guernica, rendered by different translators. The poet Ballerini's Out of London Press issued bilingual volumes of Cagnone, Tomaso Kemeny, and Giovanna Sandri, as well as an anthology that collected essays, lectures, and poems from a conference held in New York during the late 1970s, Thomas Harrison's *The Favorite Malice*. Poets associated with the postwar experimentalism, as well as various other contemporary tendencies, are represented in several other anthologies from these years – but they are conspicuously absent from William Jay Smith and Dana Gioia's *Poems from Italy*, which aims to be a representative survey of Italian poetry from its medieval beginnings.

To date, roughly twenty English-language books relating in whole or part to the experimentalist movement have been published, mostly by rather obscure small presses with limited distribution. It is no exaggeration to say that you won't find *any* of these books in your local bookstore or even in many university libraries, but you will certainly find some of Montale's books. Behind Montale's monumentalization in Anglo-American writing lies a very different poetic landscape in Italy, one where he is canonized, to be sure, but which also includes the canonical tendency I am calling, somewhat reductively, "experimentalism."

No doubt, the different reception of these Italian poetries is due to many factors, cultural, economic, ideological. The fact that Montale was awarded the Nobel Prize for Literature in 1975 accounts for some of his cultural capital here and abroad. But it can't explain the sustained attention given to his poetry by the English-language writers who have chosen to translate it, or the relative neglect bestowed on some forty years of experimentalism.

To understand this, I want to suggest, we must turn to the dominant poetics in Anglo-American culture, specifically its romantic assumptions: that the poet is a unified subjectivity freely expressing his personal experience, and that the poem should therefore be centered on the poetic I, evoking a unique voice, communicating the poet's self in transparent language, sustaining a feeling of *simpatico* in the translator. Montale's canonical status in Anglo-American writing rests on his translators' assimilation of his poetry to mainstream poetics, whereas the postwar experimentalism has been marginalized largely because it resists any such assimilation. The Montale canonized in English is actually a domesticated version shaped by a poet-oriented aesthetic and realized in the transparent discourse of fluent translation.

A case in point is Dana Gioia's version of Montale's *Mottetti*, a consecutively numbered sequence of twenty poems that forms the centerpiece of the 1939 volume *Le occasioni*. Montale's contemporaries found these poems obscure, using the term "hermeticism" (*ermetismo*) to disparage their typically modernist poetics of indirection, their recourse to ellipsis, fragmentation, heterogeneity. In an essay from 1950, "Due sciacalli al guinzaglio" ("Two Jackals on a Leash"), Montale answered his critics by claiming that the "motets" were not obscure, that although individual poems were written at various times, they constituted "an entirely unmysterious little autobiographical novel," in which he deployed some traditional cultural materials – Dante's *La Vita Nuova*, the *dolce stil novisti* – to represent his intermittent relationship with Irma Brandeis, an American Dante scholar he encountered in Florence (Montale 1982:305). Anglo-American mainstream poetics privileges the poet, so Gioia accepts Montale's defensive, slyly ironic essay at face value and asserts that the poems "form a unified sequence whose full meaning and power becomes apparent only when they are read together" (Montale 1990:11). Any obscurity is only apparent, an effect of the equally apparent discontinuity of the narrative:

> The sequence recreates *isolated* moments of insight, stripped of their nonessential elements. Everything else in the story is told *by implication,* and the reader must participate in the reconstruction of the human drama by projecting his or her own private associations to fill in the *missing* elements of the narrative.
>
> (ibid.: 16, my italics)

It is remarkable how Gioia repeatedly locates the formal elements that earned Montale the tag "hermetic" – only to explain away their existence, to "fill in" the cracks of the broken text. In Gioia's assimilation of Montale to mainstream poetics, the most important thing is to maintain the continuity of the poet's representation of his experience, insuring the coherence of the poetic subject and its control over the act of self-expression. Hence, Gioia's translation strategy is designed to make versions that "would move naturally as English-language poems," "always preferring the emotional clarity and narrative integrity of the whole poem in English to the lexicographical fidelity of the individual word," departing from Montale's lineation so as to "integrate the transposed elements tightly into a new whole" (ibid.: 21). The departures, however, are not seen as inaccuracies or domesticating revisions, but as more intimate fidelities, showing that Gioia is really *simpatico* with Montale, "faithful not only to the sense but also to the spirit of the Italian" (ibid.: 22). Here it becomes clear that the translator's feeling of *simpatico* is no more than a projection, that the object of the translator's identification is ultimately himself, the "private associations" he inscribes in the foreign text in the hope of producing a similarly narcissistic experience in the English-language reader.

The effect of mainstream poetics on Gioia's translations can be seen in his version of the sixth Italian text in the group:

> La speranza di pure rivederti
> m'abbandonava;
>
> e mi chiesi se questo che mi chiude
> ogni senso di te, schermo d'immagini,
> ha i segni della morte o dal passato
> è in esso, ma distorto e fatto labile,
> un *tuo* barbaglio:
>
> (a Modena, tra i portici,
> un servo gallonato trascinava
> due sciacalli al guinzaglio).
>
> (Montale 1984a:144)

> I had almost lost
> hope of ever seeing you again;
>
> and I asked myself if this thing

cutting me off
from every trace of you, this screen
of images,
was the approach of death, or truly
some dazzling
vision of you
out of the past,
bleached, distorted,
fading:

(under the arches at Modena
I saw an old man in a uniform
dragging two jackals on a leash).
                    (Montale 1990:35)

Gioia's version appreciably enlarges the poet's presence in the
poem with several alterations and additions. Montale's opening
lines – "La speranza di pure rivederti/m'abbandonava" (in a
rendering that follows the Italian word order and lineation, "The
hope of ever seeing you again/was abandoning me") – get
reversed, with the emphasis shifted to Gioia's "I": "I had almost
lost." Similarly, the penultimate line contains another first-person
reference, "I saw," which doesn't appear at all in the Italian text.
Gioia's other additions – "truly," "vision," "bleached," "old man" –
show an effort to make the language more emotive or dramatic, to
sketch the psychological contours of the poetic subject, but they
come off as somewhat stagy, even sentimental ("old man"). In
keeping with this emotionalizing of Montale's lexicon, Gioia uses
the phrase "approach of death" to translate "i segni della morte"
("signs of death"), diminishing the element of self-reflexivity in the
Italian, its awareness of its own status as "images" and "signs," and
replacing it with a pallid sensationalism. The English word "signs"
is currently loaded with various meanings, including a reference to
controversial foreign imports in Anglo-American literary theory
that depersonalize the text and deconstruct authorship – viz.
semiotics and poststructuralism. The avoidance of the word here
produces two notable effects: it moves the translation away from
contemporary European thinking that would question the theoretical assumptions of mainstream poetics, and it reinforces the focus
on the poet's emotional state, on the (re)presentation of Montale's
poem as (Montale's or Gioia's?) self-expression. Gioia's translation
strategy quite clearly seeks to efface Montale's modernist poetic

discourse, to remove the formal elements that made the Italian text so strikingly different to its first Italian audience, and that, if a translator tried to reproduce them in English, would result in a translation just as striking to an Anglo-American reader because of their deviation from the dominant poet-centered aesthetic.

The Italian postwar experimentalism proves recalcitrant to this assimilationist ideology in both form and theme. In its early phase, it was called the "neoavantgarde" for its return to modernist movements like Futurism, Dadaism, and Surrealism in order to develop a highly discontinuous poetic discourse that reflected on its cultural and social situation. In the preface to *I novissimi*, Giuliani outlined the experimental project as a left-wing cultural politics: language is fractured in a "schizomorphic vision" ("visione schizomorfa") which simultaneously registers and resists the mental dislocations and illusory representations of consumer capitalism (Giuliani 1961:xviii). Edoardo Sanguineti's poetry, to take one example, is a frenetic stream of episodes in the poet's life, allusions to contemporary figures and events, excerpts and applications of his readings in philosophy, literature, psychology, and social theory, punctuated with found language and references to popular culture. The experimentalism in this initial phase circulated widely in magazines and anthologies, a book series with a large trade press (Feltrinelli), and several public meetings that received substantial media attention. And the experiments took varied forms, not only writing that was much more plurivocal and heterogeneous than anything produced by Montale, but also visual poetry and collage, computer-generated texts and performance.

Experimentalism encompasses diverse poetries, and my periodizations and cultural genealogies inevitably give too neat an account (which, moreover, is interested on this occasion, pitched to demonstrate a deviation from Montale). The common experimental thread is the use of formal discontinuity to address philosophical problems raised by language, representation, and subjectivity, resembling in this such contemporary French developments as the *nouveau roman* and the emergence of poststructuralist thinking, especially in politicized versions, with the *Tel Quel* group. Indeed, the immense importance of politics to the neoavantgarde has led Christopher Wagstaff to suggest that "when, in 1968, Italy seemed to offer significant opportunities for direct political action," the movement "saw its *raison d'être* disappear," as evidenced by the demise of a central magazine, the increasing affiliations with established cultural and academic institutions, and, most tellingly, a theoretical and practical redirection (Wagstaff 1984:37).

The second experimentalist phase avoided explicit political engagement to develop more speculative projects with distinct philosophical roots (existential phenomenology, psychoanalysis, poststructuralism), exploring the conditions of human consciousness and action in powerfully indeterminate texts. The renewed emphasis on textuality was sometimes given a political inflection in theoretical statements, particularly by members of the first experimentalist phase. In an anthology that surveys Italian poetry during the 1970s, Porta argued that "the reaffirmation of the linguistic force of the I resolves the problem of the interactions between poetry and society, between poetry and reality, because the poetic I is never merely 'personal' but, just like the author, is a linguistic-collective event" (Porta 1979:27). In general, however, the post-1968 experimentalism didn't resort to the left-wing theorizations of the neoavantgarde, but rather pursued the "enamored word," as the title of one important anthology indicates, turning it into a site of uncontrollable polysemy, exposing and destabilizing the multiple determinations of subjectivity – linguistic, cultural, social (Pontiggia and DiMauro 1978). In doing this, some poets returned to the formal and thematic innovations of hermeticism, its oblique means of signification, its penchant for climactic moments. This is clear in Milo De Angelis's case: drawing not merely on hermeticism, but on such other European poets as René Char and Paul Celan, he pushes modernist fragmentation to an extreme that threatens intelligibility even while proliferating meaning.

Perhaps a poem by De Angelis, "Lettera da Vignole" ("Letter from Vignole"), can indicate how he at once resembles and differs from the early Montale. It too issues from a friendship between the poet and a woman engaged in literary activity, although not a Dantista. This is Marta Bertamini, who collaborated with De Angelis on the experimentalist magazine he founded, *niebo* (1977–1984), and on a translation from the Latin (Claudian, *The Rape of Proserpine*). Vignole is the Italian town near the Austrian border where she was born.

Udimmo la pioggia e quelli
che ritornavano: ogni cosa
nella calma di parlare
e poi la montagna, un attimo, e tutti

i morti che neanche il tuo esilio
potrà distinguere.

"Torna subito o non tornare più."

Era questa – tra i salmi
della legge – la voce
che hai ripetuto all'inizio,
la potente sillaba, prima
di te stessa.

"Solo così ti verrò incontro, ignara
nell'inverno che ho perduto e che trovo."
                    (De Angelis 1985:12)

We heard the rain and those
who were returning: each thing
in the calm of speaking
and then the mountain, an instant, and all
the dead whom not even your exile
can distinguish.

"Come back at once or don't ever come back."

This – amid the psalms
of the law – was the voice
that you repeated at the beginning,
the potent syllable, before
you yourself.

"Only then shall I come to meet you, unaware
in the winter which I lost and find."

Knowing the allusion in the title doesn't much help to fix the
meaning of this poem. The pronouns support multiple subjectivities. A word like "inverno" ("winter") sets up a fertile intertextual/
intersubjective chain: it suggests a key motif in several poets, notably
Celan and Franco Fortini (1917–), an Italian writer of politically
engaged cultural criticism and verse who early expressed his
admiration of De Angelis. Although De Angelis frequently takes
specific episodes in his own life as points of departure, his experimental poetics renders them both impersonal and interpersonal,
thickening the representation with an intricate network of images
and allusions that construct relations to other poetic discourses,
other poetic subjects, challenging any facile reduction of the text to

autobiography (whether the poet's or the reader's).

Montale is undoubtedly much easier for Anglo-American main-stream poetics to kidnap than experimentalism. In fact, it could be said that some English-language translators are responding to the traces of another poet-oriented aesthetic in Montale, "crepuscolar-ismo," a *fin de siècle* movement ("crepuscolare" means "twilight") that cultivated a private voice in conversational language, producing introspective, slightly ironic musings on prosaic experiences (San-guineti 1963). This would go some way toward explaining not only Gioia's effacement of Montale's modernism, but the recent Amer-ican fascination with younger Italian poets who seem to be returning to crepuscularism – Valerio Magrelli (1957–), for instance, whom Gioia has also championed and translated (Cherchi and Parisi 1989).

Of course, not all of Montale's English-language translators put to work an assimilationist ideology. William Arrowsmith's versions were designed precisely to respect the modernist edge of poems like *Mottetti.* In the "Translator's Preface" to *The Occasions,* Arrow-smith described his method as "resisting" any domestication of the Italian texts:

> I have conscientiously resisted the translator's temptation to fill in or otherwise modify Montale's constant ellipses, to accom-modate *my* reader by providing smoother transitions. And I have done my best to honor Montale's reticence, his ironic qualifica-tions, and evaded cadences. A chief aim has been to preserve the openness of the poet's Italian, even though this has meant resisting the genius of English for concreteness.
>
> (Montale 1987:xxi)

Arrowsmith's intention, however, was to validate, not revaluate, Montale's canonical status in Anglo-American poetry translation, and so there was no need for him to mention the postwar Italian experimentalism, let alone suggest that it was worth translating into English. Indeed, he believed that

> No Italian poet of the twentieth century has taken greater experimental risks than Montale in this book, above all in the effort to renew the Dantesque vein in terms of a sensibility that belongs so passionately to its own time and strives tenaciously to find an individual voice – a voice never to be repeated.
>
> (ibid.:xx)

The modernist translation discourse Arrowsmith recommended may have been resistant to certain Anglo-American literary values ("smoother transitions," "concreteness"), but his rationale for this discourse agreed with mainstream poetics, the romantic valorization of the poet's "voice." Obviously, Arrowsmith's translations can do little to question the shadow of neglect that Montale continues to cast on Italian experimentalists – like Milo De Angelis.

II

The irony of my situation was not lost on me. In pursuing my friend's notion of *simpatico*, I discovered an Italian writer who forced me to suspect this notion and ultimately abandon it. When I came across De Angelis's 1975 anthology selection and then got hold of his first book, what struck me most was the fact that on every level – linguistic, formal, thematic – his poems issue a decisive challenge to a poet-centered aesthetic. Their abrupt line-breaks and syntactical peculiarities, their obscure mixture of abstraction, metaphor, and dialogue give them an opacity that undermines any sense of a coherent speaking voice. They do not invite the reader's vicarious participation and in fact frustrate any reading that would treat them as the controlled expression of an authorial personality or intention. Whose – or what – voice would speak in a translation of De Angelis's poetry? Often, I should add, it is more of a question of *which* voice, since the snippets of dialogue that punctuate his texts are impossible to pin down to a distinct identity. De Angelis's poetry questions whether the translator can be (or should be thought of as being) in sympathy with the foreign author. It rather shows that voice in translation is irreducibly strange, never quite recognizable as the poet's or the translator's, never quite able to shake off its foreignness to the reader.

As I began to translate De Angelis's poems, I became aware that the notion of *simpatico* actually mystifies what happens in the translation process. Most crucially, it conceals the fact that in order to produce the effect of transparency in a translated text, in order to give the reader the sense that the text is a window onto the author, translators must manipulate what often seems to be a very resistant material, i.e., the language into which they are translating, in most cases the language they learned first, their mother tongue, but now also their own. Transparency occurs only when the translation reads fluently, when there are no awkward phrasings, unidiomatic constructions or confused meanings, when clear syntactical connections and consistent pronouns create intelligibility for the reader. When the translation is a poem in free verse, varied rhythms that avoid jogtrot meters are needed to give the language a conversational quality, to make it sound natural. Linebreaks should not distort the syntax so much as to hinder the reader's search for comprehension; they should rather support the syntactical continuity that gets him or her to read for meaning over the lines, pursuing the development of a coherent speaking voice, tracing its psychological contours. These formal techniques reveal that transparency is an illusionistic effect: it depends on the translator's work with language, but it hides this work, even the very presence of language, by suggesting that the author can be seen in the translation, that in it the author speaks in his or her own voice. If the illusion of transparency is strong enough, it may well produce a truth-effect, wherein the authorial voice becomes authoritative, heard as speaking what is true, right, obvious. Translating De Angelis's poems demystified this illusionism for me because they so obviously resist fluency, cultivating instead an aesthetic of discontinuity.

Consider a poem from *Somiglianze*, a programmatic text which gave its title to De Angelis's anthology selection:

L'idea centrale
È venuta in mente (ma per caso, per l'odore
di alcool e le bende)
questo darsi da fare premuroso
nonostante.
E ancora, davanti a tutti, si sceglieva
tra le azioni e il loro senso.
Ma per caso.
Esseri dispotici regalavano il centro
distrattamente, con una radiografia,
e in sogno padroni minacciosi
sibilanti:
"se ti togliamo ciò che non è tuo
non ti rimane niente."

                                        (De Angelis 1976:97)

The Central Idea
came to mind (but by chance, because of the scent

of alcohol and the bandages)
this careful busying of oneself
notwithstanding.
And still, in front of everybody, there was choosing
between the actions and their meaning.
But by chance.
Despotic beings made a gift of the center
absentmindedly, with an X-ray,
and in a dream threatening bosses
hissing:
"if we take from you what isn't yours
you'll have nothing left."

The Italian poem offers glimpses of a hospital setting, ominous with its suggestion of injury and death, but the actual incident is never precisely defined, and the quasi-philosophical reflections on its meaning remain abstruse, only to be further obscured by the sudden shift to dreaming and the disturbing quotation. Not only can't the reader be sure what is happening, he also doesn't quite know who is experiencing it. Until the peremptory statement from the "padroni" ("bosses"), the tone is natural yet impersonal, ruminative but not actually introspective, lacking any suggestion that the voice belongs to a particular person, let alone someone who had himself experienced the mysterious physical danger. The text does not offer a coherent position from which to understand it, or a psychologically consistent voice with which to identify. On the contrary, the fragmented syntax and abrupt line-breaks constantly disrupt the signifying process, forcing the reader to revise his interpretations. The opening lines are remarkable for their syntactical shifts and contortions, which compel some synthesis of the details just to make sense of them, but then weaken any closure with the qualification introduced by "nonostante" ("notwithstanding"). Enjambment is contradictory, schizoid, metamorphic. If "il centro" is given "distrattamente," in what sense can it be described as central? The "padroni" who are "minacciosi" ("threatening") turn "sibilanti," an Italian word often used to describe the sound of wind in the reeds, or snakes. The result of the discontinuous form of the poem is that it fails to create the illusionistic effect of authorial presence, demonstrating, with degrees of discomfort that vary from reader to reader, how much transparency depends on language, on formal elements like linear syntax and univocal meaning.

Most interestingly, De Angelis's abandonment of the formal techniques used to achieve transparency occurs in a poem whose representation of human consciousness clearly rejects romantic individualism. This is the concept of subjectivity that underlies such key affirmations of transparency as Wordsworth's theory of authorial expression in the preface to *Lyrical Ballads* (1800): "all good poetry is the spontaneous overflow of powerful feelings" (Wordsworth 1974:123). The same concept is also evident in Eliot's romantic modernism, his ultimate capitulation to the romantic cult of the author: "[poetry] is not the expression of personality," wrote Eliot at the end of "Tradition and the Individual Talent" (1919), "but an escape from personality. But, of course, only those who have personality and emotions know what it means to want to escape from these things" (Eliot 1950:10–11). De Angelis's poem, in contrast, represents consciousness, not as the unified origin of meaning, knowledge, and action, freely expressing itself in language, but rather as split and determined by its changing conditions – waking and dreaming, thought and sensory impulses, meaning and action, medical diagnoses and chance. Thus, whatever the central idea may be, it doesn't come to mind through the subject's own volition; it arises only accidentally, through various determining factors over which the subject has limited or no control, like a smell, or the possibility of death.

Because this is a foreign text that refuses the romantic aesthetic of transparency which has long dominated Anglo-American poetry, it makes any pursuit of *simpatico* difficult if not impossible for the English-language translator. "L'idea centrale" is not a congenial poem to bring into a culture that prizes individuality and self-determination to such an extent that intentionality and self-expression decisively shape its reflections on language and poetry. The continued dominance of these individualistic assumptions in contemporary Anglo-American culture inevitably makes De Angelis a minor writer in English, marginal in relation to the major English-language aesthetic, the transparent expression of authorial experience. Indeed, the dominance of individualistic assumptions makes translation itself a minor genre of writing in English, marginal in relation to writing that not only implements the major aesthetic of transparency, but bears the authorial imprimatur. Because transparent discourse is perceived as mirroring the author, it values the foreign text as original, authentic, true, and devalues the translated text as derivative, simulacral, false, forcing on translation the project of effacing its second-order status with a fluent strategy. It is here that a Platonic metaphysics emerges from beneath romantic individualism to construe translation as the copy of a copy, dictating a translation strategy in which the effect of transparency masks the mediations between and within copy and original, eclipsing the translator's labor with an illusion of authorial presence, reproducing the cultural marginality and economic exploitation which translation suffers today.[2] I was definitely attracted by the difference of De Angelis's poetry, even if it upset the Anglo-American translation practices that my friend had described so lyrically. Yet this difference was forcing me to set new goals for my work. What could I hope to achieve by translating De Angelis into English? What theory would inform my translation strategy and govern my choices?

Certainly, I could defer to the prevailing cult of the author and make my translation of "L'idea centrale" as fluent as possible, perhaps with the vain hope of edging the poem closer to transparency. Some progress in this direction can be achieved if in line 12 of the translation the verb "were" is inserted before "hissing," minimizing the fragmented syntax and giving more definition to the meaning, or if the verb "came" in the first line were given a subject, even one as vaguely defined as "it." Of course, adding "were" and "it" would not go very far toward making the text transparent, but they would at least mitigate the grammatical uneasiness usually provoked by the omission of a subject or verb in an English sentence.

My English version, however, refuses fluency. Taking its cue from De Angelis's own aesthetic, my strategy can be called resistancy: it seeks to reproduce the discontinuity of De Angelis's poem. And the translation is no doubt more discontinuous with the omission of a subject and a verb. Resistancy was also at work in my effort to heighten the abruptness of the line-breaks, their effect of forcing the reader to change expectations. In line 1 "scent," so vaguely defined that it can entertain the possibility of pleasantness, replaced two earlier choices, "smell" and "odor," both of which carry strong negative connotations and so gave too much of a foretaste of the ominous "alcohol," reducing the latter's power to evoke surprise and fear. The line-break allows "scent" to release its various possible meanings, making its juxtaposition with "alcohol" a bit more jolting. Similarly, an earlier version of line 9 began with "carelessly," but this was ultimately replaced by the more resonant "absentmindedly," which seems not only inexplicable in the context of "gift," but rather alarming: since the gift carries the important cognitive associations of "center," it offers the reader the promise of intelligibility, of some light shed on the title – which, however, the idea of absentmindedness quickly betrays.

By adopting a strategy of resistancy to translate De Angelis's poem, I have been unfaithful to, and have in fact challenged, the dominant aesthetic in the target-language culture, i.e., Anglo-American culture, becoming a nomad in my own language, a runaway from the mother tongue. At the same time, however, implementing this strategy must not be viewed as making the translation more faithful to the source-language text. Although resistancy can be said to rest on the same basic assumptions about language and subjectivity that inform De Angelis's poetry, my English version still deviates from the Italian text in decisive ways that force a radical rethinking of fidelity in translation. The kind of fidelity that comes into play here has been called "abusive" by Philip Lewis: the translator whose "aim is to recreate analogically the abuse that occurs in the original text" winds up both "forcing the linguistic and conceptual system of which [the translation] is a dependent" and "directing a critical thrust back toward the text that it translates" (Lewis 1985:43). The "abuses" of De Angelis's writing are precisely its points of discontinuity and indeterminacy. They continue to exert their force in Italian culture, on the Italian-language reader, long after the publication of *Somiglianze* In 1983, for instance, the poet Maurizio Cucchi began his dictionary entry on De Angelis by stating that "pensiero e libertà dell'immagine spesso coesistono nei suoi versi, rivelando una sottesa, insinuante inquietudine, un attraversamento sempre arduo e perturbante dell'esperienza"/"idea and freedom of image often coexist in his verses, revealing a subtending, insinuating uneasiness, an always arduous and troubling skewing of experience" (Cucchi 1983:116). My strategy of resistancy aims to reproduce this effect in English by resorting to analogous techniques of fragmentation and proliferation of meaning. As a consequence, the translation establishes an abusive fidelity to the Italian text: on the one hand, the translation resists the transparent aesthetic of Anglo-American culture which would try to domesticate De Angelis's difficult writing by demanding a fluent strategy; on the other hand, the translation simultaneously creates a resistance in relation to De Angelis's text, qualifying its meaning with additions and subtractions which constitute a "critical thrust" toward it.

For example, certain features of the syntax in my translation make it stranger than De Angelis's Italian. His first line gives a verb with no subject – "È venuta" – which is grammatically acceptable and intelligible in Italian because this particular tense indicates the gender of the subject, here feminine, almost immediately leading the Italian-language reader to the last feminine noun, which happens to be in the title, "L'idea." English sentences without subjects are grammatically incorrect and often unintelligible. By following the Italian closely and omitting the subject, therefore, I was actually moving away from the foreign text, or at least making it more difficult, more peculiar: "È venuta" seems fluent to the Italian-language reader, the upper-case "e" showing that it begins a sentence, whereas the grammatical violation in "came to mind" (with the lower case) makes it seem unidiomatic or resistant to an English-language reader – even if this is only an initial effect, which eventually forces a glance back toward the title for meaning. My translation takes a syntactical subtlety in the Italian version, the absence of any explicit subject, and distorts it, giving exaggerated emphasis to what is only gently hinted in the Italian: that the central idea always remains outside of the poem because it is never explicitly stated, perhaps because it cannot be, because it questions any form of representation, whether in language, or X-rays.

In this instance, my translation exceeds the foreign text because of irreducible differences between the source and target languages, syntactical differences which complicate the effort to produce resistancy. But the excess in the translation can also be seen in the fact that I rendered certain lines primarily on the basis of an interpretation of the poem. Because interpretation and poem are distinct entities, determined by different factors, serving different functions, leading different discursive lives, my interpretive translation should be seen as a transformation of the poem, grounded, it is true, on information about De Angelis's readings in literature, literary criticism, and philosophy, but aimed at circulating this body of writing in the English-language culture where it continues to be alien and marginal. For what De Angelis's poem shows Anglo-American readers, with all the discomfort of the unintelligible, is that European culture has decisively moved beyond romanticism, in both its nineteenth- and twentieth-century manifestations.

In his letters to me, as well as in his essays, translations and interviews, De Angelis has made clear that his poetry assimilates various literary materials (European and Eastern, classical and twentieth-century), but also that it has a distinct philosophical genealogy: he has read widely in phenomenology and psycho-analysis, yet revises them according to the new conceptions of language and subjectivity that underlie the varieties of post-structuralist thinking in contemporary French and Italian culture. An early interest in Maurice Blanchot's critical speculations about the creative process and the nature of textuality led De Angelis to the study of Heidegger and Ludwig Binswanger, and finally to a belief in the importance of Nietzsche and Lacan for any contemporary project in poetry. This aspect of De Angelis's writing was partly noted by Franco Fortini in a review of that first anthology selection: De Angelis, Fortini found, is "fascinated with the Heideggerian vortices of origin, absence, recurrence, and the danger of death" (Fortini 1975:1309). My interpretation of "L'idea centrale" argues that it reflects Heidegger's concept of "being-towards-death," but that De Angelis submits this concept to a Nietzschean revision.

In *Being and Time* (1927), Heidegger argues that human exist-ence is perpetually "falling," always already determined by con-cernful relations with people and things, its identity dispersed into the "they" – until the possibility of death appears (Heidegger 1962:219–224). The anticipation of death, the possibility of being nothing, constitutes a "limit-situation," in which the subject is forced to recognize the inauthenticity of its determinate nature and gains "a freedom which has been released from the illusions of the 'they,' and which is factical, certain of itself, and anxious" (ibid.:311). De Angelis's "L'idea centrale" exploits the potential for drama in this climactic moment of truth by sketching a hospital scene. His poem depicts being-towards-death as a state of physical and psychological extremity where the apparent unity of lived experience is split by competing representations, and conscious-ness loses its self-possession and self-consistency. "Actions" are decentered from intentionality: "their meaning" is never uniquely appropriate to the subject, but an appropriation of the subject by the "they," figured here as the "bosses" who are so "threatening" to identity because they speak "in a dream," having even colonized the unconscious. The "central idea" is that subjectivity is ultimately "nothing," mere action on which meaning is imposed, an ensemble of biological processes whose meaninglessness "despotic beings" inadvertently reveal when they attempt to master it and impose meaning through a scientific representation like X-rays. The formal peculiarities of this text – the shifts from realistic detail to abstract reflection to quoted statement, the scanty amount of information, the fragmented syntax – mimic the identity-shattering experience of being-towards-death by destabilizing the signifying process, abandoning any linearity of meaning, and unbalancing the reader's search for intelligibility.

What does become clear, however, is that De Angelis's disturbingly engimatic poem carries no suggestion that being-towards-death is the prelude to authentic existence. De Angelis resists Heidegger's idea of authenticity as being which is unified and free, which is "something of its own" and can "'choose' itself and win itself" (Heidegger 1962:68). In form and theme, "L'idea centrale" rather suggests Nietzsche's corrosive notes in *The Will to Power*, where human agency is described as "no subject but an action, a positing, creative, no 'causes and effects'" (Nietzsche 1967:331).[3] For Nietzsche, subjectivity can never be authentic, because it can never possess an essential identity: it is always a site of multiple determinations, whether produced by the grammaticality of language, the need for a subject in a sentence, or constructed by some more elaborate conceptual system or social institution, like a psychology, morality, religion, family, or job – the "bosses." De Angelis's poem calls attention to the contradictory conditions of subjectivity, which often remain unacknowledged in the "careful busying" of everyday life and need a limit-situation in order to reemerge in consciousness.

This interpretation allowed me to solve certain translation problems even as it created others. In line 3, for example, the Italian word "premuroso" can be translated variously as "thoughtful," or "attentive," or "solicitous." I chose to avoid these more ordinary meanings in favor of "careful," an equally ordinary word that has nonetheless supported a philosophical signficance in English and can bring the text closer to what I take to be its themes: Heidegger's English translators use "care" to render "Sorge," the German word with which he characterizes the nature of everyday life (Heidegger 1962:237). Similarly, in line 5, the Italian verb "si sceglieva" is ordinarily an impersonal form which does not require that a subject be specified. English sentences must have subjects, and so "si sceglieva" is often translated into English as "one chose," or the passive voice is used. Yet since my reading establishes a connection with Nietzsche's concept of human agency as subject-less action, as will or force, neither a subject nor the passive would do: I resorted to the slightly strange circumlocution, "there was choosing," and avoided any explicit subject, even in as impersonal a form as "one," while retaining a sense of forceful action. In both of these examples, the translation lost some of the ordinariness that makes the language of the foreign text especially moving and rich in possibilities – just as the use of "bosses" to translate "padroni" excluded the latter's patriarchal associations, weakening the psychoanalytic resonance of the Italian.

My interpretation undoubtedly reflects some of De Angelis's reading and thinking, but the translation solutions which it rationalizes do not make my English version any more faithful to its meaning. No, the interpretation has fixed a meaning, enabling the translation both to go beyond and fall short of De Angelis's poem. Interestingly, the interpretation also points to a logical tension in the theme, namely the contradiction of Heideggerian authenticity by Nietzschean action. My interpretive translation in effect opens up this contradiction in the poem, foregrounds it, and perhaps reveals an aspect of De Angelis's thinking of which he himself was not conscious or which, at any rate, remains unresolved in "L'idea centrale." My interpretive translation exceeds the source-language text, supplementing it with research that indicates its contradictory origins and thereby puts into question its status as the original, the perfect and self-consistent expression of authorial meaning of which the translation is always the copy, ultimately imperfect in its failure to capture that self-consistency. The fact is that the original can be seen as imperfect, fissured by conflicting ideas, by the philosophical materials it puts to work, and the translation has made this conflict clearer.

This interrogative pressure in the translation surfaces in another point of resistance, an ambiguity entirely absent from De Angelis's poem. Line 10, "and in a dream threatening bosses," adheres to the word order of the Italian text as closely as linguistic differences permit. But because "threatening" is syntactically ambiguous, applying to either "dream" (as a participle) or "bosses" (as an adjective), the line releases a supplementary meaning which proves especially resonant in the interpretive context that guided my other choices: the "bosses" can also be seen as "threatened" by the nightmarish "dream" of determinate subjectivity, or more generally the agents that direct social institutions are equally determined by the hierarchical relations in which they dominate other agents. The "dream" becomes one of subversion by the dominated, and it is the dreamer who is "threatening" and "hissing" at the "bosses." Here the abusiveness of the translation enacts an unsettling critique of the Italian text by exposing its privileging of the "bosses," its implicit representation of power and social dominance as transcending the determinations of human action.

A strategy of resistancy thus results in an abusive fidelity which constructs a simultaneous relationship of reproduction and supplementarity between the translation and the foreign text. The precise nature of this relationship cannot be calculated before the translation process is begun because different relationships must be worked out for the specific cultural materials of different foreign texts and for the specific cultural situations in which those texts are translated. This makes translation labor-intensive, but also serendipitous, with the translator poring over dictionaries, developing many alternative renderings, unexpectedly finding words and phrases that at once imitate and exceed the foreign text. "In the work of translation," Lewis notes,

> the integration that is achieved escapes, in a vital way, from reflection and emerges in an experimental order, an order of discovery, where success is a function not only of the immense paraphrastic and paronomastic capacities of language, but also of trial and error, of chance. The translation will be essayistic, in the strong sense of the word.
>
> (Lewis 1985:45)

Abusive fidelity can be achieved by various strategies of resistancy worked by various formal techniques, but more often than not the techniques surface accidentally as possibilities are tested, their effects evaluated only after the fact, when rationalization occurs.

The abuses in De Angelis's "Il corridoio del treno" ("The Train Corridor"), also from *Somiglianze*, offer another illustration:

> "Ancora questo plagio
> di somigliarsi, vuoi questo?" nel treno gelido
> che attraversa le risaie e separa tutto
> "vuoi questo, pensi che questo
> sia amore?" È buoi ormai
> e il corridoio deserto si allunga
> mentre i gomiti, appoggiati al finestrino

"tu sei ancora lì,
ma è il tempo di cambiare attese" e passa
una stazione, nella nebbia, le sue case opache.
"Ma quale plagio? Se io credo
a qualcosa, poi sarà vero anche per te
più vero del tuo mondo, lo confuto sempre"
un fremere
sotto il paltò, il corpo segue una forza
che vince, appoggia a sé la parola
"qualcosa, ascolta,
qualcosa può cominciare."
                                        (De Angelis 1976:36)

"Again this plagiary
of resemblance – do you want this?" in the cold train
that crosses the rice fields and separates everything
"you want this – you think this
is love?" It is dark now
and the deserted corridor lengthens
while the elbows, leaning on the compartment window
"you're still there,
but it's time to change expectations" and a station
passes, in the fog, its opaque houses.
"But what plagiary? If I believe
in something, then it will be true for you too,
truer than your world, I confute it always"
a trembling
beneath the overcoat, the body follows a force
that conquers, leans the word against itself
"something, listen,
something can begin."

The fragmentation of subjectivity in the Italian text is its strongest
and most striking point of resistance. The voice (or voices?) is
apparently engaged in a strange lover's quarrel, both bitter and
very abstract, where desire is structured by conflicting modes of
representation, but ultimately breaks them down. Although never
defined as a distinct identity, with a definite age or gender, the
quarrelsome voice at the opening sets up an opposition between
two concepts of "love": the first, judged false or inauthentic
("plagio"), is governed by "somigliarsi" (literally "resembling each
other"), by an identity or sameness between the lovers; the second,

implicitly favored by the voice, is an alternative governed by difference, or deviation, the invention of new "expectations" ("attese"). Yet the Italian text is already undermining this second alternative with "attese," which can also mean "delays," an ambiguity that submits the hopefulness of "expectations" to jaundiced skepticism. In fact, the quotation that begins "tu sei ancora lì" ("you're still there") can easily signify the introduction of a different voice, suggesting that maybe the one who hurled the accusation of "plagio" should be changing its expectations, that maybe the accuser should be abandoning any search for authentic existence, any effort to avoid the dishonesty of imitation, because desire always has contradictory determinations, frustrations, "delays."

The insistent questioning proceeds to the Nietzschean argument that love is yet another form of the will to power, where two lovers are locked in a struggle for dominance and each can disprove ("confuto") the other's representation of their relationship, imposing a "world" that "will be true" for both. At this point, the voices lose what vague definition they may have acquired as the text unfolded, and the two conflicting positions of intelligibility are finally abandoned by the last voice, which implicitly calls for silence, full of expectation for another, still unspoken "word" that will construct a new subject-position for "the body," a new representation for the biological "force" that threatens the linguistic basis of every relationship. The indeterminacy of the phrase "appoggia a sé la parola" ("leans the word against itself") points to the contradictory interaction between language and desire. If "itself" is read as the "force" (or "body"? – another indeterminacy, perhaps less consequential here because of the connection between "force" and "body"), the "word" receives support from, or "leans [. . .] against," the "force" as the meaning of a linguistic sign depends on the linkage between signifier and signified. Thus, desire is seen as driving language use, but also as depending on such use for its articulation. Yet if "itself" is read as "the word," in the sense of language in general, the "force" also "leans the word against" another word, circulating a chain of signifiers which defer the signified, throwing it into internal division. Here it is possible to glimpse Lacan's fundamental idea that desire is simultaneously communicated and repressed by language (Lacan 1977).

The resistancy of the translation reproduces the formal discontinuity of De Angelis's poem by adhering to its line-breaks and syntactical peculiarities. A fluent strategy could easily iron out the syntax, for example, by correcting or completing the sentence fragments – in line 7 with the substitution of the verb "lean" for the participle "leaning"; in line 10 with the insertion of a verb phrase like "go by" after the fragmentary "opaque houses." The translation, however, reproduces De Angelis's challenge to transparent discourse by using broken constructions which have the effect of throwing the reading process off-balance, aggravating the already difficult problem posed by the shifting positions of intelligibility, the dislocation of voice.

It is in the quotations that the translation is most abusive of the foreign text. To mimic the drama of this situation, I sought to make the opening forcefully colloquial, inserting the abrupt dashes and fracturing the questions in line 4 by omitting the auxiliary "do." Yet since my reading construes this text as a poststructuralist meditation on the relationship between language and desire, I sought to increase the philosophical abstraction of the English: "resemblance" replaced the more ordinary, and more concrete, phrase "resembling each other," which is actually closer to the Italian "somigliarsi." The mixture of colloquial and philosophical discourses in the translation reproduces but somewhat exaggerates the similarly discordant materials of the Italian text, its combination of concrete and abstract diction.

The resistant strategy is also evident in a tendency toward archaism in the translation, specifically the dated quality of "plagiary" and "confute" in place of the more contemporary usages, "plagiarism" and "refute." These archaic words make the quotations more unusual and distancing to the English-language reader, drawing attention to themselves as words and thus abusing the canon of transparency. The word "plagiary" is particularly useful in producing this effect: it introduces a point of polysemy which opens up a metacritical register vis-à-vis the foreign text. The Italian "plagio" signifies the action or instance of literary theft, the practice or the text, and would ordinarily be translated into English by "plagiarism"; the Italian for the agent, "plagiarist," is "plagiario." My choice of "plagiary" condenses these words and meanings: it can signify either "plagiarism" or "plagiarist," the action or the agent, the text or the subject. Combined with "resemblance" in the translation, "plagiary" becomes a pun which in itself brands any relationship based on identity as a crime against personal autonomy and individuality, a Heideggerian inauthenticity, a person-theft, conjuring up its Latin root *plagiarius* – kidnapper. But since "resemblance" also defines a mode of representation exemplified by transparent discourse, the pun on "plagiary" interrogates the subjective illusionism in transparency, its fiction of personal presence, its person-lie. The English lines, "plagiary/of resemblance," at once valorize and demystify the concept of authenticity, locating within the strident voice at the opening a different, alien voice. The strain of archaism in the translation, finally, temporalizes De Angelis's poem, suggesting that cultural forms governed by "resemblance" are situated in the past, static, unwilling to admit difference and change, but also that De Angelis's concept of the subject as determinate process departs from the individualistic evocations of older, romantic and modern poetry. The archaism in the English version goes beyond the foreign text by adding a metacommentary on its form and theme.

III

Resistancy is thus a translation strategy by which De Angelis's poems become strange to the Italian poet, as well as to the Anglo-American reader and translator. It is certain that De Angelis will not recognize his own voice in the translations, not only because his ideas and texts would seem to make such a way of reading unthinkable for him, but also because he is unable to negotiate the target language. Although he works with many languages, including Greek, Latin, French, German, and different dialects of Italian, he finds English difficult to master and can read my translations only with informants, usually native Italians who have studied English. When he does this collaborative reading, moreover, he sometimes discovers what I have been arguing, that my English loses features of the Italian texts and adds others which he had never anticipated.

The resistant strategy of my translations gives them a different, and perhaps more intense, strangeness in the target-language culture. They have enjoyed varying success with English-language readers since the late 1970s. Most of them have appeared in literary magazines, appealing to editors whose aesthetics normally diverge, both mainstream and experimentalist – although my translations have also been rejected by as many magazines.[4] The complete manuscript, a selection from De Angelis's poetry and critical prose, has received many rejections from American and British publishers, including two university presses with noted translation series – Wesleyan and P (for "prestigious": the editor at this press would not permit me to identify it). The anonymous readers' reports for these presses, written in 1987, show quite clearly that my resistant strategy was strange because it abused the transparent discourse that dominates Anglo-American poetry translation.

A reader for Wesleyan acknowledged the "difficulty" of De Angelis's Italian texts, but felt that

> Mr. Venuti's translation makes matters more difficult by being faithful to this difficulty; he has chosen *not* to choose among the many ambiguous levels of meaning of [De Angelis's] dense verse. For example, a *calcio d'angolo* remains a "corner kick," no more and no less, and, as we see clearly from its placement in the poetic line, no compromise is made for the sake of the sound in English.[5]

The sort of fidelity Wesleyan's reader preferred was evidently to the canon of transparency, which here includes univocal meaning and smooth prosody. But my translations aim to be faithful to the linguistic and cultural differences of the Italian texts, their characteristic discontinuity, the neologisms, syntactical shifts, staccato rhythms. The reader's example was taken from De Angelis's poem "Antela," whose experimentalist gestures begin in the title: a neologism combining "antenati" ("forebears") and "ragnatela" ("spider web"). My version is entitled "Foreweb." The abruptness of this poem, the dizzying succession of cryptic images, would demand considerable rewriting to produce fluent English. It would be easier, as Wesleyan evidently decided, to reject the entire manuscript.

> C'è un crimine
> non so se commesso o visto
> in un tempo senza stile, come un'aria
> di blu e di buio, che mosse
> la destra. O qualcuno
> che, morso dalla carie, urla.
> Allora anche la mosca di pezza dà
> voli indiscussi e anche
> un ginocchio ferito nel calcio d'angolo
> ricuce il maschio con la femmina.
> (De Angelis 1985:46)

There is a crime
I don't know whether committed or witnessed
in a styleless time, like a breeze
blue and dark, which moved
the right hand. Or someone
who, bitten by caries, screams.
Then even the rag-fly makes
unquestioned flights and even
a knee hurt in the corner kick
stitches male back to female.

P's anonymous reader likewise expected an assimilation of De Angelis's experimentalism to transparent discourse. The reader's comments on specific translations reveal an insistence on immediate intelligibility, criticizing archaism and polysemy in favor of current English usage. My use of the word "plagiary" in "The Train Corridor," for example, was called "really obsolete and obscure." This reader, like the one for Wesleyan, also recommended revising the Italian text, even when it contained a recognizable rhetorical device: "the discontinuity (anacoluthon) between lines 2 and 3 seems excessive, however justified by the original; a little glue seems needed."

My translations signify the foreignness of De Angelis's poetry by resisting the dominant Anglo-American literary values that would domesticate the Italian texts, make them reassuringly familiar, easy to read. And this is the reception that the translations continue to get. A selection was included in a 1991 anthology, *New Italian Poets*, a project that was initially developed by the Poetry Society of America and the Centro Internazionale Poesia della Metamorfosi in Italy and later edited by Dana Gioia and Michael Palma (Gioia and Palma 1991). The anthology received a few, generally favorable reviews in American, British, and Italian periodicals. In *Poetry Review*, however, while reflecting on the cultural differences between British and Italian poetry, the reviewer singled out (my translations of) De Angelis as an example of these differences at their most alienating:

One feature that clearly distinguishes many of these poets from their British contemporaries is a freewheeling associative imagery which doesn't feel obligated to explain itself – sudden transitions, lacunae – or to situate itself in a familiar time and place. This is at its most irksome in Milo De Angelis, whom

Palma, introducing him, suggests the reader should approach "with openness and sensitivity." If this is accomplished, the reader will be "moved by feelings and insights that, however ineffable, are genuine and profound." I did my best, but was left unmoved.

(McKendrick 1991:59)

English-language readers will tend to be both "unmoved" and "irked" by De Angelis's poetry, not only because the extreme discontinuity of the texts prevents the evocation of a coherent speaking voice, but also because he draws on philosophical concepts that remain foreign, even antipathetic, to Anglo-American culture. In a polemical essay published in 1967, Kenneth Rexroth wondered, "Why Is American Poetry Culturally Deprived?" because he "never met an American poet who was familiar with Jean Paul Sartre's attempts at philosophy, much less with the gnarled discourse of Scheler or Heidegger" (Rexroth 1985:59). Rexroth's point, that with few exceptions philosophical thinking is alien to twentieth-century American poetry, applies to British poetry as well and remains true more than twenty years later. Among the notable exceptions today are the diverse group of so-called "L=A=N=G=U=A=G=E" writers, such as Charles Bernstein, who has eroded the generic distinction between poetry and essay by drawing on various European traditions and thinkers, including Dada and Surrealism, Brecht and the Frankfurt School, post-structuralism and postanalytical philosophy (1986 and 1982).[6] Since Bernstein's aesthetic – discontinuous, opaque, anti-individualistic – has earned his writing a marginal position in American publishing, banished to the relative obscurity of the small press and the little magazine, it demonstrates that contemporary American culture is not likely to give a warm reception to a poet like De Angelis, who writes with a knowledge of the main currents in Continental philosophy (Biggs 1990). It is only fitting, then, that in 1989 my manuscript of his work was accepted for publication by Los Angeles-based Sun & Moon, a small press whose list is devoted to experimentalists like Bernstein (and whose financial problems prevented my translation from seeing print until 1994). De Angelis in fact enjoys a considerably more central position in Italian culture: his writing is published by both small and larger presses and is reviewed by noted critics in a wide range of newspapers and magazines, both local and national, little and mass-audience.[7]

Perhaps the clearest sign of his canonical status in Italy is that his first book, *Somiglianze,* was reissued in a revised edition in 1990.

If my translations of De Angelis's speculative poetry will not be immediately recognizable to the English-language reader, it is also true that I do not recognize my own voice in these translations. On the contrary, my encounter with De Angelis's texts has been profoundly estranging, and for reasons specific to my situation as a translator in contemporary Anglo-American culture: by making *simpatico* an impossible goal, the formal discontinuity of the Italian has forced me to question fluency, the dominant translation strategy in English, exposing its link to the individualism of romantic and modern theories of transparent discourse, dislodging me from the position constructed for the English-language translator by his manifold relations with editors, publishers, reviewers, and, as my friend's advice suggests, other translators. This estrangement can happen because the positioning by which a discursive practice qualifies agents for cultural production does not operate in an entirely coherent manner: a specific practice can never irrevocably fix identity, because identity is relational, the nodal point for a multiplicity of practices whose incompatibility or sheer antagonism creates the possibility for change (Laclau and Mouffe 1985:105–114). A discursive practice like translation seems particularly vulnerable to shifts in positioning, displacements of identity: its function is to work on linguistic and cultural differences which can easily initiate an interrogation of the conditions of the translator's work. Thus, although the hegemony of transparent discourse in contemporary Anglo-American culture has made fluency the hegemonic strategy in English-language translation, De Angelis's poetry can still enlist the translator in a cultural contradiction: I was led to implement a resistant strategy in opposition to the discursive rules by which my work would most likely be judged, and yet that strategy, far from proving more faithful to the Italian texts, in fact abused them by exploiting their potential for different and incompatible meanings.

The challenge which translating De Angelis's poetry poses to romantic and modern theories of discourse is quite similar to the one posed by Paul Celan's writing. In Celan's speech "The Meridian" (1960), the obscure discontinuity of his and other post-World War II European poetry – what he calls "the difficulties of vocabulary, the faster flow of syntax or a more awakened sense of ellipsis" – is associated with a rethinking of the lyric poem in its romantic and modern guises (Celan 1986:48). Celan questions the lyric project of personal expression, of evoking an individual voice: the poem "speaks only in its own, its very behalf," he states, but it "has always hoped, for this very reason, to speak also on behalf of the *strange* [...] *on behalf of the other,* who knows, perhaps of an *altogether other*" (ibid.). The poem, then, does not express an authorial self, but rather liberates that self from its familiar boundaries, becoming "the place where the person was able to set himself free as an – estranged – I," but where "along with the I, estranged and free *here, in this manner,* some other thing is also set free" – free from the appropriating power of the speaking "I," of a personal language (ibid.:46–47). The poem does not transcend but acknowledges the contradiction between self-expression and communication with some other, forcing an awareness of the limits as well as the possibilities of its language.

It is this sort of liberation that resistancy tries to produce in the translated text by resorting to techniques that make it strange and estranging in the target-language culture. Resistancy seeks to free the reader of the translation, as well as the translator, from the cultural constraints that ordinarily govern their reading and writing and threaten to overpower and domesticate the foreign text, annihilating its foreignness. Resistancy makes English-language translation a dissident cultural politics today, when fluent strategies and transparent discourse routinely perform that mystification of foreign texts. In the specific instance of Englishing De Angelis's poetry, the political intervention takes the form of a minor utilization of a major language. "Even when major," Deleuze and Guattari observe, "a language is open to an intensive utilization that makes it take flight along creative lines of escape which, no matter how slowly, no matter how cautiously, can now form an absolute deterritorialization" (Deleuze and Guattari 1986:26).[8] My translations of De Angelis's poetry obviously can never be completely free of English and the linguistic and cultural constraints which it imposes on poetry and translation; that line of escape would preempt any translation and is no more than a capitulation to the major language, a political defeat. The point is rather that my translations resist the hegemony of transparent discourse in English-language culture, and they do this from within, by deterritorializing the target language itself, questioning its major cultural status by using it as the vehicle for ideas and discursive techniques which remain minor in it, which it excludes.

The models for this translation strategy include the Czech Jew Kafka writing in German, particularly as Deleuze and Guattari read his texts, but also the Rumanian Jew Celan, who took German on lines of escape by using it to speak of Nazi racism and Hebrew culture and by exploiting to an extreme its capacity for compound words and syntactical fragmentation (see, for example, Felstiner 1983 and 1984). If the resistant strategy effectively produces an estranging translation, then the foreign text also enjoys a momentary liberation from the target-language culture, perhaps before it is reterritorialized with the reader's articulation of a voice – recognizable, transparent – or of some reading amenable to the dominant aesthetic in English. The liberating moment would occur when the reader of the resistant translation experiences, in the target language, the cultural differences which separate that language and the foreign text.

Translation is a process that involves looking for similarities between languages and cultures – particularly similar messages and formal techniques – but it does this only because it is constantly confronting dissimilarities. It can never and should never aim to remove these dissimilarities entirely. A translated text should be the site where a different culture emerges, where a reader gets a glimpse of a cultural other, and resistancy, a translation strategy based on an aesthetic of discontinuity, can best preserve that difference, that otherness, by reminding the reader of the gains and losses in the translation process and the unbridgeable gaps between cultures. In contrast, the notion of *simpatico*, by placing a premium on transparency and demanding a fluent strategy, can be viewed as a cultural narcissism: it seeks an identity, a self-recognition, and finds only the same culture in foreign writing, only the same self in the cultural other. For the translator becomes aware of his intimate sympathy with the foreign writer only when he recognizes his own voice in the foreign text. Unfortunately, the irreducible cultural differences mean that this is always a misrecognition as well, yet fluency ensures that this point gets lost in the translating. Now more than ever, when transparency continues to dominate Anglo-American culture, ensuring that *simpatico* will remain a compelling goal for English-language translators, it seems important to reconsider what we do when we translate.

Chapter 7

Call to action

The translator is the secret master of the difference of languages, a difference he is not out to abolish, but rather one he puts to use as he brings violent or subtle changes to bear on his own language, thus awakening within it the presence of that which is at origin different in the original.

Maurice Blanchot (trans. Richard Sieburth)

In the brief but provocative essay "Translating" (1971), Blanchot inverts the conventional hierarchy wherein "the original" is superior to the translation. He considers the foreign text, not as the unchanging cultural monument in relation to which the translation must forever be an inadequate, ephemeral copy, but as a text in transit, "never stationary," living out "the solemn drift and derivation ["dérive"] of literary works," constituting a powerful self-difference which translation can release or capture in a unique way (Blanchot 1990:84). This assumes the foreign text to be derivative, dependent on other, preexisting materials (a point made by Sieburth's decision to render "dérive" as two words, "drift and derivation"), but also dependent on the translation:

a work is not ready for or worthy of translation unless it harbors this difference within itself in some available fashion, whether it be because it originally gestures toward some *other* language, or because it gathers within itself in some privileged manner those possibilities of being different from itself or foreign to itself which every living language possesses.

(ibid.)

In negotiating the *dérive* of literary works, the translator is an agent of linguistic and cultural alienation: the one who establishes the monumentality of the foreign text, its worthiness of translation, but only by showing that it is not a monument, that it needs translation to locate and foreground the self-difference that decides its worthiness. Even "classical masterpieces," writes Blanchot, "live only in translation" (ibid.). And in the process of (de)monumentalizing the foreign text, the translator precipitates equally "violent or subtle changes" in the translating language. Blanchot cites "Luther, Voss, Hölderlin, George, none of whom were afraid in their work as translators to break through the bounds of the German language in order to broaden its frontiers" (ibid.:85).

The power of Blanchot's suggestive observations can be released if we translate them yet again (after Sieburth's translation and after the version presented in the foregoing commentary), situating them more locally, taking into account the material determinations of cultural practices. The difference that makes a source-language text valuable to Blanchot is never "available" in some unmediated form. It is always an interpretation made by the translator, not necessarily open to every reader, gaining visibility and privileged only from a particular ideological standpoint in the target-language culture. Every step in the translation process – from the selection of foreign texts to the implementation of translation strategies to the editing, reviewing, and reading of translations – is mediated by the diverse cultural values that circulate in the target language, always in some hierarchical order. The translator, who works with varying degrees of calculation, under continuous self-monitoring and often with active consultation of cultural rules and resources (from dictionaries and grammars to other texts, translation strategies, and translations, both canonical and marginal), may submit to or resist dominant values in the target language, with either course of action susceptible to ongoing redirection. Submission assumes an ideology of assimilation at work in the translation process, locating the same in a cultural other, pursuing a cultural narcissism that is imperialistic abroad and conservative, even reactionary, in maintaining canons at home. Resistance assumes an ideology of autonomy, locating the alien in a cultural other, pursuing cultural diversity, foregrounding the linguistic and cultural differences of the source-language text and transforming the hierarchy of cultural values in the target language. Resistance too can be imperialistic abroad, appropriating foreign texts to serve its own cultural political interests at home; but insofar as it resists values that exclude certain texts, it performs an act of cultural restoration which aims to question and possibly re-form, or simply smash the idea of, domestic canons.

Blanchot is theorizing an approach to translation based on resistance, and as his examples and the occasion of his essay make plain (it is a commentary on Walter Benjamin's "The Task of the Translator"), this is an approach that is specific to the German cultural tradition. The theory and practice of English-language translation, in contrast, has been dominated by submission, by fluent domestication, at least since Dryden. Various alternative approaches have indeed existed, including Dr. John Nott's historicist opposition to bowdlerizing, Francis Newman's populist archaism, and the polylingual experiments of Ezra Pound, Celia and Louis Zukofsky, and Paul Blackburn. Judging from their reception, however, these alternatives fell victim to their own foreignizing tendencies: their strangeness provoked harsh criticism from reviewers, and they went unread or even – in Blackburn's case – unpublished, relegated to the margins of British and American culture, neglected by subsequent translators, translation theorists, and literary scholars. For the most part, English-language translators have let their choice of foreign texts and their development of translation strategies conform to dominant cultural values in English, and among these values transparent discourse has prevailed, even if in varying forms.

Yet alternative theories and practices of translation are worth recovering because they offer contemporary English-language translators exemplary modes of cultural resistance, however qualified they must be to serve a new and highly unfavorable scene. The domesticating translation that currently dominates Anglo-American literary culture, both elite and popular, can be challenged only by developing a practice that is not just more self-conscious, but more self-critical. Knowledge of the source-language culture, however expert, is insufficient to produce a translation that is both readable and resistant to a reductive domestication; translators must also possess a commanding knowledge of the diverse cultural discourses in the target language, past and present. And they must be able to write them. The selection of a foreign text for translation and the invention of a discursive strategy to translate it should be grounded on a critical assessment of the target-language culture, its hierarchies and exclusions, its relations to cultural others worldwide. Before a foreign text is chosen, translators must scrutinize the current situation – the canon of foreign literatures in English, as well as the canon of British and American literature, set against patterns of cross-cultural exchange and geopolitical relations (for a powerful example of this sort of cultural diagnosis, see Said 1990).

The ethnocentric violence of translation is inevitable: in the translating process, foreign languages, texts, and cultures will always undergo some degree and form of reduction, exclusion, inscription. Yet the domestic work on foreign cultures can be a foreignizing intervention, pitched to question existing canons at home. A translator can not only choose a foreign text that is marginal in the target-language culture, but translate it with a canonical discourse (e.g. transparency). Or a translator can choose a foreign text that is canonical in the target-language culture, but translate it with a marginal discourse (e.g. archaism). In this foreignizing practice of translation, the value of a foreign text or a discursive strategy is contingent on the cultural situation in which the translation is made. For the translator, this value is always cast in literary terms, as a practice of writing.

Foreignizing translation is beset with risks, especially for the English-language translator. Canons of accuracy are quite strict in contemporary Anglo-American culture, enforced by copyeditors and legally binding contracts. Standard contractual language requires that the translator adhere closely to the foreign text:

> The translation should be a faithful rendition of the work into English; it shall neither omit anything from the original text nor add anything to it other than such verbal changes as are necessary in translating into English.
>
> (*A Handbook for Literary Translators* 1991:16)

Because of the legal risk, the considerable freedom of Robert Graves or the editorial emendations of Pound are not likely to be adopted by many translators today – at least not with foreign texts whose copyright hasn't yet entered the public domain. Since "faithful rendition" is defined partly by the illusion of transparency, by the discursive effect of originality, the polylingualism of the Zukofskys and Blackburn is equally limited in effectiveness, likely to encounter opposition from publishers and large segments of English-language readers who read for immediate intelligibility. Nevertheless, contemporary translators of literary texts can introduce discursive variations, experimenting with archaism, slang, literary allusion and convention to call attention to the secondary status of the translation and signal the linguistic and cultural differences of the foreign text. Contemporary translators need to develop a more sophisticated literary practice, wherein the "literary" encompasses the various traditions of British and American literature and the various dialects of English. Translators committed to changing their cultural marginality can do so only within the codes that are specific to the target-language culture. This means limiting discursive experiments to perceptible deviations that may risk but stop short of the parodic or the incomprehensible, that release the *dérive* of cultural discourses in the target language.

Translators must also force a revision of the codes – cultural, economic, legal – that marginalize and exploit them. They can work to revise the individualistic concept of authorship that has banished translation to the fringes of Anglo-American culture, not only by developing innovative translation practices in which their work becomes visible to readers, but also by presenting sophisticated rationales for these practices in prefaces, essays, lectures, interviews. Such self-presentations will indicate that the language of the translation originates with the translator in a decisive way, but also that the translator is not its sole origin: a translator's originality lies in choosing a particular foreign text and a particular combination of dialects and discourses from the history of British and American literature in response to an existing cultural situation. Recognizing the translator as an author questions the individualism of current concepts of authorship by suggesting that no writing can be mere self-expression because it is derived from a cultural tradition at a specific historical moment.

This questioning must also be conducted in the language of contracts with publishers. Translators will do well to insist on their authorial relation to the translated text during negotiations. They should demand contracts that define the translation as an "original work of authorship" instead of a "work-for-hire," that copyright the translation in the translator's name, and that offer standard financial terms for authors, namely an advance against royalties and a share of subsidiary rights sales. In the long run, it will be necessary to effect a more fundamental change, a revision of current copyright law that restricts the foreign author's control over the translation so as to acknowledge its relative autonomy from the foreign text. The foreign author's translation rights should be limited to a short period, after which the foreign text

enters the public domain, *although only for the purposes of translation.*
Given the speed with which literature currently dates as a commodity on the international book market, the prospect that translation
rights will be sold grows less likely as time passes, and the
translation of a foreign text ultimately depends on the efforts of a
translator to interest a publisher, especially in Anglo-American
publishing, where so few editors read foreign languages. If, upon
publication, a foreign text is not an instant critical and commercial
success in the culture for which it was written, it probably won't be
sought by target-language publishers. The project to translate it,
therefore, should be controlled by the translator, who, in effect,
must invent for target-language readers a foreign text that would
otherwise be nonexistent to them.

A change in contemporary thinking about translation finally
requires a change in the practice of reading, reviewing, and
teaching translations. Because translation is a double writing, a
rewriting of the foreign text according to domestic cultural values,
any translation requires a double reading – as both communication
and inscription. Reading a translation as a translation means
reflecting on its conditions, the domestic dialects and discourses in
which it is written and the domestic cultural situation in which it is
read. This reading is historicizing: it draws a distinction between
the (foreign) past and the (domestic) present. Evaluating a
translation as a translation means assessing it as an intervention
into a present situation. Reviews must not be limited to rare
comments on the style of a translation or its accuracy according to
canons that are applied implicitly. Reviewers should consider the
canons of accuracy that the *translator* has set in the work, judging
the decision to translate and publish a foreign text in view of the
current canon of that foreign literature in the target-language
culture.

It is in academic institutions, most importantly, that different
reading practices can be developed and applied to translations.
Here a double reading is crucial. A translation yields information
about the source-language text – its discursive structures, its themes
and ideas – but no translation should ever be taught as a
transparent representation of that text, even if this is the prevalent
practice today. Any information derived from the translation is
inevitably presented in target-language terms, which must be made
the object of study, of classroom discussion and advanced research.
Research into translation can never be simply descriptive; merely to

formulate translation as a topic in cultural history or criticism assumes an opposition to its marginal position in the current hierarchy of cultural practices. And the choice of a topic from a specific historical period will always bear on present cultural concerns. Yet even if research into translation cannot be viewed as descriptive, devoid of cultural and political interests, it should not aim to be simply prescriptive, approving or rejecting translation theories and practices without carefully examining their relationships to their own moments and to that of the researcher.

The translator's invisibility today raises such troubling questions about the geopolitical economy of culture that a greater suspicion toward translation is urgently needed to confront them. Yet the suspicion I am encouraging here assumes a utopian faith in the power of translation to make a difference, not only at home, in the emergence of new cultural forms, but also abroad, in the emergence of new cultural relations. To recognize the translator's invisibility is at once to critique the current situation and to hope for a future more hospitable to the differences that the translator must negotiate.

Notes

1 Invisibility

1 These cultural and social developments have been described by various commentators. My sense of them is informed especially by Mandel 1975, McLuhan 1964, Horkheimer and Adorno 1972, and Baudrillard 1983. Instrumental conceptions of language are of course not unique to the post-World War II period; they date back to antiquity in the west and have influenced translation theories at least since Augustine (Robinson 1991: 50–54).

2 Holden 1991: Chap. 1 offers a similar assessment of contemporary American poetry, although from a "centrist" position. For the historical development of transparent discourse in English-language poetry, see Easthope 1983.

3 Copyright, Designs and Patents Act 1988 (c.48), sections 1 (1)(a), 16(1)(e), 21(3)(a)(i); 17 US Code, sections 101, 102, 106, 201(a) (1976).

4 The ambiguous legal status of translation is discussed by Derrida 1985a: 196–200 and Simon 1989.

5 The UNESCO Recommendation on the Legal Protection of Translators and Translations and the Practical Means to Improve the Status of Translators (adopted by the General Conference at Nairobi, 22 November 1976), follows the wording of the Berne Convention:

> Member states should accord to translators, in respect of their translations, the protection accorded to authors under the provisions of the international copyright conventions to which they are party and/or under their national laws, but without prejudice to the rights of the authors of the original works translated.
>
> (article II.3)

6 This account of Blackburn's Cortázar project draws on documents in the Paul Blackburn Collection, Archive for New Poetry, Mandeville Department of Special Collections, University of California, San Diego: Letter to John Dimoff, National Translation Center, University of Texas, Austin, 6 May 1965; Contract with Pantheon Books for the

translation of *End of the Game and Other Stories,* 4 June 1965; Amendment to Contract with Pantheon Books, 12 May 1966; Letter to Claudio Campuzano, Inter-American Foundation for the Arts, 9 June 1966. Information concerning the "poverty level" is drawn from the *Statistical Abstract of the United States* for the pertinent years.

7   The 1969 translation rate is taken from the "manifesto" that concludes the proceedings from the landmark PEN conference held in 1970 (*The World of Translation* 1971:377). The 1979 rate is taken from my own work-for-hire contract with Farrar, Straus & Giroux for the translation of Barbara Alberti's novel *Delirium,* 29 May 1979.

8   British statistics are drawn from *Whitaker's Almanack,* American statistics from *Publishers Weekly.* I have also consulted the data in the *United Nations Statistical Yearbook, UNESCO Basic Facts and Figures, UNESCO Statistical Yearbook,* and *An International Survey of Book Production during the Last Decades* 1982.

9   Schleiermacher's theory, despite its stress on foreignizing translation, is complicated by the nationalist cultural program he wants German translation to serve: see chapter 3, pp. 101–116.

10   For the impact of poststructuralism on translation theory and practice, see, for example, Graham 1985, Benjamin 1989, Niranjana 1992, and Venuti 1992. Gentzler 1993: Chap. 6 surveys this movement.

11   The same contradiction appears in Freud's own reflections on the therapeutic/hermeneutic dilemma of psychoanalysis in *Beyond the Pleasure Principle* (1920):

> Twenty-five years of intense work have had as their result that the immediate aims of psychoanalytic technique are other today than they were at the outset. At first the analyzing physician could do no more than discover the unconscious material that was concealed from the patient, put it together, and, at the right moment, communicate it to him. Psychoanalysis was then first and foremost an art of interpreting. Since this did not solve the therapeutic problem, a further aim quickly came in view: to oblige the patient to confirm the analyst's construction from his own memory. In that endeavor the chief emphasis lay upon the patient's resistances: the art consisted now in uncovering these as quickly as possible, in pointing them out to the patient and in inducing him by human influence – this was where suggestion operating as "transference" played its part – to abandon his resistances.
>
> (Freud 1961:12)

Although Freud intends to draw a sharp distinction in the development of psychoanalysis between an early, hermeneutic phase and a later, therapeutic phase, his exposition really blurs the distinction: both phases require a primary emphasis on interpretation, whether of "unconscious material" or of "the patient's resistances," which insofar as they require "uncovering" are likewise "unconscious"; in both "the analyst's construction" can be said to be "first and foremost." What has changed is not so much "the immediate aims of psychoanalytic technique" as its theoretical apparatus: the intervening years witnessed the development of a new *interpretive* concept – the "transference." Moreover, Freud's characterization of psychoanalysis as primarily therapeutic occurs in a late text that is one of his most theoretical and speculative. Bettelheim's conception of psychoanalysis, the basis for his rejection of the *Standard Edition*, smooths out the discontinuities in Freud's texts and project by resorting to a schema of development (like Freud himself):

> The English translations cleave to an early stage of Freud's thought, in which he inclined toward science and medicine, and disregard the more mature Freud, whose orientation was humanistic, and who was concerned mostly with broadly conceived cultural and human problems and with matters of the soul.
>
> (Bettelheim 1983:32)

12   Although transparent discourse emerges in English-language translation most decisively during the seventeenth century, it has been a prevalent feature of western translation theory and practice since antiquity. This topic is treated from various perspectives by Berman 1985, Rener 1989, and Robinson 1991.

2 Canon

1   My conception of Denham and Wroth (discussed on pp. 44, 47) as "courtly amateurs" assumes Helgerson 1983.

2   For the cultural activities of exiled royalist writers, see Hardacre 1953. Steiner 1975:13–25 considers the French influence on their translations. Zuber 1968 shows the importance of D'Ablancourt to the French translation tradition.

3   The Brute legend in English historiography is treated by Parsons 1929, Brinkley 1967, Jones 1944, and MacDougall 1982. Bush 1962 offers a useful précis of the issues.

4   The historical allegory in *Coopers Hill* is elucidated by Wasserman 1959:chap. III, especially 72–76, and O'Hehir 1969:227–256. For the ideological significance of Fanshawe's and Wase's translations, see Potter 1989:52–53, 89–90 and Patterson 1984:172–176. Hager 1982 notes the domesticating impulse in Denham's translation when discussing the Laocoön passage.

5   Ogilby's version of these lines, in referring to the king's "sacred body" and to the absence of "obsequies," shares the royalism of Denham's. For the politics of Ogilby's Virgil, see Patterson 1987:169–185.

6   This relies on Easthope's account of transparent discourse in poetry and its rise during the early modern period (Easthope 1983:chap. 7).

7   Samuel Johnson admiringly discusses Denham in *The Lives of the English Poets* (1783), devoting an entire chapter to him but also commenting on his work in the chapter on Dryden.

8   Historical explanations of the heroic couplet that stress its political

function are offered, for example, by Caudwell 1973:99, 135, Korshin 1973, and Easthope 1983:119. John Milton may have set forth the first political reading of the heroic couplet when, in the prefatory statement to *Paradise Lost* (1667), he opposed the "ancient liberty" of blank verse to "the troublesome and modern bondage of Riming."

9   The subscription lists for Pope's Homer are discussed by Rogers 1978, Hodgart 1978, and Speck 1982. Hodgart observes that the list for the *Iliad* "reveals a decided Tory–Jacobite tendency" (Hodgart 1978:31).

10   For the emergence and function of the "public sphere" in the eighteenth century, see Habermas 1989, Hohendahl 1982, and Eagleton 1984.

11   Alison describes the extremely favorable reception of Tytler's treatise – "The different reviewers of the day, contended with each other in the earliness of their notice, and in the liberality of their praise" – concluding that "after the experience of fifteen years [and five editions], it may now be considered as one of the standard works of English criticism" (Alison 1818:28).

12   For the ideological standpoint of the *Edinburgh Review,* see Clive 1957: Chap. 4, Hayden 1969:8–9, 19–22, and Sullivan 1983b:139–144.

13   *Blackwood's* also ran a favorable review of the second volume of Rose's Ariosto (*Blackwood's* 1824). For the ideological standpoint of this magazine, see Hayden 1969:62–63, 73 and Sullivan 1983b:45–53.

14   These remarks assume the cultural histories of Abrams 1953 and Foucault 1970.

15   For the ideological standpoints of these magazines, see Roper 1978:174–176, 180–181, Hayden 1969:44–45, 73, and Sullivan 1983a:231–237 and 1983b:57–62.

16   The parentage of Lamb and Caroline St. Jules is discussed by Posonby 1955:2–5, Stuart 1955:160–163, 184, and Cecil 1965:27.

17   Quinlan notes that "the taste for Evangelical literature had eventually pervaded all ranks of society. Even among the upper classes there were many, like Lord Melbourne, who read theology and biblical criticism for pleasure" (Quinlan 1941:271).

18   Lamb's politics is also discussed by Dunckley 1890:83–84, 106–107. Quinlan notes that "as compared with the strict Evangelicals who indiscriminately banned all novels and plays, the expurgators might consider themselves liberals, taking a middle course at a time when the most severe censors could not tolerate polite literature in any form" (Quinlan 1941:229).

3 Nation

1   English renderings of Schleiermacher's lecture are taken from Lefevere 1977:67–89, French renderings from "Des différentes méthodes du traduire," trans. Berman 1985:279–347. Quotations of the German follow Schleiermacher 1838:207–245.

2   Sheehan 1989:157–158 describes the different German cultural

constituencies during this period.

3 For surveys of German nationalism in the eighteenth and early nineteenth century, see Sheehan 1989:371–388 and Johnston 1989:103–113.

4 Lefevere's choice of "the Germans translate every literary Tom, Dick, and Harry" to render Schlegel's "die Deutschen sind ja Allerwelts-übersetzer" is typical of his strong reliance on fluent strategies that draw on contemporary English idioms.

5 For critiques of Schleiermacher's hermeneutics along these lines, see, for example, Palmer 1969:91–94 and Gadamer 1970:68–84. Two expositions of Schleiermacher's hermeneutics which make clear but do not critique its individualism are Forstman 1968 and Szondi 1986.

6 Steiner 1974:234 *et passim* has so far been the only translation theorist writing in English who recognizes the importance of Schleiermacher's lecture – but for rather different reasons from those set forth here and in Berman 1984:248–249n.

7 In this passage Lefevere is quoting Nida 1964:159. Lefevere later reaffirmed his view of Schleiermacher's theory by asserting that "the second part of his famous maxim, 'move the author towards the reader,' [is] the only viable one" (1990:19). Lefevere's latest work shows a much greater concern for the cultural and social determinants of translation (Lefevere 1992a), although he feels that a foreignizing method like Schleiermacher's is obsolete

> because the audience for it has almost ceased to exist[,] the educated reader who was able to read original and translation side by side and, in doing so, to appreciate the difference in linguistic expression as expressing the difference between two language games.
>
> (Lefevere 1992b:5)

My argument, however, is that foreignizing translation can appeal to diverse cultural constituencies, monolingual as well as educated, but also that foreignizing translation discourses can be perceived without recourse to a comparison with the foreign text (even if such a comparison is certainly illuminating).

8 The account of Newman's career and opinions presented in the following pararaphs draws on the *DNB*, Sieveking 1909, and Newman's three-volume selection of his many lectures, pamphlets, and articles (Newman 1869, 1887, and 1889).

9 For the diversity of the Victorian reading audience, see Altick 1957. For the meanings and uses of English archaisms, I have relied on the *OED*.

10 Newman referred to the "modern Greek Epic metre" in his 1851 review article, where he quoted from "a well-known patriotic address stimulating the Greeks to free themselves from Turkey" (Newman 1851:390). His use of the "modern Greek Klephtic ballad" is noticed in the *North American Review* 1862a:119. Hobsbawm discusses the role

of the "klephts" in the Greek nationalist movement (Hobsbawm 1962:173–174).

11 For liberal historiography, see Butterfield 1951, Burrow 1981, and Culler 1985. Newman's other historical writings also reveal Whig assumptions. A liberal teleology shaped the lessons he drew from historical "contrasts" and frequently issued into a utopianism, both democratic and nationalistic:

> We [...] can look back upon changes which cannot be traced in antiquity: we see the serf and vassal emancipated from his lord, the towns obtaining, first independence, next coordinate authority with the lords of the land. When the element which *was* weaker gradually works its way up, chiefly by moral influences and without any exasperation that can last long, there is every ground to hope a final union of feeling between Town and Country on the only stable basis, that of mutual justice. Then all England will be blended into one interest, that of the *Nation*, in which it will be morally impossible for the humblest classes to be forgotten.
>
> (Newman 1847a:23)

Newman treated capitalist economic practices with the same Whiggish optimism, asserting that because "all-reaching Commerce touches distant regions which are beyond the grasp of politics" geopolitical relations will eventually be characterized by "peace" (ibid.:33).

12 The divided reception of the controversy becomes evident in a brief survey of the reviews. Arnold's recommendation of hexameters for Homeric translation was accepted in the *North American Review* 1862a and 1862b. More typical were reviews that accepted Arnold's academic reading of Homer, but rejected his recommendation of hexameters as too deviant from English literary tradition: see, for example Spedding 1861 and the *North British Review* 1862. Near the end of the decade, Arnold's "brilliant contribution" to the controversy was still being mentioned in reviews of Homeric translations (*Fraser's Magazine* 1868:518). Newman, in contrast, had few supporters. John Stuart Blackie seems to have been unique in agreeing with Newman's reading of Homer and recommending a rhymed ballad measure for Homeric translation (Blackie 1861).

13 Lattimore insisted that "my line can hardly be called English hexameter" because it lacks the regularity of nineteenth-century hexameters (he cited Longfellow). But he made clear the domestication at work in his version: he agreed with Arnold's reading of Homer and aimed to adapt his six-stress line to "the plain English of today" (Lattimore 1951:55). The first paperback edition of Lattimore's *Iliad* appeared in 1961; by 1971 the translation had been reprinted twenty-one times.

4 Dissidence

1   My concept of foreignizing translation as a "dissident" cultural practice is indebted to Alan Sinfield's work on political forms of literary criticism, notably 1992. Especially pertinent to the politics of foreignizing translation is Sinfield's remark that "political awareness does not arise out of an essential, individual, self-consciousness of class, race, nation, gender, or sexual orientation; but from involvement in *a milieu, a subculture*" (Sinfield 1992:37).

2   Williams 1958: Chap. 2 has clarified this point. My argument concerning Tarchetti's cultural politics implicitly takes issue with Carsaniga:

> In their loathing for everything bourgeois, the *scapigliati* found it necessary to break with the Manzonian tradition and its ideological mystifications; on the other hand their antisocial instincts prevented them from achieving an authentic realist art. [.. .] Tarchetti, who had been an acute observer and critic of the distorting disciplines of military life, took refuge in mysticism.
>
> (Carsaniga 1974:338)

Such comments tend to make the naive equation between realism and reality, failing to take into account the ideological determinations of literary form.

3   Costa and Vigini 1991 indicates that few book-length translations of foreign fantastic narratives were available in Italy before Tarchetti began writing and publishing: there were three editions of Hoffmann's tales (1833, 1835, and 1855) and *Storie incredibili* (1863), which contained translations of Chamisso's *Peter Schlemihls wundersame Geschichte* and Poe's "The Murders in the Rue Morgue" and "The Oval Portrait." The Italian versions of Poe's texts were made from Baudelaire's French translations. Rossi 1959:121–125 sketches the Italian reception of Poe.

4   From its very first issue, *The Keepsake* published Oriental tales and poems with titles like "Sadak the Wanderer. A Fragment," "The Persian Lovers," and "The Deev Alfakir" (Reynolds 1828:117–119, 136–137, 160–169).

5   These clauses are taken from my contracts with American publishers for translations of several Italian-language books: Barbara Alberti, *Delirium*, Farrar, Straus & Giroux, 29 May 1979, p. 1; *Restless Nights: Selected Stories of Dino Buzzati*, North Point Press, 15 September 1982, p. 2; and I. U. Tarchetti, *Fantastic Tales*, Mercury House, 3 July 1991, p. 5.

5 Margin

1   Pound expresses this sort of elitism in his introduction to *Sonnets and Ballate of Guido Cavalcanti* when he refers to "*voi altri pochi* [you other few] who understand" (Anderson 1983:19). Other reviewers sym-

pathetic to Pound's modernist translation projects include Murphy 1953, Ferlinghetti 1953, and *The New Yorker* 1954.

2   Davie's commentary on Pound's writing includes two books, 1964 and 1976. Homberger discusses Davie's "sustained and occasionally bitter attack upon the intention behind the Cantos" (Homberger 1972:28–29).

3   See also Stern 1953:

> What is peculiar in Pound's translating shows up mostly in the famous versions of Cavalcanti and Arnaut Daniel. Away from the didactic context, Pound has tended to burden some of the translations with an antique weight (perhaps in order to carry what has since become staple or cliché or what has since vanished altogether from the tradition). [...] The finest English verse in *The Translations* comes in *The Seafarer* and in the Chinese poems of *Cathay*. There whatever is sporty or cagy or antique or labyrinthine in other sections of the book drops away and we have the pure, emotionally subtle, lovely verse which most English readers have Pound alone to thank for knowing.
>
> (Stern 1953:266, 267)

Edwin Muir similarly praises "all the translations in the book except those from Guido Cavalcanti," adding, somewhat eccentrically, that "the poems from the Provençal and the Chinese bring off the miracle" (Muir 1953:40).

4   Fitts's changing attitude toward Pound's writing is documented by the two reviews printed in Homberger 1972, the first a very enthusiastic assessment of *A Draft of XXX Cantos* from 1931, the second a curt dismissal of *Guide to Kulchur* from 1939 (Homberger 1972:246–255, 335–336). Carpenter 1988:507, 543 also notes Fitts's negative reviews of Pound. Pound, in turn, felt that even Fitts's positive reviews were misguided (Carpenter 1988:478). Laughlin seems to have indulged Fitts's criticisms, since he invited Fitts "to check and correct the classical allusions" in *The Cantos* (ibid.:687).

5   The translation is reprinted, without the Latin texts, in Zukofsky 1991, where the dates of composition, 1958–1969, are given in square brackets. Cid Corman, who was in correspondence with Louis Zukofsky and published some of the Catullus translation in his magazine *Origin*, notes that it involved "at least 8 or 9 years' labor" (Corman 1970:4). Celia Zukofsky later made clear the division of labor (Hatlen 1978:539n.2). Pound's influence on the Zukofskys' Catullus can be inferred from Ahearn 1987:200, 203, 208, 218.

6   I have learned much about the language of the Zukofskys' Catullus from Guy Davenport's brief but incisive essays, 1970 and 1979. See also Gordon 1979 and Mann 1986, who presents an astute discussion of the cultural and political issues raised by the translation.

7   Not surprisingly, Raffel reviewed Apter's study very favorably (Raffel 1985), and his own study of Pound's writing (Raffel 1984) includes a chapter on the translations, but entirely omits any discussion of

the Cavalcanti and Daniel versions. See also Lefevere's negative evaluation of the Zukofskys' Catullus (Lefevere 1975:19–26, 95–96). "The result," Lefevere concluded, "is a hybrid creation of little use to the reader, testifying at best to the translator's linguistic virtuosity and inventiveness" (ibid.:26). Lefevere's recent work aims to be "descriptive" instead of "prescriptive," so he refrains from judging the Zukofskys' Catullus, although pointing out that it has "never achieved more than a certain notoriety as a curiosum doomed not to be taken seriously" (Lefevere 1992a:109).

8   I cite the Blackburn–Pound correspondence from Paul Blackburn, Letters to Ezra Pound, Collection of American Literature, Beinecke Rare Book and Manuscript Library, Yale University, and Ezra and Dorothy Pound, Letters to Paul Blackburn, Paul Blackburn Collection, Archive for New Poetry. Neither collection contains Blackburn's first letters to Pound in 1950. Some of the correspondence is dated, either by the correspondents or by archivists; dates I have conjectured on the basis of internal evidence are indicated with a question mark. My reading of Blackburn's relationship to Pound is indebted to Sedgwick 1985.

9   This publishing history is reconstructed from documents in the Paul Blackburn Collection, Archive for New Poetry: M. L. Rosenthal, Letters to Emile Capouya, 17 July and 2 August 1958; Capouya, Letter to John Ciardi, 27 June 1958; Ciardi, Letter to Capouya, 2 July 1958; Capouya, Letter to Ramon Guthrie, 18 July 1958; Guthrie, Letter to Capouya, 24 July 1958; Guthrie, Report on Blackburn's *Anthology of Troubadors*; Capouya, Letters to Blackburn, 12 September 1958, 8 October 1958, 31 October 1958, 8 December 1958, 26 March 1965; R. Repass, Memo (Contract Request for Blackburn), 29 September 1958; Herbert Weinstock, Letter to Blackburn, 11 June 1963; Daniel R. Hayes, Letter to Blackburn, 7 June 1963; Arthur Gregor, Letter to Blackburn, 1 September 1965; M. L. Rosenthal, Letters to Blackburn, 8 February 1957, 16 March 1958, 14 June 1958, 22 July 1959, 1 November 1965.

10   "Agreement of Representation (Contract)," 11 August 1959, Paul Blackburn Collection, Archive for New Poetry. Sales figures for the Cortázar translations (cited on pp. 265–266) are taken from royalty statements in the Blackburn Collection. Blackburn's correspondence as Cortázar's agent documents the increasing American interest in the Argentine writer's fiction.

11   This catalogue of writers is drawn from various reviews of Blackburn's Cortázar: Coleman 1967, Kauffman 1967, Davenport 1967, *Time* 1967, MacAdam 1967, Stern 1967, *Times Literary Supplement* 1968.

6 Simpatico

1   Montale's seven Italian collections are *Ossi di seppia* (1925), *Le occasioni* (1939), *La bufera e altro* (1956), *Satura* (1971), *Diario del '71 e del '72* (1973), *Quaderno di quattro anni* (1977), and *Altri versi e poesie*

disperse (1981), now gathered in Montale 1984a. William Arrowsmith was completing translations of *Cuttlefish Bones* and *Satura* when he died in 1992; Jonathan Galassi is currently completing a translation of Montale's first three books. Montale's Italian texts have also been the object of free adaptations in English: see, for example, Lowell 1961:107–129 and Reed 1990.

2   These reflections on romantic individualism and its degrading of translation rely on Derrida 1976 and Deleuze 1990:253–266.

3   See also *On the Genealogy of Morals*:

> A quantum of force is equivalent to a quantum of drive, will, effect – more, it is nothing other than precisely this very driving, willing, effecting, and only owing to the seduction of language (and of the fundamental errors of reason that are petrified in it) which conceives and misconceives all effects as conditioned by something that causes effects, by a 'subject,' can it appear otherwise.
>
> (Nietzsche 1969:45)

Deleuze 1983: 6-8 offers an incisive exposition of Nietzsche's "philosophy of the will."

4   The magazines that have published my translations of De Angelis's poetry include *American Poetry Review, Paris Review, Poetry,* and *Sulfur.* The translations have been rejected by *Antaeus, Conjunctions, Field, New American Writing, The New Yorker,* and *Pequod,* among others.

5   Letter from Peter Potter, Assistant Editor, Wesleyan University Press, 24 November 1987.

6   For a selection from the writing of this loosely associated group, see Messerli 1987. For discussions of the theoretical differences between the L=A=N=G=U=A=G=E group and the romanticism which dominates contemporary American poetry, see Perloff 1985 and Bartlett 1986.

7   De Angelis's poetry has been reviewed in little magazines like *Produzione e cultura,* in the widely circulated literary tabloid *Alfabeta* (now defunct), and in mass-audience magazines like *L'Espresso* and *Panorama.* Newspapers that have printed reviews of his books include *La Gazzetta di Parma, La Stampa,* and *Corriere della Sera.*

8   Derrida similarly notes that "there are, in one linguistic system, perhaps several languages, or tongues. [...] There is impurity in every language," and he concludes that "translation can do everything except mark this linguistic difference inscribed in the language, this difference of language systems inscribed in a single tongue" (1985b:100). I am arguing that it is precisely this difference that the strategy of resistancy is designed to mark, the differences among languages, but also within them.

Bibliography

Abrams, M. H. (1953) *The Mirror and the Lamp: Romantic Theory and the Critical Tradition*, Oxford: Oxford University Press.

Adams, R. M. (1979) "From Langue d'Oc and Langue d'Oïl," *New York Times Book Review*, 25 February, pp. 14, 36.

The Adventures of Catullus, and History of His Amours with Lesbia. Intermixt with Translations of his Choicest Poems. By several Hands. Done from the French. (1707), London: J. Chantry.

Ahearn, B. (ed.) (1987) *Pound/Zukofsky: Selected Letters of Ezra Pound and Louis Zukofsky*, New York: New Directions.

Alison, A. (1818) *Memoir of the Life and Writings of the Honourable Alexander Fraser Tytler, Lord Woodhouselee*, Edinburgh: Neill & Co.

Allen, D. M. (ed.) (1960) *The New American Poetry*, New York: Grove.

Altick, R. (1957) *The English Common Reader: A Social History of the Mass Reading Public, 1800–1900*, Chicago: University of Chicago Press.

Amos, F. R. (1920) *Early Theories of Translation*, New York: Columbia University Press.

Anderson, B. (1991) *Imagined Communities: Reflections on the Origin and Spread of Nationalism*, rev. edn, London and New York: Verso.

Anderson, D. (1982) "A Language to Translate Into: The Pre-Elizabethan Idiom of Pound's Later Cavalcanti Translations," *Studies in Medievalism* 2:9–18.

—— (ed.) (1983) *Pound's Cavalcanti: An Edition of the Translations, Notes, and Essays*, Princeton: Princeton University Press.

Annan, N. (1944) "Books in General," *New Statesman and Nation*, 18 March, p. 191.

Anti-Jacobin Review; and Protestant Advocate (1821) Review of G. Lamb's Translation of Catullus, 61:13–19.

Apter, R. (1986) "Paul Blackburn's Homage to Ezra Pound," *Translation Review* 19:23–26.

—— (1987) *Digging for the Treasure: Translation after Pound* (1984), New York: Paragon House.

Arnold, M. (1914) *Essays by Matthew Arnold*, London: Oxford University Press.

—— (1960) *On the Classical Tradition*, ed. R. H. Super, Ann Arbor:

University of Michigan Press.

Athenaeum (1886) Review of *The Iliad of Homer*, trans. Arthur Way, 10 April, pp. 482–483.

Bakhtin, M. (1984) *Rabelais and His World* (1964), trans. H. Iswolsky, Bloomington: Indiana University Press.

Balderston, D. (1992) "Fantastic Voyages," *New York Times Book Review*, 29 November, p. 15.

Baldick, C. (1983) *The Social Mission of English Criticism: 1848–1932*, Oxford: Clarendon Press.

Ballantyne, A. (1888) "Wardour-Street English," *Longman's Magazine* 12 (October):585–594.

Ballerini, L. and Milazzo, R. (eds) (1979) *The Waters of Casablanca*, Chelsea 37.

Barnard, M. (ed. and trans.) (1958) *Sappho: A New Translation*, Berkeley and Los Angeles: University of California Press.

—— (1984) *Assault on Mount Helicon: A Literary Memoir*, Berkeley and Los Angeles: University of California Press.

Bartlett, L. (1986) "What Is 'Language Poetry'?" *Critical Inquiry* 12:741–752.

Bassnett, S. (1980) *Translation Studies*, London and New York: Methuen.

Baudrillard, J. (1983) *Simulations*, trans. P. Foss, P. Patton, and P. Beitchman, New York: Semiotext(e).

Belsey, C. (1980) *Critical Practice*, London and New York: Methuen.

Beltrametti, F. (1976) *Another Earthquake*, trans. P. Vangelisti, San Francisco and Los Angeles: Red Hill.

Benjamin, A. (1989) *Translation and the Nature of Philosophy: A New Theory of Words*, London and New York: Routledge.

Berengo, M. (1980) *Intellettuali e librai nella Milano della Restaurazione*, Turin: Einaudi.

Berman, A. (1984) *L'Épreuve de l'étranger: Culture et traduction dans l'Allemagne romantique*, Paris: Gallimard.

—— (1985) "La traduction et la lettre, ou l'auberge du lointain," in *Les Tours de Babel: Essais sur la traduction*, Mauvezin: Trans-Europ-Repress.

Bernstein, C. (1986) *Content's Dream: Essays 1975–1984*, Los Angeles: Sun & Moon.

—— (1992) *A Poetics*, Cambridge, Massachusetts: Harvard University Press.

Bettelheim, B. (1983) *Freud and Man's Soul*, New York: Alfred Knopf.

Bevington, M. M. (1941) *The Saturday Review, 1855–1868: Representative Educated Opinion in Victorian England*, New York: Columbia University Press.

Biggs, M. (1990) *A Gift That Cannot Be Refused: The Writing and Publishing of Contemporary American Poetry*, New York: Greenwood.

Blackburn, P. (1953) "Das Kennerbuch," *New Mexico Quarterly* 23 (Summer):215–219.

—— (ed. and trans.) (1958) *Anthology of Troubadours – translated from the 12th and 13th C. Occitan by Paul Blackburn*, Unpublished Manuscript, Paul Blackburn Collection, Archive for New Poetry, Mandeville Department of Special Collections, University of California, San Diego.

—— (1962) "The International Word," *Nation*, 21 April, pp. 357–360.

—— (1963) "The Grinding Down," *Kulchur* 10 (Summer):9–18.

—— (trans.) (1966) *Poem of the Cid*, New York: American R.D.M. Corporation.

—— (1985) *The Collected Poems of Paul Blackburn*, ed. E. Jarolim, New York: Persea.

—— (ed. and trans.) (1986) *Proensa: An Anthology of Troubadour Poetry* (1978), ed. G. Economou, New York: Paragon House.

Blackie, J. S. (1861) "Homer and his Translators," *Macmillan's Magazine* 4:268–280.

Blackwood's Edinburgh Magazine (1818) "Observations on Catullus, Suggested by a Piece of French Criticism," 2:486–490.

—— (1823) "New Poetical Translations – Wiffen – Rose – Gower," 14:26–39.

—— (1824) "The Second Volume of Rose's Ariosto," 15:418–424.

Blanchot, M. (1990) "Translating" (1971), trans. R. Sieburth, *Sulfur* 26:82–86.

Bonifazi, N. (1971) *Il racconto fantastico da Tarchetti a Buzzati*, Urbino: STEU.

—— (1982) *Teoria del fantastico e il racconto fantastico in Italia: Tarchetti, Pirandello, Buzzati*, Ravenna: Longo.

Borges, J. L. (1962) *Ficciones*, ed. A. Kerrigan, New York: Grove.

Bowdler, T. (ed.) (1818) *The Family Shakespeare. In Ten Volumes 12mo. In which nothing is added to the Text; but those Words and Expressions are omitted which cannot with Propriety be read aloud in a Family*, London: Longman.

Brady, P. V. (1977) "Traps for Translators," *Times Literary Supplement*, 25 February, p. 201.

Braun, R. E. (1970) "The Original Language: Some Postwar Translations of Catullus," *The Grosseteste Review* 3,4:27–34.

Brinkley, R. (1967) *Arthurian Legend in the Seventeenth Century* (1932), New York: Octagon.

British Critic (1798) Review of J. Nott's Translation of Catullus, 10:671–673.

British Quarterly Review (1865) "Homer and his Translators," 40 (April):290–324.

Brooke, S. (1898) *English Literature from the Beginning to the Norman Conquest*, New York and London: Macmillan.

Brower, R. (ed.) (1959) *On Translation*, Cambridge, Massachusetts: Harvard University Press.

Brownjohn, A. (1969) "Caesar 'Ad Some," *New Statesman*, 1 August, p. 151.

Bunting, B. (1936) Review of E. Stuart Bates, *Modern Translation, Criterion* 15:714–716.

Burgess, A. (1990) "On Wednesday He Does His Ears," *New York Times Book Review*, 14 October, p. 11.

Burrow, J. W. (1981) *A Liberal Descent: Victorian Historians and the English Past*, Cambridge: Cambridge University Press.

Bush, D. (1962) *English Literature in the Earlier Seventeenth Century 1600–1660*, 2nd edn, Oxford: Clarendon Press.

Butler, H. E. and Cary, M. (eds) (1927) *C. Suetoni Tranquilli Divus Iulius*, Oxford: Oxford University Press.

Butterfield, H. (1951) *The Whig Interpretation of History*, New York: Scribner.

Caesar, A. (1987) "Construction of Character in Tarchetti's *Fosca*," *Modern Language Review* 82:76–87.

Cagnone, N. (1975) *What's Hecuba to him or he to Hecuba?* trans. David Verzoni, New York, Norristown, and Milan: Out of London.

Campbell, G. (ed. and trans.) (1789) *The Four Gospels, Translated from the Greek. With Preliminary Dissertations, and Notes Critical and Explanatory.*, London: A. Strahan & T. Cadell.

Carpenter, H. (1988) *A Serious Character: The Life of Ezra Pound*, Boston: Houghton Mifflin.

Carsaniga, G. M. (1974) "Realism in Italy," in F. W. J. Hemmings (ed.) *The Age of Realism*, Harmondsworth: Penguin.

Castronovo, V., Fossati, L. G., and Tranfaglia, N. (1979) *La stampa italiana nell'età liberale*, Rome and Bari: Laterza.

Caudwell, C. (1973) *Illusion and Reality: A Study of the Sources of Poetry* (1937), New York: International Publishers.

Cecil, D. (1965) *Melbourne*, London: Constable.

Celan, P. (1986) "The Meridian," in *Collected Prose*, trans. R. Waldrop, Manchester: Carcanet.

Chandler, A. (1970) *A Dream of Order: The Medieval Ideal in Nineteenth-Century English Literature*, Lincoln: University of Nebraska Press.

Cherchi, P. and Parisi, J. (1989) "Some Notes on Post-War Italian Poetry," *Poetry* 155 (October–November):161–167.

Christ, R. (1984) "Translation Watch," *PEN American Center Newsletter* 53 (Winter):8.

Cixous, H. (1974) "The Character of 'Character'," trans. K. Cohen, *New Literary History* 5:383–402.

Clive, J. (1957) *Scotch Reviewers: The Edinburgh Review, 1802–1815*, Cambridge, Massachusetts: Harvard University Press.

Cohen, J. M (1962) *English Translators and Translations*, London: Longmans, Green & Co.

Coleman, A. (1967) "Everywhere Déjà Vu," *New York Times Book Review*, 9 July, p. 5.

Commager, S. (1971) Review of Three Catullus Translations, *New York Times Book Review*, 15 August, pp. 4, 35.

Conquest, R. (1970) "The Abomination of Moab," *Encounter* 34 (May):56–63.

Coogan, D. (1970) "Catullus," *Chelsea* 28:113–118.

Corke, H. (1967) "New Novels," *The Listener*, 8 June, pp. 761–762.

Corman, C. (1970) "Poetry as Translation," *The Grosseteste Review* 3, 4:3–20.

Cortázar, J. (1964) "Continuidad de los Parques," in *Final del juego*, Buenos Aires: Editorial Sudamericana.

—— (1965) *The Winners*, trans. E. Kerrigan, New York: Pantheon.

—— (1966) *Hopscotch*, trans. G. Rabassa, New York: Pantheon.

—— (1967) *End of the Game and Other Stories*, trans. P. Blackburn, New York: Pantheon.

—— (1969) *Cronopios and Famas*, trans. P. Blackburn, New York: Pantheon.

—— (1973) *All Fires The Fire*, trans. Suzanne Jill Levine, New York: Pantheon.

Costa, C. (1975) *Our Positions*, trans. P. Vangelisti, San Francisco and Los Angeles: Red Hill.

Costa, M. and Vigini, G. (eds) (1991) *CLIO: catalogo dei libri italiani dell'ottocento (1801–1900)*, Milan: Editrice Bibliografica.

Crusius, L. (1733) *The Lives of the Roman Poets. Containing A Critical and Historical Account of Them and their Writings, with large Quotations of their most celebrated Passages, as far as was necessary to compare and illustrate their several Excellencies, as well as to discover wherein they were deficient*, London: W. Innys, J. Clarke, B. Motte, J. Nourse.

Cucchi, M. (1983) *Dizionario della poesia italiana: i poeti di ogni tempo, la metrica, i gruppi e le tendenze*, Milan: Mondadori.

Culler, A. D. (1985) *The Victorian Mirror of History*, New Haven, Connecticut: Yale University Press.

D'Ablancourt, N. P. (trans.) (1640) *Les Annales de Tacite. Première Partie. Contenant la vie de Tibère*, Paris: Jean Camusat.

Davenport, G. (1967) "And a Cool Drink by the Hammock," *National Review*, 25 July, pp. 811–812.

—— (1970) "Louis Zukofsky," *Agenda* 8(3–4):130–137.

—— (1979) "Zukofsky's English Catullus" (1973), in C. F. Terrell (ed.) *Louis Zukofsky, Man and Poet*, Orono, Maine: National Poetry Foundation.

Davie, D. (1953) "Translation Absolute," *New Statesman and Nation*, 5 September, pp. 263–264.

—— (1964) *Ezra Pound: Poet as Sculptor*, New York: Oxford University Press.

—— (1976) *Ezra Pound*, New York: Viking.

Dawson, J. (1966) *Friedrich Schleiermacher: The Evolution of a Nationalist*, Austin and London: University of Texas Press.

De Angelis, M. (1975) "L'idea centrale," in M. Forti (ed.) *L'almanacco dello Specchio* 4:371–391.

—— (1976) *Somiglianze*, Milan: Guanda.

—— (1985) *Terra del viso*, Milan: Mondadori.

—— (1994) *Finite Intuition: Selected Poetry and Prose*, ed. and trans. L. Venuti, Los Angeles: Sun & Moon.

Dejeanne, J. M. L. (ed.) (1971) *Poésies Complètes du Troubadour Marcabru* (1909), New York: Johnson.

Deleuze, G. (1983) *Nietzsche and Philosophy*, trans. H. Tomlinson, New York: Columbia University Press.

—— (1990) *The Logic of Sense*, trans. M. Lester with C. Stivale, ed. C. V. Boundas, New York: Columbia University Press.

Deleuze, G. and Guattari, F. (1986) *Kafka: Toward a Minor Literature*, trans. D. Polan, Minneapolis: University of Minnesota Press.

Denham, J. (ed. and trans.) (1656) *The Destruction of Troy, An Essay upon the Second Book of Virgils Æneis. Written in the year, 1636*, London: Humphrey Moseley.

—— (1969) *The Poetical Works*, ed. T. H. Banks, 2nd edn, Hamden, Connecticut: Archon.

Derrida, J. (1976) *Of Grammatology*, trans. G. C. Spivak, Baltimore and London: Johns Hopkins University Press.

—— (1982) "Différance," in *Margins of Philosophy*, trans. A. Bass, Chicago: University of Chicago Press.

—— (1985a) "Des Tours de Babel," trans. J. F. Graham, in J. F. Graham (ed.) *Difference in Translation*, Ithaca, New York: Cornell University Press.

—— (1985b) *The Ear of the Other: Otobiography, Transference, Translation*, ed. C. McDonald, trans. A. Ronell and P. Kamuf, New York: Schocken.

Dickstein, M. (1992) Review of G. Celati, *Appearances*, trans. S. Hood, *New York Times Book Review*, 29 November, p. 18.

Dryden, J. (1956) "Preface to *Ovid's Epistles*" (1680), in E. N. Hooker and H. T. Swedenberg, Jr (eds) *The Works of John Dryden*, vol. I, Berkeley and Los Angeles: University of California Press.

—— (1958) "Dedication of the *Æneis*" (1697), in J. Kinsley (ed.) *The Poems of John Dryden*, vol. III, Oxford: Clarendon Press.

—— (1962) "Preface to *The Rival Ladies*" (1664), in G. Watson (ed.) *Of Dramatic Poesy and Other Critical Essays*, vol. I, London: Dent.

Dublin University Magazine (1862) "Homer and his Translators," 59 (June):643–654.

Dunckley, H. (1890) *Lord Melbourne*, London: Sampson Low, Marston, Searle and Rivington.

Eagleton, T. (1984) *The Function of Criticism: From The Spectator to Post-structuralism*, London: Verso.

Easthope, A. (1983) *Poetry as Discourse*, London and New York: Methuen.

Edinburgh Review (1820) Review of T. Mitchell's Translations of Aristophanes, 34:271–319.

Edwards, J. (1954) "Pound's Translations," *Poetry* 83:233–238.

Eliot, T. S. (1928) "Baudelaire in Our Time," in *For Lancelot Andrewes: Essays on Style and Order*, London: Faber & Gwyer.

—— (1950) *Selected Essays*, New York: Harcourt, Brace & World.

Elton, C. A. (ed. and trans.) (1814) *Specimens of the Classic Poets, In a Chronological Series from Homer to Tryphiodorus, Translated into English Verse, And Illustrated with Biographical and Critical Notices*, 3 vols, London: Robert Baldwin.

Eshleman, C. (1989) "The Gull Wall," in *Antiphonal Swing: Selected Prose, 1962–1987*, Kingston, New York: McPherson.

European Magazine, and the London Review and Literary Journal (1793), Review of A. F. Tytler, *Essay on the Principles of Translation*, 24:186–189, 278–282.

Fagles, R. (trans.) (1990) Homer, *The Iliad*, ed. B. Knox, New York: Viking.

Farina, S. (1913) *La mia giornata: Care ombre*, Turin: Società Tipografico-Editrice Nazionale.

Faulkner, P. (ed.) (1973) *William Morris: The Critical Heritage*, London: Routledge & Kegan Paul.

Faxon, F. W. (1973) *Literary Annuals and Giftbooks. A Bibliography, 1823–1903. Reprinted with Supplementary Essays*, Pinner, Middlesex: Private Libraries Association.

Feldman, G. (1986) "Going Global," *Publishers Weekly*, 19 December, pp. 20–24.

Feldman, R. and Swann, B. (eds) (1979) *Italian Poetry Today*, St. Paul, Minnesota: New Rivers.

Fell, C. (1991) "Perceptions of Transience," in M. Godden and M. Lapidge (eds) *The Cambridge Companion to Old English Literature*, Cambridge: Cambridge University Press.

Felstiner, J. (1983) "Paul Celan in Translation: 'Du Sei Wie Du'," *Studies in Twentieth-Century Literature* 8:91–100.

——— (1984) "Paul Celan's Triple Exile," *Sulfur* 11:47–52.

Ferlinghetti, L. (1953) "Among the New Books," *San Francisco Chronicle*, 4 October, p. 26.

Fiedler, L. (1962) "Sufficient unto the Day" (1955), in W. Phillips and P. Rahv (eds) *Partisan Review Anthology*, New York: Holt, Rinehart & Winston.

Fischbach, H. (1992) "The Mutual Challenge of Technical and Literary Translation: Some Highlights," *Sci-Tech Newsletter*, January, pp. 3–5.

Fitts, D. (1954) "The Tea-Shop Aura," *New Republic*, 4 January, pp. 18–19.

——— (ed. and trans.) (1956) *Poems from the Greek Anthology*, New York: New Directions.

——— (1958) *The Poetic Nuance*, New York: Harcourt, Brace.

Flad, B. (1992) "A Speech for the Defense of the Visible and Audible Translator," *Translation Review* 38–39: 40–41.

Forstman, H. J. (1968) "The Understanding of Language by Friedrich Schlegel and Schleiermacher," *Soundings* 51:146–165.

Fortini, F. (1975) "The Wind of Revival," *Times Literary Supplement*, 31 October, pp. 1308–1309.

Foucault, M. (1970) *The Order of Things: An Archaeology of the Human Sciences*, New York: Random House.

——— (1977) "Nietzsche, Genealogy, History," in *Language, Counter-Memory, Practice: Selected Essays and Interviews*, eds and trans D. F. Bouchard and S. Simon, Ithaca, New York: Cornell University Press.

Fowler, H. W. (1965) *A Dictionary of Modern English Usage*, ed. E. Gowers, New York and Oxford: Oxford University Press.

Frank, J. (1961) *The Beginnings of the English Newspaper 1620–1660*, Cambridge, Massachusetts: Harvard University Press.

Fraser's Magazine (1868) "Translations of the *Iliad*," 78 (October): 518–531.

Frémy, D. and M. (eds) (1992) *Quid 1992*, Paris: Laffont.

Frere, J. H. (1820) Review of T. Mitchell's Translations of Aristophanes, *Quarterly Review* 23:474–505.

Freud, S. (1960) *The Psychopathology of Everyday Life* (1901), trans. A. Tyson, ed. J. Strachey, New York: Norton.

——— (1961) *Beyond the Pleasure Principle* (1920), ed. and trans. J. Strachey, New York: Norton.

Gadamer, H.-G. (1970) "The Problem of Language in Schleiermacher's Hermeneutic," trans. D. E. Linge, in R. W. Funk (ed.) *Schleiermacher as Contemporary*, New York: Herder and Herder.

Gall, S. (1980) "Ramon Guthrie," in K. L. Rood (ed.) *Dictionary of Literary Biography 4: American Writers in Paris, 1920–1939*, Detroit: Gale.

Gardam, J. (1990) "The Institute of Translation and Interpreting Survey of

Rates and Salaries," *Professional Translator and Interpeter* 1:5–14.
Genest, J. (ed.) (1832) *Some Account of the English Stage from the Restoration in 1660 to 1830*, vol. VIII, Bath: H. E. Carrington.
Gentleman's Magazine (1798) Review of J. Nott's translation of Catullus, 68:408.
—— (1825) "John Nott, M.D.," 95:565–566.
—— (1834) "Hon. George Lamb," 104:437–438.
Gentzler, E. (1993) *Contemporary Translation Theories*, London and New York: Routledge.
Giddens, A. (1979) *Central Problems in Social Theory: Action, Structure, and Contradiction in Social Analysis*, Berkeley and Los Angeles: University of California Press.
Gioia, D. and Palma, M. (eds) (1991) *New Italian Poets*, Brownsville, Oregon: Story Line Press.
Giuliani, A. (ed.) (1961) *I novissimi: Poesia per gli anni '60*, Milan: Rusconi and Paolazzi.
Glenny, M. (1983) "Professional Prospects," *Times Literary Supplement*, 14 October, p. 1118.
Goldin, F. (ed. and trans.) (1973) *Lyrics of the Troubadours and Trouvères: An Anthology and a History*, Garden City, New York: Doubleday.
Gordon, D. M. (1979) "Three Notes on Zukofsky's Catullus," in C. F. Terrell (ed.) *Louis Zukofsky, Man and Poet*, Orono, Maine: National Poetry Foundation.
Gozzano, G. (1981) *The Man I Pretend to Be: The Colloquies and Selected Poems of Guido Gozzano*, ed. and trans. M. Palma, Princeton: Princeton University Press.
—— (1987) *The Colloquies and Selected Letters*, ed. and trans. J. S. Nichols, Manchester and New York: Carcanet.
Graham, J. (ed.) (1985) *Difference in Translation*, Ithaca, New York: Cornell University Press.
Graham, S. (1953) "Pound Sterling," *Poetry Review* 44:472–479.
Grannis, C. B. (1991) "Balancing the Books, 1990," *Publishers Weekly*, 5 July, pp. 21–23.
Grant, M. (ed.) (1980) Gaius Suetonius Tranquillus, *The Twelve Caesars*, trans. R. Graves, Harmondsworth: Penguin.
Graves, R. (trans.) (1957) Gaius Suetonius Tranquillus, *The Twelve Caesars*, Harmondsworth: Penguin.
—— (1965) "Moral Principles in Translation," *Encounter* 24:47–55.
Grove, R. (1984) "Nature Methodiz'd," *Critical Review* 26:52–68.
Guthrie, R. (1923) *Trobar Clus*, Northampton, Massachusetts: S4N.
—— (1927a) *A World Too Old*, New York: Doran.
—— (1927b) *Marcabrun*, New York: Doran.
—— (1929) *The Legend of Ermengarde*, Paris: Black Manikin.
—— (1970) *Maximum Security Ward 1964–1970*, New York: Farrar, Straus & Giroux.
Habermas, J. (1989) *The Structural Transformation of the Public Sphere: An Inquiry into a Category of Bourgeois Society*, trans. T. Burger with F. Lawrence, Cambridge, Massachusetts: MIT Press.
Hager, A. "British Virgil: Four Renaissance Disguises of the Laocoön

Passage of Book 2 of the *Aeneid*," *Studies in English Literature 1500–1900*, 22(1982):21–38.

A Handbook for Literary Translators (1991), 2nd edn, New York: PEN American Center.

Hardacre, P. H. (1953) "The Royalists in Exile during the Puritan Revolution, 1642–1660," *Huntington Library Quarterly* 16:353–370.

Harrison, T. J. (ed. and trans.) (1983) *The Favorite Malice: Ontology and Reference in Contemporary Italian Poetry*, New York, Norristown, and Milan: Out of London.

Hatlen, B. (1978) "Catullus Metamorphosed," *Paideuma* 7:539–545.

Hawkins, T. (ed. and trans.) (1625) *Odes of Horace, The best of Lyrick Poets, Contayning much morality, and sweetness, Selected, and Translated by S:T:H:*, London: W. Lee.

Hayden, J. O. (1969) *The Romantic Reviewers, 1802–1824*, Chicago: University of Chicago Press.

Heidegger, M. (1962) *Being and Time*, trans. J. Macquarrie and E. Robinson, New York: Harper and Row.

Helgerson, R. (1983) *Self-Crowned Laureates: Spenser, Jonson, Milton, and the Literary System*, Berkeley and Los Angeles: University of California Press.

Hermans, T. (1985) "Images of Translation: Metaphor and Imagery in the Renaissance Discourse on Translation," in T. Hermans (ed.) *The Manipulation of Literature: Studies in Literary Translation*, London: Croom Helm.

Hill, H. C. (1970) "Transonance and Intransigence," *The Grosseteste Review* 3(4):21–25.

Hingley, R. (ed. and trans.) (1964) *The Oxford Chekhov*, vol. III, London and New York: Oxford University Press.

Hobsbawm, E. J. (1962) *The Age of Revolution: 1789–1848*, New York: New American Library.

Hodgart, M. (1978) "The Subscription List for Pope's Iliad, 1715," in R. B. White, Jr (ed.) *The Dress of Words*, Lawrence, Kansas: University of Kansas Libraries.

Hohendahl, P. E. (1982) "Literary Criticism and the Public Sphere," trans. R. L. Smith and H. J. Schmidt, in *The Institution of Criticism*, Ithaca, New York: Cornell University Press.

Holden, J. (1991) *The Fate of American Poetry*, Athens, Georgia: University of Georgia Press.

Holyday, B. (trans.) (1635) *Aulus Persius Flaccus His Satyres. Translated into English, By Barten Holyday, Master of Arts, and student of Christ Church in Oxford. And now newly by him reviewed and amended. The third Edition*, London: R. Higginbotham.

Homberger, E. (ed.) (1972) *Ezra Pound: The Critical Heritage*, London and Boston: Routledge & Kegan Paul.

Honig, E. (1985) *The Poet's Other Voice: Conversations on Literary Translation*, Amherst: University of Massachusetts Press.

Hooley, D. M. (1988) *The Classics in Paraphrase: Ezra Pound and Modern Translators of Latin Poetry*, Selinsgrove, Pennsylvania: Susquehanna University Press.

Horkheimer, M. and Adorno, T. (1972) *Dialectic of Enlightenment*, trans. J. Cumming, New York: Continuum.

Houghton, W. E., Houghton, E. R. and Slingerland, J. H. (eds) (1987) *The Wellesley Index to Victorian Periodicals, 1824–1900*, 5 vols, Toronto: University of Toronto Press.

Howard, H. (trans.) (1557) *Certain Bokes of Virgiles Aenaeis turned into English meter by the right honorable lorde, Henry Earle of Surrey*, London: R. Tottel.

An International Survey of Book Production during the Last Decades (1982), Paris: UNESCO.

Jackson, R. (1981) *Fantasy: The Literature of Subversion*, London and New York: Methuen.

Jameson, F. (1979) *Fables of Aggression: Wyndham Lewis, the Modernist as Fascist*, Los Angeles and Berkeley: University of California Press.

Jiménez-Landi, A. (1974) *The Treasure of the Muleteer and Other Spanish Tales*, trans. P. Blackburn, Garden City, New York: Doubleday.

Johnston, O. W. (1989) *The Myth of a Nation: Literature and Politics in Prussia under Napoleon*, Columbia, South Carolina: Camden House.

Jones, E. (1944) *Geoffrey of Monmouth 1640–1680*, Berkeley: University of California Press.

Jonson, B. (1968) *The Complete Poetry of Ben Jonson*, ed. William B. Hunter, Jr, New York: Norton.

Kaplan, B. (1967) *An Unhurried View of Copyright*, New York: Columbia University Press.

Kauffmann, S. (1967) "Real and Otherwise," *New Republic*, 15 July, pp. 22, 36.

Keeley, E. (1990) "The Commerce of Translation," *PEN American Center Newsletter* 73 (Fall):10–12.

Kemeny, T. (1976) *The Hired Killer's Glove*, trans. T. Kemeny, New York, Norristown, Milan: Out of London.

Korshin, P. J. (1973) *From Concord to Dissent: Major Themes in English Poetic Theory 1640–1700*, Menston, England: The Scolar Press.

Krapp, G. P. and Dobbie, E.V.K. (eds) (1936) *The Exeter Book*, New York: Columbia University Press.

Kratz, D. (1986) "An Interview with Norman Shapiro," *Translation Review* 19:27–28.

Lacan, J. (1977) "The Subversion of the Subject and the Dialectic of Desire in the Freudian Unconscious," in *Écrits: A Selection*, trans. A. Sheridan, New York: Norton.

Laclau, E. and Mouffe, C. (1985) *Hegemony and Socialist Strategy: Toward a Radical Democratic Politics*, trans. W. Moore and P. Cammack, London: Verso.

Lamb, G. (ed.) (1816) *Shakespeare's Timon of Athens, As Revived at the Theatre Royal, Drury-lane, On Monday, Oct. 28, 1816. Altered and Adapted for Representation, By the Hon. George Lamb*, London: C. Chapple.

—— (ed. and trans.) (1821) *The Poems of Caius Valerius Catullus Translated. With a Preface and Notes, By the Hon. George Lamb*, 2 vols, London: John Murray.

Latham, W. (trans.) (1628) *Virgils Eclogues Translated into English: By W. L.*

Gent., London: W. Jones.

Lattimore, R. (ed. and trans.) (1951) *The Iliad of Homer*, Chicago: University of Chicago Press.

Lecercle, J.-J. (1990) *The Violence of Language*, London and New York: Routledge.

Lefevere, A. (1975) *Translating Poetry: Seven Strategies and a Blueprint*, Assen: Van Gorcum.

—— (ed. and trans.) (1977) *Translating Literature: The German Tradition from Luther to Rosenzweig*, Assen: Van Gorcum.

—— (1981) "German Translation Theory: Legacy and Relevance," *Journal of European Studies* 11:9–17.

—— (1990) "Translation: Its Genealogy in the West," in S. Bassnett and A. Lefevere (eds) *Translation, History and Culture*, London and New York: Pinter.

—— (1992a) *Translation, Rewriting and the Manipulation of Literary Fame*, London and New York: Routledge.

—— (ed. and trans.) (1992b) *Translation/History/Culture: A Sourcebook*, London and New York: Routledge.

Levy, C. (1991) "The Growing Gelt in Others' Words," *The New York Times*, 20 October, p. F5.

Levy, E. (1966) *Petit Dictionnaire Provençal–Français* (1909), Heidelberg: Carl Winter Universitatverlag.

Lewis, P. E. (1985) "The Measure of Translation Effects," in J. Graham (ed.) *Difference in Translation*, Ithaca, New York: Cornell University Press.

Locher, F. (ed.) (1980) *Contemporary Authors*, vols 93–96, Detroit: Gale.

London Magazine (1824) "Rose's Orlando Furioso," 9:623–628.

London Quarterly Review (1858) "Horace and his Translators," 104 (October):179–198.

—— (1874) "The Odes of Horace and Recent Translators," 42 (April and July):1–27.

Lorca, F. G. (1979) *Lorca/Blackburn: Poems of Federico Garcia Lorca*, trans. P. Blackburn, San Francisco: Momo's.

Lottman, H. R. (1991) "Milan: A World of Change," *Publishers Weekly*, 21 June, pp. S5–S11.

Lowell, R. (1961) *Imitations*, New York: Farrar, Straus & Giroux.

MacAdam, A. (1967) "A Life without Patterns," *New Leader*, 11 September, pp. 19–20.

McDougal, S. Y. (1972) *Ezra Pound and the Troubadour Tradition*, Princeton: Princeton University Press.

MacDougall, H. A. (1982) *Racial Myth in English History: Trojans, Teutons, and Anglo-Saxons*, Hanover, New Hampshire: University Press of New England.

McKendrick, J. (1991) "Italians for Anglosassoni," *Poetry Review* 81, 3 (Autumn):58–59.

McLuhan, M. (1964) *Understanding Media: The Extensions of Man*, New York: McGraw-Hill.

Macmillan's Magazine (1861) "Homer and His Translators," 4:268–280.

McPeek, J. A. S. (1939) *Catullus in Strange and Distant Britain*, Cambridge,

Massachusetts: Harvard University Press.

Makin, P. (1978) *Provence and Pound*, Berkeley and Los Angeles: University of California Press.

Mandel, E. (1975) *Late Capitalism*, trans. J. De Bres, London: New Left Books.

Mann, P. (1986) "Translating Zukofsky's Catullus," *Translation Review* 21–22:3–9.

Marcus, J. (1990) "Foreign Exchange," *Village Voice Literary Supplement*, 82 (February):13–17.

Mariani, G. (1967) *Storia della Scapigliatura*, Caltanisetta and Rome: Sciascia.

Marsh, P. (1991) "International Rights: The Philosophy and the Practice," *Publishers Weekly*, 12 July, pp. 26–27.

Martin, C. (ed. and trans.) (1990) *The Poems of Catullus* (1979), Baltimore and London: Johns Hopkins University Press.

Mayor, A. H. (1932) "Cavalcanti and Pound," *Hound & Horn* V(3) (April–June):468–471.

Mellor, A. K. (1988) *Mary Shelley: Her Life, Her Fiction, Her Monsters*, New York and London: Methuen.

Mercurius Politicus, Comprising the Sum of Foreine Intelligence, with the Affairs now on foot in the three Nations of England, Scotland, & Ireland. For Information of the People. Numb. 306. From Thursday April 17: to Thursday April 24, 1656.

Messerli, D. (ed.) (1987) *"Language" Poetries: An Anthology*, New York: New Directions.

Michener, C. (1980) "Laughter Goes Into Exile," *Newsweek*, 24 November, p. 108.

Montale, E. (1959a) *Poems by Eugenio Montale*, ed. and trans. E. Morgan, Reading, England: University of Reading.

—— (1959b) *Selected Poems of Montale*, ed. and trans. George Kay, Edinburgh: Edinburgh University Press.

—— (1966) *Selected Poems*, ed. G. Cambon, New York: New Directions.

—— (1970a) *Provisional Conclusions*, ed. and trans. E. Farnsworth, Chicago: Henry Regenry.

—— (1970b) *Xenia*, trans. G. Singh, Los Angeles: Black Sparrow, and New York: New Directions.

—— (1971) *The Butterfly of Dinard*, trans. G. Singh, Lexington: University Press of Kentucky.

—— (1973) *Mottetti*, trans. L. Kart, San Francisco: Grabhorn Hoyem.

—— (1976a) *New Poems: A Selection from Satura and Diario del '71 e del '72*, ed. and trans. G. Singh, New York: New Directions.

—— (1976b) *A Poet in Our Time*, trans. A. Hamilton, London: Boyars.

—— (1978) *The Storm and Other Poems*, trans. C. Wright, Oberlin: Oberlin College.

—— (1980a) *It Depends: A Poet's Notebook*, trans. G. Singh, New York: New Directions.

—— (1980b) *Xenia and Motets*, trans. K. Hughes, London: Agenda.

—— (1982) *The Second Life of Art: Selected Essays*, ed. and trans. J. Galassi, New York: Ecco.

—— (1984a) *Tutte le poesie*, ed. G. Zampa, Milan: Mondadori.

—— (1984b) *Otherwise: Last and First Poems*, trans. J. Galassi, New York: Random House.

—— (1985) *Bones of Cuttlefish*, trans. A. Mazza, Oakville, Ontario: Mosaic.

—— (1986) *The Storm and Other Things*, trans. W. Arrowsmith, New York: Norton.

—— (1987) *The Occasions*, trans. W. Arrowsmith, New York: Norton.

—— (1990) *The Motets of Eugenio Montale; Mottetti: Poems of Love*, trans. D. Gioia, St. Paul, Minnesota: Graywolf.

Monthly Magazine (1821) Review of G. Lamb's Translation of Catullus, 52:33–36.

Monthly Review (1792), Review of A. F. Tytler, *Essay on the Principles of Translation*, 8:361–366.

—— (1797) Review of J. Nott's Translation of Catullus, 24:275–278.

—— (1822) Review of G. Lamb's Translation of Catullus, 97:1–13.

Moore, N. (1971) "Hot Cat on a Cold Tin Roof Blues (or, Get Your Boots Laced, Fullus – Here Comes That Guy 'Cat'Ullus," *Poetry Review* 62:179–187.

Muir, E. (1953) "New Poems for Old," *Observer*, 2 August, p. 40.

Murphy, R. (1953) "The Art of a Translator," *Spectator*, 18 September, p. 303.

Mynors, R. A. B (ed.) (1969) Virgil, *Opera*, Oxford: Clarendon Press.

National Review (1860) "The English Translators of Homer," 11 (October):283–314.

Newman, F. W. (1841) *Introductory Lecture to the Classical Course*, London: Simpkin, Marshall and Co., and J. Green.

—— (1847a) *Four Lectures on the Contrasts of Ancient and Modern History*, London: Taylor and Walton.

—— (1847b) *On the Relations of Free Knowledge to Moral Sentiment*, London: Taylor and Walton.

—— (1851) "Recent Translations of Classical Poets," *Prospective Review*, 7 (August):369–403.

—— (ed. and trans.) (1853) *The Odes of Horace*, London: John Chapman.

—— (ed. and trans.) (1856) *The Iliad of Homer*, London: Walton and Maberly.

—— (1861) *Homeric Translation in Theory and Practice. A Reply to Matthew Arnold, Esq.*, London and Edinburgh: William and Norgate.

—— (1869) *Miscellanies*, vol. I, London: Trübner and Co.

—— (1887 and 1889) *Miscellanies*, vols II and III, London: Kegan Paul, Trench.

New Republic (1955) "Selected Books," 16 May, p. 46.

New Yorker (1954) "The Translations of Ezra Pound," 1 May, p. 112.

Niccolai, G. (1975) *Substitution*, trans. P. Vangelisti, San Francisco and Los Angeles: Red Hill.

Nida, E. A. (1952) *God's Word in Man's Language*, New York: Harper & Brothers.

—— (1964) *Toward a Science of Translating. With Special Reference to*

Principles and Procedures Involved in Bible Translating, Leiden: Brill.

—— (1975) *Customs and Cultures: Anthropology for Christian Missions* (1954), South Pasadena, California: William Carey Library.

Nida, E. A. and de Waard, J. (1986) *From One Language to Another: Functional Equivalence in Bible Translating*, Nashville: Thomas Nelson.

Nietzsche, F. (1967) *The Will to Power*, trans. W. Kaufmann and R. J. Hollingdale, New York: Vintage.

—— (1969) *On the Genealogy of Morals*, trans. W. Kaufmann and R. J. Hollingdale, New York: Vintage.

Niranjana, T. (1992) *Siting Translation: History, Poststructuralism, and the Colonial Context*, Berkeley and Los Angeles: University of California Press.

North American Review (1862a) "On Translating Homer," 94 (January):108–125.

—— (1862b) "Newman's Homeric Translation," 94 (April):541–545.

North British Review (1862) "Recent Homeric Critics and Translators," 72 (May):345–380.

Nott, J. (ed. and trans.) (1778) *Kisses: A Poetical Translation of the Basia of Joannes Secundus Nicolaius. With the Original Latin, and An Essay on his Life and Writings. The Second Edition, With Additions*, London: J. Bew.

—— (ed. and trans.) (1782) *Propertii Monobiblos; or, That Book of the Elegies of Propertius, Entitled Cynthia; Translated into English Verse: With Classical Notes*, London: H. Payne.

—— (ed. and trans.) (1787) *Select Odes, from the Persian Poet Hafez, Translated into English Verse; with Notes Critical, and Explanatory*, London: T. Cadell.

—— (ed. and trans.) (1795) *The Poems of Caius Valerius Catullus, in English Verse, with the Latin Text revised, and Classical Notes. Prefixed are Engravings of Catullus and his Friend Cornelius Nepos. Two Volumes*, London: Joseph Johnson.

Ogilby, J. (ed. and trans.) (1654) *The Works of Publius Virgilius Maro. Translated, adorn'd with Sculpture, and illustrated with Annotations, By John Ogilby*, London: T. Warren.

O'Hehir, B. (1968) *Harmony from Discords: A Life of Sir John Denham*, Berkeley and Los Angeles: University of California Press.

—— (ed.) (1969) *Expans'd Hieroglyphicks: A Critical Edition of Sir John Denham's Coopers Hill*, Berkeley and Los Angeles: University of California Press.

Osmond, T. S. (1912) "Arnold and Homer," in W. P. Ker (ed.) *Essays and Studies By Members of the English Association*, vol. III, Oxford: Clarendon Press.

Ossman, D. (1963) *The Sullen Art: Interviews with American Poets*, New York: Corinth Books.

Packard, W. (ed.) (1987) *The Poet's Craft: Interviews from the New York Quarterly* (1974), New York: Paragon House.

Palmer, R. E. (1969) *Hermeneutics: Interpretation Theory in Schleiermacher, Dilthey, Heidegger, and Gadamer*, Evanston, Illinois: Northwestern University Press.

Pannwitz, R. (1917) *Die Krisis der europäischen Kultur*, Nurenberg: H. Carl.

Parsons, A. E. (1929) "The Trojan Legend in England: Some Instances of its Application to the Politics of the Times," *Modern Language Review* 24:253–264, 394–408.

Patterson, A. (1984) *Censorship and Interpretation: The Conditions of Writing and Reading in Early Modern England,* Madison: University of Wisconsin Press.

—— (1987) *Pastoral and Ideology: Virgil to Valéry,* Berkeley and Los Angeles: University of California Press.

Penna, S. (1982) *This Strange Joy: Selected Poems,* ed. and trans. W. S. Di Piero, Columbus, Ohio: Ohio State University Press.

Perkin, J. (1989) *Women and Marriage in Nineteenth-Century England,* London: Routledge.

Perkins, D. (1987) *A History of Modern Poetry: Modernism and After,* Cambridge, Massachusetts: Harvard University Press.

Perloff, M. (1985) "The Word as Such: L=A=N=G=U=A=G=E Poetry in the Eighties," in *The Dance of the Intellect: Studies in the Poetry of the Pound Tradition,* Cambridge: Cambridge University Press.

Phaer, T. (ed. and trans.) (1620) *The Thirteene Bookes of Aeneidos. The first twelue being the worke of the Diuine Poet Virgil Maro; and the thirteenth, the Supplement of Maphaus Vegius. Translated into English Verse, to the first third part of the tenth Booke, by Thomas Phaer, Esquire: and the residue finished, and now newly set forth, for the delight of such as are studious in Poetry, by Thomas Twyne, Doctor in Physike,* London: B. Alsop.

Picasso, P. (1968) *Hunk of Skin,* trans. P. Blackburn, San Francisco: City Lights.

Piccolo, L. (1972) *Collected Poems of Lucio Piccolo,* trans. R. Feldman and B. Swann, Princeton: Princeton University Press.

Piola-Caselli, E. (1927) *Trattato del Diritto di Autore,* 2nd edn, Naples: Marghieri.

Pontiggia, G. and Di Mauro, E. (eds) (1978) *La parola innamorata: i poeti nuovi 1976–1978,* Milan: Feltrinelli.

Pope, A. (ed. and trans.) (1967) *The Iliad of Homer* (1715–20), in Maynard Mack (ed.) *The Twickenham Edition of the Poems of Alexander Pope,* vol. VII, London: Methuen, and New Haven, Connecticut: Yale University Press.

Porta, A. (1978) *As If It Were a Rhythm,* trans. P. Vangelisti, San Francisco and Los Angeles: Red Hill.

—— (ed.) (1979) *Poesia degli anni settanta,* Milan: Feltrinelli.

—— (1986a) *Invasions: Selected Poems,* ed. P. Vangelisti, trans. A. Baldry, P. Vangelisti, and P. Verdicchio, San Francisco and Los Angeles: Red Hill.

—— (1986b) *Passenger: Selected Poems,* ed. and trans. P. Verdicchio, Montreal: Guernica.

—— (1987) *Kisses from Another Dream,* trans. A. Molino, San Francisco: City Lights.

—— (1992) *Melusine,* trans. A. Molino, Montreal: Guernica.

Portinari, F. (1989) "Milano," in A. Asor Rosa (ed.) *Letteratura italiana. Storia e geographia, III,* Turin: Einaudi.

Posonby, V. B. (ed.) (1955) *Georgianna; Extracts from the Correspondence of*

Georgianna, Duchess of Devonshire, London: John Murray.
Potoker, E. M. (1965), Review of H. Böll, *Absent Without Leave*, trans. L. Vennewitz, *Saturday Review*, 11 September, p. 42.
Potter, L. (1989) *Secret Rites and Secret Writing: Royalist Literature, 1641–1660*, Cambridge: Cambridge University Press.
Pound, E. (1950) *The Letters of Ezra Pound, 1907–1941*, ed. D. D. Paige, New York: Harcourt, Brace & World.
────── (1952) *The Spirit of Romance* (1910), New York: New Directions.
────── (1953) *Translations*, New York: New Directions.
────── (1954) *Literary Essays*, ed. T. S. Eliot, New York: New Directions.
────── (1956) *Selected Poems*, New York: New Directions.
────── (1960) *The ABC of Reading* (1934), New York: New Directions.
Publishers Weekly (1963) "Statistics for 1962: Subject Analysis of American Book Production," 21 January, pp. 40–44.
Quarterly Review (1823) Review of L. Ariosto, *Orlando Furioso*, trans. W. S. Rose, 30:40–61.
────── (1888) "Matthew Arnold," 167 (October):398–426.
Quasimodo, S. (1968) *The Selected Writings of Salvatore Quasimodo* (1960), ed. and trans. A. Mandelbaum, New York: Minerva.
────── (1980) *The Tall Schooner*, trans. M. Egan, New York: Red Ozier.
────── (1983) *Complete Poems*, trans. J. Bevan, London: Anvil.
Quinlan, M. (1941) *Victorian Prelude: A History of English Manners, 1780–1830*, New York: Columbia University Press.
Quinn, S. M. B. (1972) *Ezra Pound: An Introduction to the Poetry*, New York: Columbia University Press.
Raffel, B. (1969) "No Tidbit Love You Outdoors Far as a Bier: Zukofsky's *Catullus*," *Arion* 8:435–445.
────── (1984) *Ezra Pound, The Prime Minister of Poetry*, Hamden, Connecticut: Archon.
────── (1985) "Pound and Translation," *Literary Review* 28:634–635.
Reed, J. (1990) *The Coastguard's House*, Newcastle upon Tyne: Bloodaxe.
Rener, F. M. (1989) *Interpretatio: Language and Translation from Cicero to Tytler*, Amsterdam: Rodopi.
Rexroth, K. (1985) "Why Is American Poetry Culturally Deprived?" (1967), in *TriQuarterly* 20 63:53–59.
Reynolds, B. (1950) *The Linguistic Writings of Alessandro Manzoni: A Textual and Chronological Reconstruction*, Cambridge: Heffer.
Reynolds, F. M. (ed.) (1828) *The Keepsake for MDCCCXXVIII*, London: Hurst, Chance and Co.
Rider, H. (1638) *All The Odes And Epodes of Horace. Translated into English Verse: By Henry Rider, Master of Arts of Emanuel Colledge in Cambridge*, London: R. Rider.
Robinson, D. (1991) *The Translator's Turn*, Baltimore and London: Johns Hopkins University Press.
Rogers, P. (1978) "Pope and his Subscribers," *Publishing History* 3:7–36.
Roper, D. (1978) *Reviewing before the Edinburgh: 1788–1802*, Newark, Delaware: University of Delaware Press.
Ross, A. (1989) *No Respect: Intellectuals and Popular Culture*, New York and London: Routledge.

Rossetti, D. G. (ed. and trans.) (1981) *The Early Italian Poets* (1861), ed. Sally Purcell, Berkeley and Los Angeles: University of California Press.
Rossi, S. (1959) "E. A. Poe e la Scapigliatura Lombarda," *Studi americani* 5:119–139.
Said, E. W. (1978) *Orientalism*, New York: Pantheon.
——— (1990) "Embargoed Literature," *Nation*, 17 September, pp. 278–280.
Sandri, G. (1976) *From K to S: Ark of the Asymmetric*, trans. F. Pauluzzi, New York, Norristown, and Milan: Out of London.
Sanguineti, E. (1963) "Da Gozzano a Montale," in *Tra Libertà e Crepuscolarismo*, Milan: Mursia.
Saturday Review (1861) "Homeric Translators and Critics," 27 July, pp. 95–96.
Scarles, C. (1980) *Copyright*, Cambridge: Cambridge University Press.
Scarron, P. (1988) *Le Virgile Travesti* (1648–49), ed. J. Serroy, Paris: Bordas.
Schleiermacher, F. (1838) *Sämmitliche Werke. Dritte abteilung: Zur Philosophie, Zweiter Band*, Berlin: Reimer.
——— (1890) *Selected Sermons*, ed. and trans. M. F. Wilson, New York: Funk and Wagnalls.
——— (1977) *Hermeneutics: The Handwritten Manuscripts*, ed. H. Kimmerle, trans. J. Duke and J. Forstman, Missoula, Montana: Scholars Press.
Sedgwick, E. K. (1985) *Between Men: English Literature and Male Homosocial Desire*, New York: Columbia University Press.
Sereni, V. (1971) *Sixteen Poems*, ed. and trans. P. Vangelisti, San Francisco and Los Angeles: Red Hill.
Shakespeare, W. (1959) *Timon of Athens*, ed. H. J. Oliver, London: Methuen.
Sheehan, J. J. (1989) *German History, 1770–1866*, Oxford: Oxford University Press.
Shelley, M. W. (1976) *Collected Tales and Stories*, ed. C. E. Robinson, Baltimore and London: Johns Hopkins University Press.
Sieveking, I. S. (1909) *Memoir and Letters of Francis W. Newman*, London: Kegan Paul, Trench, Trübner and Co., Ltd.
Simon, S. (1989) "Conflits de juridiction: La double signature du texte traduit," *Meta* 34:195–208.
Sinfield, A. (1989) *Literature, Politics, and Culture in Postwar Britain*, Berkeley and Los Angeles: University of California Press.
——— (1992) *Faultlines: Cultural Materialism and the Politics of Dissident Reading*, Berkeley and Los Angeles: University of California Press.
Sinisgalli, L. (1988) *The Ellipse: Selected Poems*, ed. and trans. W. S. Di Piero, Princeton: Princeton University Press.
Skone James, E. P., Mummery, J. F., Rayner James, J. E., and Garnett, K. M. (1991) *Copinger and Skone James on Copyright*, 13th edn, London: Sweet and Maxwell.
Smith, D. M. (1969) *Italy: A Modern History*, 2nd edn, Ann Arbor: University of Michigan Press.
Smith, L. R. (ed. and trans.) (1981) *The New Italian Poetry*, Berkeley and Los Angeles: University of California Press.
Smith, W. J. and Gioia, D. (eds) (1985) *Poems from Italy*, St. Paul,

Minnesota: New Rivers.
Spatola, A. (1975) *Majakovskiiiiiij*, trans. P. Vangelisti, San Francisco and Los Angeles: Red Hill.
—— (1977) *Zeroglyphics*, San Francisco and Los Angeles: Red Hill.
—— (1978) *Various Devices*, ed. and trans. P. Vangelisti, San Francisco and Los Angeles: Red Hill.
Spatola, A. and Vangelisti, P. (eds) (1982) *Italian Poetry, 1960–1980: from Neo to Post Avant-garde*, San Francisco and Los Angeles: Red Hill.
Speck, W. A. (1982) "Politicians, Peers, and Publication by Subscription, 1700–50," in I. Rivers (ed.) *Books and their Readers in Eighteenth-Century England*, Leicester: Leicester University Press.
Spectator (1918) "The Gate of Remembrance," 20 April, p. 422.
Spedding, J. (1861) "Arnold on Translating Homer," *Fraser's Magazine* 63 (June):703–714.
Stallybrass, P. and White, A. (1986) *The Politics and Poetics of Transgression*, London: Methuen.
Stapylton, R. (trans.) (1634) *Dido and Aeneas. The Fourth Booke of Virgils Aeneis Now Englished by Robert Stapylton*, London: W. Cooke.
Steiner, G. (1974) *After Babel: Aspects of Language and Translation*, London, Oxford, New York: Oxford University Press.
Steiner, T. R. (ed.) (1975) *English Translation Theory 1650–1800*, Assen: Van Gorcum.
Steiner, W. (1992) "The Bulldozer of Desire," *New York Times Book Review*, 15 November, p. 9.
Sterling, J. A. L. and Carpenter, M. C. L. (1986) *Copyright Law in the United Kingdom*, Sydney and London: Legal Books.
Stern, D. (1967) "Straight and Nouveau," *Nation*, 18 September, pp. 248–249.
Stern, R. G. (1953) "Pound as Translator," *Accent* 13(4) (Autumn):265–268.
Stewart, S. (1980) "The Pickpocket: A Study in Tradition and Allusion," *MLN* 95:1127–1154.
Stock, N. (1982) *The Life of Ezra Pound*, rev. edn, San Francisco: North Point.
Stone, L. (1977) *The Family, Sex and Marriage in England, 1500–1800*, New York: Harper and Row.
Storie incredibili (1863), Milano: Daelli.
Strabo (1930) *The Geography of Strabo*, ed. and trans. H. L. Jones, London: William Heinemann Ltd, and New York: G. P. Putnam's Sons.
Stracher, C. A. (1991) "An Introduction to Copyright Law for Translators," *Translation Review* 36–37:12–14.
Stuart, D. M. (1955) *Dearest Bess: The Life and Times of Lady Elizabeth Foster, afterwards Duchess of Devonshire*, London: Methuen.
Stubbs, J. (1968) "Looking-glass Land," *Books and Bookmen* May, p. 26.
Sturgeon, T. (1990) "Doing That Medieval Thing: Paul Blackburn's Medieval Premises," *Sagetrieb* 9:147–168.
Sullivan, A. (ed.) (1983a) *British Literary Magazines: The Augustan Age and the Age of Johnson, 1698–1788*, Westport, Connecticut and London: Greenwood.

——— (1983b) *British Literary Magazines: The Romantic Age, 1789–1836*, Westport, Connecticut and London: Greenwood.

——— (1984) *British Literary Magazines: The Victorian and Edwardian Age, 1837–1913*, Westport, Connecticut and London: Greenwood.

Szondi, P. (1986) "Schleiermacher's Hermeneutics Today," in *On Textual Understanding and Other Essays*, trans. H. Mendelsohn, Minneapolis: University of Minnesota Press.

Tarchetti, I. U. (trans.) (1869a) Carlo Dickens, *L'amico comune*, Milano: Sonzogno.

——— (trans.) (1869b) J. F. Smith, *Fasi della vita o Uno sguardo dietro le scene*, Milano: Sonzogno.

——— (1967) *Tutte le opere*, ed. E. Ghidetti, 2 vols, Bologna: Cappelli.

Thomas, A. (ed.) (1971) *Poésies complètes de Bertran de Born* (1888), New York: Johnson.

Time (1967) "Unease in the Night," 11 August, p. 80.

Times Literary Supplement (1961) "On Translating the Bible," 17 February, p. iv.

——— (1967) "Anatomy of a Publication," 11 May, p. 399.

——— (1968) "Experiment with Rabbits," 14 March, p. 245.

——— (1969) "Recapitulations," 20 February, p. 180.

Todd, J. (ed.) (1985) *A Dictionary of British and American Women Writers, 1660–1800*, Totowa, New Jersey: Rowman and Allanheld.

Todorov, T. (1975) *The Fantastic: A Structural Approach to a Literary Genre*, trans. R. Howard, Ithaca, New York: Cornell University Press.

Townshend, A. (1983) *The Poems and Masques of Aurelian Townshend*, ed. C. Brown, Reading, England: Whiteknights Press.

Tytler, A. F. (1978) *Essay on the Principles of Translation*, ed. J. F. Huntsman, Amsterdam: John Benjamins.

Underdown, D. (1960) *Royalist Conspiracy in England 1649–1660*, New Haven, Connecticut: Yale University Press.

Ungaretti, G. (1958) *Life of a Man*, ed. and trans. A. Mandelbaum, London: Hamish Hamilton, New York: New Directions, and Milan: Scheiwiller.

——— (1969) *Selected Poems*, ed. and trans. P. Creagh, Harmondsworth: Penguin.

——— (1975) *Selected Poems of Giuseppe Ungaretti*, ed. and trans. A. Mandelbaum, Ithaca, New York: Cornell University Press.

Updike, J. (1981) "Books," *New Yorker*, 3 August, pp. 92–93.

Venuti, L. (ed.) (1992) *Rethinking Translation: Discourse, Subjectivity, Ideology*, London and New York: Routledge.

Vicars, J. (1632) *The XII Aeneids of Virgil, the most renowned Laureat Prince of Latine-Poets; Translated into English deca-syllables, By John Vicars*, London: N. Alsop.

Von Hallberg, R. (1985) *American Poetry and Culture, 1945–1980*, Cambridge, Massachusetts: Harvard University Press.

Wagstaff, C. (1984) "The Neo-avantgarde," in M. Caesar and P. Hainsworth (eds) *Writers and Society in Contemporary Italy*, New York: St. Martin's Press.

Ward, A. (1974) *Book Production, Fiction and the German Reading Public*,

1740–1800, Oxford: Oxford University Press.

Wasserman, E. (1959) *The Subtler Language: Critical Readings of Neoclassic and Romantic Poems*, Baltimore: Johns Hopkins University Press.

Watt, I. (1957) *The Rise of the Novel*, Berkeley and Los Angeles: University of California Press.

Weber, H. (1812) *Tales of the East: Comprising the Most Popular Romances of Oriental Origin; and the Best Imitations by European Authors: With New Translations, and Additional Tales, Never Before Published*, vol. II, Edinburgh: James Ballantyne and Company.

West, P. (1970), Review of G. G. Márquez, *One Hundred Years of Solitude*, trans. G. Rabassa, *Book World*, 22 February, p. 4.

Westminster Review (1862) "On Translating Homer," 77:150–163.

Whicher, G. (1953) "Reprints, New Editions," *New York Herald Tribune*, 25 October, p. 25.

―――― (1954) Review of *The Translations of Ezra Pound*, *American Literature* 26:119–121.

Whiteside, T. (1981) *The Blockbuster Complex: Conglomerates, Show Business, and Book Publishing*, Middletown, Connecticut: Wesleyan University Press.

Whitfield, S. J. (1991) *The Culture of the Cold War*, Baltimore and London: Johns Hopkins University Press.

Willey, B. (1956) *More Nineteenth-Century Studies: A Group of Honest Doubters*, New York: Columbia University Press.

Williams, R. (1958) *Culture and Society 1780–1950*, New York: Harper and Row.

Wilson, E. (1946) "Books," *New Yorker*, 13 April, p. 100.

Wilson, P. (1982) "Classical Poetry and the Eighteenth-Century Reader," in I. Rivers (ed.) *Books and their Readers in Eighteenth-Century England*, Leicester: Leicester University Press.

Wiseman, T. P. (1985) *Catullus and His World: A Reappraisal*, Cambridge: Cambridge University Press.

Wollstonecraft, M. (1975) *A Vindication of the Rights of Woman*, ed. M. Brody, London: Penguin.

Woodmansee, M. (1984) "The Genius and the Copyright: Economic and Legal Conditions of the Emergence of the 'Author'," *Eighteenth-Century Studies* 14:425–448.

Wordsworth, W. (1974) *The Prose Works of William Wordsworth*, eds W. J. B. Owen and J. W. Smyser, vol. I, Oxford: Oxford University Press.

The World of Translation (1971), New York: PEN American Center.

Wroth, T. (1620) *The Destrvction of Troy, or The Acts of Æneas. Translated ovt of the Second Booke of the Æneads of Virgill That peerelesse Prince of Latine Poets. With the Latine Verse on the one side, and the English Verse on the other, that the congruence of the translation with the Originall may the better appeare. As also a Centurie of EPIGRAMS, and a Motto vpon the Creede, thereunto annexed. By Sʳ THOMAS WROTHE, Knight*, London: T. Dawson.

Zanzotto, A. (1975) *Selected Poetry of Andrea Zanzotto*, ed. and trans. R. Feldman and B. Swann, Princeton: Princeton University Press.

Zuber, R. (1968) *Les "Belles Infidèles" et la formation du goût classique: Perrot d'Ablancourt et Guez de Balzac*, Paris: Colin.

Zukofsky, L. (1991) *Complete Short Poetry,* Baltimore and London: Johns Hopkins University Press.

Zukofsky, L. and Zukofsky, C. (1969) *Catullus (Gai Catulli Veronensis Liber),* London: Cape Goliard Press, and New York: Grossman.

Zwicker, S. N. (1984) *Politics and Language in Dryden's Poetry: The Arts of Disguise,* Princeton: Princeton University Press.

Index